# Black Religion
# and
# Black Radicalism

# Black Religion
# and
# Black Radicalism

*An Interpretation of the Religious History
of African Americans*

## GAYRAUD S. WILMORE

Third Edition, Revised and Enlarged

ORBIS BOOKS

Maryknoll, New York 10545

The Catholic Foreign Mission Society of America (Maryknoll) recruits and trains people for overseas missionary service. Through Orbis Books, Maryknoll aims to foster the international dialogue that is essential to mission. The books published, however, reflect the opinions of their authors and are not meant to represent the official position of the society.

This edition copyright © 1998 by Gayraud S. Wilmore
Published by Orbis Books, Maryknoll, NY 10545

First edition published in the C. Eric Lincoln Series on Black Religion by Anchor Press/Doubleday, 1973

Second edition, revised and enlarged, copyright © 1983 by Gayraud S. Wilmore, published by Orbis Books, Maryknoll, NY 10545

Manufactured in the United States of America

---

**Library of Congress Cataloging-in-Publication Data**

Wilmore, Gayraud S.
    Black religion and Black radicalism : an interpretation of the
religious history of African Americans / Gayraud S. Wilmore. — 3rd
ed., rev. and enl.
      p.  cm.
    Includes bibliographical references and index.
    ISBN 1-57075-182-X (pbk.)
    1. Afro-Americans—Religions.   2. Radicalism—United States.
3. United States—Religion.   4. United States—Politics and
government.   5. United States—Social life and customs.   I. Title.
BR563.N4W53   1998
200'.89'96073—dc21                      97-45085
                                                   CIP

# Contents

# Introduction to the Second Edition

The first edition of this book appeared in 1973. It was a year of ill fortune for both black religion and black radicalism. Richard Milhous Nixon was elected to his second term as president, and we now know that he began forthwith to use the Federal Bureau of Investigation and other government agencies to infiltrate and create suspicion and internecine warfare among militant movements in the black community. The national movement of black religious radicalism that had provided such a hospitable climate for the inauguration of the C. Eric Lincoln Series on black religion, of which this was the third volume, experienced frustration and dwindling support under the secrecy and repression of the pre-Watergate years.

From the beginning of Nixon's second term to the election of Ronald Reagan in 1980, ideological clarity, solidarity, and social activism among blacks in the United States noticeably decreased. And as goes the black community, so goes the black church. The 1970s saw the diminution of the influence of such formerly important black church-related groups as the Interreligious Foundation for Community Organization (IFCO), the Southern Christian Leadership Conference (SCLC), the National Office of Black Catholics (NOBC), and the National Conference of Black Churchmen (NCBC). The large black denominations, somewhat belatedly, began to express selected emphases of the black theology that was being developed in the annual conferences and study commissions of the NCBC.

New activist coalitions such as the National Black Pastors Conference, Partners in Ecumenism, the National Black Seminarians Conference, and the Congress of National Black Churches appeared on the scene as the first groups mentioned above began to lose momentum in the mid-1970s. But although the condition of the black poor was more desperate in 1982 than in 1972, the masses, for reasons that cannot be dealt with here, seemed less responsive to the leadership of left-of-center black church-sponsored organizations than they had been since the Angela Davis affair at the end of the 1960s.

It has been encouraging to me that since 1976, when *Black Religion and Black Radicalism* went out of print, many persons have been interested in a new edition. In view of the related articles and books published since

the first edition, many of them following up hunches and research suggestions made in the first edition, it seemed appropriate to prepare a
revised edition that would not only correct some of the errors of the original volume, but expand upon it at points where further research made
new information available or provided fresh insights. I have attempted to
do so by many revisions in the text and by more extensive notes.

The point needs to be made that although religion is not playing the
role today that it played ten years ago, and in spite of the fact that some
doubt may be cast upon its efficacy as conditions in the black community
worsen, there is still a need to recall the route we took to reach where we
are today—if only to see where we went astray. But more than that.
There are still black church members, or those preparing in theological
schools to lead church members, who refuse to accept that institution's
withdrawal from the struggle for black liberation. Black Christians continue to demand from us the kind of scholarship that can, at one and the
same time, deal honestly with facts, uncover truth, and lead the reader
toward a religious commitment to help remake the world and not be satisfied simply to dissect it. There may be good and valid arguments to the
contrary, but it is my opinion that what we call "the movement" is by no
means played out today. It is my opinion that some persons are still
searching for historical foundations within the heritage of black religion
to undergird the continuing struggle for justice and liberation.

It is true, nevertheless, that in times such as these one may question
the wisdom of a book that intends to demonstrate the historical relationship between black religion and black radicalism. Vincent Harding
in the late 1960s identified the mainstream of black thought and action
as radicalism. His work, more than any other except that of W. E. B. Du
Bois, provoked me to turn from social ethics to history. In his new
book—unaccountably, from my viewpoint—Harding is less sanguine
about the term "radicalism" and seems to favor the idea of protest
demanding a fundamental transformation of human relationships
(*There is a River: The Black Struggle for Freedom in America*, Harcourt Brace
Jovanovich, 1981). Nevertheless, in a review of the book in the *New York
Times*, November 1, 1981, Eric Foner correctly remarks that Harding
interprets American history as having produced "a radical viewpoint that
regards white society as having an 'illness' deeper than racism, a sickness
of the soul. . . ."

That is the kind of radicalism with which I believe black religion has
had a vacillating and paradoxical relationship for at least three hundred
years. The term serves better than any other I can think of to express the
insistent theme within black church history that white society and white
Christianity were sick unto death and that sickness could be cured only
by a radical *metanoia*.

It is true that the term "radicalism" is elusive if one attempts to locate it
somewhere between traditional Marxism and international terrorism.

But in black intellectual history there were other options. Radicalism had to do with the assumption that race and color are at the root of the problems of Western civilization and that the only lasting solution would require a transformation of human relationships that would amount to a national conversion involving the recognition of the dignity and equality of blacks.

Radicalism is, perhaps, a relative term depending in any case upon who is trying to upset which convention against what kind of odds. In a classic essay, "Radicalism and Conservatives," Kelly Miller, dean at Howard University from 1907 to 1918, does not so much define those terms as take for granted that in the context in which blacks use them both refer to opposition to white racism and it is impossible for any thoughtful black person not to be opposed to his or her status in American society. "Radical and conservative Negroes agree as to the end in view, but differ as to the most effective means of attaining it. The difference is not essentially one of principle or purpose, but point of view." Miller proceeds thence to contrast the tactics of the Douglass-Trotter-Du Bois tendencies against those of Booker T. Washington and his friends. The classification of the former as radical and the latter as conservative has endured through the years.

My book accepts that classic differentiation among Afro-Americans, but goes further to attempt to isolate a radical tradition that has ebbed and flowed in black religion. One cannot help noticing that both Vincent Harding and Manning Marable have emphasized the "spiritual strivings" that characterize the black struggle as the ebb and flow of a body of water. Marable uses the image of "Blackwater," and Harding reminds us that "There is a River."

This bubbling, meandering stream rises somewhere in the dim history of the black worshiping community. Over the years it has taken on sharpened definition in the black church and in its affiliated agencies, so that it is possible to say today—going beyond Kelly Miller's assimilationism—that there are three characteristics of the radical tradition in black religion: (1) the quest for independence from white control; (2) the revalorization of the image of Africa; and (3) the acceptance of protest and agitation as theological prerequisites for black liberation and the liberation of all oppressed peoples. Such an analysis will place more emphasis upon the black church's affinity to the radicalism of Trotter and Du Bois than to the conservatism of Washington. But its greatest concern—and this is the constructive task of this book—will be to demonstrate that there has been and continues to be a significant difference between black religion and white religion in their approaches to social reality and social change—whether in reference to theological liberalism or to fundamentalism. Because of that fact alone I am prepared to argue that black faith has been "more radical" in the proper sense of that much-maligned term.

This enlarged revision was made possible by a sabbatical leave granted me by the Board of Trustees of the Colgate Rochester/Bexley Hall/Crozer Theological Seminary, Rochester, New York. I am grateful to my colleagues, especially to the members of the Black Church Studies faculty team, and Mrs. Sylvia Jemison, program secretary, for their willingness to take up my academic and administrative responsibilities during a leisurely period of writing in the Methodist manse and the Anglican rectory on Green Turtle Cay in the Bahamas. I am grateful to Reverend Donald H. Smith, rector of St. Peter and St. Ann Parish, Abaco, and the church people of the beautiful Abaco cays, for the many courtesies extended to me during my sabbatical.

It will be immediately evident that many scholars have contributed in one way or another to this revision. I should like also to acknowledge my debt to my own students these past ten years. Many classroom discussions and semester papers helped me to see deficiencies that would have otherwise passed unnoticed. The work of John W. Blassingame, Charles Long, Leonard Barrett, Eugene Genovese, Mechal Sobel, Albert J. Raboteau, Randall Burkett, James H. Cone, and others too numerous to mention, not only stimulated me to go back and revisit the effort I made in 1970, but also reinforced my confidence in the basic soundness of my initial interpretation of black religious history.

The concept of black radicalism continues to be ill-defined in scholarly circles. But there is little doubt that the data support the contention that there were distinctive and disruptive survival and liberation motifs in the development of religion among Afro-Americans, and that whatever impetus for fundamental change in American society did come out of the black community had indispensable support, if not its inception, in black religious institutions.

*Gayraud S. Wilmore*
*Rochester, NY*

# Introduction to the Third Edition

To make such a confession may strike the reader as an act of false humility, but I am of the honest opinion that the continuing popularity of this book, first published in 1973, is less a compliment to its author than an indication of the compelling nature of its subject matter. With the exception of a few notable writers—Carter G. Woodson, Joseph R. Washington, C. Eric Lincoln, and Lawrence Mamiya among them—one is hard put to find either black or white scholars of religion who have essayed to survey in one volume the whole turbulent sweep of African American history in an effort to satisfy the desire to understand and appreciate the meaning of the black religious experience as expressed in the churches, religious institutions, and movements of the African American people over the past three hundred years.

What are the primordial sources of black religion? What are the connecting links and commonalities existing between black Christianity and black Islam, black Judaism, and African Traditional Religions? What has been the special relevance of the Christian faith in ancient and modern Africa to African American churches? What are the essential marks of black religions in South America, Central America, and the Caribbean, and how do they compare with the defining characteristics of black religion in the United States? What is the relationship between survival, self-development or elevation, and liberation motifs or tendencies in the history of African American Christianity? How do black churches in the United States differ from white churches in Europe and North America? And what is the significance of those differences for the dissolution or the renewal of Christian faith in the twenty-first century?

Such questions would challenge the mettle of the most perspicacious graduate student one can imagine sitting for qualifying exams for a doctorate in African American religious studies today, but these and many no less difficult questions continue to intrigue and frustrate ordinary people and keep them reading books like this one. Increasing numbers of African American professors are being invited to give public lectures or write books on these questions and are themselves supporting the Society for the Study of Black Religion, the Kelly Miller Smith Institute on Black Church Studies at Vanderbilt University, and the black history and theology sections of the annual meetings of the American Academy of Religion in order to equip themselves to meet the demands of students and the reading public. George W. Williams, Carter G. Woodson, W. E. B. Du Bois, and Ruby F. Johnston would be particularly pleased to see how seriously this scholarship is taken into account and appreciated in both the black churches and the academy today.

Because so many interesting questions keep being raised and so many readers continue to search for answers in books like *Black Religion and Black Radicalism*, this year in its twelfth printing, the editor of Orbis Books, Robert Ellsberg, spent more than two years trying gently to inveigle me into preparing yet a third edition, once again "revised and enlarged." I finally agreed, but somewhat reluctantly. Having retired from the faculty of the Interdenominational Theological Center in 1990, I consider myself pretty much out of touch with the recent and most sophisticated developments in the discipline of African American religious history as it is taught and written about these days. One needs to be reading as many new books, journal articles, and doctoral dissertations in the field as possible to ensure that judgments made with boundless confidence fourteen years ago have not been overturned by the new findings of former students and colleagues who are still foraging in the archives and/or teaching. I have not been idle in retirement, occasionally lecturing and reading papers here and there since 1990, but I am by no means as certain about my knowledge of the history and especially about the present state of black religion as when I was in the classroom almost every day.

The obvious remedy for this condition, familiar to many tired and most retired professors, would be to spend several quiet months catching up, and then go over every page of the text being revised so as to make whatever trivial or drastic changes seem necessary. I must confess that I did not hie off to the Bahamas with a trunk full of books and journals, and did not make as many drastic changes as, perhaps, I should have made. There are just too many more important things that one must hasten to do at this stage of life, while it is still light—for the time is shorter than it has ever been. I did, however, read every line of the previous edition and found, not to my surprise, many places where I know better today than I did in 1983. In most of them the reader will find emendations made under the pressure of being fully cognizant that this was probably the last time the writer would be able to say something more clearly and convincingly than he did the first time.

The ways in which my mind has changed since 1983 will be evident in this revised text. For one thing, the new Chapter 1 will show my belated respect for the neglected work of African and African American scholars on Africa in the ancient world, the significance of the Nile Valley civilizations in the history of religions in Africa, and the new interest of students and church members in the extent to which we can be confident that God's revelation was alive and well in Africa before the coming of the white man. Being fortunate enough to join the faculty of ITC prior to the retirement of the acknowledged "dean" of black biblical studies, the distinguished emeritus Professor Charles B. Copher, helped open my eyes to the critical importance of the African past for any comprehensive examination of the meaning of religion, especially the religion of the first Africans to set foot in the New World. That particular angle of research was missing from the second "revised and enlarged" edition, and I have tried to correct the omission in this one.

The studies of the slave narratives by Dwight N. Hopkins, George C. L. Cummings, Will Coleman, Cheryl J. Sanders, and other younger scholars have underscored and elaborated certain assumptions some of us made earlier about the religion of the slaves and the nascent theology that developed from it. This "second generation" of black theologians and ethicists, thanks to the celebrated scholar who has been their inspiration, James H. Cone of Union Seminary in New York, has made African American religious and church history more indispensable for black theology than it was in the early days of the movement. I only regret that this third edition does not make as much use of their data and insights as I would have preferred. The fault is mine, but I have been in too much of a hurry to get this revision out before the hard drive of my antique computer crashes. Even now my monitor's screen is wavering wearily!

For the same reason of haste, perhaps the greatest deficiency of this enlarged edition is my failure to include much of the fresh data and critical perceptions about black religion and the churches that have recently come from womanist scholars. Throughout my perusal of the material in Chapters 2 to 7, I was conscious of how much we male historians of religion have misconstrued certain developments by leaving out or understating the contributions of African American women—our sisters, mothers, grandmothers, and great-grandmothers. The amount of neglected historical information that has been uncovered by Evelyn Brooks Higginbotham, Margaret Washington Creel, Cheryl Gilkes, Diana L. Hayes, Delores Williams, Marcia Riggs, Mozella Mitchell, and too many other women scholars to mention here, is an embarrassment to all the men who have written in this field for more than a century. This revised work does not begin to reflect adequately the full scope of their contributions, but I hope that the changes to inclusive language and the small additions I have made here and there in the text will testify to my awareness of the difference their scholarship is making in our understanding of the history of African American religion and theology.

Finally, I wish I had dealt in greater depth with the creativity and complexity of Pentecostal history than I did in the earlier volume. Atlanta, where the Charles H. Mason Theological Seminary of the Church of God in Christ is located on the campus of ITC, is a perfect place to pursue such a study, and I should have taken greater advantage of it in those last years of my teaching career. If I ever write another book on African American religion, which is highly doubtful, I would pay much more attention to black Holiness, Pentecostal, and Spiritual churches and the work of Leonard Lovett, James S. Tinney, David Daniels, Hans Baer, Walter Hollenweger, Roswith Gerloff, and Kofi Opoku, all of whom have greatly enriched the history of the black church with their studies of charismatic movements, and their prophets and prophetesses in West Africa, Great Britain, the Caribbean, and the United States. I would say the same thing about the latest work that has been done on black Roman Catholic history by Cyprian Davis, Jamie Phelps, Shawn Copeland, Albert Raboteau, Diana L. Hayes, and others. The reader will not find enough on black Islam, Roman Catholicism, and Pentecostalism in this volume, and I regret that limited space and time precluded the treatment they all deserve in a book on black religion.

To have included all the wealth of scholarship from the last quarter of the twentieth century in the present volume would have required a much larger book than Orbis envisioned and more work than I could have successfully completed in the six months I had for getting a revised manuscript to Maryknoll. The breadth of African American religious scholarship today is astounding, considering where black church history and theology were in the first half of the century. We urgently need a monumental synthetic work—something on the order of Sydney E. Ahlstrom's *A Religious History of the American People*—but none of the three editions of my book ever intended to equal that magnificent achievement, if indeed it were ever within my competence to produce such. But with all the newly unearthed material screaming to be collated and made accessible to African American clergy and laity, I cannot doubt that sometime in the next century we will have such a work—finally, an appropriate and respectable consummation of the dreams and pioneering efforts of Carter G. Woodson, Mark Miles Fisher, and W. E. B. Du Bois.

Notwithstanding all these inexcusable demurrers, I believe that this third edition is more accurate and useful than the first two. I am content that although my mind has changed about some things during the past fourteen years, my basic presuppositions and arguments concerning the nature and history of African American religion, particularly of black Christianity, remain fairly intact. The ambivalent relationship between black religion and political radicalism which I explained, at least to my own satisfaction, in the Introduction to the second edition, which one should read before reading this, has been strenuously tried but not found wanting by most colleagues. It is always tempting to impose a theoretical template upon data relating to the ebb and flow of black religiosity, from the "invisible institution" of the churches under slavery to the black mega-churches at the end of the twentieth century, but historiography is a notoriously inexact science, if science at all, and what I have done with the concepts of survival, elevation, and liberation is the result of considered judgments about, corrections of, and the fine tuning of the material I have worked on throughout my teaching career. Readers should find that because of certain qualifications I have made in Chapter 10 this edition is more faithful to the data I used earlier in arriving at the idea of black survival and liberation. This change, I trust, will help us make more sense of the kaleidoscopic profusion of persons, events, and movements that make up the long and complex history of the African American religious experience in the United States.

For many years I have admired the work that Vincent Harding has done since the 1960s at the Institute of the Black World, which was originally headquartered in Atlanta. His writings and speeches have influenced me probably more than I realize. Like Vincent, I have always considered myself an activist scholar of the black world, who has never been satisfied merely to study history, but wanted to influence it by passionate involvement in the struggle for the liberation and advancement of black people. I am delighted with the thoroughness and technical precision of many of our younger black scholars in religion and philosophy, but it was never my purpose in life to produce knowledge about African Americans for its own sake, or the sake of the academy. My greatest concern about younger scholars is that they seem less personally involved in the continuing struggle than my generation was, our excesses and deficiencies notwithstanding.

I continue to be more interested in producing work that will contribute to the ongoing life and mission of the church and to the struggle for justice and humanization that has, with fair consistency, marked its journey through the African American communities of North America. If this third and final edition of the book, which for the last twenty-four years has been the most successful attribute of my vocation, helps black and white Christians to understand the African American church and the particular mission God has given to it, I will go to my rest more than satisfied.

Finally, I cannot close without expressing thanks and paying a tribute to Lee Wilmore, my loving wife for fifty-three years, without whose uncomplaining patience, perceptive understanding, and quiet encouragement the three versions of this work would never have seen the light of day. May that wise lady continue to look over my shoulder—encourage, scold, prod or rein me in, as occasion demands.

*Gayraud S. Wilmore*
*Atlanta, June 1997*

# Acronyms

| | |
|---|---|
| AACC | All African Conference of Churches |
| ACS | American Colonization Society |
| ACU | African Christian Union |
| AME | African Methodist Episcopal |
| AMEZ | African Methodist Episcopal Zion |
| AOC | African Orthodox Church |
| ATR | African Traditional Religions |
| BEDC | Black Economic Development Conference |
| CNBC | Congress of National Black Churches |
| CNEA | Colored National Emigration Association |
| CORE | Congress of Racial Equality |
| IFCO | Interreligious Foundation for Community Organization |
| ITC | Interdenominational Theological Center |
| NAACP | National Association for the Advancement of Colored People |
| NCBC | National Committee of Black Churchmen (earlier, NCNC) |
| NCC | National Council of Churches |
| NCNC | National Committee of Negro Churchmen (later, NCBC) |
| NOBC | National Office of Black Catholics |
| RAM | Revolutionary Action Movement |
| SCLC | Southern Christian Leadership Conference |
| SNCC | Student Non-Violent Coordinating Committee |
| SPG | Society for the Propagation of the Gospel |
| UNIA | Universal Negro Improvement Association |
| WCC | World Council of Churches |

## CHAPTER 1

# African Beginnings

*Always Africa is giving us something new or some metempsychosis of a world-old thing. On its black bosom arose one of the earliest, if not the earliest self-protecting civilizations. . . . Nearly every human empire that has arisen in the world, material and spiritual, has found some of its greatest crises on this continent of Africa. . . . As Mommsen says, "It was through Africa that Christianity became the religion of the world."*

W. E. B. Du Bois, 1915

In 1973 the Abuna, or Patriarch, of the Ethiopian Orthodox Church, Theophilus, visited Boston where he was the honored guest of the African Studies Program of Boston University. The African American clergy of the city were especially invited to attend one of the meetings at which he spoke, and about fifty of them came on campus to receive him warmly. In the course of his remarks the Abuna reminded the black ministers that the church he presided over in Addis Ababa was founded in the fourth century A.D. and was one of the oldest in Christendom. Since its establishment was second only to the Coptic Church of Egypt, it antedated all the Christian communions of Europe and America except the Church of Rome. For that reason, he said, not to mention others that had to do with the needs of black people on both sides of the Atlantic, African Americans ought to recognize Ethiopian Orthodoxy as the parent of all baptized Christians of African descent, "so come home to your Mother Church—she stands ready to welcome you!"

The idea was neither novel nor unreasonable. For over a hundred years various gestures had been made suggesting that a union between the descendants of the African slaves and the ancient churches of Africa was not only appropriate in the eyes of many African Americans, but earnestly sought by Coptic and Ethiopian Christian leaders. The Confession of Alexandria, issued by the General Committee of the 114 member churches of the All African Conference of Churches in February 1976, recognizes the priority of the churches of Egypt and Ethiopia, a priority gratefully acknowledged by many African and African American Christians.[1] References to "the God of Ethiopia" and Psalm 68:31 which, in the Authorized Version, prophesies that "Ethiopia shall soon stretch out her hands unto God," abound in the early writings and speeches of black leaders in North America and the Caribbean. In the nineteenth and early twentieth centuries African Americans closely identified with what was then the only independent black nation in their Motherland, with the exception of Liberia. They were jubilant when Emperor Menelik II turned back Italian arms at Adowa in March 1896 and angered by the refusal of the League of Nations and the U.S. government to come to the aid of Emperor Haile Selassie when fascist Italy unleashed its revenge on Abyssinia with the invasion of 1935.[2]

It was not surprising, therefore, that over the years some black Christians in North America and the Caribbean, whether wisely or unwisely, would dream about settling in Ethiopia and that some who elected not to emigrate would consider aligning their churches with either the Coptic Church of Egypt or the Ethiopian Orthodox Church. After the Garvey movement reawakened African American interest in Ethiopia and the Ethiopian Orthodox Church freed itself from the control of the Alexandrian Patriarchy in 1948 and became a member of the World Council of Churches, almost every major city in the United States had at least one black preacher or self-styled prophet who organized what purported to be a branch of Ethiopian Orthodoxy in the black ghetto. So when the Abuna Theophilus addressed African American clergy in Boston in 1973 he had behind him a long and complex history of vague yearnings and aspirations, on the part of both Addis Ababa and a segment of independent African American churches, to forge some kind of ecclesiastical union among the black churches of the United States, Jamaica, and other islands of the Caribbean, and the ancient church of Ethiopia over which he was Patriarch.[3]

The event in Boston had no significant consequence for relations between African and African American Christians in the last quarter of the twentieth century, but it does serve to bracket the fourth century A.D., and the rise of Christianity in East Africa as a beginning point, at least in the minds of many people on both continents, for examining the history of black Christianity. It is no accident that African American spokespersons of the nineteenth century popularized the idea that the history of black religion, including Christianity, begins not among the slaves of pious whites in New England and Virginia, or on the plantations of South Carolina and Georgia, but in Africa—with the religion of the ancient Egyptians, which had a powerful effect upon early Christianity and should be regarded as the most prominent of the African Traditional Religions that originated in the Nile Valley.[4] Black scholars of the nineteenth and early twentieth centuries sought to demonstrate tenuous connections between the first African Christian churches in North America, Egyptian religion prior to Christianity, and the ancient black churches of Ethiopia and Nubia. They did not have all the technical information and equipment that modern scholarship requires to unravel the mysteries of these putative connections, but neither do most of us today. In any case, they knew that the line of relationship did not run from the slave church in America to Rome, Wittenberg, Geneva, and Canterbury, as much as it did to Thebes, Axum, Meroe, and Accra.

The first eleven chapters of George Washington Williams's monumental *A History of the Negro Race in America, 1619–1880*, deal with the presence of black people in the Bible, the achievements of the Hamitic race, which belie the spurious curse of Noah in Genesis 9:25–27, and the origin of black Christianity in ancient Africa.[5] Others before and since have refused to accept the assumption of many white scholars that the place to commence any discussion about black Americans is their debarkation on the quays of Jamestown, Charleston, and New Orleans. William Jacob Walls, the forty-second bishop and scholarly historiographer of the African Methodist Episcopal Zion Church, begins his history of the denomination with a discussion of African civilization and religion—particularly with Africa as the true place of origin of black Christianity in the Western world.[6] During the apogee of black consciousness and the rise of the black studies movement in the 1960s and 1970s, numerous scholars who wrote articles and books about black culture and religion returned to the earlier practice of commencing the black story with the African story. Although some of their conclusions may have been hyperpolemic and based on less than exhaustive research, their contributions corrected the gross misconceptions of black history by others, and opened up the rich vein of African–African American cross-cultural exchanges and relationships previously overlooked or disparaged.[7]

Thus, this interpretation of African American religion, with its checkered implications for radical political and cultural action, begins appropriately with a brief discussion of religion in Africa. My purpose is to illustrate the continuities and discontinuities which continue to influence and reshape the worship styles, spirituality, and belief structures of black Christians in America.[8] I return to this subject in Chapter 2 where the discussion proceeds essentially along the lines followed in the two previous editions of this book. But here I want to trace the evolution of Christianity in Africa, its encounter with African Traditional Religions, Judaism, and Islam (not to mention other ancient and more recent religions whose impact upon modern Africa we cannot explore in this volume). We are about, therefore, to reconnoiter the fertile terrain of religiosity which all of these ways of behaving and believing created in the areas whence the majority of slaves came to populate the New World and eventually to found the African American churches we have today.

## AFRICAN TRADITIONAL RELIGIONS

African Traditional Religions (ATR) is the term used to designate the primal, basically monotheistic if operationally polytheistic and heterogeneous religions of Africa that stretch backward into the dim reaches of prehistory and forward, in many localized forms and languages, into modern Africa. It is the worship of God and gods, closely identified with primordial ancestors, tribal histories, and founders of ethnic groups and civilizations, that exists in all parts of the continent. Despite wide variations, ATR seem to hold in common, nevertheless, some values, beliefs, and practices across the more than five-thousand-mile stretch from Dakar in Senegal to Ras Hafun, at the easternmost tip of Somalia.

Generally speaking, these religions have no sacred scriptures, single founder, central temple or sanctuary, schools of prophets, ecclesiastical organization, or sacerdotal officialdom in the sense that we understand these things in the West. They are family- and clan-centered religions, pragmatic in their relation to and effect upon the totality of daily existence, and firmly ecological and anthropocentric in their ontology. African Traditional Religionists regard God, natural phenomena, and the ancestors as intrinsically related to each other, and the traditionalist's primary interest in them is not philosophical, but practical, that is, how they together affect the lives of human beings.[9]

Since Egypt is definitely in Africa and over the centuries both contributed to and borrowed from the religions of black people in the Upper Nile Valley, we are obliged to regard Egyptian religion as an early example of ATR under the special ecological and sociopolitical conditions of the Delta, between roughly 6000 and 3200 B.C. Little is known of the evolving Egyptian civilization during that early period, but it is certain that the people were racially mixed, with both Caucasoid and Negroid characteristics, intermingled, separated, and varied in intensity from time to time and place to place according to migrations from both the North and the South.

The field is fraught with uncertainties and speculations, but according to such scholars of early Egyptian religion as E. A. Wallis Budge, Norman Lockyer, and John G. Jackson, astronomy and religion were closely intertwined in Kemet, or predynastic Egypt, and worship of the moon and stars preceded the deification of the sun and the institution of sacred kingship which also developed in other parts of Africa. We are skirting the borders of an extremely complex area of study that cannot be thoroughly explored here, but two main points stand out: first, that in addition to the divinity of the kings or pharaohs of Egypt, the great sun god, Ra or Re, who personified the physical sun, was the central figure of this Nilotic ATR, and the legends that surround him cannot help but remind Christians of the Holy Trinity, which was to be deified almost two millennia later. Concerning the influence of ancient Egyptians upon Christianity much later, Noel Q. King writes of Egyptian Christianity:

A study of the history of Coptic art reveals yet other glories of this church. She was not afraid to take over motifs from the old Egyptian religion and from Hellenism. The ideal statue-form of the Holy Mother Isis in her blue robe, and her divine infant Horus, became a standard Christian nativity setting. The *ankh,* the hieroglyph for life, was combined with the cross in iconography to be a symbol of resurrection after death.[10]

Second, Budge and many black and white scholars have been convinced for a long time that these ancient Egyptians belonged to the African race,

and especially [to] that portion of it which lived in the great tract of country which extends from ocean to ocean, right across Africa, and is commonly known as the Sudan, i.e., the country *par excellence* of the Blacks.[11]

The rich mythology of Egyptian religion involves many twists and turns in the story of Osiris who, in a later version reported by Plutarch, after marrying his sister, Isis, is slain by his evil brother Set. The widowed queen-Goddess, Isis, gives birth to a son, Horus, and after bringing Osiris back to life, sees Horus become a king and rule the earth as the third person of the new Egyptian trinity of Osiris, Isis, and Horus. The myth of the death and resurrection of Osiris, as well as the fascination of the ancient Egyptians with the idea of life after death, has been thought by many to have been related to the death of every setting sun and its rising again in the new dawn.

The great religious reformer of dynastic Egypt was the Pharaoh, Amenhotep IV, or Akhenaton (1367–1350). Akhenaton spurned the polytheism of his predecessors and restored an earlier monotheism with the worship of "Aten, the Solar Disk." His attempt to reform Egyptian religion failed, however, and the gods of Nubia, the territory south of the first cataract on the Nile which had made a large contribution to the culture of the Delta, became even more influential in dynastic Egypt.

## JUDAISM IN AFRICA

Some would argue that Judaism is almost as indigenous to ancient Africa as African Traditional Religion. Certainly from the descent of the Jacob family into Egypt (Genesis 46:1) there must have been an intimate relationship between the religion of Israel and the religions of Lower and Upper Egypt. Given the henotheistic climate in which the Torah took shape, we are able to hypothesize the ferocity of the struggle that ensued for centuries between Yahweh and foreign deities. Nor is it always clear who won. Borrowings went on incessantly between the peoples of that time, and there is no reason to assume that the religions of the Hyksos invaders and African Traditional Religions, particularly Egyptian religion, did not infiltrate Judaism to become part and parcel of the religion of the ethnically mixed slaves whom Moses led out of bondage sometime between 1290 and 1224 B.C.

Ethiopian history, steeped in an impressive biblical tradition, records that the Queen of Sheba, Makeda, came away from her visit to Solomon (I Kings 10:1–13) with more than royal bounty. A son born to them, called Menelik, became the first Emperor of Ethiopia, the "Conquering Lion of the Tribe of Judah," the ancestor, in unbroken line, of Haile Selassie. Although the birth of Menelik is not mentioned in the Hebrew Bible and reposes in the cloudy atmosphere of legend, the idea that Judaism was introduced to Ethiopia through this union and the transfer of the Ark of the Covenant from Jerusalem to Makeda's home, in what later became the Ethiopian province of Tigre, has been believed by millions of Ethiopians for centuries and rests upon no more flimsy a foundation than some of the "historical facts" that European and American Christians take for granted.[12] It is unquestionable that a strong Judaic presence infused the ATR that lies behind Ethiopian Christianity and strengthens the contention that Judaism is semi-indigenous to Africa.

Prior to the refuge Mary and Joseph sought for the baby Jesus in the Jewish ghetto of what is today Cairo, millions of Jews were scattered all over the ancient world—from the borders of Nubia southeast across the Arabian peninsula and northwest across Roman Africa to what is now Mauritania.[13] The Ethiopians, therefore, had a long-standing relationship with Judaism and other Semitic religions. Some authorities who may be dubious about the story of Menelik will, nonetheless, give the early date of 300 B.C. for the emergence of the Falasha, or Black Jews of Ethiopia, who practiced an eccentric form of Judaism and possessed an apocryphal literature in the sacred language of Ge'ez. The world was suddenly awakened to the existence of the Falasha when the Israelis finally recognized their existence as black Jews in 1975 and began airlifting them to Israel for settlement. By 1990 approximately 1,200 had been resettled through the efforts of the American Association for Ethiopian Jews.

## THE FIRST "VISIT" OF CHRISTIANITY

Christianity may be regarded as the third major religion, after African Traditional Religions and Judaism, to be so intimately identified with Africa in its first century as to be practically indigenous, or as in the case of Judaism, at least semi-indigenous to the continent. The gospel made its first appearance in Africa not in the Delta region, but in the Upper Nile Valley through Judich, the "Ethiopian" eunuch who was baptized at an oasis on a desert road between Jerusalem and Gaza by Philip, the Evangelist (Acts 8:26–40).[14] The ancient Greeks knew all of Africa south of the First Cataract as either Ethiopia or Kush. Actually Judich came from the kingdom of Meroë, in what was later called Nubia, or in modern times, the Sudan.

We know nothing about his missionizing efforts after he returned home, praising God for sending Messiah Jesus as his Savior, for evidently no church took root in Nubia before A.D. 600. But it is very unlikely that Judich was silent once he returned to the court of the Candace, or queen. The eunuch, barren as the desert in which Philip found him, may well have fertilized the religious soil of the Upper Nile Valley and opened the way for ATR in that area to assimilate Byzantine Christianity when it finally came. But that can only be conjecture.

African Christianity took root first in Egypt. That much is clear to people in that part of the world and should be graciously accepted by the rest of us. Records which are solid to Eastern Christians, though generally unknown and if known, uncertain, to most European and American Christians, report that John Mark, the author of the Second Gospel, a Cyrenian Jew and erstwhile companion of the Apostle Paul, established the first African Christian church that we know about as early as A.D. 42. In the year 68 when St. Mark was martyred in Alexandria, the first person he had converted, a cobbler named Anianos, had already been made a bishop. It was from their joint ministrations that Christianity blossomed in the Delta and Upper Egypt before the end of the second century.[15] By the time of the episcopate of Demetrius of Alexandria (189–232), Christianity was well on its way among the Copts, the native Egyptian population which had adhered to the worship of Osiris, and the story of its tortured expansion through the next three centuries involves many Nubian and other black African converts whose martyred blood enriched the soil of the Egyptian desert.[16]

Blacks from Africa served in the Roman army in the first years of the Christian era, and many were evidently converted to Christianity. Black Roman Catholics today like to recall that St. Maurice was a black African general who, while his legion was stationed in Switzerland in the latter part of the third century, refused to lead it against the Bagaudae, after discovering that the fierce white Gallic tribesmen were also Christians. Maurice and his men were executed by Augustus Maximilian for their insubordination to the Roman's command to slaughter the Bagaudae and for refusing to sacrifice to pagan gods. After that part of Switzerland became Christian, a basilica, later the center of the monastery of St. Maurice-en-Valais, was built on the site of the martyrdom. This St. Maurice (not to be confused with St. Maurice of

Apomea, immortalized in the El Greco painting) has always been portrayed in many European cathedrals and churches with black African features. He is still the patron saint of infantry soldiers and swordsmiths in Savoy, Sardinia, and Cracow, Poland.[17]

## CHRISTIANITY IN ETHIOPIA

In Egypt and the rest of the Graeco-Roman world Christianity was confined to the lower levels of society for three centuries. Just the opposite happened in Ethiopia. There, according to the contemporary church historian, Rufinus, it was introduced to the royal court by two young men of Tyre who fell into the hands of hostile Axumites when their vessel put ashore for provisions on the way to India. The entire crew and accompanying travelers were put to death, but the young men, Frumentius and Aedesius, were taken to the king who befriended them and appointed Aedesius, the younger, to be his cupbearer and Frumentius his private secretary. When the king died, the queen-mother prevailed upon the two youths to remain in Axum and assist in administering the kingdom and raising her son, destined to become Ezana, king of Axum, the first Christian ruler in Africa—the African Constantine.

When they were free to depart the kingdom, Aedesius returned to Tyre, but Frumentius remained to help establish a small Christian community at court and among a few traders along the coast. Sometime later he reported its existence to Bishop Athanasius in Alexandria and was consecrated bishop himself between 341 and 346 by Athanasius and sent back to Axum to continue the evangelization of the Ethiopians. The date of Ezana's conversion is given by most scholars as 330. There seems to be little doubt that the king adopted the Christian faith and brought his entire kingdom into the church. A Greek inscription belonging to him has been discovered. It begins: "In the faith of God and the power of the Father, the Son and the Holy Ghost." Also, coins that were minted in the early part of Ezana's reign bear the pagan symbol of the crescent and disk, while those minted later in his reign carry the sign of the Cross. Thus did Christianity become the state religion of a black kingdom, Ethiopia, a mere four centuries after the birth of Christ.[18]

Not without a struggle with paganism the Christian faith finally replaced the cults of the Sabaeans and other immigrants in Ethiopia during the next two centuries. Real resistance was encountered from the Agaw section of the population, some of whom worshiped water, trees, and certain idols, and from another segment which had been drawn to Judaism; but the faith spread rapidly in both Ethiopia and Yemen. One group of ancient chronicles speaks of the propagation of Christianity as the work of certain monks such as Abba Yohannes, who founded the monastery of Debra-Sina, or Abba Libanos, who is said to have been sent to Ethiopia at the instigation of St. Pachomius, with whom he had been associated in Upper Egypt. Libanos was only one of many Ethiopian hermit monks who withdrew from the world to almost inaccessible monasteries and churches hewn out of the high cliffs in the wastelands of Ethiopia where they subsisted on a meager fare, including bitter herbs and unripe bananas.[19] Early monasticism in both Egypt and Ethiopia involved many black Christians who upheld the new faith in Messiah Jesus with a fervor and dedication unmatched in the history of the church outside of Africa. A rivalry even grew up between various monasteries, each vying with the other for the greater holiness, recounted in a series of biographies of the so-called Nine Saints, to whom is attributed the later development of the Ge'ez liturgy and literature. The Nine Saints were anti-Chalcedonians from Constantinople and Syria who had been persecuted by the Roman Emperor, harried to the Egyptian desert, and thence to Ethiopia where they undertook the massive task of Christianizing the populace by producing the Ethiopic version of the Bible from a Syrio-Greek text, probably in the sixth century.

Of special interest to African and African American historians is the strikingly African character of early Ethiopian Christianity. The strenuous effort of the Christian nations of the West to make contact with a legendary Prester John, reputed to be a Christian ruler in Abyssinia who would help them out-flank Islam in Asia Minor and Africa, brought the Portuguese envoy, Pedro de Covilham, into contact with the Ethiopian church after 1487. Covilham was well received by the Ethiopians, but not permitted to leave. Groves reports that in 1520 a Portuguese embassy, bent upon uprooting the church from its heterodoxy and placing it under the spiritual authority of the Roman pontiff, found in Ethiopia a form of Christianity that had existed for more than a thousand years, but which was radically different from the form of the faith practiced by Europeans.

> The chaplain to the embassy, Francisco Alvarez, wrote an account of the country and their visit. . . . He gives a valuable account of Christian practice as he found it observed. . . . Thus the shouting and leaping in connexion with worship he admits may be accepted as done to the glory of God. . . . He frankly expressed to the *abuna* (the head of the Abyssinian Church) his amazement at the ordaining of children and even infants in arms as deacons, to which the old man replied that they would learn, and that he was very old and it might be long before his successor could be appointed from Cairo.[20]

The Jesuits tried their best to win Ethiopia for the Church of Rome for over a hundred years, but without notable success. Many of them complained about the "corruptions" that had crept into the Ethiopian church as a result of its separation from Roman Catholicism. Jerome Lobo, a Jesuit who remained in the country after his order had been

expelled by Fasiladas in 1633, gives an even more graphic picture of the
tumultuous public worship he witnessed.

> They sing the Psalms of David of which as well as other parts of the
> Holy Scriptures, they have a very exact translation in their own lan-
> guage. . . . The instruments of musick made use of in their rites of
> worship, are little drums, which they hang about their necks, and
> beat with both hands. . . . They begin their consort by stamping their
> feet on the ground, and playing gently on their instruments, but
> when they have heated themselves by degrees, they leave off drum-
> ming and fall to leaping, dancing, and clapping their hands, at the
> same time straining their voices to their utmost pitch, till at length
> they have no regard either to the tune, or the pauses, and seem
> rather a riotous, than a religious assembly. For this manner of wor-
> ship they cite the Psalm of David, 'O clap your hands all ye nations'.
> Thus they misapply the sacred Writings, to defend practices, yet
> more corrupt than those I have been speaking of.[21]

Father Lobo's misapplication of European norms to the Africanized
Christianity he found in Ethiopia underscores both the divergence of
the faith in black Africa from what Iberian Catholicism regarded as
authentic New Testament Christianity, and the impossibility of any easy
reconciliation that would render the Jesuits' arrogant and even militant
incursions acceptable to the Ethiopians. A mission of six Capuchin friars
soon followed, but it too failed when four of the missionaries were killed.
The Muslim Turks, at the request of Emperor Fasiladas, successfully cut
off any priests who attempted to reach the country. Groves adds, with
cryptic understatement, "The net result of the Jesuit mission was to render the Abyssinians bitterly hostile to the Roman Catholic Church, and
this attitude lasted long."

## THE CHURCH OF NUBIA

As we have noted, Judich, the "Ethiopian" eunuch, was the first
Christian convert to enter the area the ancients knew as Kush or Nubia—
the lands lying south of the First Cataract. It was to the city of Meroë that
he returned to his queen circa A.D. 37 and, presumably, brought her the
exciting news that the God of Israel whom he formerly worshiped had a
Son whose name was Jesus, and that his Father had raised him from the
dead. If the Meroë royal family and nobility had been persuaded by Judich
and a church formed at that time, it would have antedated both the
Coptic Church of Egypt and the Ethiopian Orthodox Church. What the
early existence of such a church in the heart of Africa might have meant
for the evangelization of the continent, the subsequent resistance thrown

up against Islam, and the interdiction of the overland and Atlantic slave trade, challenges our most unrestrained imagination. But as far as we know, the Meroitic kingdom was not Christianized by Judich, and it was not until the sixth century that the church was to be founded in Nubia by Byzantine missionaries.

In A.D. 500 the land that Arab authors knew as *Bilad an-Nuba*, or the country of Nubia, included Nobatia, lying between the First Cataract (Aswan) and the southern tip of the Second Cataract; Makuria, not well defined but located somewhere between the Second Cataract and Kabushiya—its capital being Dongola; and Alodia, or Alwa, the land extending from Kabushiya or Meroë to the confluence of the Blue and White Niles—its capital being Soba, a few miles east of present-day Khartoum. Perhaps the most important of these people were the Nobatae because, in order to protect the southern border of Egypt at the Aswan cataract from a warlike people called the Blemmyes, a branch of the Beja, the Roman emperor Diocletian (284–304) invited the Nobatae to settle down as a buffer state between Egypt and the Blemmyes raiders.[22] It was, therefore, to the Nobatae that the first Christian missionaries, an imperial delegation from Constantinople, anti-Chalcedonians, came sometime around A.D. 543.

The Nobatae and other people inhabiting the Upper Nile Valley were adherents of an African Traditional Religion not unlike that found in other parts of the continent. They had a multiplicity of gods and goddesses, chief among whom was the Egyptian goddess Isis. According to one authority, however, an even greater god among the people near the border between Egypt and the Sudan was the sun-god Mandulis; and in Upper Nubia, Amon, the god of fertility whose cult originated in Pharaonic times. Other divinities of the Nubians were Horus, represented by a man's body with a hawk's head, and Arensnuphis, depicted as a hunter and worshiped by both the Nubians and the Beja. Like the Egyptians, the Nubians possessed a firm belief in life after death. In the royal tombs, unearthed in Qustul and Ballana in 1930 and since the Second World War, archaeologists discovered that the dead were entombed with horses, cattle, and many earthly artifacts placed there so that they could be used by the kings when they reached the other world.[23]

According to the *Ecclesiastical History* of a contemporary, Bishop John of Ephesus, the Empress Theodora in Constantinople dispatched to the Nobatae around 543 Julian, an elderly presbyter of the Patriarch Theodosius of Alexandria. Julian had heard of a black people beyond the frontier of Egypt and was filled with a great passion to take the gospel to them. The Empress, who happened to share with Theodosius and Julian a Monophysite Christology, was almost thwarted by her husband, the Emperor Justinian, in her intention to be the first to bring the gospel to Nubia. Justinian, not to be outdone, tried to send a rival Orthodox mission with great gifts for the king and people of Nobatia, but Theodora succeeded in having the mission delayed until after Julian and his entourage could reach the country. Having failed to supersede the Monophysite embassy to the Nobatae, the Orthodox mission turned to the neighboring kingdom of Makuria, which adopted the Chalcedonian or Melkite faith.[24]

After the death of Julian, a pious missionary by the name of Longinus was made bishop by the Monophysite Patriarch Theodosius and sent to Nobatia to replace him. Longinus was received with great joy and remained in the country for six years. He was the one who organized the Nubian church. He introduced the liturgy in Greek, the language of Byzantium, and, crossing over Makuria at the risk of his life from the new Christians who had been won over to the Chalcedonian theology, entered the kingdom of Alodia, or Alwa, where he successfully founded a church that, along with the church in Nobatia, was loyal to the Monophysite see of Alexandria.

Thus, the early evangelization of Nubia was marked by a see-sawing and occasionally violent competition between episcopal proponents of the two prevailing views of the nature of Christ. In any case, by 580 Christianity had become the official religion of the three Nubian kingdoms, and a Byzantine form of the faith triumphantly raised the Cross over the holy places and shrines of African Traditional Religion in the heartland of black Africa. Perhaps no part of church history has been more neglected in Europe and North America, and unfortunately by Africans and African American believers, than the story of Christianity in Nubia. That story is an essential part of what some have called the first "visit" of Christianity to Africa—a period of six hundred years, extending from the conversion of the Ethiopian eunuch in about A.D. 37 and the coming of John Mark to Alexandria a few years later, to the courageous mission of Bishop Longinus to the people of Alwa in Upper Nubia during the second half of the sixth century.

Despite incursions from the East by Axumites, from the North by Persians, and the virtual encirclement of Nubia by Arabian Muslims in the seventh century, Christianity took root in the Upper Nile Valley and the black churches and monasteries of Nubia flourished for more than eight hundred years. Scholars do not give a definite date for its final demise as a result of internal weakness, the failure to develop a native clergy, and the persistent onslaught of Islam, but dissension among members of the royal families in the thirteenth century was aggravated by the conspiracy of some of them with the Sultan Baybars in Egypt. This brought on the replacement of Christian kings by Muslim kings in Dongola. A series of crises after 1260 precipitated the collapse of Nubia and the practical disappearance of Christianity over the next two or three hundred years. Even so, the longevity of Nubian Christianity is remarkable. Between 1974 and 1976 documents were discovered at Ibrim that mention Christian kings, bishops, and other officials of several

Christian principalities which continued after the fall of Dongola to the Muslim Kanz family. These and other documents suggest that perhaps one of those kingdoms, Dotawo, may have existed as late as 1464.

According to Fantini, the Portuguese, Francisco Alvarez, traveled to Ethiopia and Nubia in 1520. After returning home in 1527 he wrote a report which contained the following remark of John, a Syrian, who accompanied him on the Nubian leg of the long journey: "There are in it [Nubia] 150 churches which still contain crucifixes and figures of Our Lady and other figures painted on the walls and all old." "He also reported," writes Fantini, "that the inhabitants had lost their faith, but had not yet become Muslims. 'They live in the desire of being Christians.' "[25]

## ISLAM IN AFRICA

The fourth great religion of Africa is Islam, which from its inception encompassed significant elements of the other three—African Traditional Religion, Judaism, and Christianity—and, on that account, presented itself to the world as the final and most complete revelation of God, known by his true name as Allah, with the Prophet Muhammad as his preeminent representative on earth. Islam's relationship to Africa was fundamental and instantaneous. One of the first converts to the new faith was a black man, Bilal, an African who lived in Mecca and became the first muezzin—the official who calls the faithful to prayer. Ibrahim Abu-Lughod writes concerning the critical period before the hegira from Mecca in A.D. 622:

> Muhammad counselled about 40 of his disciples to seek refuge in Ethiopia, a country whose economic, cultural, and political links with Arabia are historic, and where they would be tolerated by its emperor and would preach the new faith as well. This very early coincidence of the Islamic presence in Africa made it possible to view Islam as a religious belief-system as indigenous to Africa as it was to West Asia.[26]

After the death of the Prophet in 632, when Muslim armies swept everything before them in Persia and Syria-Palestine, one of his generals, Amr Ibn al As, stormed into Egypt. The conquest was sudden and widespread. Shortly after 640 the Nile Valley, from Alexandria to the First Cataract, was in Muslim hands, although the Coptic Church was tolerated because Christians and Jews were considered "People of the Book." Coptic remained the language of the liturgy; Arabic gradually became the language of many of the common people and Islam their religion. In 641 Amr Ibn al As sent a military expedition across the southern border of Egypt, passing through Nobatia and reaching as far as the plain of Dongola before his army had to retreat in face of the unerring accuracy of the Nubian bowmen. Several peace treaties with the Nubians did not prevent them, along with the Beja, from continuing to conduct raids across the border. Intermittent warfare and temporary peace settlements, requiring the Nubians to pay tributes of slaves to their Arab overlords, existed for five hundred years. With the beginning of the dynasty of King George I in Dongola, which lasted well into the eleventh century, a period of relative quiet prevailed in Nubia despite the unease of the church as many Christians converted to Islam. One Bishop Abba Kyros, who occupied the episcopal see of Faras from 862 to 897, during the reign of George I, even bore the prestigious title of "Metropolitan," indicating, among other things, that Islam did not greatly interfere with ecclesiastical organization (Nubia continued under the Patriarch of Alexandria) and showed more willingness to permit Christians to go on with their normal church life than European Christians were ever willing to grant the followers of Muhammad.

The story of Islam's dramatic sweep through Cyrenaica to Morocco and ultimately across the Mediterranean to Spain is well known and need not be discussed here. It still comes as a shock to many African Americans, however, to discover that "black Moors" not only conquered Catholic Spain, but "blackenized" it and established outposts in Europe that lasted almost to the end of the fifteenth century. The softness and resilience of Iberian Catholicism as compared, for example, with Northern European Protestantism, can be partly accounted for by the long residence of a thoroughly Africanized Islam in Spain and Portugal.

One of the great Muslim teachers of the early eleventh century, Abadallah Ibn Yasin, went into a spiritual retreat or *ribat* in North Africa to prepare himself and his followers for a great expansion of the faith. Those who were with him, called the Almoravids, were the people who, after their teacher's death, descended like locusts upon ancient Ghana and presided over its disintegration in 1076. While occasional Berber jihads in the Western Sudan during the Middle Ages made converts by the edge of the sword, many more were made by the patient proselytizing of traders, travelers, secretaries, and scholars who traversed the savanna lands south of the Sahara, built great centers of learning at Jenne and Timbuktu on the Niger, and were responsible for the remarkable flowering of Islam in the West African kingdoms of Ghana, Mali, and Songhai.

Islam proceeded south of the Sahara with a markedly different strategy from that of the Christian crusaders of Europe used against the Muslims in Asia. In the first place, its straightforward and uncomplicated theology, resting upon the so-called five pillars of duty,[27] made Islam easily understood by ordinary people. While powerful rulers like Mansa Musa of Mali and Askia Muhammad of Songhai were great patrons of Islamic culture as well as military leaders, the conquest of the Western

Sudan was accomplished by a relatively small army of the faithful who made peaceful and perhaps more effective proselytizers.

> They lived their own social life, marrying women of the countries where they were, but making them into Muslims and bringing up their children as good Muslims, educated in Muslim learning. They did not interfere in local politics to any great extent, and had a kind of special position when any local wars broke out. They traded over a vast area, exchanging the goods of the more northerly areas for gold, cola nuts, and slaves of the south. Oral tradition in northern Ghana still tells how the Gonja conquerors were met by a family of Muslim clerics who agreed to go forward with them, calling for God's blessing on what they were doing and advising them as they went along.[28]

African Traditional Religions, in those areas of the Western Sudan where the Muslims carved out a foothold from which they have not been dislodged to this day, rarely experienced at the hands of Islam the bitter antagonism they experienced from Protestant Christianity when the evangelical missionary societies arrived near the end of the eighteenth century. Islam sometimes blended imperceptibly with ATR, content to permit Africans to call themselves Muslims without demanding more than minimal changes in belief structure and lifestyle. Much of West African culture, in terms of totem, rites of purification and invocation, reverence of the ancestors, and the use of amulets and talismans, was left undisturbed as long as the pillars of Islam were upheld and Allah was entreated to make a person "a better Muslim." It may be said that in consequence ATR was enriched by the Arabic language, the Arabic emphasis on education and the universal brotherhood of a highly diverse humanity, rather than rudely stamped out by stern and often racist expatriates bent upon condemning everything African and saving the souls of the heathen.

## THE SECOND "VISIT" OF CHRISTIANITY

Christianity made its second "visit" to Africa in the same century that Columbus thought he had discovered a new route to India across the western sea. It was Portugal, a small country with fewer than two million inhabitants, that essayed to explore the coastline of Africa beyond the Canaries and Cape Bojador and carry the banner of Catholic Christianity to "the black Moors" they might encounter along the way. Prince Henry, justifiably dubbed "The Navigator," directed the enterprising Portuguese explorers voyage by perilous voyage, between 1430 and his death in 1460, until the Senegambia had been reached and the sea lanes opened further south to Sierra Leone, the Gold Coast, Benin—and then in rapid stages—

to the Cape of Good Hope, rounded by Vasco da Gama on the 25th of December, 1497.

Already in 1442 some two hundred African slaves and a quantity of gold dust were brought back to Portugal by Gil Eannes, one of Prince Henry's captains, and after forts had been established on the Guinea coast the influx of slaves increased with each voyage. When the Congo was reached and Diego Cam returned home in 1485, he brought back slaves who were baptized. Later they boarded ship again and returned with Eannes and a large number of priests to begin the evangelization of the Congolese.[29] By 1492 the mission to the Congo was proceeding apace. At the capital, two hundred miles inland from the coast, the king and queen were baptized under the Christian names of John and Leonora. The Bishop of São Tomè, an island off the Guinea coast, was unable to take up residence in the new Christian kingdom, and consecrated for the purpose a Congolese who studied in Lisbon and was probably the first black African to become a Roman Catholic bishop. Some authorities believe that the young man was none other than Alfonso, the crown prince. In any case, it is reported that his son, Henry, was educated in Lisbon and Rome and ordained to the priesthood. In 1518 the son became titular bishop of Utica and was appointed Vicar Apostolic of the Congo by Pope Leo X.[30]

Thus, the Congo became the first Christian state in West Africa, but the faith was little more than a thin veneer that barely covered the royal family and a few nobles. No more so, of course, than in parts of Europe during the same period where animist worship of trees, stones, and springs existed under a patina of Christianity.[31] During the Roman Catholic effort in the Congo an appeal came up from the chief of a people further south, a vassal of King John of the Congo. Sometime later an expedition set out and established Christianity in Angola by 1574, but with no greater depth among the populace.

Despite these deficiencies it appears that the Portuguese were able to plant Christian churches in West Africa in the fifteenth and sixteenth centuries, and many young Africans were sent to Europe to train for holy orders. But always the roots were shallow. The commercial interests of Portugal and the political machinations of the kings, vying with each other for ascendancy, the demand of the missionaries for monogamy which threatened traditional marriage, the paltry instruction the people received before mass baptisms and the subsequent lack of pastoral attention, and—most of all—the beginning of the Atlantic slave trade, conspired to undermine the evangelizing effort.

By the end of the sixteenth century both Christian and Portuguese influence in West Africa had practically disappeared, albeit, as happened similarly in Nubia after the triumph of Islam, the faint afterglow of Catholicism suffused the attenuated memory of succeeding generations well into the nineteenth century. Holman Bentley, upon arriving in the

Congo in 1879, reported that he found "the sad relics of failure" used as fetishes by African Traditional Religionists. The chief and people paraded a large crucifix and some images of saints around the town in time of drought. Some of the older people were called *minkwilizi* (believers) and functioned at great funerals using some of the relics of Christian worship.[32]

## THE THIRD "VISIT" OF CHRISTIANITY

The third "visit" of Christianity to Africa came in the late eighteenth and early nineteenth centuries when African American slaves, who had evacuated the American colonies with the British during the Revolutionary War and were rewarded with their freedom, together with native African Christians, undertook the task of evangelizing their "heathen" brothers and sisters. One African historian calls the second visit of Christianity to Africa, which began with the Portuguese effort in the fifteenth century, "the era of frustration," and the third visit and more hospitable reception given to the faith between 1787 and 1893, "the era of promise."[33] Certainly the founding of the British colony of Sierra Leone for the repatriation of slaves from England and those intercepted by the British navy on the high seas was the most important factor in the success of the Protestant effort. It began when 411 ex-slaves, including sixty or seventy white women prostitutes from London who were to be their wives, sailed from Plymouth and landed at what was called the Province of Freedom on May 9, 1787.[34]

But the promise of the Sierra Leone settlement, conceived by Granville Sharp and other British abolitionists as a bulwark against the continuation and proliferation of the slave trade, was moot until the arrival of the former American slaves from Nova Scotia—under the leadership of the black former British army sergeant, Thomas Peters, and the highly regarded white abolitionist and naval officer, John Clarkson. An evangelistic motive was a major factor in bringing the group of black Methodist settlers, who embarked under the spiritual leadership of Boston King, and a smaller group of black Baptists under David George, a former slave from Silver Bluff, South Carolina. The fleet of fifteen ships carrying 1,190 passengers, including 456 children, lowered anchor in the Sierra Leone River on March 16, 1792.[35] This part of the story belongs to the rise of missionary emigrationism among African American Christians which will be discussed in the next chapter.

The dream that Christians in England had that Sierra Leone would become a beacon of evangelical light for the Dark Continent was never fully realized, but the gospel did go abroad from the colony, articulated by black men and women. This time the church took root, as also occurred in the United States as black preachers gradually took over their own congregations. It can be said, therefore, that Christianity found a permanent home in West Africa and in Black America about the same time, under black leadership in both places. In 1820 Christian churches were established in Liberia by African American ex-slaves who had been liberated by one means or another and who had returned to their Motherland.

The major burden of this successful third "visit" of Christianity, this time to West Africa, was borne by African sons and daughters themselves—converts like William Wade Harris, a Grebo of Liberia; Thomas Birch Freeman, who was born in England of a mixed marriage; Samuel Adjai Crowther, who had a tragic career as the first African bishop of the Anglican church; James "Holy" Johnson, a Yoruba, who became a bishop of the Anglican Synod of Nigeria; and Mother Martha Davies, of Freetown, Sierra Leone, who with nine other Creole mothers founded a "Confidential Band" in 1907, restricted to married church women.[36]

Since the 1960s African Americans have been interested in what they might learn about their African Christian heritage from research into the nature of the groups in Africa that rejected missionary Christianity from Europe and North America and established their own independent churches. In that direction may lie the answer to questions African American theologians and church leaders are asking about God's revelation to Africa prior to the arrival of whites and how what theologians call "common revelation" can be made coherent with biblical revelation. Instead of the history of missionary Christianity in West Africa, more relevant to the black churches of the United States may be the history of such independency movements as the Church of the Lord (Aladura) of Nigeria, the Kimbanguist Church of Zaire, the Cherubim and Seraphim Church of Nigeria, and the Army of the Cross of Christ Church of Ghana.[37]

## WEST AFRICA AND AFRICAN AMERICAN RELIGION

More research is needed before we can determine the extent to which both Judeo-Christian and Muslim ideas and practices were mixed, if only on the surface, with the traditional religions of West Africa. Many of the slaves who were brought to America had already been introduced to Islam, and some may well have brought some attenuated knowledge of Christianity. Given the longevity of Nubian Christianity and its decay and leaching, via ancient caravan routes, into Darfur, Bornu, and possibly as far as Northern Nigeria and the eastern bank of the Niger, the cultures and religions of the Western Sudan were probably not as isolated and quarantined as some have supposed. Even contacts that were more distant than Nubia were known. "Roman beads," writes H. H. Johnston, "are dug up in Hausaland and are obtained from the graves of Ashanti chiefs," and "Christianized Berbers from North Africa even carried Jewish and Christian ideas of religion as far into the Dark Continent as Borgu, to the west of the Lower Niger."[38] Given the fact that Johnston was infected with the Second Hamitic hypothesis that any evidences of high civilization in the Western Sudan must have come from the east, we should be suspicious of some of his claims, but it comes as no surprise that there were and continue to be borrowings back and forth among Christianity, Islam, and ATR from the eleventh century forward. The three faiths accommodated themselves to each other both in West Africa and in America. "God," claimed some of the Muslims imported to Georgia, "is Allah, and Jesus Christ is Mohammed—the religion is the same, but different countries have different names."[39]

The assimilation of Islam and Christianity into ATR should no more prejudice the original values inherent in the traditional religions of West Africa than the other way around. Students of West African societies insist upon an independent development of many religious ideas in ATR that found their way into both ancient and new churches in Africa and today can enrich both Christianity and Islam outside of Africa. Kofi Asare Opoku, a critic of missionary Christianity and European anthropologists who still maraud across West Africa to the Gulf of Guinea in search of material for doctoral dissertations, writes:

> The West continues to hold up to Africa its perverted image of the African past, and anything that does not fit into that image is dismissed or attributed to non-African sources. Westerners attributed the Yoruba statues to Egyptian influence, the art of Benin to Portuguese creation, and the architectural ruins of Great Zimbabwe to the Arabs. . . . In recent years, Carl Sagan could write, in connection with the astronomical knowledge of the Dogon of West Africa: "I picture a Gallic visitor to the Dogon people. . . . He may have been a diplomat, an explorer, an adventurer, or an early anthropologist."[40]

## THE AFRICAN INHERITANCE

We cannot delve into the complexities of ATR during the past five hundred years. Some features that were retained in the Caribbean neo-African cults and black religion in the United States will be dealt with in the next chapter. Here it is sufficient to note that our study of "African beginnings" not only shows the antiquity of the black Christian church but also indicates that many of the great religious ideas of Judaism, Christianity, and Islam arose spontaneously not only in Egypt, but at about the same time far to the west, within the great bend of the Niger and the Congo rivers. Despite significant differences, the essential truths of African Traditional Religions, Judaism, Christianity, and Islam anticipate, recapitulate, and reinforce one another in divers times and places across the broad stretch of sub-Saharan Africa. Thus, we acknowledge the mystery of the universal revelation of God given to the African people long before the arrival of Christianity from Europe and North America, or Islam from Arabia, and thus, with reference particularly to Christianity, the relative ease and alacrity with which many Africans who were taken into slavery in the New World adopted the Christian faith and syncretized it with the ATR that they brought with them across the Atlantic.

Monotheism or "monarchial polytheism"; the concept of a High God and lesser divinities who open the way, serve, or are the messengers of God; the voluntary recession or forced separation of God from the creation, requiring appeasement through blood sacrifice, redemptive suffering, and other means of reconciliation and reunion; the necessity of rites of purification, glorification, thanksgiving, and supplication; the reality of many gradations of power—from personal charisma, to impersonal spiritual forces that can do good or evil, to the omnipotence of a Supreme Being—and power's residence in both the visible and invisible worlds; the belief in moral rectitude, human solidarity, in a life after death, and a final judgment—all of these more or less characteristic aspects of African Traditional Religions from Senegambia, around the Gulf of Guinea, to the Congo and Angola (not to mention Equatorial and Southern Africa), find correspondences in the Judeo-Christian tradition. The tremendous proliferation and popularity of the independent or "instituted" Christian churches in Africa since the latter half of the nineteenth century bear eloquent witness to the affinity between the traditional religions and Christianity when accorded mutual respect and enrichment in the people's devotional life. Many observers recognize the possibilities inherent in this affiliation and its implications for the history of Christianity and the future of Christian belief disengaged from European cultural and religious hegemony.

> The love affair between Christ and the church on the African continent goes back two millennia. At the present time the church has a future and possibilities more dazzling than anything we can imagine, if only she can dissociate herself from some of the misdeeds of her rascally self-appointed friends of the past (and of the present in southern Africa). Perhaps, at last we may be allowed to discern her as she really is, in all her beauty, black and comely and arrayed as a bride for her Lord.[41]

Having explored the taproot of Christianity as it developed, disappeared from sight, and returned to Africa again to be reconstituted and reinterpreted under the pressure of European proselytization, Islam, the

Atlantic slave trade, native evangelists, and the fluctuating resistance of African Traditional Religions, we are now ready to turn to black religion's progress in the New World. Thus, we leave behind the crucible of West Africa where the spiritual gifts and sensibilities of African Americans were melted and molded prior to the Middle Passage and then underwent resurgence in the "invisible institution" of the brush arbor churches of Plantation America. There, despite the ignorance, prejudice, and repression of white Christians, African spirituality found refuge in the religion of the slave—until freedom came and the essence of that ancient spirituality could reassert itself in the great African American churches of the twentieth century.

## CHAPTER 2

# The Religion of the Slave

*Perceiving from the readiness of these answers that the subject
had been a familiar one with him, I immediately asked: "The black
people talk among themselves about this, do they: and they think so,
generally?"*

*"Oh, yes, sir; dey talk so: dat's what dey tink."*

*"Then they talk about being free a good deal, do they?"*

*"Yes, sir. Dey—dat is, dey say dey wish it was so; dat's all dey talk,
master—dat's all, sir."*

Frederick Law Olmsted
*A Journey in the Seabord Slave States,* 1856

From the beginning the religion of the descendants of the Africans
who were brought to the Western world as slaves has been something
less and something more than what is generally regarded as
Christianity. Under the circumstances, it could not have been otherwise. The religious beliefs and rituals of a people are inevitably and
inseparably bound up with the material and psychological realities of
their daily existence. Certainly the realities of this world for the slaves
were vastly different from those of the slavemasters. In a way, the slavemasters understood this better than did their preachers and missionaries. Few planters or overseers were ever so sanguine as the
missionaries about the possibility of master and slave sharing the same
religion.

The Reverend James Ramsey, an indefatigable and pious slaveholding
preacher who spent eighteen years preaching to the slaves in the West
Indies, may have been one exception. In an essay published in 1784 he
made the following interesting and rather uncommon observation:

Master and slave are in every respect opposite terms; the persons to
whom they are applied, are natural enemies to each other. Slavery,
in the manner and degree that it exists in our colonies, could never

have been intended for the social state; for it supposes tyranny on one side, treachery and cunning on the other. Nor is it necessary to discuss which gives first occasion to the other.[1]

Such unvarnished good sense should be a requirement for any serious discussion of what characterized the religion of the African slaves once the confusion about whether baptism necessitated granting them freedom was over and they had become the objects of systematic evangelization. The most immediate and determinative reality in the life of most slaves was their bondage in this strange land, thousands of miles from the sacred earth in which were interred the bones of their ancestors and where the gods of their fathers walked and talked with men and women. The religion of the whites, first Roman Catholicism and later Protestantism, could make effective contact with the slave's religious experience in Africa, but the consequences were never so flattering to the superior power of the European version of the true faith as the missionaries wanted to believe.

The religious inclinations of blacks in the United States, the West Indies, Central and South America today, almost five hundred years later, are largely predisposed to the beliefs and practices of the Judeo-Christian tradition. But the Christianity that developed among successive generations of the descendants of the first slaves brought to this part of the world is a different version of the Judeo-Christian tradition than that professed by the descendants of the slavemasters—whether Catholic, Protestant, or Jew. Without going into details at this time, it should be noted that in recent years historians of religion and other scholars have been uncovering a form of belief and practice in the religious institutions of African Americans that may be categorized as "black religion." They have sought to indicate the points at which black religion not only differs from what most white religionists believe, but where knowledge of black faith may help scholars understand something about the most elemental religious consciousness which humans have expressed, for, generally speaking, religion has functioned closer to the survival needs of blacks in America than it has to those of whites.[2]

Since the early 1960s black believers—Protestants, Catholics, Muslims, Jews, and African traditionalists—have attempted to express what they believed were some of the distinctive attributes of African American religion—the "spiritual strivings" (Du Bois)—of oppressed and scattered Africans who refused to surrender their humanity under enslavement and never lost sight of the freedom and justice they believed were God-given. During the 1960s black writers such as St. Clair Drake, Yosef ben-Jochannan, John G. Jackson, Chancellor Williams, Leonard Barrett, Joseph R. Washington, and Ulysses D. Jenkins contributed to this "sense of ethnic differentness" by exploring the roots of African American culture and religion in the African past. The consequence as we saw in Chapter 1 is a general search, still going on today, for a spiritual renewal in the diaspora that can be related to the past and the future of Africa as well as America.

In Africa itself, particularly in the ecumenical centers and universities, scholars of both Christian and Islamic persuasion have inquired into the meaning and significance for the future of the continent when Christianity, Islam, African Traditional Religions, and the new secularism of a free and democratic nation encounter one another at *Orita*, the Yoruba word for "where the ways come together." Today the urgency of the task is accentuated by the termination of the old-fashioned missionary strategy on the part of the churches of Europe and North America, and the fact that a new, indigenous form of African Christianity—unabashed by its differences from the white Christianity of the West—is taking root among African peoples.

Meanwhile, in the United States, the American Muslim Mission (formerly the Nation of Islam), which produced Malcolm X, a man whom many blacks consider one of the great martyrs of our time, and the quasi-religious groups that sponsor African culture among black Americans or gather around various institutions in urban centers, like Albert B. Cleage's (Jaramogi Abebe Agyeman) Shrine of the Black Madonna, are continual reminders that black religion is a complex concatenation of archaic, modern, and continually shifting belief systems, mythologies, and symbols, none of which can be claimed as the exclusive property of any one religious tradition—yet sharing a common core related to Africa and racial oppression. Many poets, preachers, academicians, and charismatic leaders of the masses continue to excavate the roots of black culture from the slag heap of history that has largely ignored it. They are finding that the deepest meaning of the black experience lies in the variegated religious and philosophical acquirements of African Americans. The broad consensus among them is that it is through religious doors that contemporary African Americans may have to walk to find their authentic identity as a people.

It is the purpose of this book to continue this search for meaning and direction by an analysis of the development of black religion in America from the period of slavery to the emergence of the new theological currents that black church members brought to the civil rights movement of the 1960s, currents that were further developed in what is called the black theology movement.

The analysis is basically historical. Its major presupposition is that, notwithstanding elements of white evangelicalism in the mainstream of black faith, there was from the beginning a fusion between a highly developed and pervasive feeling about the essentially spiritual nature of historical experience, flowing from the African traditional background, and a radical secularity related both to religious sensibility and to the experience of slavery and oppression. This fusion accounts for the most significant characteristics of black religion. The dialectical relationship of these two elements of the black religious consciousness was institutionalized in the historical black churches and in the communal and associational groupings that grew up around them and have not entirely severed their connection with the churches. The revitalization and revolutionary movements that developed in the black community whenever an inveterate white racism backlashed to check progress toward liberation drew upon the resources of this distinctive religious orientation to interpret the meaning of the black experience and to strengthen the ability of the masses to face and deal with calamity.

## WHITE CHRISTIANITY AND BLACK RELIGION

What we may call "white Christianity" in Europe and North America has made a deep and lasting impression upon blacks everywhere, including Africa. But blacks have used Christianity not so much as it was delivered to them by racist white churches, but as its truth was authenticated to them in the experience of suffering and struggle, to reinforce an enculturated religious orientation and to produce an indigenous faith that emphasized dignity, freedom, and human welfare.

Most sociologists of religion will agree that religion does much of the same thing for all sorts and conditions of peoples. But it is a matter of serious debate whether a specific religion of a specific people can be transmitted in toto to another people—even in the same geographical location—without certain substantive changes due to ethnicity, custom, social structure, and many other factors. Especially is this true when one people is free and another is enslaved.

The questions that existence presents to the religious sensibility and imagination of a person who is relatively free to determine his or her own style of life and vocation are existentially different questions from those that the religious introspection of a slave predicates and seeks to answer. The matter seems almost too commonplace to belabor. And yet many persons express surprise and not a little vexation at the suggestion that there have been in the past, and to some significant extent continue into the present, important discontinuities between Christianity as practiced by white Americans and Christianity as practiced in the still largely segregated African American communities of the Western hemisphere.

Newbell Niles Puckett, who was usually prejudiced in his estimate of blacks, nevertheless makes a telling remark in commenting upon the similarities and dissimilarities between Negro and Anglo-Saxon folk religion:

The mere fact that a people *profess* to be Christians does not necessarily mean that their Christianity is of the same type as our own.

The way in which a people interpret Christian doctrines depends largely upon their secular customs and their traditions of the past. There is an infinite difference between the Christianity of the North and South in America, between that of city and country, and between that of whites and colored, due in the main to their different modes of life and social backgrounds. Most of the time the Negro outwardly accepts the doctrines of Christianity and goes on living according to his own conflicting secular mores, but sometimes he enlarges upon the activities of God to explain certain phenomena not specifically dealt with in the Holy Scriptures.[3]

It is true that the first independent black churches, the African Baptist and African Methodist, patterned their orders of worship and creeds after the white churches from which they separated in the latter half of the eighteenth century. But it is also true, and even more significant, that these churches called themselves "African" and developed, particularly in the South, out of that so-called "invisible institution," the slave church. From the beginning these churches developed what whites recognized as a "Negro style" of devotion and belief. Whatever those first gatherings of slaves for religious purposes outside the supervision of whites may have been like, it is inaccurate to think of the religious institutions that made their first appearance among blacks as "churches" in the sense of the European or American model. According to Du Bois:

> It was not at first by any means a Christian Church, but a mere adaptation of those heathen rites which we roughly designate by the term Obe Worship, or "Voodooism." Association and missionary effort soon gave these rites a veneer of Christianity, and gradually, after two centuries, the Church became Christian, with a simple Calvinistic creed, but with many of the old customs still clinging to the services.[4]

Later we shall have occasion to examine the relationship between African American religion and vodun. There is considerable discussion today about the precise manner in which the earliest teachings of Christianity were absorbed by the slaves who were brought to North America from Africa or the Caribbean. We have certain statements by slaves of the period, the later slave narratives, reports of missionaries, and the WPA material collected between 1936 and 1938 from former slaves or their children. But we lack many written descriptions of the accommodation to Christianity by priests and medicine men, and the exact methods by which they developed a system of religion that contained elements of both Euro-American and African beliefs. Moreover, complete freedom of expression by those slaves who had previously been religious leaders in Africa would have required the absence of any white person. Whites would have been offended by the obvious corruption of Christian worship, as they understood it. And the implicit psychological independence would have been considered dangerous. Accordingly, we have few records of such meetings held in the absence of whites, though it cannot be doubted that they were held, particularly in those areas where several slaves were able to come together and were sufficiently isolated to hold religious services without white supervision.

It is not certain how much exposure any individual slave had to Christianity prior to the systematic mission inaugurated in 1701 by the Society for the Propagation of the Gospel of the Anglican Church. Slavery had existed since about 1505 under Roman Catholic indulgence in the Spanish West Indies in Latin America. By the middle of the sixteenth century some African slaves from the Gulf of Guinea in West Africa had been introduced to Protestantism by Captain John Hawkins, the English privateer and adventurer.[5] Inasmuch as many of the first slaves to be brought to the North American colonies came from the Antillean subregion of the Caribbean, it is possible that some of them had already made a partial transition from their native religion to Christianity prior to being evangelized on the mainland. Brawley tells us that some of the slaves brought to the West Indies after 1517 had been educated as Muslims or as Catholics, and that in 1540 there was a Negro in Quivira, Mexico, who had actually taken holy orders. By 1542 the Roman Catholic Church had established three Brotherhoods of the True Cross of Spaniards, two of which were dedicated to missionizing blacks and Amerindians.[6]

These facts leave open the possibility that, when the English colonists turned from their earlier indifference to the Christianization of their slaves and began to give them religious instruction, there were some ready for thorough indoctrination because they had already heard something about Christianity. Some may have already emerged as religious leaders who were beginning to work out some accommodation, as we saw in Chapter I, between ATR and Christianity. We do not know for sure, and in the absence of solid evidence we are obliged to move cautiously with this kind of speculation.

We do know that some of the early preachers to the slaves were not whites, but former African priests or religious specialists of one sort or another who possessed unusual gifts of leadership and persuasion. One source that has been mentioned is Dahomey, where dynastic quarrels produced such leaders among those sold to the white traders as slaves. Some of the victims were not only the defeated chiefs and their families, but also their priests and diviners. Herskovits has pointed out that the most intransigent among those conquered by the Dahomeans were the local priests of the river cults. Although compliant priests were retained in order not to incur the wrath of their gods, those who resisted—for example, the priests serving the river gods in what is now the nation of

Benin—were sold to the slavers and probably ended up in the New World.[7] Herskovits comments on the implications of this for the development of resistance among the slaves:

> What, indeed, could have more adequately sanctioned resistance to slavery than the presence of priests who, able to assure supernatural support to leaders and followers alike, helped them fight by giving the conviction that the powers of their ancestors were aiding them in their struggle for freedom.[8]

Whatever leadership roles they may have played, it is certain that by the beginning of the eighteenth century there were a few black Christians in some of the English colonies—most of them worshiping in congregations with their masters or, if they were freed, with their white neighbors—albeit under the conditions of racial segregation.[9] It was not until after the Revolution that black preachers began to be licensed by the denominations. Previously they were recognized by their own people and exercised what was later called "jackleg" ministries whenever opportunity was given and the slaves were able to assemble under their leadership.

What do we know about the main features of this black religion prior to the founding of the first black churches? In one of the most thorough studies of the nature of slave religion Eugene Genovese writes:

> In the southern United States the combination of hostile white power, small plantation and farm units, and the early closing of the slave trade crushed much of the specific African religious memory. But since the denominations could not easily absorb the African impulse, they found themselves defeated by it in two sometimes complementary ways: large residues of "superstition" remained in the interstices of the black community; and Afro-Christianity arose as something within the Euro-Christian community and yet remained very much without.[10]

We have enough evidence from various sources to establish the fact that black religion in the United States, as in the Caribbean and Latin America, was a resilient form of the Judeo-Christian faith fused to an African base. The summary statement by Du Bois that it was characterized by "the Preacher, the Music, and the Frenzy" cannot be far from the truth.[11] E. Franklin Frazier recognized the presence of these elements, but emphasized also the importance of the white Protestant influence—particularly the use of the Bible in the development of early black Christianity. It is true that despite the illiteracy of the vast majority the slaves were greatly attracted to what they considered "the sacred book" and they gave rapt attention to its reading by missionaries and their own black preachers, many of whom had learned the Bible "by heart." In the biblical stories, psalms, and accounts of miracles they found the conviction and hope that a better life was possible for them in this world and, with even more certainty, in the world beyond. Frazier writes:

> It was from the Bible that the slaves learned of the God of the white man and of his ways with the world and with men. The slaves were taught that the God with whom they became acquainted in the Bible was the ruler of the universe and superior to all other gods. They were taught that the God of the Bible punished and rewarded black men as well as white men. Black men were expected to accept their lot in this world and if they were obedient and honest and truthful they would be rewarded in the world after death.[12]

In slave autobiographies and descriptions of religious services there are indications of the importance of Scripture, even though it was more often than not rendered according to the personal idiosyncrasies of the preacher. But even more prominent is the highly charged emotionalism of the services, the "mourners' bench," the shouting, handclapping, holy dancing, and the picturesque imagery of the sermon and the spiritual songs.[13] The slaves made an adaptation to Christianity that rendered it something more than a dispassionate system of theology and a code of behavior. They accepted the spirited, evangelical interpretation of the Baptist and Methodist preachers and imitated them, but they also went beyond that understanding of the faith to fashion it according to their own social, recreational, and personal spiritual needs.

One of the outstanding missionaries during the first part of the nineteenth century was a Presbyterian, Reverend Charles Colcock Jones. With true Calvinistic zeal for purity of doctrine, Jones complained of perversions of the gospel among the newly converted slaves on the plantations he served. He was particularly exercised over their propensity to antinomianism, the heretical belief that the moral law is of no effect to one who has come under the dispensation of Jesus Christ. Jones observed about the religious practices he witnessed:

> True religion they are inclined to place in profession, in forms and ordinances, and in excited states of feeling. And true conversion, in dreams, visions, trances, voices—all bearing a perfect or striking resemblance to some form or type which has been handed down for generations, or which has been originated in the wild fancy of some religious teacher among them.[14]

Jones described the slaves' concept of the Supreme Being and of the person of Christ as indefinite and confused. In this connection it is interesting to note that the spirituals rarely express explicit christological interest. Jesus is simply identified as the Lord who befriends us and is concerned about our problems. There is little interest in theological arguments for his divinity. As far as Christ is concerned some of the slaves ministered to by Jones had heard of someone by that name, but did not know who he was, or were inclined to identify him with Muhammad, the prophet of Allah.

> The Mohammedan Africans remaining of the old stock of importations, although accustomed to hear the Gospel preached, have been known to accommodate Christianity to Mohammedanism. "God," they say, "is Allah, and Jesus Christ is Mohammed—the religion is the same, but different countries have different names."[15]

It was reported that in Georgia some slaves had a religion of their own based on their own experiences, the experience of God with them, and various revelations and visions.[16] Even though "churched Negroes" respected the Bible and learned to read it before they could read much of anything else, there was a contempt among many slaves for "book religion." They rejected it not merely because they had to depend upon oral instruction, but because they had considerable self-esteem and confidence in their own manner of believing in and worshiping God. "The Spirit within" was considered superior to the Bible as a guide for their religious knowledge. One informant discovered that the slaves on his plantation were adverse to the Bible because they had been told by their masters that it upheld slavery.[17]

C. C. Jones reported in the Tenth Report of the Association for the Religious Instruction of the Negroes in Liberty County, Georgia, an interesting incident in this regard:

> I was preaching to a large congregation on the Epistle to Philemon; and when I insisted on fidelity and obedience as Christian virtues in servants, and upon the authority of Paul, condemned the practice of running away, one-half of my audience deliberately rose up and walked off with themselves; and those who remained looked anything but satisfied with the preacher or his doctrine. After dismission, there was no small stir among them; some solemnly declared that there was no such Epistle in the Bible; others, that it was not the Gospel; others, that I preached to please the masters; others, that they did not care if they never heard me preach again.[18]

The togetherness of the slaves in their own community is another aspect of the style of religious life that many white missionaries could neither understand nor appreciate. Members of the same church were sometimes sacrally bound not to reveal each other's sins. One need not suspect some profound theological aberration for such conspiracies, particularly in view of the fact that for the slavemaster by far the most heinous sins were rebelliousness, stealing, sabotage, and malingering. Jones, however, had a keen smell for what he considered antinomianism among his charges. He found all kinds of degradation and immorality among those who had been baptized and professed to be Christians. In one place he remarks: "That which would be an abominable sin, committed by a church member with a worldly person, becomes no sin at all if committed with another church member." Believers felt that they must "Bear one another's burdens and so fulfill the law of Christ."[19]

Joseph B. Earnest supports Jones's suspicion of religious lawlessness among the slaves. He observed that "frequently sins are committed during, or immediately after, a religious service."[20] This may be an exaggeration, but one can believe the story he tells of an old Negro who testified in church that he had cursed some, stolen some, drunk some whiskey, and had certainly committed other sins during this life but, thank God, he had never lost his religion.

Newbell Niles Puckett held that the African concept of sin, which survived to some degree in the early black churches, had to do with a broken relationship with the gods rather than an offense against another person. It was an offense, a neglect, or ill-advised act against the spirits that was judged sinful—whether committed consciously or accidentally. Hence, he concluded, there was resident in the Christianity of the southern Negro, following the West African practice, almost no connection between morality and religion:

> An Arkansas Negro considered it all right to conjure inasmuch as he had "surrance er salvation," and most of the conjure-doctors with whom I have come in contact are unusually religious and ostentatious in their church obligations—some of them even being ministers.[21]

Puckett's racism makes him suspect, and although Albert J. Raboteau may be correct when he implies that one cannot find much evidence of slave preachers practicing conjury, there is evidence of a relationship between conjuration and black religion. The testimonies of ex-slaves make clear that good church members took pains to avoid conjurers, but it is not clear that the reverse was true. When William Adams, the ex-slave conjurer from Texas, said that "De old folks in dem days knows more about de signs dat de Lawd uses to reveal His laws dan de folks of today," he was talking about a form of religion in which conjuration was tacitly accepted and secretly if not openly practiced by religious persons.[22] Puckett's statement that some of the practitioners were ministers is not difficult to believe if we understand conjury in a broad rather than narrow sense, and as benign as well as hostile. Nor should we be surprised at the excuses Earnest reports some slaves gave for what he considered sinful.

The issue is whose morality is at question under the circumstances and what is the proper role for religion in a struggle for survival.

What Earnest, Puckett, and others refused to acknowledge was the appropriateness of the slaves' use of the Bible and supernatural power to counteract the willpower of their oppressors. Leonard Barrett shows the function of black religion in Jamaica during the same period when the myalmen, or "good" conjurers, were gradually taking over religious authority from the more hostile obeah practitioners. The same process may well have occurred in the American South.[23] Just as craft and cunning were used to deal with the dominating power of the whites, so were those darker aspects of the supernatural that are sometimes called "the wrath of God" invoked by the religious specialists among the slaves to frustrate and punish their tormentors.

Religious purists who complain that any black religion that may have evolved from practices as superstitious and retaliatory as conjury must be regarded more with embarrassment than praise have the same problem as some of the missionaries. They fail to understand how the slave looked upon and evaluated the hypocrisy of the white Christianity he or she experienced. Their frequent refusals to be disciplined by the moral strictures of the slavemaster's religion suggest a moral integrity and spirit of resistance that could be expressed with impunity only in religious form. The missionary was looking for purity of doctrinal belief and daily life in accordance with the accepted standards of Christianity. Nothing could have been further from the existential situation in which the slaves found themselves or more remote from the basic religious orientation such a situation provoked.

The slaves had small concern for doctrinal fidelity, but not because there was no theological or moral content in the religions they practiced in Africa, or in the adaptations they were obliged to make to Christianity. Actually the hierarchical structure and pragmatic quality of the African religions that were partly carried over into the Afro-Catholic cults of Haiti, Cuba, and Bahia maintained the basic ontological and soteriological emphases that are present in the traditional religions and some of the independent churches of Africa today. The absence of theological interest among the slaves was due, most of all, to the practical and experimental nature of their religion in which the existence of a Supreme Being, the reality of the spirit world, and the revelatory significance of symbols and myths were all taken for granted and required no explicit theological formulation in the Western sense. Indeed, what they already believed about nature, human beings, and God was more firmly corroborated by their experience than by any catechesis that had to conform to the institution of slavery.

The slaves were uneducated, by Western standards, but they were by no means ignorant. Almost immediately they recognized the gross inconsistency between the allegation that this all-powerful God of the whites could care so much about their eternal salvation while remaining indifferent to the powerlessness and wretchedness of their condition. Even though they adopted the outward appearance of Christian conversion, they took from it only what proved efficacious for easing the burden of their captivity and gave little attention to the rest. They were aware that the God who demanded their devotion, and from whom came the spirit that infused their secret meetings and possessed their souls and bodies in the ecstasy of worship, was not the God of the slavemaster, with his whip and gun, nor the God of the plantation preacher, with his segregated services and injunctions to servility and blind obedience.

Well into the nineteenth century the slaves relied upon the most elemental presuppositions of a religious way of life to give consolation and meaning to their suffering. Whatever specific beliefs may have been salvaged from Africa, or from the breaking-in period in the Caribbean, they came under the most vigorous assault by the North American missionaries and plantation preachers. The polytheistic aspect of traditional African religion had to be surrendered under great duress despite the fact that the idea of a Supreme Being was not foreign to Africans. Yet the spirits of the ancestral gods, disembodied and depersonalized, invaded the interstices of the objective world and impregnated the imagination with an interminable variety of the ghosts, witches, talking animals, and supernatural phenomena that comprised the folklore of the southern black. The harsh, oppressive conditions of daily life, especially for field hands, rendered this animated, divinized environment generally hostile in the mind of one in slavery—for it could scarcely avoid being the subconscious manifestation of the nightmarish reality of every waking hour. We have today a more optimistic picture of the period between sundown and sunrise in the slave quarters than previously, but it cannot be denied that the obvious disorganization and dehumanization of the social situation at best served to undergird a fatalistic and demonic side of everyday existence.

The overarching question was one of survival—mental and physical—and whatever slaves could appropriate from the conjurer, or later from the charismatic Christian preacher, to deal with the aleatory quality of their situation and to ward off the evil influences around them was seized upon as a gift from "de Lawd" who had not seen fit to extricate them from their plight, but nevertheless provided some means of preserving health and sanity in the midst of it. This is not to suggest that slaves did not find joy and consolation in their religion. Slave religion did indeed address the serious problems of survival by falling back upon some of the more malevolent possibilities of an earlier tradition. But there was another side.

The grim determination and punctiliousness with which many Protestants went about the business of saving the souls of the heathen was foreign to the basic sensibilities of African and African American religions. For the slave, reverence toward God was, first of all, the joyous affirmation of God's presence and providence. Once the spirit came near, one opened himself or herself to it with a vivaciousness and abandon that were expressed most satisfactorily in song and dance. The secular and the sacred met and embraced each other in the bodily celebration of the homologous unity of all things—the holy and profane, good and evil, the beautiful and dreadful. To give oneself up with shouts of joy and "singing feet" to this wholeness of being, to the ecstatic celebration of one's creaturehood, and to experience that creaturehood taken up and possessed by God in a new state of consciousness, was to imbibe the most restorative medicine available to the slave.

The brooding melancholy of the Negro spirituals has led some to believe that the religion of the slave was one of unrelieved gloom and grief—a religion of lost souls flailing hopelessly against a wall of darkness. The slaves knew sorrow and misery, but they knew it as an inevitable part of the natural life, of creaturely existence, and they lowered themselves into its depths in funeral rituals and in mournful songs and spirituals. What appears to be wallowing in sorrow as a poor, demoralized human being was more a way of *feeling into* life in its nether dimensions, of being more deeply nourished by the power of the inscrutable and tragic in life, without an awareness of which human beings cannot fully realize themselves and their place in the mysterious womb of the universe.

The dominant motif then of slave religion was affirmation and joy—even carnal pleasure had its prominent place. Such a religion bound men and women to the organic, vitalistic powers of creation—to the powers that they believed could provide for and sustain those who joyfully acknowledged and served the Creator. Behind the recognition that in existence there is some radically opposing force, some intrinsic mischief that we must somehow overcome or learn to control, was an even greater recognition that life is good and is to be savored and enjoyed while it lasts.

The curious mixture of zeal and carelessness that resulted from the fusing of Christianity with the religions the slaves brought with them from Africa was an unending puzzlement to those missionaries who arduously labored to get them to contemplate the state of their souls with fear and trembling. The preachers could never understand the humor and light touch with which the slaves handled sacred things, a habit the preachers charged to stupidity or a lack of refinement. The shouts of a Saturday night over the spirits in a bottle of rum and the shouts of a Sunday morning over the Holy Spirit sounded suspiciously alike to the white missionaries. They shared their uneasiness about it with one another, but were wary of admitting it to their patrons. How could one exult so vociferously over the ritual and ceremony of Christianity, on the one hand, and, on the other, take the solemn moral requirements of the faith with such lightheartedness? If such moral gymnastics as some of the Christian slaves exhibited were permitted, how were the preachers and their slaveholding sponsors to judge whether such persons had experienced a genuine conversion and could be trusted to be obedient slaves?

Some of the missionaries confessed that they did not know how to deal with this dilemma. William Capers, the famous Methodist missionary, in a letter to Wilbur Fisk, complained of nursing the slaves through a probationary period for church membership, only to have them fall away into their old habits because, as he put it, "the prevalent conceit that sin is sin for white men not negroes . . . [held] a fond control over them."[24] Backsliding, jumping from one denomination to another to secure better personal advantages, and distorting Christian teachings to fit their own preferences were reported by whites as proof of the religious immaturity and childishness of their black converts. Their extreme excitability in prayer and praise, often exhibited with subtle traces of sensuality, their exaggerated imitation of white piety—which in the next moment would slip into boisterousness and a playful disregard for the sanctity of worship—gave some observers the general impression that "the Negroes play at religion" and were incapable of Christianization by the accepted norms of whites.

But it is incontestable that what whites regarded as incapacity and childishness was more often a completely different approach to religion, a different view of the world, and a studied avoidance of white control. Slave religion was partly a clandestine protest against the hypocrisy of a system that expected blacks to be virtuous and obedient to those who themselves lived lives of indolence and immorality in full view of those they purported to serve as examples. The Reverend Charles C. Jones did well to warn inexperienced missionaries about naivety in assuming that slaves had swallowed all their teachings. He said that such unsuspecting preachers, "beholding their attention to the preaching of the Gospel, adapted to their comprehension, and hearing the expressions of their thankfulness for the pains taken for their instruction, come to the conclusion that they are an unsophisticated race."[25]

The preacher, said Jones, could take nothing for granted when dealing with these blacks. He must not mistake outward manifestations of piety for true conversion if he did not want, in the end, to be frightened away from the mission field in astonishment or disgust:

> He discovers deism, skepticism, universalism. As already stated, the various perversions of the Gospel, and all the strong objections which he may perhaps have considered peculiar only to the cultivated minds, the ripe scholarship and profound intelligence of critics and philosophers![26]

All of its deficiencies and excesses notwithstanding, the religion that the slaves practiced was their own. It was unmistakably the religion of an oppressed, but not entirely conquered, people. It had, of course, common features with Euro-American Protestantism and, in the French-speaking and Spanish-speaking Caribbean, with Roman Catholicism. But it was not forged in the drawing rooms of the elegant mansions of Virginia and South Carolina, or in the segregated galleries of the northern churches. It was born out of the experience of being black and understanding blackness to be somehow connected with being held in bondage and needing to be free. Its most direct antecedents, as far as Christianity was concerned, were the quasi-religious meetings that took place on the plantations, unimpeded by white supervision and under the leadership of the first generation of African priests who were to become preachers. It was soon suppressed and dominated by the religious instruction of the Society for the Propagation of the Gospel in Foreign Parts and the Baptist, Methodist, and Presbyterian churches. But the black faith that evolved from the coming together of diverse religious influences became a *tertium quid,* something distinctly different from any of its major contributors.

Both the slave congregations of the South—"the invisible institution"—and the more or less free black churches of the North developed a religion that masked a sublimated outrage balanced with patience, cheerfulness, and a boundless confidence in the ultimate justice of God. As the religion of a subjugated people, it had both positive and negative effects upon those who participated in it. It served, in formal and informal ways, to order and interpret an existence that was characterized on the one hand by repression, self-abnegation, and submissiveness, and on the other by subterfuge, opportunism, and the joyous affirmation of life despite tribulation.

It would be helpful at this point to examine somewhat more closely the African religious background that provided a rapidly disintegrating but persistent base upon which the institutions of the slave were erected. It is not the purpose of this discussion to make a comparative analysis of Christianity and the traditional religions of West Africa or their adaptation in the Caribbean during the period of slavery. Such a task belongs properly to the fields of anthropology and the history of religions. Scholars have adequately demonstrated the continuities and discontinuities. It is now clear that black religion in North America had roots in Africa and the Caribbean as well as in the Great Awakenings of the eighteenth and nineteenth centuries.[27]

## THE AFRICAN SUBSTRATUM

What many Europeans and Americans once regarded as a lower form of animism and pagan superstition in Africa is now recognized as highly involved ontological and ethical systems. This is partly because African scholars began to examine their own religions without the deferential accession to imported norms and values. On their part, African American scholars have become more appreciative of their own African past and now generally hold that the slaves who were imported to the New World were not completely divested of their belief systems. Whatever was their precise nature, it is certain that those beliefs were not as unenlightened and preposterous as we once believed. The traditional religions of Africa have a single overarching characteristic that survived in an attenuated form for generations—a powerful belief that the individual and the community were continuously involved with the spirit world in the practical affairs of daily life.

African religions know nothing of a rigid demarcation between the natural and the supernatural. All of life is permeated with forces or powers in some relationship to human weal or woe. Individuals are required, for their own sake and that of the community, to affirm this world of spirit that merges imperceptibly with the immediate, tangible environment. One enters into communion with this other reality in a prescribed way to receive its benefits and avoid its penalties. The Supreme Being, ancestors, spirits resident in or associated with certain natural phenomena, and living humans who possess gifts of healing or of making mischief, were all united in one comprehensive, invisible system that has its own laws which sustain the visible world and ordinary life for the good of all.

Considerable injustice was done to the true nature of these beliefs by the early missionaries and others who could regard them only as "ignorant superstitions" or "dark and cruel fetishism." Even Du Bois, commenting upon obi or obeah worship, which he attributed to slaves who were transported to the West Indies, uncritically identified this form of religion with nature worship and witchcraft. What is suggested thereby is that we are dealing here with a perversion of the natural revelation of God, the weird concoction of a race of religious fanatics and charlatans. A somewhat more sophisticated analysis assumed that these religions were basically animistic and should be understood primarily as sorcery and magic. But such terms are pejorative and the implication, when applied to the seminal religion of the slaves, is that they were ignorant and uncivilized persons; that to the degree that some vestige of the old beliefs survived, it must be responsible for the hysteria, degradation, and destructiveness of black religion.

African scholars have thrown a different light on these ancient structures of belief and practice and, therefore, on what may have been the true meaning of the religious background the slaves brought to the New World.[28] Although many questions are still unanswered, it is possible to correct some popular presuppositions about the barbarity (as compared, let us say, to Christianity's part in the extermination of the Amerindians) and inferiority of what the adherents of the traditional religions believed in the past and continue to believe today.

Formerly the major emphasis was on the assumption of a strong predisposition for animism and nature worship. It is interesting to note that when American and European anthropologists did not understand what they were observing in a primal religion, the term "animism" usually cropped up. In the case of Africa it implied that the people found their gods in the sun, moon, stones, rivers, and in countless other natural objects or phenomena that had been desacralized in the West for a long time. The missionaries, in both America and Africa, assumed that this was an idolatrous practice having no soteriological or ethical meaning that could be related to the religion of Jesus.

Protestants, perhaps more than Catholics, were horrified by the native religions reported by travelers to West Africa. By the seventeenth and eighteenth centuries the Reformation was still a relatively recent occurrence and Protestantism, especially the churches strongly influenced by Puritanism, was still reacting to what it considered the idolatry and paganism of Roman Catholicism. Both Iberian Catholicism and Islam were less intolerant of the religious practices of Africans. But most Protestant missionaries saw little in them that represented "a preparation for the gospel." The use of charms, magic, ghosts, and witches was deplored as satanism. No religion that was essentially polytheistic, that countenanced polygamy, that made so much of ancestors, spirits, and the phenomena of nature, could provide an acceptable ground for Christianization. It first had to be stamped out to make way for the gospel.

But the religions of Africa, for all their exotic peculiarities and strangeness to the European mind, were by no means crude and unenlightened. John S. Mbiti and others have shown that the widespread belief that the Africans worshiped nature and venerated animals as gods is a gross misunderstanding. Although the heavenly bodies and some animals, such as lizards and snakes, often have a place in African religions, they are only two of several categories of being. They are symbolic representations of the living, pulsating environment in which humans subsist and through which we are related to the spirits of natural things and the ancestors, but preeminently with a Supreme Being, the God who is above all gods and who is known as Creator, Judge, and Redeemer.[29]

Concerning this "nature worship" Mbiti has this to say about the central place of the sun in the religions of such peoples as the Ashanti and Igbo, two West African groups from which a considerable number of slaves were brought to the Americas:

Among many societies, the sun is considered to be a manifestation of God Himself. . . . There is concrete indication that the sun is considered to be God, or God considered to be the sun, however closely these may be associated. At best, the sun symbolizes aspects of God, such as His omniscience, His power, His everlasting endurance, and even His nature.[30]

By far the most familiar criticism one hears of African religions is what Westerners regard as the inordinate reliance upon "medicine men," "conjurers," and other practitioners who are thought to dabble in magic or possess supernatural powers. Popular opinion has made such specialists little more than religious impostors and racketeers who make their living off the fears and gullibilities of primitive persons. As we have seen from Herskovits, not a few of them may have been among the shipments of slaves from Dahomey and Togo, and it is they who may have formed the original cadres out of which the earliest black preachers began to emerge before they were recognized and instructed by whites. This partially explains the low estate in which most black preachers were held by the colonists before they became dependable representatives of the status quo.

It is true that all kinds of religious specialists must have been included among the slaves—from high priests and priestesses to village diviners and root doctors. It is necessary, however, to differentiate between the various roles those persons played and evaluate the contribution each made to the survival of the slave community. It is important to note, for example, that it is not certain that "conjurer" and "medicine man" are terms that can be employed indiscriminately to comprehend both good and bad magic. The term "medicine man" should be reserved for what we would call good magic. The conjurer, or witch doctor, plied his trade more frequently for antisocial purposes and was the object of fear among most African peoples. Such persons were sought out by those who wished to harm or destroy others. And because it was possible for bad magic to be turned back against the one who desired to use it for his or her own purposes, the conjurer was hated as well as feared. This was the person often blamed for whatever went amiss in the natural course of events and in the tempestuous interpersonal relationships under the conditions of slavery. In Africa a witch or conjurer was sometimes driven from the village, if not hunted down and slain.

On the other hand, the medicine man in African societies was a source of help and healing for the community in which he lived. Mbiti speaks of him as "the greatest gift" to the community and as "both doctor and pastor." He not only made use of plants, herbs, and minerals in his healing art, but was called upon for other ministrations. He gave such advice and counsel as persons needed to make themselves more productive and effective in the various departments of daily life—whether as warriors, farmers, husbands, or wives. He was, in other words, the precursor of the first "exhorters," "householders," or slave preachers who, with and without certification by white churches became the religious leaders of the black community. Mbiti gives a summary description of this religious specialist in Africa:

> In short, the medicine-men symbolize the hopes of society; hopes of good health, protection and security from evil forces, prosperity

and good fortune, and ritual cleansing when harm or impurities have been contracted. These men and women are not fools; they are on the average, intelligent and devoted to their work, and those who are not simply do not prosper or get too far.[31]

This is, of course, a description of medicine men in contemporary Africa, but it is a considerably more dependable picture of the religious practitioners occasionally mentioned by white preachers and missionaries than the one we have from popular prejudice. This is not to deny that there were slaves who were the operators of a fraudulent mumbo-jumbo and who made a good living from the fear and credulity of their neighbors. Any inspection of the classified section of the *New York Amsterdam News*, the *Chicago Defender*, and other black newspapers across the country will attest to the fact that this kind of business is still carried on among certain segments of the black community. But most of the so-called conjure-men and "voodoo doctors" who rose to prominence in the secret meetings of the slaves were men of ability and integrity who took their vocations with the utmost seriousness. They were leaders who, in Mbiti's terms, symbolized the hopes of the community, who came to be called "Reverend," and were sought out for spiritual counsel and healing by both blacks and whites.[32]

Originally, the prophets and preachers who evolved out of the African medicine men among the slaves attempted to direct the propitious, health-giving forces of nature to those who, despite the devastation of their ancestral culture, still believed in the efficacy of the spirit world and the protection of the gods and the spirits of the departed. They sold amulets, charms, "gre-gre bags" or "hands" (small parcels containing bits of paper, bones, or potions that were hung around the neck for protection and good luck). But their services were by no means confined to the use of magic. They also interpreted the meaning of events and called the people to a sense of solidarity, pride, and the first stirrings of resentment against their oppressors. Returning once more to Herskovits's theory that a specific group of priests were among the slaves brought from Dahomey, we cite again his argument about their role:

> It is apparent that here is a mechanism which may well account for the tenaciousness of African religious beliefs in the New World, which . . . bulk largest among the various elements of West African culture surviving. What could have more effectively aided in this than the presence of a considerable number of specialists who could interpret the universe in terms of aboriginal belief? What, indeed, could have more adequately sanctioned resistance to slavery than the presence of priests who, able to assure supernatural support to leaders and followers alike, helped them fight by giving

the conviction that the powers of their ancestors were aiding them in their struggle for freedom?[33]

The point I am stressing is that the early spiritual leaders among the slaves in the Caribbean and North American colonies were the representatives of the traditional religions of Africa that we are beginning to understand and appreciate today. What they brought to Christianity were attitudes and perspectives both in agreement and at variance with missionary teaching. For all of what has seemed to Westerners to have been weird and outlandish practices, these men and women retained an instinctive intelligence about existence, physical and mental health, and the presence in life of that which is radically antagonistic to and irreconcilable with the best interests of the community. They had a concept of a Supreme Being who was involved in the practical affairs of life, but in a different way than the Judeo-Christian God. This Being was approachable through many intermediaries, but was known by various names, including Father and Mother, and whose power was supreme over all other powers of the universe. It was not only in the identification of the healing properties of plants and minerals, or in the exorcism of demonic influences, that these medicine men-preachers contributed to the security of the uprooted slave. What became most significant for a later period was the fact that they recognized the relationship between "bad magic" as whites practiced it and the dehumanizing situation in which they and their people found themselves.

## VODUN

In describing the corruption of African religions in the New World, several writers have settled upon the term vodun, or voodooism, as the one that best sums up the various strains of African religions that became a residual mixture in the slave community.[34] Whether or not this expedient is permissible depends to some extent on how one defines vodun. It is widely accepted that the beliefs and rituals that cluster around the basic character of vodun—if, indeed, not the cult itself— were vestigial remains of African religions that syncretized with Roman Catholicism in the West Indies and Latin America. There are undeniable affiliations between the traditional mythologies of West Africa, particularly of Dahomey and Nigeria, and the *vodu* invoked in the temples of Haiti today.[35] We know that for the first thirty-five or forty years of slavery on the mainland, most of the slaves came from Africa by way of the West Indies. If any considerable number were brought from Hispaniola (present-day Haiti and the Dominican Republic), we should not be surprised to find the influence of vodun.

According to Parrinder, the term *vodu* originated with the Ewe (a tribe from the area of what was called the Gold Coast) and is derived from *vo* ("apart"), which has roughly the same meaning as our word "holy" (set apart for sacred use). The word we mentioned earlier as used by Du Bois in his description of slave worship—obi or obeah—refers to the use of charms or fetishes for the purpose of bewitching others or shielding oneself from harm. It is sometimes associated with the practice of vodun. The slaves from Dahomey and Togo went mainly to Hispaniola and it is to them that this tradition is ascribed. Those who were brought to Jamaica also came primarily from the Gold Coast, and Parrinder finds the Jamaican obeah a derivative of the Twi *obayifo*, which he translates simply "witchcraft" and does not associate with snake worship as others do vodun.[36]

Vodun, however, was and is more than ophiolatry and trickery. Its devotees "believe in one supreme God, too good to get angry," and they find in him the same succor and help that others find in the God of the so-called higher religions. What remains in the slums of Port-au-Prince, Harlem, and New Orleans, exploited by pretenders, can only be an impoverished relic of the original. But during slavery it had a close relationship to the theologies and cosmologies of West Africa. Metraux finds that the most important of its divinities still belong to West Africa, where there are shrines for them in towns and villages from Senegal to Angola:

> Moreover . . . the main divinities [of the vodun pantheon] are still classified according to the tribe or region from which they originate. Thus we have Nago gods, Siniga (Senegalese), Anmine (Minas), Ibo, Congo and Wangol (Angolese) gods. Some gods even carry as an epithet the name of their African place of origin: for instance, Ogu-Badagri (Badagri is a town in Nigeria) and Ezili-Freda-Dahomey (Ezili of Whydah-Dahomey).[37]

Vodun should be understood as a conglomeration of half-remembered, partially "dereligionized" beliefs and rites that came out of the Caribbean area. It had its antisocial and destructive aspects, to be sure, but it was not the morbid, menacing superstition that is essentially cannibalism, the criminal use of poison, and sexual cohabitation with snakes—as it is so often pictured in American motion pictures and comic books. French and English travelers and missionaries who were exposed to the traditional religions of Africa and their adaptations in the Caribbean were terrified by what they regarded as their blood-curdling and diabolical character. But modern investigation has thrown light on vodun's fundamentally religious nature, its proximate relationship to the traditional religions of West Africa, and the way it has been both functional and dysfunctional—like all religions—in the lives of individuals and society. The vodun that was extant among West Indian slaves at the end of the eighteenth century was close to, if not in fact, an organized church—with its temples, its *bokono* (magicians) and *vodu-no* (priests) who had been trained in Africa, its elaborate ritual, ceremonial dancing, and hymnody. In all probability it had already been infiltrated by Roman Catholicism and in turn was recreating out of Catholic Christianity a religion with a distinctive African flavor, much more sensitive to the reality and immediacy of the supernatural, and more aware of the nebulous demarcation between the secular and the sacred.

As the American slaves must have known it, vodun was the worship of "an all-powerful and supernatural being," symbolized by a serpent, but also personified by a hierarchy of gods closely resembling those of Dahomean mythology.[38] It was, in substance, a religion of the people, explaining for them the nature of the world in which they lived, the terrifying experiences of their captivity in a strange land, and the means by which they could protect themselves from ever-present evil under the skilled guidance of medicine men and priests. The slaves sought deliverance from evil that was seen and unseen through faithfulness to the great vodun even while they showed reverence to the lesser *loa* who surrounded him and were eventually identified with the saints of the Roman Catholic Church. Rather than merely a vengeful stratagem to punish those one hated (although, as we shall see, it served that purpose in insurrections), vodun was as much a religion as the Christianity of the plantation owners and missionaries. The vodun was a god of goodness, not of satanic evil. As Metraux points out regarding its modern version (which he believes has changed little from earlier times), the spirits do not engage in criminal acts, but behave in conformity with the normative mores and conventions of society.[39]

For the purposes of this discussion it is necessary to understand vodun and obeah to some extent as responses to the demoralizing conditions of slavery and one means by which slaves made some adjustment to the condition of their bondage. What we know about the revolutionary proclivities of the slaves who practiced vodun in Haiti and elsewhere raises a question about whether it had something to do with what we noted earlier as obstreperous elements in the religion of blacks on the mainland who were infiltrated by those from Haiti and elsewhere. We know, of course, about Louisiana, but vodun went far afield from Creole culture. Folklorists find it in many places throughout the South before and after the Civil War. Indeed, it found its way into some of the storefront cults and occult shops of Harlem and other ghettos of the North, and, with the addition of more recent immigrants from the Caribbean, it can be found in several American cities today. We know also that vodun has always been vulnerable to antiwhite feelings among oppressed blacks. Wherever we find it converging with non-Christian, cultic elements in black religion we can expect to find a militant, religiously inspired rejection of white values and control.

Those who today speak disparagingly of vodun, santeria, shango, and other forms of African religion in the New World usually refer to the criminal aspects and the unending spirals of fear in which adherents seem to be caught—the feeling of having to turn to magic to defend oneself and to exact retributive justice from others. This well may be. All societies find a way to provide more or less socially acceptable, but frequently devastating, outlets for fears, prejudices, and petty jealousies. There are no laws against politely snubbing one's mother-in-law, refusing to answer the telephone when one knows a neighbor needs help, selling jet fighters to a friendly nation, or defoliating the forests of an enemy. But these examples represent negative and sometimes neurotic reactions to problems and frustrations, from interpersonal to international. Where social situations are fraught with conflict and tension, whether in an affluent suburb or an overcrowded ghetto, the techniques for survival and self-gratification become ruthless and destructive, no matter how natural or genteel they may seem in terms of accepted norms.

In a so-called primitive society the same conditions obtain for dealing with or getting back at someone, and the fetishistic or conjural instrumentalities employed seem no more exotic and no more or less effective to those who use them than those that are used by a supposedly enlightened and civilized society. Mbiti has written concerning the difficult human conditions under which sorcery and witchcraft developed in an African village:

> The environment of intense relationship favors strongly the growth of the belief in magic, sorcery, witchcraft, and all the fears, practices and concepts that go with this belief. I do not for a moment deny that there are spiritual forces outside man which seem sometimes to function within human history and human society. But the belief in the mystical power is greater than the ways in which that power might actually function within the human society. African communities in the villages are deeply affected and permeated by the psychological atmosphere which creates both real and imaginary powers or forces of evil that give rise to more tensions, jealousies, suspicions, slander, accusations and scapegoats. It is a vicious cycle. . . . It is hard to describe these things: one needs to participate or grow up in village life to get an idea of the depth of evil and its consequences upon individuals and society. A visitor to the village will immediately be struck by African readiness to externalize the spontaneous feelings of joy, love, friendship and generosity. But this must be balanced by the fact that Africans are men, and there are many occasions when their feelings of hatred, strain, fear, jealousy and suspicion also become readily externalized. *This makes them just as brutal, cruel, destructive and unkind as any other human beings in the world.*[40]

If this can be said about persons under the ordinary conditions of village life in Africa, what can be expected of them, or of any human beings, under the conditions of slavery as it was practiced in the Americas? Whole villages were sold into bondage. Persons were uprooted and transported across the Atlantic Ocean to be set down on plantations where men, women, and children were little more than beasts of burden. It was in this bitter and inflammatory situation that vodun and obeah flourished in their most hostile form as the African slaves strove with one another and their masters over the means of basic survival, color, status, and the brutality of forced labor. The intimidation and hatred that witchcraft and conjury often represented came to be part of a religion that sought to deal with the enigmatic questions of good and evil, life and death, and the cause of undeserved suffering at the hands of whites. This was the inevitable consequence of slavery and it could be only a matter of time and opportunity for the violent impulses released by such a religion to be turned against the real enemy in vindictiveness and revenge.

This is what eventually happened in Haiti. When the slaves revolted in 1791, sending tremors of hope and excitement among blacks throughout the world, all of the powers of vodun were invoked. The leaders of the revolution later tried to make it the state religion, holding that it was the mystical powers of the priests that gave the black soldiers the feeling of invincibility that drove the English, Spanish, and, finally, the army of Napoleon into the sea. Although Toussaint L'Ouverture himself was a staunch Roman Catholic, before his career as a guerilla he had been a medicine man, or root doctor. Once, on the arrival of the French expeditionary forces under Leclerc, Toussaint sought divination from a vodun priest at the fort of Crete-á-Pierrot.[41] Dessalines, his successor, had been a plantation slave. Tradition has it that he knew vodun better than Toussaint and deliberately incited the Congolese and Guinean slaves to practice it on the eve of battle as a means of obtaining invulnerability. The doubt that some historians cast over whether Dessalines, who was deified in the vodun pantheon, had real sympathy with the cult because he later attempted to stamp it out seems not well founded merely on that account. Christian princes in Europe were known to have been great patrons of the church during times of war, but feared and suppressed the papacy and the radicals of the Reformation once peace had been won and their political problem solved.

The fact is that the Haitian nationalists found in vodun a spiritual force that could not be separated from the people's yearning for liberation. The maroons, or fugitive slaves, who held out in the mountains and spurred the slave rebellions of 1758 and 1790, had their priests with them who faithfully practiced vodun rites. Around 1758 a prophet or magician named Makandal began to preach the destruction of the whites by poisoning. He was later burned at the stake at Limbe in northern Haiti, but legends about his escape from the fire continued for years. The name of Makandal, along with that of Toussaint L'Ouverture and Jean Jacques Dessalines, was traditionally invoked by members of the cult to inspire anticolonial resistance.[42] Dantes Bellgarde, in his *Histoire de peuple haïtien*, writes that "the slaves found in Voodoo the ideal stimulus for their energy—since Voodoo had become less of a religion than a political association—a sort of 'black carbonaro.' "[43] As we shall see, this transmutation of spiritual energy into a political movement for freedom has been an inherent characteristic of black religion from the slave period. It played an important part in slave insurrections in the United States and in the militancy of a significant sector of the black church down to the present.

Notwithstanding the efforts of the early missionaries to introduce the slaves to a religion that demythologized the elemental powers of the primitive consciousness and encouraged escape from the world and submission to slavery in the hope of paradise in an afterlife, the fact remains that religion had a much more practical and immediate role to play among the slaves. Whether the missionaries desired it or not, Christianity had to provide *some* aspects of spirituality that were continuous with the African experience—as happened in the case of vodun in Haiti, or *santeria* in Cuba—and the most notable were those that dealt with the curative, shielding, self-gratifying powers of a deity. As much as he might have quoted John 3:16 as the cornerstone of the true faith, the missionary could not evade the fact that his "only begotten Son of God" performed miracles, cast out demons, waged a continuous struggle against Satan, and gave to those who followed him the power to do the same. All this was translated into a religious pragmatism by which the slaves dealt with the most destructive and threatening aspects of their real situation. Moreover, the missionary could not, in good conscience, depreciate the presence and work of the Holy Spirit in the life of the believer. This work could readily be interpreted by the slaves as identical with conjuration and spirit possession in their ancestral religions. Even with the exclusion of other factors, this alone assured a measure of self-determination and continuity with the past, by diverting certain biblical and theological conceptions of Christianity into structures of belief and practice that more adequately served the needs of the slaves. Those needs had to do with physical survival, psychic stability, and ultimately with political liberation.

The implications of the doctrine of "the freedom of the Christian," basic to the New Testament and Reformation theology, had no difficulty being recalled by the churches during the War of Independence. It was, however, assiduously avoided by most missionaries in their instructions to blacks. Having convinced the slaveowner that the religious conversion of his human property would not result in capital loss but greatly increase his profits, the missionary reduced Christian theology and ethics to their most simplistic and innocuous affirmations. A favorite text was Ephesians 6:5, "Servants be obedient to them that are your masters according to the flesh, with fear and trembling, in singleness of your heart, as unto Christ." By the middle of the nineteenth century several catechisms were available for oral instruction, such as Charles C. Jones's catechism for Presbyterian slaves and Bishop Capers's "A Catechism for little Children and for Use on the Missions to the Slaves in South Carolina."[44] Most of these outlined the basic tenets of orthodoxy with suitable ethical injunctions calculated to inculcate monogamy, honesty, industriousness, and to discourage temptations to insurrection. One such document inquired of the slave: "What did God make you for?" The answer: "To make a crop." "What is the meaning of 'Thou shalt not commit adultery'?" The answer: "To serve our heavenly Father, and our earthly master, obey our overseer, and not steal anything."[45]

Whereas all the missionaries deplored what they regarded as obstinacy and superstition among the slaves and made a major effort to dethrone heathenism, a few early Quakers and Methodists made an abortive attempt to sensitize their converts to the implications of Christianity for human justice and equality. The Quaker George Fox and the Methodist Francis Asbury at first sought voluntary manumission from the slave-owners as an expression of the genuineness of their own conversion and repentance for the sin of trafficking in human flesh. When this method proved to be of no avail in the face of the sheer economic advantage of slavery, more radical itinerant white preachers actually instigated slave uprisings and few of them were apprehended in the process. The consequence throughout the South was a fear and suspicion of strangers who came among the blacks with the professed purpose of evangelizing. In most cases such unsolicited preaching was strictly forbidden, or, if permitted, carefully regulated and kept under surveillance.

All in all, it is fair to say that the opening up of the whole issue of human equality in the context of the gospel, and the moral right of the slave to escape or resist enslavement, was due in some measure to the agitation of a few intrepid whites who transmitted the egalitarian spirit of the American Revolution and radical Christianity to the secret gatherings of slaves. These early Christian abolitionists helped to fan the winds of prophecy that broke over the Denmark Veseys and Nat Turners in the tumultuous period of protest and rebellion that preceded the Civil War. Even the most conservative teachings could be exploited in a negative way to turn the religiosity of the slaves and the organizational potential of their churches into intrigue. The fears of the slaveowners were essentially well founded. They knew instinctively that any attempt to educate or indoctrinate their workers would, in the long run, change the precarious relationship between master and slave. For this reason many of them opposed any kind of religious instruction, preferring to maintain law and order by brute force rather than by a paternalistic Christian education.

The planters were assisted in this determination by the colonial governments. As early as 1715 North Carolina passed an act declaring that any master or slaveowner who permitted "Negroes to build . . . any house under the pretense of a meeting-house upon account of worship, shall be liable to a fine of fifty pounds."[46] In 1723 Maryland voted to restrict independent religious meetings among Negroes, and by 1770 Georgia had forbidden slave assemblies under the penalty of "twenty-five stripes, with a whip, switch or cow-skin." Thus, the American colonies, prior to the Revolutionary War, kept the overt religious life of the slaves under severe restrictions. Du Bois writes, however:

> Whether or not such acts tended to curb the really religious meetings of the slaves or not it is not easy to know. Probably they did, although at the same time there was probably much disorder and turmoil among the slaves, which sought to cloak itself under the name of the church.[47]

In summary, we can say that despite the deliberate distortion of Christian doctrine and stringent restrictions upon religious activity, a distinctive African American form of Christianity—actually the new religion of an oppressed people—slowly took root in the black community. This black folk religion contained a definite moral judgment against slavery and a clear legitimation of resistance to injustice. White antislavery radicals, the precursors of Lovejoy and John Brown, contributed to the militancy of some black Christians and to the spirit that created the independent black churches. But we have made the point that there was something else that made religion among the slaves different from the Christianity of the white churches. It was the slaves' African past that did most to influence their style of religious life, their rejection of the spiritual and political despotism of the whites, and made the most important contribution to the black Christian radicalism of the nineteenth century.

## CONCLUSION

Drawing on the work of Du Bois and Herskovits rather than E. Franklin Frazier and Stanley Elkins, I have attempted to show the indomitable humanity of the slaves and the credibility of the African background thesis in plantation America. In an area of scholarly dispute where the primary source materials are sparse on either side, ideological leanings are all too apparent. There is no disguising the fact that I have chosen to lean in the direction of the strength of the African inheritance rather than the putative irresistibility of the Euro-American acculturation process as it supposedly works in contact with "less civilized" cultures.

There is as much evidence that certain retentions from Africa persisted in African-American religion in the South as there is that the slaves collapsed before the juggernaut of evangelism and were revived in the pure white garments of Euro-American Christianity.

I have also contended that there is sufficient data to show that the first religious leaders recognized by the slaves as such were not those appointed out of their number by white missionaries, because their conversions seemed to be the most authentic, but those men and women who had either learned their priestcraft in Africa, or were taught by someone else who had. Moreover, the maleficent aspect of the lore these specialists had mastered could not help but be used against the whites until it was clear, as Genovese believes, that it did not work as it did against blacks. It was by some such process of demonstrated ineptitude and eventual pacification that practitioners of bad magic gradually became or yielded to practitioners of good magic. The end result was the taking on of more and more of the language, ritual trappings, and symbolization of Christianity until the old African religions were overpowered and the first Christian exhorters began to emerge as confidants and assistants of the itinerant white preachers.

Elements within African religion that could be used for resistance to acculturation and domination, however, did not totally disappear. Vodun as it was utilized by Toussaint and Dessalines in Haiti could not be summoned for spiritual reinforcement in the Virginia and South Carolina insurrections, but a basically African orientation against the black magic of white oppression and the total subsumption of everything black under everything white persisted within the African American folk religion of a later period.

This is to say that an essential ingredient of black Christianity prior to the Civil War was the creative residuum of the African religions. The defining characteristic of that spirituality was its spontaneous fascination with, and unselfconscious response to, the reality of the spirit world and the intersection between that world and the world of objective reality. Such an ontology called for the release of the human spirit, the sacred vessel in which the vital forces of the universe coalesce, from every power—whether of humans or the gods—that would exercise unauthorized dominion over it. Those who profess such a religion cannot be bound by anyone or anything indefinitely. Freedom is intrinsic to its very nature.[48] The African attitude literally created the image of the preexistent God in the freedom of the religious imagination and opened human life to the influence of divinity that flowed out of history and the natural world. The liberation of the whole person—body, mind, and spirit—from every internal and external constraint not deliberately and purposely elected was the first requirement for one who would be possessed by the Spirit. God alone had the authority to command, to invoke life and death, blessing and cursing, although it is clear that God customarily exercised this power through many intermediaries. But the indispensable condition for life and human fulfillment in the religious and philosophical tradition of Africa was freedom—the untrammeled, unconditional freedom to *be*, to exist, and to express the power of being, fully and creatively, for the sheer joy and profound meaning of *Muntu*, man in the genderless sense of basic humanity.

It was from within an African religious framework that the slaves made adjustments to Christianity after hearing the gospel. The influences of the African religious past extended into their new life, first in the Caribbean and later in the United States and, far from being completely obliterated, were reshaped by the circumstances of enslavement. Slavery, as a matter of fact, only served to drive those influences from the past beneath the surface by force and terror. But instead of decaying there, the African elements were enhanced and strengthened in the subterranean vaults of the unconscious from whence they arose—time and time again during moments of greatest adversity and repression—to subvert the attempt to make the slave an emasculated, depersonalized version of a white person.

Christianity alone, adulterated, otherworldly, and disengaged from its most authentic implications—as it was usually presented to the slaves—could not have provided the slaves with all the resources they needed for the kind of resistance they expressed. It had to be enriched with the volatile ingredients of the African religious past and, most important of all, with the human yearning for freedom that found a channel for expression in the early black churches of the South.

Joseph R. Washington, Jr., made a significant contribution in the 1960s to the discussion about black folk theology when he observed:

> Born in slavery, weaned in segregation and reared in discrimination, the religion of the Negro folk was chosen to bear the roles of both protest and relief. Thus, the uniqueness of black religion is the racial bond which seeks to risk its life for the elusive but ultimate goal of freedom and equality by means of protest and action. It does so through the only avenues to which its members have always been permitted a measure of access, religious convocations in the fields or in houses of worship.[49]

But this religion, as the common sense orientation, sagacity, and lifestyle of the folk, went far beyond religious convocations in fields and churches. It permeated the wit and wisdom, the music and literature, the politics and prophecy of a wide spectrum of black life in the highly secularized urban areas of the North, as well as in the rural communities of the South. It was the soil out of which grew the syncretistic, militant black nationalism and the African culture interests of many cults in the ghettos of Harlem, Watts, Chicago, and other communities. It erupted intermittently, like an underwater volcano, in the music of Mahalia Jackson and

Duke Ellington and in the writings of some who are otherwise as far apart as James Baldwin and Amiri Baraka. It inundated the black churches of the South and many in the North during the height of the civil rights movement when Dr. Martin Luther King, Jr., was its high priest and the Southern Christian Leadership Conference its institutional "church." In a later chapter I shall examine the contribution of black folk religion to the radical stance of that sector of the church that embraced the concept of black power in the mid-1960s. It suffices, at this point, simply to note that those strains of black religion that have been least influenced by white Christianity have played an important role in the quest for racial justice and are inseparable from black culture as a whole.

But we must go on now to see how this substratum of the religion of the slaves affected the long struggle against slavery. One way to tell that story is to investigate the role religion played in three of the most important slave revolts of the nineteenth century.

## CHAPTER 3

# Not Peace, but the Sword

*The slaveholders of the present generation, if cloven down by God's judgment, cannot plead that they were unwarned. . . . Well may the God of the oppressed cry out against them, "because I have called and ye have refused. . . . Therefore will I laugh at your calamity and mock when your fear cometh. When your fear cometh like desolation and destruction like a whirlwind, then shall ye call but I will not answer. "*
Theodore Weld to Angelina Weld, Feb. 6, 1842

With the publication in 1938 of Joseph C. Carroll's *Slave Insurrections in the United States, 1800–1865*, a new interest began in what had been a neglected area of black history. Some attention to the matter had been given in a few monographs and in larger works on the general moral and social conditions of the slaves. It was left to the radical abolitionists and a few black preachers such as Henry H. Garnet and Henry M. Turner to make the American public aware, before the end of the nineteenth century, that blacks had never been content in their bonds, and that from the beginning of slavery they had made a persistent effort to free themselves.

Nevertheless, many white Americans have a picture of the slave as a rather good-natured coward. Why did the blacks not revolt long before 1861? The popular view has been that the slaves who came from Africa, unlike the Native Americans, did little to secure their freedom except beg for it, occasionally purchase it on patently unfair terms, or pray for it with manacled hands uplifted to God to the accompaniment of "Swing Low, Sweet Chariot."

One reason for the widespread misunderstanding about the true situation concerning organized resistance was the paucity of available information due to the suppression of news or rumors that would serve to stimulate hope and thereby trigger more uprisings. The trials of conspirators by self-appointed, or even legitimate, authorities were often conducted in secrecy, although the grisly remains of a lynching party were sometimes left on display to remind others what they might expect from such adventures. But by and large, there was little inclination on the part of the slaveholding establishment to ignite the fires of freedom—particularly among the class of free Negroes—or to encourage conspiracies with northern abolitionists by broadcasting the true extent of insurrectionary activity. Undue publicity could only risk sending out the signal that at last the situation in the slave states was ripe for revolution.

Consequently, in addition to the numerous revolts that we know about, there must have been many more that have never come to light.[1] The widespread fear of insurrections that is manifest in all the public and private records of the period seem out of all proportion to the actual number of events that have been recorded. It now seems clear that, notwithstanding the suppression of information, the whole issue of insurrections was underplayed—partly because of that peculiar racist predisposition of many to remember the Negroes as docile, accommodating collaborators in their own misery, waiting for whites to give them their freedom.

If there was little scholarly treatment of this subject before Carroll's book, there has been even less on the role of religion—and specifically the role of black religionists—in slave plots and rebellions. It is, of course, well known that white abolitionists, many motivated by Christianity, stirred up discontent and instigated some of the desperate attempts to run away or foment rebellion following upon their visits to the plantation country—often from Massachusetts and Connecticut. Quaker and Methodist attacks on the institution of slavery were no secret to the slaves. James Redpath of Malden, Massachusetts, who wrote a book on his travels through the South, said frankly that the slaveholding class ought to be exterminated and the overseers driven into the sea, "as Christ once drove the swine; or chase them into the dismal swamps and black morasses of the South. . . . I would slay every man who attempted to resist the liberation of the slaves."[2] Among white northerners Redpath was rare, but not unique. There were a few such persons among the Baptist and Methodist missionaries, and they left a legacy of secret rebelliousness among the slaves with whom they came in contact. But there has been almost no sustained inquiry into the question of the slave preachers themselves, or the religiously motivated slave leaders, whether or not they were members of the clergy. To what extent were these men and women the instigators of insurrection? And how did they put the resources of religion—their Africanized Christianity—to the service of resistance to slavery?

## BLACK RELIGION AND BLACK INSURRECTION

The relationship between black religion and the slave insurrections deserves more study than has been given to it.[3] This chapter cannot present a full treatment of the problem. What is intended here is a reminder of the religious background of the slave's discontent and an examination of the religious attitude of some of the major propagandists and conspiracies about which we have knowledge. More extensive and detailed research on this matter must be left to others. Although it would be a huge overstatement to say that every black congregation was a seedbed of revolution and every black preacher a Nat Turner in disguise, there is good reason to believe that religion was considerably more involved than most available records would seem to indicate.

White preachers and missionaries protested that their charges would never countenance such "gross immorality" as rebellion. Needless to say, they would have been painfully embarrassed if the matter proved to be the contrary. They labored among the blacks at the behest of the slave owners and the slightest indication that their ministrations, consciously or unconsciously, were sowing seeds of rebellion would have brought immediate dismissal, if not worse. There were frequent enough occasions when white men were known to be involved in uprisings to raise suspicions whenever trouble broke out among seemingly well-disciplined slaves. And it would be even more likely to suspect a fire-eating Baptist or Methodist circuit-rider who lacked common sense enough to "love niggers." As the editor of the Baton Rouge *Gazette* wrote in 1841:

> We need not wonder if deeds of blood and murder should take place if incendiary preachers are allowed to hold forth with impunity at camp meetings and other places where our slaves congregate, and baldly make appeals to the worst passions of human nature. A stop must be put to the ranting and raving of these wolves in sheep's clothing.[4]

As early as 1732, Governor Drysdale, in a message to the Virginia House of Burgesses, remarked on the difficulty the colony was having in detecting and punishing slave insurrections. That year the legislature passed new laws concerning the control of slaves, because the regulations then in effect were "found insufficient to restrain their tumultuous and unlawful meetings, or to punish the secret plots and conspiracies carried on amongst them."[5] These "tumultuous and unlawful meetings" were, in all probability, religious meetings where the emotions of the slaves, whipped to a frenzy by a preacher, rose to such an intensity that they were extremely vulnerable to an appeal, in the context of a sermon or prayer, to throw off their chains in an uprising.

White missionaries were not infrequently suspected of being implicated in slave plots. That some of them had serious religious objections to slavery and may have encouraged insurrection is evident. The charge was made by the Charles Town, South Carolina, grand jury on March 17, 1741, that a journal of "enthusiastic prophecys" of the destruction of the town and the liberation of the slaves contained the signature of one Hugh Brian. Under the influence of this white man, according to one record, "great bodys of Negroes have assembled together on pretense of religious worship."[6]

In the Archives of Virginia, *Executive Papers*, dated September 5, 1789, appears the complaint of a Holt Richardson of King William County, of certain insurrectionary activities related to religion in that vicinity:

> I have appointed Paterrolers to Keep our Negroes in order & to search all Disorderly houses after night & unlawful Meetings & where they find a large quantity of Negroes assembled at night to take them up & carry them before a justice which has been done, but we have a sett of disorderly People who call themselves Methodists and are joined by some of those who call themselves Baptist, who make it a rule two or three times each week to meet after dark & call in all the Negroes they can gather & a few whites & free mulatoes who pretend under the clock [*sic*] of Religion to meet at a School house where no one lives & there they pretend to preach & pray with a sett of the greatest Roges of Negroes in this County & they never break up till about two or three o'clock in the morning & those Negroes who stays with them goes through the neighborhood & steele everything theat they can lay their hands on & our Negroes are not to be found when we are in want of them, but are at some such meetings and I have ordered the Paterrolers to go to such unlawful meetings & to take up all Negroes that they should find at such places.[7]

The Nat Turner revolt greatly heightened the suspicion that religion was a primary factor in slave uprisings. Governor John Floyd in his message to the Virginia legislature on December 6, 1831, expressed the opinion that the spirit of insubordination and insurrection among the slaves had its origin in "Yankee pedlars and traders" who taught that "God was no respecter of persons—the black man was as good as the white" and "that the white people rebelled against England to obtain freedom, so have blacks a right to do so." He further blamed the Turner revolt on the Negroes' reading of the Bible, David Walker's and William Lloyd Garrison's writings, and the turning of this knowledge into conspiratorial purposes through the instigation of "black preachers."[8]

One reason for the relative paucity of data on this aspect of the slave revolts is not difficult to surmise. In the first place, little is known about the content of slave preaching when whites were not in the congregation.

Secondly, what travelers such as Olmsted and some of the early historians have given us about the otherworldliness of the black preacher and the slave church, they received from the blacks themselves, who were not about to tell whites all they knew about the complicity of their own preachers in unlawful activity. Many plots were aborted because of the betrayal by a house slave who had been promised his or her freedom for the information. But such disclosures usually came at the time the insurrectionists were moving from talk to action—usually on the eve of an attack. There must have been considerable talk in churches and elsewhere that never came to the attention of the masters. The very fact that rebellion and religion were associated with each other in the minds of many black preachers—particularly those who ran away and returned to preach secretly—means that the religious atmosphere was charged and would have exploded many more times, by the incitement of a preacher or inspired lay person, had not the odds been so heavily weighted against the possibility of success.

In the third place, much of our knowledge of preachers and churches during the antebellum period comes from the reports of white missionaries who usually went to great pains to prove to the churches that Christianity was good rather than dangerous for the slaves. The original objection of the slaveowners to the conversion of their slaves and even the holding of religious services on the plantations was that itinerant abolitionist ministers, or over-enthusiastic black exhorters, would take advantage of the situation and distort the message of the gospel into a summons to secular freedom. White pastors and missionaries, having difficulty enough persuading the white population to accept Christianity, were not in the habit of revealing to the slaveowners the strange and devious translations their teachings were subjected to in the hearts and minds of the slaves. There was among their charges, in fact, a deepseated longing for deliverance and a seizing upon every rumor that might suggest that it was at hand.

Successful revolutions do not occur without planning and organization. Persons must come together at some time. What better time than on Sundays when there was some leisure, when they could visit each other on nearby plantations, and when the whites were in their own churches? What better place to talk about freedom than a religious gathering? In church a sense of personal worth and dignity was evoked. The passion for deliverance from the bondage of sin could easily slip over into a desire to be delivered also from the sins of the whites who flourished like the green bay tree while they continued to treat blacks like beasts of the field.[9]

The planters suspected that this kind of talk was going on in clandestine church meetings, at feasts and burials. There is good evidence to prove that they were not mistaken. Enough mischief seeped out of the meetinghouses and field worship services for them to tighten security by the middle of the eighteenth century. In the Carolinas and Virginia, night patrols were on the prowl to interrupt church services held in some part of the plantation that was out of the sight and earshot of whites. Slaves who were caught at such meetings had to use every artifice not to be taken to the authorities or have their Bibles confiscated. Black preachers could expect to be severely whipped for leading such meetings no matter how harmless they may in fact have been.

To some degree slave discontent was due also to the various kinds of resistance literature circulating from the time of the Revolutionary War to the Civil War. Before considering specific conspiracies related to religion, it is necessary to understand the supportive role that this literature—slave petitions, antislavery tracts and pamphlets—played in awakening the religious sensibilities of both slave and free, setting the stage for all kinds of resistance.

From 1688, when the Quakers of Germantown, Pennsylvania, raised their famous questions against slavery, to 1829, when the Appeal of David Walker made its first appearance, a steady stream of broadsides and pamphlets—many of them religiously inspired—circulated throughout the country. Although the vast majority of blacks were illiterate, many who had learned to read, both slaves and freepersons, eagerly absorbed the nutriment of freedom that flowed from the pages of this prolific literature. Many who could not read for themselves heard it read aloud or discussed by others, for such material—although suppressed in the slave states—was secretly distributed by free blacks and sympathetic whites.

The period immediately preceding and following the American Revolution produced a climate of opinion generally favorable to the expression of ideas concerning human rights and the legitimacy of rebellion against tyrannical power. By the end of the century the Haitian and French revolutions had added fuel to the fire. For a time the atmosphere buzzed with the militant rhetoric of Patrick Henry, Tom Paine, and the polemics of early Methodist objectors to slavery such as Freeborn Garretson and Bishop Francis Asbury. The famous Methodist General Conference held during the Christmas season of 1784 viewed slavery as "contrary to the golden laws of God" and struck a responsive chord among many evangelicals in the South as well as in Philadelphia and New York. For some southern churchmen voluntary manumissions became an expression of religious conviction. Antislavery tracts began to multiply toward the end of the eighteenth century when it became clear that slavery—now made more profitable by the mechanization of cotton production—was becoming what appeared to be a permanent fixture in the economy of the South.

In fact, fewer blacks were drawn to the Methodists, who were forced to suspend the implementation of the 1784 declaration in less than twelve months, than to the Baptists. Among the latter there were splinter groups that rallied against slavery, such as one called the Emancipating Baptists. The Reverend David Barrow of Virginia and later Kentucky, an Emancipating Baptist, published a pamphlet entitled "Involuntary, Unmerited, Perpetual, Absolute, Hereditary Slavery,

Examined on the Principles of Nature, Reason, Justice, Policy, and Scripture," which became a part of the arsenal of incendiary materials used by the early Baptist emancipationists.[10] In addition, between 1773 and 1779, in the wake of the spirit of liberty accompanying the war, a series of public petitions written by individuals or groups of slaves set forth the black person's own disputation against his or her bondage in terms of natural law and Scripture. In ungrammatical English but with perfect clarity, one such slave petition was sent in 1774 to the colonial legislature by a group in Massachusetts. An example of the way such statements employed religious arguments for the abolition of slavery is evident in the following excerpt:

> There is a great number of us sencear members of the Church of Christ, how can the master and the slave be said to fulfill that Command Live in love, let Brotherly Love contuner and abound, Beare yea one anothers Bordenes. How can the master be said to Beare my Borden when he Beares me down with the Have chanes of slavery and operson against my will and how can we fulfill our parte of duty to him whilst in this condition and as we cannot serve our God as we ought whilst in this situation.[11]

A similar appeal was forwarded in May 1779 to the General Assembly of Connecticut by the slaves of the towns of Stratford and Fairfield. A fragment reads:

> We perceive by our own Reflection, that we are endowed with the same Faculties with our masters, and there is nothing that leads us to a Belief, or Suspicion, that we are any more obliged to serve them, than they us, and the more we Consider of this matter, the more we are Convinced of our Right (by the laws of Nature and by the whole Tenor of the Christian religion, so far as we have been taught) to be free; we have endeavored rightly to understand what is our Right, and what is our Duty, and can never be convinced that we were made to be Slaves. Altho God almighty may justly lay this, and more upon us, yet we deserve it not, from the hands of Men. We are impatient under the grievous Yoke, but our Reason teaches us that it is not best for us to use violent measures, to cast it off; we are also convinced that we are unable to extricate ourselves from our abject State, but we think we may with the greatest Propriety look up to your Honours, (who are the fathers of the People) for Relief.[12]

The majority of these documents from the pre-abolitionist period, and many that resulted from the organized activity of blacks in the North, indicate the extent to which the slaves appealed from their religious convictions to the consciences of white religionists. Some of the earliest statements were voted on and distributed by African societies, counterparts of the Free African Society organized in Philadelphia by Richard Allen and Absalom Jones in 1787. The antislavery pronouncements of the first independent black churches, the sermons and addresses against slavery by northern black preachers, are all a part of this dissident literature. There were also the speeches of Christian laymen, such as James Forten of Philadelphia, and the articles and editorials of the first black newspaper *Freedom's Journal,* published in New York City by the Reverend Samuel E. Cornish and John B. Russwurm in 1827.[13]

All, or certainly a large amount, of this evocative witness against slavery from the pens of black men and women fell into the eager hands of slaves at one time or another, even in the South, where restrictions against such propaganda were more assiduously enforced. Such material was often smuggled into coastal cities by sailors and commercial agents. Despite the fact that most slaves could not read, they "read it" nevertheless—in the curious manner by which many learned how to read the Bible before they knew the alphabet. They were able to glean from it the knowledge that other persons, black as well as white, were condemning the institution of chattel slavery and calling upon the resources of the Christian faith and the founding documents of American democracy to abolish it.

### Young's Ethiopian Manifesto

In February 1829 there appeared an unusual pamphlet by one Robert Alexander Young, a free black of New York, entitled "The Ethiopian Manifesto, Issued in Defense of the Blackman's Rights, in the Scale of Universal Freedom." In this work, and others of similar genre, it is possible to see an element of early black religion that nurtured the struggle for freedom: a deep-lying African spirituality, a kind of God-madness, an enthusiasm for dream interpretation, visions, and prophecy. These tendencies were unfettered and enhanced when black men and women, in the groaning and travail of their spirits, attempted to apply biblical categories to their understanding of and attitude toward their oppression. With the mystical sense of prophecy and divine intervention that both laity and clergy found in the Scriptures—particularly in the apocalyptic writings—they were able to invoke a power that required no human justification, a power that gave them license to become oracles against the whites in vindication of their own people.

Under the sanction of this kind of religious intuition and in the language of mysticism, Young appealed to blacks of all nations to take stock of the injustices visited upon them by whites and to prepare for the revelation of God's judgment. It was an unmistakable call to a more militant posture, if not to revolution.

Young placed the responsibility for freedom squarely on the shoulders of blacks themselves. He believed that God had decreed of the human person "that either in himself he stands, or by himself he falls." He prophesied to the slaveowners that destruction would be the consequence of their evil work, even as their own consciences condemned them:

Weigh well these my words in the balance of your conscientious reason, and abide the judgment thereof to your own standing, for we tell you of a surety, the decree hath already passed the judgment seat of an undeviating God, wherein he hath said, "surely hath the cries of the black, a most persecuted people, ascended to my throne and craved my mercy; now, behold! I will stretch forth mine hand and gather them to the palm, that they become unto me a people, and I unto them their God."[14]

One of the striking differences between the black church of the early nineteenth century and that of today is the thorough knowledge of the Scripture its members possessed—particularly of the Old Testament. This knowledge is evident in the writings and speeches of both laity and clergy. The Bible was, of course, regarded by black and white alike as the inspired word of God. Quotations, poetic allusions, and literary devices from the King James Version made up much of the stylistic embroidery of many erudite writings of the period. But the black Christian, under the influence of educated clergy and gifted lay persons such as Robert Young and David Walker, felt a special affinity to the people of the Old Testament. The God of Israel was the Lord of hosts, the God of battles who swept his enemies before the faces of his people. The great prophets who had fought against the idolatry, hypocrisy, and social injustice of Israel and Judah in the pre-exilic period were familiar allies in the crusade against his cries to God for vindication perfectly suited the religious sentiment of the slaves.

But the preeminent relevance of the Old Testament for blacks, as many of the most famous spirituals bear witness, was found in the story of the Exodus. The Egyptian captivity of the people of Israel, their miraculous deliverance from the army of Pharaoh, and their eventual possession of the land promised by God to their ancestors—this was the inspiration to which the black believer so often turned in the dark night of the soul.

Whenever the Judeo-Christian tradition is made known to an oppressed people, the scenario of election, captivity, and liberation in the Old Testament seems to have a special appeal. The story of the deliverance of Israel from slavery has always been understood as the prototype of nationalistic redemption—the divine revelation of the transhistorical meaning of historical experience.

In the antebellum days black prophets avidly seized upon this revolutionary hermeneutic and bore home its foreboding implications to white America. The Ethiopian Manifesto of Robert Alexander Young makes the message clear:

> Ah, doth your expanding judgment, base slaveholder, not from here descry that the shackles which have been by you so undeservingly forged upon a wretched Ethiopian's frame, are about to be forever from him unlinked. Say ye, this can never be accomplished? If so, must indeed the power and decrees of Infinity become subservient to the will of depraved man. But learn, slaveholder, thine will rests not in thine hand; God decrees to thy slave his rights as a man.[15]

Young's mystical vision in 1829 was that a Black Messiah who would champion the cause of "the degraded of this earth" was to come. He would call the slaves to a life of adamantine asceticism, including a prohibition against cohabitation, until freedom was attained or racial suicide came in preference to the ignominy of slavery. The theme of the Black Messiah has occurred periodically in the United States, the West Indies, and Africa ever since. Young's challenge to blacks throughout the world is certainly one of the earliest expressions of militant Pan-Africanism, which was not to come into full bloom until 1945 when the Fifth Pan-African Congress met in Manchester, England.

Young's prophecy of a black savior was one of the many messages to "the Ethiopians" that he claimed to have read in "an instructive Book," which goes unnamed. However, Young's Black Messiah—in view of the preparation made for his coming—resembles the New Testament Christ:

> As came John the Baptist, of old, to spread abroad the forthcoming of his master, so alike are intended these our words, to denote to the black African or Ethiopian people, that God has prepared for them a leader, who awaits but his season to proclaim to them his birthright. How shall you know this man? By indubitable signs which cannot be controverted by the power of mortals, his marks being stamped in open visage, as equally so upon his frame, which constitutes him to have been particularly regarded in the infinite work of God to man.[16]

### Walker's "Appeal to the Coloured Citizens of the World"

The Ethiopian Manifesto shocked both blacks and whites, but an even more powerful piece of propaganda to be written by a black was the famous "Appeal to the Coloured Citizens of the World" by David Walker. It appeared later in the same year as Young's Manifesto. Walker's pamphlet attracted wider attention among both friends and foes of slavery and was published in three editions—the first in September 1829, seventy-six pages, and the third, of eighty-eight pages, the next year. It is not known how many copies of the Appeal were distributed, but hundreds must have found their way into the South; there are several indications of their being circulated among slaves.[17]

Even more than the Ethiopian Manifesto, Walker's Appeal is steeped in biblical language and prophecy. It is one of the most remarkable religious documents of the Protestant era, rivaling in its righteous indignation and radicalism Luther's "Open Letter to the Christian Nobility of the German Nation," published in Wittenberg in 1520. A comparative study of these two documents reveals striking similarities. Both men were addressing themselves to their own oppressed and beleaguered people out of a last-ditch, desperate situation that called for the most basic alteration of the religious and civil order. Both believed that God had commanded them to pronounce judgment against powers that seemed almost as indestructible as they were corrupt. Both were aware that such audacity might cost them their lives.

The pugnacious German reformer has been universally recognized as one of the greatest religious leaders of all time and one whose work resulted in what was the most important movement in the history of Western Christianity. David Walker, on the other hand, has been shamefully neglected by church historians. Yet his genius and contribution as a lay theologian and prophet of radical religion is indisputable. His critique of the deep corruption of the American church and society is unparalleled in American literature, and it is impossible to calculate the influence it had in quickening the passion for revolt among blacks in the tumultuous decades preceding the Civil War.

We learn from Henry Highland Garnet's brief sketch of Walker's life that he was born in Wilmington, North Carolina, on September 28, 1785. The son of a free mother and a slave father, as a boy Walker developed a deep hatred for slavery and determined to quit the South for some part of the country where it did not exist. Vowing to "be avenged for the sorrow which my people have suffered," he left North Carolina and settled in Boston, where he learned to read and write. In 1827 he entered the clothing business on Brattle Street in Cambridge.[18] According to one report he kept a "slop shop" that was frequented by sailors who pawned their clothing for drinks.[19] Walker married in 1828 and began the scholarly study that is everywhere reflected in his writings. His house became a refuge for fugitive slaves and "the home of the poor and needy." He became the Boston agent of *Freedom's Journal* and spoke frequently on the subject of slavery to small, informal audiences. By 1828 his speaking had gained considerable notice and he was just beginning to lecture to large audiences before his untimely death.[20]

Walker probably made the several excursions from Boston to the South that are mentioned in the Appeal. After its initial publication his life was in great danger from enraged slaveholders whose network of spies and informers extended as far north as New England. Garnet, whose information came from Mrs. Dewson, Walker's widow, writes that Walker was advised to flee to Canada for his life. But he refused to leave Boston, saying, "I may be doomed to the stake and the fire, or to the scaffold tree, but it is not in me to falter if I can promote the work of emancipation."[21]

The cause of his death on June 28, 1830, at the early age of forty-four—possibly while the third edition of his work was just beginning to be distributed—remains shrouded in mystery. Many believed that he was poisoned, but his biographer expresses no opinion of his own except to say that "he died in Bridge Street."[22] It is more than probable that Walker was murdered, and it would not be far afield, under the circumstances of those days, to surmise that he was betrayed by a black, even as the Christ to whom he had dedicated his life's work was betrayed by one of his own.

David Walker's fierce excoriation of Christianity is possibly the most devastating since Voltaire's *Catéchisme de l'honnête homme.* And yet he was far from being an atheist. He never surrendered his faith to cynicism. The truth of the gospel and the mission of Christianity in the world were being hindered by the system of slavery, and it was his singular purpose to call all true believers to its defense. We know that he was a faithful member of the Methodist Church in Boston. In the Appeal he held in highest esteem the venerable Richard Allen, the first bishop of the African Methodist Episcopal Church. His Appeal is actually a religious document though not taken as such by many. Not only is its theme of sin and retribution based on a biblical view of the justice of God and the redemption of human history through the power of love, but the entire work is explicitly "dedicated to the Lord."[23] The writer adds the following observation to this dedication:

> Some of my brethren, who are sensible, do not take an interest in enlightening the minds of our more ignorant brethren respecting this BOOK, and in reading it to them, just as though they will not have either to stand or fall by what is written in this book. Do they believe that I would be so foolish as to put out a book of this kind without strict—ah! very strict commandments of the Lord?—Surely the blacks and whites must think that I am ignorant enough.—Do they think that I would have the audacious wickedness to take the name of my God in vain?[24]

In Article I, "Our Wretchedness in Consequence of Slavery," Walker compares slavery in the United States with slavery in ancient civilizations and advances the argument that in the history of the world no people has been as degraded and dehumanized as the Negroes in America. In this context his crowning example is the way the Jews fared under Egyptian captivity. He traces the biblical story from Joseph—who was sold into slavery by his brothers—to Moses, in order to demonstrate that through all their trials in Egypt the Israelites were never subjected to the "insupportable insult" that they were not to be regarded as members of the human family.

Unprecedented racism and the deliberate attempt to strip every vestige of humanity from black flesh is the biting accusation that Walker hurls into the faces of the white Christians of America. His conclusion is that they must surely be afflicted with some innate devilishness ("acting more like devils than accountable men") that they would not hesitate to put themselves in the place of the Creator himself. Thus, an ironic swipe at Thomas Jefferson's well-known theory of black inferiority:

> Now suppose God were to give them more sense, what would they do? If it were possible, would they not *dethrone* Jehovah and seat themselves upon his throne? I therefore, in the name and fear of the Lord God of Heaven and of earth, divested of prejudice either on the side of my colour or that of the whites, advance my suspicion of them, whether they are *as good by nature* as we are or not. Their actions, since they were known as a people, have been the reverse. I do indeed suspect them, but this, as I before observed, is shut up with the Lord, we cannot exactly tell, it will be proved in succeeding generations.[25]

Article III is entitled "Our Wretchedness in Consequence of Ignorance." Here Walker condemns whites for withholding enlightenment from the slaves. He makes a sharp attack on the ignorance and treachery of blacks against one another in the interest of the oppressor and urges them to educate themselves. It is in this section that he presents a frontal assault on "the preachers of the religion of Jesus Christ" and, in some of the harshest language of the book, points to the patent falsity of white Christianity and the impending fate of the church of the slaveholders:

> They have newspapers and monthly periodicals, which they receive in continual succession, but on the pages of which, you will scarcely ever find a paragraph respecting slavery, which is ten thousand times more injurious to this country than all the other evils put together; and which will be the final overthrow of its government, unless something is very speedily done; for their cup is nearly full.—Perhaps they will laugh at or make light of this; but I tell you Americans! that unless you speedily alter your course, *you* and your *Country are gone*!!!!!! For God Almighty will tear up the very face of the earth!!![26]

The final section, entitled "Our Wretchedness in Consequence of the Colonizing Plan," begins with a repudiation of Henry Clay and the whole scheme of black colonization that had been advanced as a solution to the race problem since 1713, but most actively and successfully since the Revolutionary War.

In the third edition Walker supplements the original version of this concluding section with additional material dealing with legal prohibitions against black education and what he considers an acceptable alternative to forced colonization: voluntary black emigration to parts of the British Empire, or to Haiti. He then adds a list of "the cruelties inflicted on us by the enlightened Christians of America."

Here as elsewhere Walker speaks of white Americans as "our natural enemies"—a designation that arises from his interpretation of the history of American civilization. He believed that God had given up on this civilization ("they have got to be hardened in consequence of our blood") because of its unremitting brutality. But he clarifies what he means by the natural enmity he sees between black and white:

> I say from the beginning, I do not think we were natural enemies to each other. But the whites having made us so wretched, by subjecting us to slavery, and having murdered so many millions of us, in order to make us work for them, and out of devilishness. . . . Consequently they, themselves, (and not us) render themselves our natural enemies, by treating us so cruel.[27]

The Appeal is a summons to black manhood and womanhood. It is Walker's call to rebellion, to throw off the chains of slavery and fight in self-defense for freedom and dignity in the name of the Lord of hosts. The strategy for battle is as direct as it is sanguinary:

> If you commence, make sure work—do not trifle, for they will not trifle with you—they want us for their slaves, and think nothing of murdering us in order to subject us to that wretched condition—therefore, if there is an *attempt* made by us, kill or be killed. . . . Look upon your mother, wife and children, and answer God Almighty! and believe this, that it is no more harm for you to kill a man, who is trying to kill you, than it is for you to take a drink of water when thirsty;—in fact, the man who will stand still and let another murder him, is worse than an infidel, and, if he has common sense, ought not to be pitied.[28]

Walker cannot understand how it is possible for whites to expect blacks to do anything less than reject their proffered friendship until they repent of their sins before God:

> But Americans, I declare to you, while you keep us and our children in bondage, and treat us like brutes, to make us support you and your families, we cannot be your friends. You do not look for it, do you?[29]

Although it is a stringently militant document, Walker's Appeal does not represent unmitigated hostility and hatred of all whites. The spirit of his writing strains toward some kind of resolution of the problem of race *without* violence—if white America would have it so. In that sense the Appeal is consonant with the dominant mood and motif of traditional black radicalism in the United States from the earliest slave petitions to the writings of contemporary black theologians. In Walker the theme of reconciliation arises again and again, but always out of a solemn recognition of the inevitability of whites reaping what they have sown, of facing the necessity of true repentance for the sins of the past, and of bringing racism and oppression to an end without further delay.

Walker acknowledges those whites who have been the friends of freedom and states that only their faithfulness has sustained the nation in the past and will save it in the future:

> What would have become of the United States of America, was it not for those among the whites, who not in words barely, but in truth and in deed, love and fear the Lord. . . . They are indeed, the salt of the earth. Remove the people of God among the whites, from this land of blood and it will stand until they cleverly get out of the way.[30]

Through all the blood and fire, an ultimately hopeful spirit breathes through Walker's writing as he calls upon white Christians to count the cost of racial peace and to humble themselves before God in order that friendship and brotherhood can bless the land that must otherwise be soaked in blood.

Toward the end of the book in a plaintive, almost wistful, change of mood, he addresses himself to those whites who may still be reading his words:

> Throw away your fears and prejudices then, and enlighten us and treat us like men, and we will like you more than we do now hate you. . . . Treat us then like men, and we will be your friends. And there is not a doubt in my mind, but that the whole of the past will be sunk into oblivion, and we yet, under God, will become a united and happy people. The whites may say it is impossible, but remember that nothing is impossible with God.[31]

David Walker's Appeal struck fear into the hearts of whites in the South, and the authorities immediately sought its suppression. The mayor of Savannah, where sixty copies were discovered, wrote to Mayor Harrison Gray Otis of Boston demanding that something be done to restrain the publication and distribution of "this highly inflammatory work." Otis replied that he was powerless to stop it under the law. He did, however, issue a warning to captains of vessels putting out from Boston harbor to be careful to see that they were not carrying it aboard their ships.[32] The editor of the *Columbian Sentinel* called it "one of the most wicked and inflammatory productions ever issued from the press" and said that banning it from Georgia was more than justified in order to secure "the immediate safety of the whites."[33]

It is not certain that Nat Turner read or was directly influenced by the Appeal, but it is not inconceivable that he could have known both Walker's and Young's writings. We know that the publication of the Appeal sent warning signals throughout the eastern seaboard states. Although many opposed its bellicose spirit and its call for the violent overthrow of slave power, others secretly welcomed the way it narrowed the issue to immediate emancipation as the only reasonable safeguard against a revolt. Black preachers in the North pretended to be shocked by its ferocity, but made good use of it for their own purposes. Among whites it was the subject of much thought and discussion in antislavery circles. Actually it marked the beginning of the increased militancy of Garrison, Weld, Birney—and later the martyrdom of Elijah Lovejoy and John Brown.[34]

Literature of this character played a significant role in reminding the slaves that it was not only against the law of nature and the principles of democracy that they should forever be patient in bondage, but more than that: it was contrary to the will and purpose of God. Through the distribution of such tracts and pamphlets in the religious gathering of slaves, they came to know that there were other blacks in the North who were prepared to join them with brains and brawn if ever the blow for freedom were struck. Richard Allen, Daniel Coker, David Walker, and others like them were known among blacks as deeply religious leaders who shared a common hatred of slavery and were ready to push the whole institution over the precipice at the right time. Black ministers could not openly sanction violence and maintain their own personal safety or continue to cultivate helpful contacts with white abolitionists such as Garrison and the Tappan brothers, who deplored such tactics. But they kept their own counsel and few of them were attracted to the pacifist movement. Most vacillated back and forth between violence and nonviolence as a solution to slavery, but in their most discouraged moments could say with Samuel Cornish, the black Presbyterian preacher and publisher, that "offensive aggression" could be "indispensable to . . . personal liberty and rights."[35]

## PRE–CIVIL WAR INSURRECTIONS

To what extent did religious factors, such as the leadership or conspiracy of religious leaders, have to do with violent resistance to slavery?

Detailed investigation into the precipitants of rebellion would be required to give a complete answer to the question. Extensive research into each instance of conspiracy or rebellion is outside the limits of this study. It is possible, nevertheless, to discern some of the linkages between religion and some of those revolts for which adequate data are available.

Needless to say, it is not possible at every point to differentiate between the role played by what we call black religion and white Christianity as it was preached and practiced by the religiously motivated among white abolitionists. In one sense the two traditions were imperceptibly merged in the religion of antislavery itself, which brought blacks and whites together in many societies and conventions of the nineteenth century. Black and white abolitionists who went into the South to agitate and organize the Underground Railroad were generally inspired by the same biblical texts and infused with the same Christian spirit. But there were some notable differences.

In the application of religion to the struggle for freedom, few whites were as radical in their interpretations of scriptural injunctions to resist tyranny as Denmark Vesey, David Walker, and Nat Turner. Few white Christians were able to take interracial friendship so seriously as to be willing not only to free the slaves, but to accept blacks as their equals.[36] Few white abolitionists understood, or were prepared to accept, the role of what they considered pagan religious practices. Most of them rejected the involvement of this kind of religion in the slave revolts in Haiti, Jamaica, and elsewhere in the hemisphere. They would have recoiled from the thought that this menacing black spirituality had anything to do with Christianity.

In his discussion of some of the causes of the insurrections, Herbert Aptheker points out that it was the general assumption that they were caused primarily by the activity of Methodist and Quaker missionaries, and that without their instigation blacks would not have become so infected with the fever for revolt.[37] He goes on to say that although this popular view may be true, it is impossible to substantiate it with fact. His own conclusion is that the fundamental factor provoking rebellion was "the social system itself"—the system of slavery and "the degradation, exploitation, oppression, and brutality which it created."[38]

There is no doubting that any inquiry into the role of religion in fomenting insurrections must give considerable credit to the fact that radical white Christians taught the blacks how to read the Bible in such a way as to discover how their faith addressed the question of human liberation. That assumption, however, should not lead us to believe that black religion was inconsequential, and black preachers so lacking in indignation, that only the ethical revivalism of evangelicals and the inspired teachings of "white ministers and religious ladies" could have provided blacks with a theology of revolution and the spiritual dynamism to act it out. We have already taken note that whites were involved in some of the plots, but even the most irrepressible abolitionists were quick to deny that they had any part in violence, and there is little discernible causal relationship between them and the slave insurrections.

To the extent that religion is at least *one* important factor among others in some of the major insurrections or conspiracies, it must be said that it did not emanate from the white churches of the South, the North, or even from the disreputable Methodist itinerants and the Emancipating Baptists. It sprang rather from the religious imagination of the slaves themselves and from those former slaves who escaped to become pastors of churches, or to sit in the pews of the newly independent black congregations of Baltimore, Wilmington, Philadelphia, New York, and Boston.

W. E. B. Du Bois, whose understanding of the origin and nature of black religion is incomparable, tells us that slavery represented in the minds of the transplanted Africans the dark triumph of evil. They called up all of the resources of their religion to express and activate the spirit of resistance—in their hearts if not in their hands.[39] As for free blacks of the North in this regard, Du Bois writes:

> The free Negro leader early arose and his chief characteristic was intense earnestness and deep feeling on the slavery question. Freedom became to him a real thing and not a dream. His religion became darker and more intense, and into his ethics crept a note of revenge, into his songs a day of reckoning close at hand. The "Coming of the Lord" swept this side of Death, and came to be a thing hoped for in this day. . . . This desire for freedom seized the black millions still in bondage, and became their one ideal of life. . . . For fifty years Negro religion thus transformed itself and identified itself with the dream of Abolition, *until that which was a radical fad in the white North and an anarchistic plot in the white South had became a religion to the black world.*[40]

It was this pervasive radicalism just under the surface of black religion in the antebellum period that gave it an ethical base more pliant and consequently more easily adapted to the exigencies of a one-sided struggle than did either the evangelical Protestantism of the mainline white churches, or the Christian abolitionism of the Tappans and other white friends. There were exceptional individuals—the radical Methodist evangelist Orange Scott, and later Elijah Lovejoy, Theodore Parker, and the redoubtable John Brown. But although they were looked upon as dangerous mutants in the evolution of white Christianity in the United States, black Christians, for the most part, have regarded the leaders of the slave insurrections as exemplary heroes of black history.

One of the earliest conspiracies that had more than a passing connection with religion occurred in the Northern Neck region of Virginia as early as 1687.[41] Suspicion of the true character of the incident, which is said to have involved a large number of slaves, arises from the fact that the plot developed in connection with mass funerals that the slaves were permitted to hold during that early period. Such funerals were, of course, religious events. Usually held at night, they were intensely emotional experiences in which charismatic black religious leaders whipped the mourners into a frenzy that could readily be turned into riot.[42] Reports of the Northern Neck rebellion are extremely sparse. Few books and no newspapers were published in the country prior to 1700.[43] But we know that the leaders were arrested and executed, and the authorities issued a ban against public funerals.

Prohibitions of funerals, holiday festivals, and other types of slave gatherings where religious excitement could provide an excuse for conspiracy became the law in many parts of the South and the West Indies. In this connection it is worth noting the comment by Joseph Carroll on another Virginia insurrection involving some two hundred blacks. It took place not far from the scene of the Northern Neck rebellion on a Sunday in October 1722:

> Sunday was a favorite day on which the slaves often planned outbreaks, because it was easy to get together on Sunday. . . . The slaves were given a deal of liberty in assembling for religious worship. Hence the religious services were the great incubators where Slave Insurrections were hatched. Fortunately for the ruling class this plot [in October 1722] was discovered just in time to be nipped in the bud.[44]

In 1712 a famous insurrection broke out in New York City. It was thought to be related to a school for young blacks founded in 1704 by Elias Neau, an agent for the Society for the Propagation of the Gospel.[45] The plot was actually brewed by blacks of the Cormantee and Pappa tribes from West Africa who, "with the aid of a conjurer, believed that they had made themselves invulnerable."[46] Early in the morning of April 7, slaves set fire to the house of Peter van Tilburgh and shot at the whites who came to extinguish the blaze. They were finally subdued and the incident ended with eight or ten white persons killed and eighteen or more blacks executed. It is clear that some kind of African religious specialists were involved in the plot. The rebels, in keeping with an African custom, sucked the blood of each other's hands as a bond and pledge of secrecy.

The uprising may have been in some degree unintentionally related to Elias Neau's religious instruction. The French catechist conducted classes in Christian education and was at first accused of having encouraged a desire for freedom as part of his instruction. Although a formal inquiry into the matter exonerated Neau and his catechumens, one eyewitness account acknowledged that at least one of the black students was in the plot. Another student was condemned on "slander evidence," and two Roman Catholic blacks were implicated, but saved at the last moment. Later investigation ascertained that an African witch doctor and recent arrivals from the Slave Coast were the chief conspirators.[47]

The governor apologized to Neau and attempted to protect the missionary from the hostility of the still unconvinced white population. Nevertheless, the fact that some of his students, together with black Catholics, were on the edge of the circle of the accused plotters and carried on the insurrection under the incitement of an African witch doctor gives reason to suspect that some volatile combination of Christianity and African religion was one of the precipitants of the revolt. The white community continued for some time to associate the school with the uprising, and it was not safe for Neau to be seen on the streets until tempers had cooled.

Rumors of freedom were rife in slave country. Frequently they gave rise to expectations that were followed by dismay when hopes were dashed. Such was the case in 1730 in colonial Virginia, where the word spread among slaves that the newly arrived Colonel Spotswood had been empowered by the king of England to free all slaves who had received baptism.

This custom, first introduced by the Portuguese in Africa, had never been mandatory in America.[48] In the eighteenth century, however, the fact that the matter was debated in church and civil courts caused considerable confusion. Many slaves desired to be baptized with the hope that their status would thereby be improved. Most of them received it, however, with little or no religious instruction. The relationship thus established between religion, baptism, and personal freedom continued to further mystify the sacrament among the slaves and convinced some that their adoption of the master's religion made them as good a person as he was and as free.

In 1730 Virginia authorities became aware of many gatherings and meetings among blacks with "loose discourses" on the topic of liberty.[49] Leaders were arrested and soundly whipped. But six weeks later two hundred slaves in Norfolk and Princess Anne counties assembled on Sunday and chose new leaders to take charge of their intended revolt.[50] The plot was discovered and four of the leaders were tried and executed.

During the 1730s slaveowners faced a serious problem when their slaves began escaping to St. Augustine, Florida, where the Spanish were in control. Hostility against Roman Catholics ran high in the towns along the Atlantic seaboard. Although never proved, it was generally believed that a Catholic priest was involved in a slave insurrection planned in Prince George County, Maryland, in 1739.[51] Enmity between the English and the Spanish made the latter encourage slaves to escape to Florida, and a royal decree of October 1733—which secret informers brought into the plantation country—promised them safe residence and freedom.

During 1739 and 1740 there were at least three insurrections in South Carolina believed to have been instigated by Catholic priests. Although it is well to be wary of widespread Protestant prejudice when evaluating these reports, the fact that many of the slaves in South Carolina were from Angola and had already been converted to Roman Catholicism made them prime targets for propaganda from Florida. Some of them must have associated freedom with the Catholic Church and would have been strongly drawn to the Catholic establishment in St. Augustine.[52]

The most serious incident during this period occurred when some seventy-five slaves burned buildings and killed whites as they marched toward St. Augustine shouting slogans of liberty with colors flying and drums beating. They were met ten miles south of Stono, South Carolina, by a better armed detachment of militia and were defeated after a sharp engagement in which at least twenty-five whites and fifty slaves were slain.[53]

Two years later, in September 1741, fires broke out in Charles Town that were attributed to blacks who were said to have been on the brink of revolt. The complicity of religion in this incident is found in a report to the grand jury of the town concerning a book signed by Hugh Brian, a white man, which contained "sundry enthusiastic Prophecys, of the destruction of Charles Town, and deliverance of the Negroes from their Servitude, and that by the Influence of ye said Hugh Brian, great bodys of Negroes have assembled together on pretense of religious worship."[54]

It is difficult to know what role to assign to religious influences such as inflammatory preaching and conjury in the strange conspiracy of blacks and four disreputable whites that created such a sensation in New York City during the same year. An extended description of the plot from contemporary newspaper accounts indicates that a man named John Ury, identified as a Roman Catholic priest but claiming to be an Anglican clergyman, and a John Romme (who told blacks that he possessed a charmed life) were involved in a plan to set fire to the town and plunder its inhabitants. Punishment was exacted indiscriminately as far as blacks were concerned. Thirty-one slaves were hanged or burned at the stake "amid prayers, imprecations and shrieks of agony."[55]

We shall have occasion later to look at the role of black Christians in the increasing disposition of blacks to abandon the moral suasion philosophy of white abolitionists, giving aid to fugitives, supporting conspiracies in the West Indies, and encouraging nationalistic movements in Africa. The point here is that in the numerous slave revolts prior to 1800, religious factors of one sort or another were frequently present. Sometimes visionary whites, foreigners to their own society's values, were involved. At other times conjurers or witch doctors, who apparently were sometimes in the background, were called upon to provide inconspicuous supporting services. At still other times black preachers—unordained and illiterate men of extraordinary intelligence—kept the pot boiling by relating slavery to white immorality, and freedom to black salvation through Jesus Christ.

If fewer black religious leaders came forward in the United States than in the movement of African independent churches in the latter part of the nineteenth and early twentieth centuries, it is only because slavery in this country, particularly in those areas where blacks were in the majority, was highly institutionalized and made a stronger effort to bring religion under its control. The American slaves had no strong, uniform religious tradition to fall back upon. Their practice of the new religion they were developing at the time was under closer surveillance than any other activity of their leisure time. What black preachers in America did to foment discontent and resistance to bondage, they did not so much by example and open exhortation as by suggestion and innuendo, as we find used in such spirituals as "Steal Away," "O Mary, Don't You Weep," and "Joshua Fit de Battle of Jericho".[56]

The ability of these men and women to carry on clandestine warfare under the noses of their captors should not be discounted merely because of the scarcity of documented incidents involving their leadership. The most intelligent among them would have been able to stay in the background and watch their mischief take its course in undermining a system they could not shake by direct assault.

The popular assumption is that revolts like Turner's in Virginia or Chilembwe's in Nyasaland were seldom led by black preachers in the United States because their religion was mainly otherworldly and they themselves were generally little more than kindly, foot-shuffling clowns. Nothing could be further from the truth. The men and women who took charge of building the institution of religion in the slave community were not the ignorant buffoons they are often made out to be by the "cultured despisers" of black faith. Their restraint in leading open slave rebellion had nothing to do with either otherworldliness or cowardice. We must assume that they understood the power of their own charisms, but also the odds against success under the circumstances. They knew what to expect from the slaveholders if rebellion should break out among untrained and unarmed slaves. A few religious leaders, as we shall see, dared to risk insurrection under these very conditions, but the majority moved with caution and decided to let whites fight the matter out among themselves in the war they knew would come in God's own time.

Slave preachers, reinforced by their African background, understood well the awe-inspiring power of the Spirit. It was for them not merely a source of interior, personal freedom; it also represented the judgment, the vengeance of God, who required the blood of sacrifice as propitiation for mortal sin. Like Moses with the serpent in the wilderness, the preacher held great power in his hands when he stood before his people. His lineal relationship to the shaman, the witch doctor, and the other religious specialists who communed with the nature spirits and the ancestors on the banks of the Nile and the Congo, made him deeply sensitive to the mysteriousness of faith and its capacity to take possession of persons and drive them into frenzy. The exorcism of the demonic spirits, which lie beneath the surface of the soul, as the New Testament bears witness, is never completely predictable in its results. The full power of primitive religion can bring forth uncontrollable forces of good and evil, intertwined and inseparable. In African religion, as we have seen, the line that makes it possible for us to differentiate between such forces is barely discernible.

It is almost impossible for persons accustomed to a structured, intellectual religious experience to understand the immediate, involuntary impulse to throw oneself wholly into the spell of elemental powers when they are called forth by evocative exhortation and ritual in the context of deprivation and oppression. The slave preacher approached those powers boldly, but with deep respect. One phrase, one careless word or gesture could transform a religious meeting into a boiling caldron of emotion that would send the hearers pouring out of the brush-arbor church and into the homes of the slavemasters to kill and burn. It was rare for a preacher who was fully aware of this possibility to permit hysteria to advance to such a boiling point of fanaticism.

During the civil rights period of the 1960s, many observers in the South came to appreciate the power of black faith and the restraint of black preachers under certain conditions. James Bevel, Hosea Williams, Jesse Jackson, and other leaders demonstrated an ability to use religious emotion to reach the masses even more effectively than Dr. Martin Luther King himself. On many occasions they closed the switch that could have transformed the singing, shouting congregation of poor blacks into a mob that would have swept out of the black section of some southern town and into the white neighborhoods with torch and gun. The civil rights preachers restrained themselves and their people by correctly assessing the situation and restraining the spirit. Every Sunday in the churches of the black community—North and South—old-style preachers exercise that same restraint, bringing their congregations to the height of religious hysteria with the "gravy" of homiletical peroration, and at the climax "sitting down in the storm." The traditional preacher knows when enough is enough—when one more swell of emotion could cause physical injury to those inundated by it. Worshipers have been known to throw themselves against hot stoves, to rip and tear clothing, to break up chairs, and generally to pull, like Samson, the temple down upon themselves. It is precisely for this reason, however, that the Spirit usually operates under an implicit social control.

If one can speak of the slave preachers as conservative, it was this tremendous power and the recognition of its dangers that made them so. But they were certainly not conservative in what they desired for their people. They knew the misery and injustice the people suffered daily. They knew how defenseless they were against the patrols, militia, and soldiers who were instantaneous in response to the first indication of trouble. Many preachers must have thought that one day the sign would be given by God to release "the power" and let it do its will. But they bided their time. Perhaps more often in solitude than in public, they prayed for the Day of the Lord that is not light but darkness. That sign for which they looked was finally given to Vesey, Turner, and other visionaries and prophets on both sides of the Atlantic who led their people in violent opposition to white oppression.

Most of the preachers in the United States stopped short of insurrection. They lived and worked in the time between the recognition of just grievances and the opportunity to do something effective to cast them off. The time for black unity and for understanding the purposes of God on the wilderness side of the Jordan had not yet come for them. In this interim period they turned to the vision of what lay on the other side of victory. The golden streets, the rivers of milk and honey, the melodious harps and trumpets of the angels, the golden crowns and shining robes that awaited those who shall overcome. The preacher's creative rendition of the eschatological passages of the Old and New Testaments became his second option—a means of drawing the people from the edge of doom that he knew was just beyond the peak of rage that their religion masked but also nourished against the day of reckoning. He continued, therefore, to preach what in his own situation he considered the pragmatic implications of the message that Christ had made everyone free, that the day would surely come when the truth of the gospel of liberation would be manifest.

The otherworldliness of slave preaching was an interim strategy. It was the deliberate choice of the preacher to give his people something to which they could attach their emotions—something to substitute for the immediate, uncontrollable, and probably ill-fated decision to strike, then and there, for freedom. He, therefore, gave relief from the tragedy of slavery, a modicum of comfort in the presence of the overwhelming reality of defeat and despair. Black religion may have been otherworldly, but it was not otherworldly-quietistic, but otherworldly-disruptive. Oppressors have never been able to relax in the presence of this kind of otherworldliness. During slavery it was a way of already living in that *other* world of transcendent freedom. Its purpose and meaning have not greatly changed in the traditional churches, sects, and cults of the black community today. To let "this little light shine" in the dark corners of the white world meant that whatever the black Christian did received transcendent meaning, not from the present of injustice, but from the future of truth, justice, and divine retribution already breaking in upon this world in many hidden and deceptive ways. Subterfuge, sabotage, trickery, foot-dragging, and other behavioral patterns of day-to-day resistance were insinuated into the intercourse with whites in the guise of stupidity and obsequiousness, as a tactic of survival.[57]

It does not follow from this, as some have supposed, that basic dignity was thus compromised. The effect of underground resistance was a sense of divine vindication and rectitude because the oppressor's power was being frustrated and his sin uncovered and punished. In the absence of opportunity and means of fomenting successful insurrections, this kind of attack on the flanks and from the rear of the enemy—a psychological guerrilla warfare—was the conspiratorial response of blacks to white oppression. And no one could have given it a better ideological interpretation than the preachers. The justification did not come from the often imitative theology of the antebellum black church, but in the realized eschatology of preaching—its response to the absurdity of the situation, its appropriation of a radical ethic of resistance, and its formulation and recommendation of subtle and concealed norms for interracial contact and confrontation.

## CHAPTER 4

# Three Generals in the Lord's Army

*Up, Afric, up; the land is free*
*It sees no slave to despot bow.*
*Our cry is Liberty—*
*On; strike for God and vengeance now*
 *Fly, tyrants fly,*
 *Or stay and die.*
*No chains to bear, no scourge we fear;*
*We conquer, or we perish here.*

By V. Said to have been sung by
slaves in insurrection.
*The Liberator,* July 23, 1831

One of the most important slave revolts in the United States occurred in 1800, the year Thomas Jefferson was elected president. In Haiti, Toussaint L'Ouverture had all but completed a successful revolution against slavery. The great black liberator defeated the invading English army and had assumed command of the entire island as general-in-chief. Slaves throughout the New World were emboldened by these events and a spirit of rebellion was in the air. The nineteenth century began with a dire warning to believers in the innate inferiority of blacks and the system of human bondage. Before it was over both belief and system would have suffered an irreparable loss.

### GABRIEL, THE BLACK SAMSON

A young man of twenty-five named Gabriel, slave of Thomas Prosser, whose plantation was just outside the city of Richmond, Virginia, was moved with his brother Martin to strike the first blow for liberty in the new century. A man of impressive physical and mental capacities, Gabriel was also a student of the Bible and was strongly drawn by reli-

gious convictions to lead an insurrection. His favorite biblical hero was
Samson. In imitation of the great judge of the Hebrew people, Gabriel
wore his hair long in compliance with Judges 16:17, "There hath not
come a razor upon mine head; for I have been a Nazarite unto God from
my mother's womb: if I be shaven, then my strength will go from me,
and I shall become weak, and be like any other man."

Gabriel believed that God had marked him from childhood to be a
deliverer of his people.[1] Throughout the summer of 1800 he frequently
made this divine election known to several men with whom he associated. He interpreted to them the various parts of Scripture that he
believed referred to the condition of the Negro in slavery and the necessity of rising up against the Philistines—the slaveholders. The exploits of
Samson in Judges 15 had particular significance to Gabriel as he laid
careful plans to sow destruction throughout Henrico County and lead
the slaves to the establishment of a new black kingdom in Virginia with
himself as ruler. Judges 15:14–15, 20 reads:

> And when he came unto Lehi, the Philistines shouted against him:
> and the Spirit of the Lord came mightily upon him, and the cords
> that were upon his arms became as flax that was burnt with fire, and
> his band loosed from off his hands. And he found a new jawbone of
> an ass, and put forth his hand, and took it, and slew a thousand men
> therewith. . . . And he judged Israel in the days of the Philistines for
> twenty years.

In this passage Gabriel saw his own name as the new black Samson who
was called to bring down the kingdom of slavery and institute on
American soil what Toussaint was able to create in the Caribbean—a free
black people established as a nation. His plan was to kill all the whites
who were encountered, seize arms and ammunition from the Richmond
arsenal, loot the state treasury, and, if possible, strike an agreement with
the remaining slaveholders for the liberation of all who were still slaves.
Various estimates have been made of how many were involved in the
action itself. According to the official report, about one thousand actually met at the rendezvous outside the city. But because of a great storm
that struck the area on the evening of August 30, when the attack was supposed to have been launched, the plan had to be abandoned. Gabriel's
people did not enter Richmond, but disbanded in confusion—possibly
believing that a sign from heaven that the time was not ripe had been
given in the unusual storm or that the plan was unacceptable to God.[2]
According to Gabriel's own testimony, he had about ten thousand men
ready to go into battle. Other witnesses at the trial gave estimates of two
thousand and six thousand. The governor of Mississippi said that as many
as fifty thousand slaves were in complicity with Gabriel.[3]

The plot was probably the first well-planned, consciously political revolution in a long history of slave uprisings on the mainland. The slaves were obviously organized. There was to be a cavalry and an infantry. Gabriel was given the title of general. The Haitian revolution was undoubtedly the model, but religious factors played a more important role in justifying the Gabriel insurrection than in the one led by Toussaint L'Ouverture. If the revolt failed, the plan was to retreat into the mountains and carry on a protracted warfare as a maroon community, or guerrilla band. But even before the storm broke on the night of August 30, two slaves—Tom and Pharaoh—revealed the plot to their master, Mosby Sheppard of Richmond. Guards were posted at the penitentiary arsenal and cavalry was dispatched on a patrol of all roads leading from Prosser's farm to the city.

An attack might well have been put into effect during the next two or three days, but because of some failure in logistics—perhaps the problem of communicating new orders to all the dispersed units—conspirators began to be apprehended by the state militia and patrols early in September. Governor Monroe secured all strategic points in the vicinity of Richmond during the next several days while continuing to arrest suspects. On September 12 five slaves were executed. Three days later, five or six more met the same fate. All in all, thirty-five were hanged, one committed suicide, and four escaped.[4]

Gabriel attempted to flee. Despairing of trying to reorganize his scattered forces, he went aboard a schooner lying in Norfolk harbor and lay in hiding for eleven days. In the end he was once again betrayed. He was arrested on September 24, 1800, and executed on October 7.

Despite his failure General Gabriel had reminded the people of Virginia and the nation of the fact that the temper of the times—the spirit of Jeffersonian democracy, the spirit of the Haitian revolution, and the egalitarianism issuing from the French Revolution of 1789—made it impossible not to expect blacks to demand the application to themselves of the human rights and the principles of democracy to which others had appealed. As one Virginia journalist of the period wrote: "This doctrine of equality cannot fail in producing either a general Insurrection or a general emancipation."[5] Because of their support of emancipation, Gabriel had ordered that all Methodists, Quakers, and Frenchmen be spared by the rebels. Thereby, his own deep religious motivation reached out to the two church groups he believed to be on God's side against slavery, and to Frenchmen because the government of France had recognized the new black nation in the West Indies.

The immediate reaction of the slaveholders to these events was fear and suspicion. Restrictions on the movements of slaves were tightened, and a public guard instituted in Richmond as a precaution against future outbreaks.

Other rebellions came hard upon the Gabriel affair. Slave revolts occurred frequently after 1800 in South Carolina, North Carolina,

Georgia, Louisiana, and Mississippi. In the two last-named states, agitation for restrictions on religious activities by slaves became prominent after several attempted rebellions prior to 1812.[6] Slave discontent flared throughout Virginia for months. Plans were laid and uncovered, and several local attempts were carried out—none with success. There were instances of the use of poison in connection with some of the plots. This practice was related to the complicity of vodun in some of the incidents. For example, in 1802 a slave named Dick, of Mecklenburg County, was convicted of conspiring to poison his master, "and believed he could accomplish his purpose by beating up leaves with snake heads and leaving the combination at the door of his master."[7] In 1805 there was an insurrection in Wayne County, North Carolina, where the method of poisoning was attributed to the influence of West Indians among the slaves.[8]

Richard Byrd of Smithfield, Virginia, wrote to Governor John Tyler on May 30, 1810, about an insurrectionary plan for Whitsunday in North Carolina. A boy, after being flogged, revealed that operations were to begin in North Carolina, and that the insurgents were to come into Virginia to help the slaves there. Such information was transmitted from church to church by itinerant preachers who went back and forth among them. Indeed, Byrd was confident that slave preachers were involved and used religious meetings for the purpose of organizing the rebellion. He referred particularly, in this regard, to a "General Peter," of Isle of Wight County, who had been in communication with the slaves of North Carolina.[9]

Another instance of the influence of religion in slave uprisings is recorded for 1816 in Spottsylvania and Louisa counties, Virginia. Although it is not clear who had the most influence over whom in the plot, a white man named George Boxley, proprietor of a country store, was implicated with blacks. Carroll writes concerning Boxley, who was said to have been the leader of the slaves:

> He was a visionary character, somewhat like John Brown. He participated in the religious gatherings of the Negroes and told his experiences along with the rest, as Negroes are accustomed to do on such occasions. Among other things that the Lord had done for him, Boxley told the Negroes that a little white bird had brought him a holy message, which was that he was to deliver his fellowmen from bondage. On the basis of this religious superstition he enlisted many Negroes in his project for an insurrection.[10]

Here again we see the readiness of the slaves for revolt when they were persuaded that divine sanction had been given to a charismatic leader. In the same year as the Boxley incident the Camden, South Carolina, *Gazette* reported another insurrectionary attempt in which "those who were most active in the conspiracy occupied a respectable stand in one of the churches, several were professors [of the faith] and one a class leader." Slave preachers used the church meeting because the church proved to be one of the places, perhaps the only one, where blacks could gather and be motivated to join together in conspiracy against the system. Although some of these leaders were self-serving opportunists who manipulated credulous slaves, many others—like General Gabriel— were sincere believers who knew that the great prophets of the Old Testament set themselves unswervingly against human injustice and called down the wrath of God upon those who victimized the poor. They had not the slightest doubt that this same God of the prophets brooded over the captivity of the Africans and wanted the leaders of the people to lead them—the new Israelites—to freedom.

## DENMARK VESEY, METHODIST CONSPIRATOR

Denmark Vesey, the leader of the famous slave insurrection in South Carolina some twenty-two years after the Richmond event, purchased his freedom from a Captain Joseph Vesey in 1800, the year that General Gabriel made his move. Captain Vesey had acquired Denmark on one of his voyages as a slavetrader and gave him considerable freedom as his personal servant. As a result of his intelligence and wide travels as a cabin boy, Denmark had become an unusually cultured and sophisticated man by the time he decided to lead a revolt.[11] After leaving the service of his former master, he settled down in Charleston to work as a carpenter. For the next twenty years he studied everything he could get his hands on and became a respected leader in the little community of free blacks that had grown up in Charleston. In fact his influence extended beyond the city. His travels to the islands and into the interior of the plantation country brought him into contact with persons in various sections of the state. Everyone esteemed him a person of extraordinary intellectual ability and someone who had a future as a leader of his people.[12]

Among the things that interested Vesey and engaged him in many talks and conversations with individuals and groups were the inflammatory pamphlets that had been brought into the Charleston area from free black communities outside the South—including one said to have originated in Sierra Leone.[13] It is worth noting that the black Methodists with whom Vesey was closely involved could have been in contact with friends who had been in that colony since 1820, or with black Baptists from the United States who had been working there since as early as 1792. It is quite possible that a spirited black religion, shot through with elements of political radicalism, had already begun to be communicated back and forth across the Atlantic by 1822. Sailors like Vesey were excellent messengers for such a purpose and port cities like Charleston were ready-made lairs for conspiracies.

Vesey had an absorbing interest in black religion. Like Gabriel and Martin Prosser, he was engrossed in the study of the Scriptures and brought to his investigations some interpretations that were decidedly unorthodox and possibly African or West Indian in origin.[14] He applied himself particularly to the study of two suggestive passages from the Old Testament. The first was from Zechariah 14:

> Behold, a day of Jehovah cometh, when thy spoil shall be divided in the midst of thee. For I will gather all nations against Jerusalem to battle; and the city shall be taken, and the houses rifled, and the women ravished; and half of the city shall go forth into captivity, and the residue of the people shall not be cut off from the city. Then shall Jehovah go forth, and fight against those nations, as when he fought in the day of battle.

The second passage bears closer examination. It was from a part of the Bible slave preachers often turned to in their sermons and it inspired one of the best known of the Negro spirituals—"Joshua Fit De Battle of Jericho." The story of the siege of the Canaanite city is strongly suggestive of the conspiratorial process of a slave insurrection. Denmark Vesey, with an intuitive sense of the mystical and a good grasp of Scripture, must have seen parallels between the children of Israel—after they crossed the Jordan and stood before the cities that barred their way into the Promised Land—and the situation of blacks. Had they not been brought across the Atlantic Ocean to the New World for a purpose? Only the rich and powerful of America stood between them and their destiny as a free and chosen people in this new country. All of the connections with the Old Testament story were obvious.

In the biblical story, even before Joshua crossed over from Shittim, he had sent spies into the land to ascertain the weaknesses of the enemy. They were befriended in Jericho only by a harlot, Rahab. When the city was taken she and her family were spared. The utmost secrecy had to be maintained, but when the time was ripe terror had to be struck into the hearts of the defenders. Evidently, the children of Israel, though well organized for the battle, were poorly armed for it. Joshua 6:9 speaks of "armed men" preceding the seven priests who were to blow on trumpets of rams' horns; immediately behind the priests was the ark of the covenant, followed by all the others—who had only their voices to raise against the Canaanites. The Lord himself, in the form of an angel with a drawn sword in his hand—"prince of the host of Jehovah"—came before Joshua and consecrated the ground on which he stood. Like all the battles of the Israelites, this was a holy war. Without their God they could accomplish nothing. Denmark Vesey was convinced that the same was true for the slaves he had been called to lead to freedom.

During the six days in which the Israelites surrounded the city, Joshua commanded the people: "Ye shall not shout, nor let your voice be heard, neither shall any word proceed out of your mouth, until the day I bid you shout; then shall ye shout" (Josh. 6:10). On the seventh day and on the seventh turn around the city walls—when the priests blew on the ram's horn trumpets—Joshua ordered his people to shout:[15]

> So the people shouted, and the priests blew the trumpet: and it came to pass, when the people heard the sound of the trumpet, that the people shouted with a great shout, and the wall fell down flat, so that the people went up into the city, every man straight before him, and they took the city. And they utterly destroyed all that was in the city, both men and women, both young and old, and ox and sheep, and ass, with the edge of the sword [6:20–21].

There is no record of how Vesey treated this dramatic story when he told it to the slaves. It deserves to be quoted at some length because we know that Vesey was fascinated by it and often used it in addresses when he was recruiting followers. Under such circumstances it is reasonable to assume that he applied the biblical story to his own situation. He also told stories from Greek mythology, such as that of Hercules and the wagoner, as well as other Bible stories from which one could inculcate self-respect and fearlessness.[16] Vesey was known to hold up the example of Toussaint L'Ouverture and the Haitian rebels as heroic examples for the American slaves.

One of Vesey's most trusted companions was the slave of Paul Pritchard, Gullah Jack, who worked through a group known as the Gullah Society. It met regularly, and its members were bound to Jack "by a shrewd combination of magic and discipline."[17] Jack himself was a native African conjurer who had the reputation of being invulnerable. He instructed those who joined the conspiracy to eat nothing but parched corn and ground nuts on the fateful day. They were also told to keep a piece of crab claw in their mouths as a protection against being harmed in the attack. Whatever may have gone on in the religious meetings held during the months of planning, it is clear that Denmark Vesey and Gullah Jack, each drawing upon the reservoir of his own religious convictions, were able to work together in preparing the hearts and minds of those who were to participate in the insurrection.

Church meetings provided the opportunity for indoctrination and planning. In 1800 South Carolina had passed a law forbidding all black religious meetings between sunset and sunrise.[18] But out of respect for a petition of the Charleston Baptist Association, this prohibition was amended in 1803 to permit class meetings until nine o'clock at night, providing a majority of whites were present. In 1819 this requirement was also dropped and religious gatherings of blacks were deemed lawful if at least one white person attended.

Actually, as Woodson and others indicate was the case in other parts of the South, many of these laws against religious assemblies were honored more in the breach than in the observance. Much depended upon the climate of white security at any given time. The slaves met with their own preachers behind closed doors whenever things were relatively quiet. As soon as the rumor of an uprising was noised abroad, or some misconduct resulted from a meeting, the whites were terrified and regulations were again stringently enforced.

In his excellent study of the Denmark Vesey insurrection, John Loften quotes from a writer in *The Times* of Charleston:

> Almost every night there is a meeting of these noisy, frantic worshippers. . . . Midnight! Is that the season for religious convocation? Even allowing that these meetings were conducted with propriety, is that the accepted time? That the meeting of numerous black people to hear the scripture expounded by an ignorant and (too frequently) vicious person of their own color can be of no benefit either to themselves or the community is certain; that it may be attended with many evils is, I presume, obvious to every reflecting mind.[19]

It is most significant in connection with the Vesey plot that the black Methodists, organized as a national denomination in 1816, were involved in the 1822 conspiracy and in almost continuous difficulty with the Charleston authorities from 1817 to the ill-fated attempt. Denmark Vesey was a member of the Hampstead church, one of several black congregations that broke away from the white denomination that year. The class system of the independent African Methodist Association of Charleston was used as a recruitment and indoctrination vehicle as well as a communications network for the revolt. All the leaders were members of the new independent black church. Many of them were class leaders and at least one was a preacher.[20]

The Reverend Morris Brown, who later became a bishop of the African Methodist Church, was a secret counselor to the group.[21] Brown was away "on church business" when the insurrection took place. He was forced to leave the state when he returned to Charleston and was fortunate enough to get safely away to Philadelphia where he became a protégé of Bishop Richard Allen, who probably knew and approved of his actions.

The black Methodists of Charleston provided an excellent pool of dissidence and conspiracy. In 1817, as a result of complaints from white Methodists who were incensed with their schismatic tendencies, 469 members of one of the separated congregations were arrested. In 1818 the Hampstead church itself was accused of being in violation of the law prohibiting assembly, and on a Sunday in June of that year 140 members were arrested. The next day the city council sentenced a bishop and four ministers to one month in prison or exile from the state. Eight ministers were sentenced to ten lashes or ten dollars each.[22] Vesey was an influential member of the most troublesome congregation. He must have been as bitter about this interference as anyone else. It can only be a matter of conjecture how much this continuous harassment confirmed him and others in their determination to strike out not only for ecclesiastical freedom, but for political liberty as well. In any event, the Hampstead congregation was strongly implicated, and the church building was destroyed in the white backlash that followed.

Vesey had done his preparatory work well. Between three and nine thousand blacks were ready to move on signal. The area of operation was to extend for eighty miles from Charleston. The date was originally set for July 14, 1822, but was later changed to Sunday, June 16. Having only homemade weapons, in addition to a few guns and swords, several groups were to supply themselves with arms from gunshops and the arsenal shortly upon entering the city. According to carefully laid plans, once the attack had been launched it was anticipated that not only many other slaves would join in, but also "several white men of low character"—the symbol of Rahab and her household?[23] Monday Gell, one of Vesey's lieutenants, had even written to President Boyer of Haiti, informing him of the intended "stroke for liberty" and seeking his cooperation.[24]

Against the protests of some of his followers, Vesey insisted that the Lord had commanded that not a soul was to be spared, with the exception of the whites already mentioned. All the other whites were to be destroyed and the city set on fire in several places simultaneously. It is a mark of the determination of those men, and of the ultimate nature of their commitment, that they did not shrink from extreme violence to property and indiscriminate slaughter. They were, after all, property themselves, but they were prepared to destroy everything, including themselves. As for the killing, not only did they have the biblical precedent before them and believed themselves to be instruments of God's terrible wrath, but they also knew, as David Walker pointed out later, that once they had begun, only total extermination, as lamentable as that may seem, could hope to succeed in such an impossible situation. They could expect no mercy if they failed.

On the afternoon of May 25, 1822, a slave of Messrs. J. and D. Paul named William approached another slave, Devany, of Colonel Prioleau, and told him what was about to take place. William offered to take Devany to one of the leaders who would take his name and give him an assignment. Devany, a house servant, could not contain himself. When his master Prioleau returned to town from a trip to the country, he revealed the secret to him, and all was lost. By five o'clock on May 30 both Devany and William had been arrested and were being interrogated for further information, the whole business being kept as secret as possible. The official record states:

Things remained in this state for six or seven days, until about the 8th of June, when William, who had been a week in solitary confinement, beginning to fear that he would soon be led forth to the scaffold, for summary execution, in an interview with Mr. Napier (one of the committee appointed to examine him) confessed, that he had for some time known of the plot, that it was very extensive, embracing an indiscriminate massacre of the whites, and that the blacks were to be headed by an individual, who carried about with him a charm which rendered him invulnerable. He stated, that the period fixed for the rising, was on the second Sunday in June. This information was without delay conveyed to his excellency the Governor, and a Council forthwith convened.[25]

By ten o'clock on Sunday night, June 16, Charleston was surrounded by a strong force of militia and police. The plan of Vesey and his companions could not be put into effect without certain disaster. By June 18 ten slaves were under arrest. Among them were Peter Poyas and Mingo Harth, two of Vesey's trusted lieutenants. On June 28 Ned and Rolla Bennett (slaves of Governor Thomas Bennett of South Carolina) and Batteau Bennett, Peter Poyas, Jesse Blackwood, and Denmark Vesey were summarily sentenced to death. All of them were executed on July 2. Those who were still at large made an attempt to rally on Sunday night, June 16, and again on the day of the execution, but it was much too late. By this time the town was thoroughly prepared. When Gullah Jack, the Angolan conjurer, was arrested three days after the execution of the six, the leadership had been decisively shattered. Within thirty days 131 persons were arrested. Thirty-seven were executed, 43 transported out of the state or banished from the United States, and 48 whipped and discharged, there being no evidence against them.[26] Vesey and most of the doomed leaders died in silence, following the counsel of Peter Poyas who had warned against including "house niggers" in the plot because they could not be trusted to remain silent. At the end he said to the others, "Do not open your lips; die silent as you shall see me do."[27]

As happened following the Gabriel plot, the Charleston conspiracy, rather than dampening the ardor for revolt, encouraged conspiracies in other communities of the state and throughout the South.[28] Fires of an incendiary nature broke out in several places during the next few years. When the slaves were unable to do anything else, they frequently turned to the torch and poison to express their grievances. Once again an attempt was made by the whites to increase suppression by various regulations: forbidding the hiring out of slaves, forcing free blacks of fifteen years or older to have a guardian who controlled their behavior, prohibiting assembly, forbidding the instruction of slaves in reading or writing, and barring entrance to the state by any black person from Mexico, the West Indies, or Latin America.[29] Black crews of ships entering Charleston harbor were required to remain on their vessels or suffer imprisonment.

After the wholesale executions, northern newspapers began to write about how South Carolina justice was meted out to slaves, the "bloody sacrifice," and "the great sacrifice of human lives" that had occurred without any white persons having been struck a blow. An editorial debate ensued between the Charleston *City Gazette* and newspapers in New York, Philadelphia, Boston, and other cities. In many parts of the nation antislavery sympathies were fanned and Northerners began to talk about the administration of justice in the South. The dismal failure and the terrible consequences were the price that had to be paid by blacks to shake the consciences of Americans. Black Christians continued to believe that God was aligned with them against the iniquitous system of slavery. They came to the conclusion that after the blood of their martyrs had soaked the red clay of Dixie, many whites—in a tragic and cataclysmic struggle—would pay with their own lives for the blasphemy of holding in chains other human beings created in God's image.


## NAT TURNER, BAPTIST PROPHET OF REBELLION

Before the tremors of the South Carolina earthquake had died away, the ground was being prepared for a new and more serious insurrection—this time farther north: the revolt of the Baptist preacher Nat Turner, in Southampton, Virginia. Despite contemporary reports of the incident and the official record of Turner's famous confession, the sad truth is that most white Americans to whom his name is familiar became acquainted with Nat Turner during the late 1960s through the fictionalized version of his life in the Pulitzer prize-winning book *The Confessions of Nat Turner*, by William Styron.[30]

The misfortune is that the book distorted known facts about Turner during one of the most critical periods of race relations in the history of the nation. It received, nevertheless, extravagant praise from some of America's leading literary critics and angered blacks everywhere. There is little question but that its popularity was in large measure due to the fact that the white community—weary of the civil rights movement and in the midst of a backlash against black radicalism—was looking for some way to discredit the authenticity of the struggle. A quasi-historical repudiation of its roots served that purpose splendidly. The young militants of the black power movement, which came into prominence in 1966, not only reminded white America of its guilt, but also represented an inexplicable and frightening departure from what most whites had come to regard as the paradigm: the nonviolent direct action program of Dr. Martin Luther King, Jr. Many readers of Styron's best-selling book could imagine that the author had brilliantly uncovered something significant about black militancy—its paradoxical love-hate syndrome, its lust for power, and its futility—that others lacked the courage to disclose. *The Confessions of Nat Turner* was, therefore, not only a travesty of history in the eyes of the black community, but also contributed to the gullibility and miscalculation of the liberal community at a time when the movement for legitimate power should have been seriously regarded, if not appreciated, by thoughtful white Americans.

In the introduction to a critical response by ten black writers, John Henrik Clarke asked about the effect of Styron's book upon white readers: "Why had the book received so much applause from the established press and a large number of well-known scholars who, in praising this book, display their ignorance of the true story of the Nat Turner revolt? Have they failed to see Nat Turner as a hero and revolutionist out of fear that they might have to see H. Rap Brown and Stokely Carmichael the same way?"[31]

It is necessary for anyone recalling the crisis in Southampton County, Virginia, during the summer of 1831 to correct the degrading image of Turner that was thrust upon an already miseducated public by the fictional portrayal. The picture of Turner as "a fanatical black man who dreams of going to bed with white women, who holds nothing but contempt for his fellow blacks, and who understands, somewhat, the basic human desire to be free, but still believes in the basic humanity of some slaveholders" must be replaced with what we actually know about him.[32] It is necessary, in other words, to make a sensitive and intelligent inquiry into the historical data available in order to surmise what manner of man Turner was and what were the forces, within and without, that drove him to take violent reprisal against the slaveholders for his oppression.

The most important thing to know about Turner is that he was a representative of an important group of slave preachers who discovered something white Christians had attempted to conceal from the slaves for more than two hundred years. Nat Turner, like others whose names are buried under the debris of the citadel of American slavery, discovered that the God of the Bible demanded justice, and to know God's Son, Jesus Christ, was to be set free from every power that dehumanizes and oppresses. Turner discovered his manhood in the conception of the Christian God as one who liberates. His fanatical attempt to authenticate that manhood in blood was the inevitable consequence of the fanatical attempt of whites to deny it. Styron's frequent biblical quotations and references to Turner's inner life never lifted this essential fact about the man to the level of significance. Hence, what must be regarded as the major point in an attempt to write fiction tolerably faithful to history failed to come through.

Even a casual reading of the 1831 text of the confession to Thomas R. Gray will make clear that Turner's conversion to Christianity and his development as a slave preacher are basic to any understanding of what motivated him. He was born on October 2, 1800, the slave of Benjamin Turner. At a very early age it was obvious to everyone who came in contact with him that Nat was a precocious child. This belief was reinforced in the minds of his mother and father by certain birthmarks that, according to African custom, indicated the unusual mental abilities associated with a "witcheh-man," a conjurer.[33] Throughout his childhood they strengthened Nat in the belief that he was indeed intended for some great purpose.

His paternal grandmother had a decisive influence on him. She was a member of the Methodist church called Turner's Meeting House, where slaves of the Turner family had worshiped with their masters and mistresses from the late colonial period. Benjamin Turner believed in promoting religion on his plantation and conducted prayer meetings for the family. The slaves were included in these meetings and it was in such an atmosphere of evangelical piety that Nat came into a knowledge of the faith. He also was supported in a belief that everyone else shared: that God had ordained him for a special vocation. Surrounded by such influences his childhood was exceptional for a slave. Opportunities were given to him that were denied to others. He astonished his master and the entire household by the facility with which he learned to read and write. Much of his free time was spent in meditation and prayer, but sometimes he stole off to carry on various mysterious experiments with paper and gunpowder.

Nat's superior ability partly separated him from the other slaves, but not entirely. Even though he was "marked to be a preacher," the blacks in the neighborhood took him with them when, as he says, "they were going on any roguery." Apparently he did not participate in the stealing on such occasions, but had the confidence of his fellows as one who could help them plan their forays. The fact that he participated at all in this particular activity is an interesting commentary on what the slaveholding class considered a common fault among their Negroes. What these men were about was underground resistance to the system—as benign as that system may have been in Southampton County, Virginia, at the time. It is unthinkable that an intelligent slave like Turner had not considered the moral implications of these episodes during his frequent meditations. His recollection of it in the confession shows no sign of remorse, for he says plainly: "Growing up among them, with this confidence in my superior judgment, and when this, in their opinion, was perfected by Divine inspiration ... became the subject of remark by white and black."

The text of Luke 12:31, "But rather seek ye the kingdom of God; and all these things shall be added unto you," struck Nat Turner as having peculiar relevance during this period. We cannot know precisely what meanings he attached to these words, but the context is highly suggestive in light of his subsequent development as a messianic figure. The nations of the world seek material things, and these indeed are needful for life, but the followers of Jesus shall not only receive them in abundance, but much more, when the kingdom of God shall come in secrecy and great power. Hence, Luke 12:35, 39–40, 49–51 reads:

> Let your loins be girded about, and your lights burning. . . . And this know, that if the good man of the house had known what hour the thief would come, he would have watched, and not have suffered his house to be broken through. Be ye therefore ready also: for the Son of man cometh at an hour when ye think not. . . . I am come to send fire on the earth; and what will I if it be already kindled? But I have a baptism to be baptized with; and how am I straitened till it be accomplished! Suppose ye that I am come to give peace on earth? I tell you, Nay; but rather division.

The context of this remarkable passage, which made such an impression on Turner, tells us that the messianic vocation that will usher in the kingdom of prosperity and power is symbolized not by peace, but the sword. When dubious about what spirit had prompted Nat to concentrate upon this passage, Gray questioned him about it. He replied without hesitation that it was the spirit of the prophets of the Old Testament. At the beginning of his ministry he had already perceived a close relationship between Jesus of Nazareth and the great prophets who had called down the wrath of God upon their enemies.

This is all the more remarkable when we remember that such an interpretation of Jesus was far from the interpretation given by the missionaries. For them Jesus was the meek and mild exemplar of the faith—the lamb of God slain from the foundation of the world whose obedience to *his* Master, God the Father, was the model for the slave. We can well imagine that this was the picture painted by Benjamin Turner in his frequent prayer meetings. Nat Turner's appropriation of another kind of Lord, his recognition of the meaning of Jesus and the kingdom in relation to the prophets of God's justice on behalf of the oppressed, adumbrated the black theology which developed among black preachers from Henry Highland Garnet to Martin Luther King, Jr.—Jesus as the protagonist of radical social change.

Nat's father had escaped from slavery when Nat was a child by running away from the Turner plantation, never to return. The same desire possessed his son. Nat had always believed that it was revealed to his family and friends that he had too much intelligence to be a slave and would never give satisfactory service to any master. He began to tell the other slaves what he planned to do, describing his purposes as a fulfillment of divination. For thirty days he remained in the woods, but finally—to the astonishment of his fellow slaves—returned to the plantation, saying that the Spirit had directed him to do so. Drewry comments on the passage of Scripture thought to have influenced Nat's decision to terminate his escape and continue his ministry:

> The reason he returned was that he imagined the spirit appeared to him and told him that he had his wishes directed toward the things of this world and not to the Kingdom of Heaven, and that he should return to the service of his earthly master, "for," said the spirit, "he who knoweth his master's will and doeth it not shall be beaten with many stripes, and thus have I chastened you."[34]

Drewry implies that Nat was harassed by the feeling of having betrayed his master and that he returned partly out of guilt for running away. That Nat would have confused his earthly master's will with that of his heavenly master seems most unlikely. Mike Thelwell's interpretation of the return to slavery is also questionable. Thelwell credits Nat's use of the words of Luke 12:47 to a brilliant thrust of irony by which Nat sought to disarm his master. The truth, says Thelwell, is that Turner feigned repentance and pretended to be "the faithful darky—well-steeped in the acceptable slave morality."[35]

There is no reason why we should not assume that "the master's will" meant nothing less to Nat than the will of Christ. He did say that "the reason of my return was that the Spirit appeared to me and said I had my wishes directed to the things of this world and not to the Kingdom of Heaven." He had, in other words, been disobedient to his calling. Instead of remaining on the plantation and waiting for the Day of the Lord, about which he had been secretly preaching, he had yielded to impatience, to the temptation to escape alone. He had evaded the terrible work God had called him to do and had thought selfishly only of his own freedom and the material success that awaited him in the North.

We have Turner's own rendition of the parable about being ready for the parousia—the second advent of Christ—which is found, interestingly enough, in his favorite chapter of the New Testament, Luke 12.[36] The faithful and wise steward in the parable is the one who remains at his post and watches for the Lord's coming. He is to be rewarded by being made ruler over the entire household:

> But and if that servant says in his heart, My lord delayeth his coming; and shall begin to beat the man-servants and maidens, and to eat and drink, and to be drunken; The lord of that servant will come in a day when he looketh not for him, and at an hour when he is not aware. . . . *And that servant who knew his lord's will, and prepared not himself, neither did according to his will, shall be beaten with many stripes.*

Nat Turner had become weary—waiting for the sign that the Day of Judgment had come. He had weakened under the burden that had been his as a leader of the slaves and had run away, only to be driven back by a relentless spirit that had pursued him. His was the classic dilemma of the prophets of the Old Testament from Moses to Amos. They could always find an excuse for refusing the mantle of the prophetic calling. But in the end—contrary to their own preferences—they were drawn irresistibly to the awesome responsibility.

Shortly after Nat returned to the plantation, he had a remarkable vision in which white and black spirits were engaged in a great battle with blood flowing in streams. The voice that spoke out of that vision reminded him that the lot had fallen to him to suffer what had to be suffered in obedience to his calling. "Such is your luck," said the voice, "such you are called to see, and let it come rough or smooth, you must surely bear it." There was no escape from God's will. That will was destined to be performed by none other than Nat Turner, and in no other place than Southampton County, Virginia.

After 1825 a series of extraordinary experiences occurred to Turner as he redoubled his efforts to attain true holiness. He began to see strange signs in the heavens and interpreted them as miraculous depictions of Christ's outstretched hands on the cross. During this period he believed that he had been given true knowledge of the faith and was qualified to think of himself as a minister of the gospel. From that time forward he began to preach to the slaves and extend himself beyond the immediate neighborhood. One account has it that by 1828 he was preaching to large gatherings as far away as Hertford County, North Carolina, at the Barnes Methodist church.[37]

One day while laboring in the fields he found blood on the corn, which he took to be a sign of Christ's blood "returning to earth again in the form of dew." He also reported strange hieroglyphic characters on leaves in the woods, "and numbers, with the forms of men in different attitudes, portrayed in blood." It is impossible to say very much about these phenomena. Down through the ages mystics have repeated such unfathomable occurrences, leaving it to us to believe or disbelieve as we choose. Remembering the destiny toward which Nat Turner was drawn with increasing rapidity by that time, one thinks of Stephen (Acts 7:54 ff.), who gazed into heaven and saw the glory of God, and Jesus standing at his right hand, before he was stoned to death. We can only say that the great founders of the world's religions, and some of their most renowned disciples, had experiences similar to Nat Turner's. The world has been puzzled by their visionary experiences, but the power of their lives was sufficient to convince millions that wonders most persons are too spiritually blind to see were in fact revealed to prophets and mystics.

In the absence of any indication of where he received such information, there is certainly no reason to accept the opinion of Drewry that

Nat wrote the hieroglyphics and quotations on leaves and blades of fodder. Drewry writes that "he spat blood at pleasure, but it proved to be the coloring matter of the log-wood, stolen from his master's dye pots."[38] Before he was hanged, Nat declared that after his execution it would grow dark and rain for the last time. Although Drewry reports that it actually did rain and that "there was for some time a dry spell," it is interesting that he does not venture some natural explanation of that rather remarkable instance of the mystery that surrounded Nat Turner.[39]

In any event, some believed that Nat was a man of God and not a practitioner of humbuggery. One such person was a white man named Ethelred T. Brantley, a respectable overseer. Drewry comments on Brantley, "after his intercourse with Nat no one would have anything to do with him."[40] The good church people of Southampton refused Nat permission to be baptized with Brantley. It must have caused something of a scandal in the community that such a highly regarded white man would have fallen under the spell of a fanatical slave preacher, for we learn from Gray's *Confessions* that "many who reviled us" were present when Turner and the overseer, like Philip and the Ethiopian eunuch with roles reversed, went down into the water together.

This episode was followed by another vision on May 12, 1828, when Turner received the unmistakable sign that he should prepare for the great work—the apocalyptic struggle with the serpent, which to him must have symbolized the system of slavery. The white slaveholders who had been first in this world would now become last in the kingdom. And the slaves, who had been made last, would—as Scripture clearly prophesied—become first. Turner's own words describe what happened:

. . . and on the appearance of the sign [the eclipse of the sun in February 1831] I should arise and prepare myself, and slay my enemies with their own weapons. And immediately on the sign appearing in the heavens, the seal was removed from my lips, and I communicated the great work laid out for me to do, to four in whom I had the greatest confidence [Henry Porter, Hark Travis, Nelson Williams, and Sam Francis are referred to here]. It was intended by us to have begun the work of death on the 4th of July last—

Two years and nine months intervened before Nat felt that he had received the sign. It came in the form of a solar eclipse in February 1831. The realization that the time had come at last, and sinking deeper into that agony of spirit one experiences when wrestling with God over a great decision that can be neither accepted nor evaded, brought Turner down with an illness sometime prior to the July date that had been set earlier. July 4 passed without incident. But the postponement served to force him and his men to review repeatedly the earlier plan. Still doubt lingered, for his confession mentions that new schemes were formed and rejected as they weighed divine necessity against the reasonable possibility of success.

Nat, the prophet—austere and aloof—trusted his accomplices, but had ceased associating intimately with them, probably because he had more confidence in their toughness and courage than in the genuineness of their religious dedication. The men themselves, however, seem to have held him in awe to the end. If their religion was not distinguished by asceticism and the outward signs of beatitude, it was, nevertheless, characterized by the confidence blacks have always vested in the preacher who could convince them that he walked with God in their stead, and whose words of truth thundered against their own unbelief.

Sometime in August a strange atmospheric phenomenon occurred across the sky over Virginia and North Carolina. It extended over a period of three days and was known as the "Three Blue Days" of 1831.[41] It seemed to Nat—after his sickness of July had passed and after he had all but exhausted the discussion about alternative strategies—that this was the sign he had been waiting for. We do not know whether or not the image of the Passover supper Jesus had with his disciples was in his mind when he, Henry, and Hark—the two beloved disciples?—met in the woods for a supper of barbecue and brandy on the Sunday afternoon of August 21. With all that had gone before to bring him to that moment, it would have been strange indeed if he did not have some sense of reenacting the Communion on that occasion. The surroundings fitted the mood. The site they chose for the meal was in the woods near the Cabin Pond—considered taboo because of superstitions connected with the burning of a slave there for having whipped his master to death.[42]

Four others had joined Hark and Henry: Sam Francis, Jack Reese, Nelson Williams, and Will Francis.[43] Was Will Francis, as Styron imagined, strangely different than the others? Did Nat have an overpowering sense that this might be the Judas come to betray him? If so, he was immediately reassured. When, upon arriving late for the rendezvous, he found Will there, he questioned him sharply about why he had come. Will's reply should leave no doubt about what was uppermost in the minds of the little band that night. He answered that his life "was worth no more than the others, and his liberty was as dear to him." When asked whether he was determined to win his freedom regardless of what he might have to do, Will replied that he would win it, or lose his life in the attempt.

The late nineteenth-century black historian George W. Williams claimed that Nat Turner gave a speech that Sunday night at the Cabin Pond. Among other things, Nat is reported to have said that God had appointed that night for the black race to be delivered from slavery, and that the war should be waged "upon a Christian basis."[44] No verbatim account of what was actually said was recorded, but the speech that Williams supposes to have come from the lips of Nat Turner is believable. Turner was a preacher and he would not have failed to use the dramatic setting of that Sunday night to preach to the little congregation as he had never preached before. It would have been more like the Nat Turner that Williams wrote about than the one pictured by Styron to have plainly shown to his companions the justice of what they were about to do, according to Scripture, and on the basis of the revelations he had received.

Before midnight, with only a hatchet and a broadax, they set out for the home of the man who at the time was Nat's own master, John Travis. At the Travis house they slaughtered everyone—Travis, his wife, and five others. They took what guns and ammunition they could find, and, dressing their lines like infantrymen, they marched off to perform the bloodiest slave insurrection in American history. By Tuesday morning, August 23, at least seventy slaves had killed fifty-seven whites in a twenty-mile area of the Boykins district of Southampton County.[45]

There is no point in going into the gory details. They are recounted with amazing candor and without remorse in Turner's confession. The plan was ultimately to take the county seat, Jerusalem (now Courtland, Virginia), and there to furnish themselves with weapons and ammunition. Somewhere on the main road between Cross Keys and Jerusalem, in a field in front of the residence of a prosperous planter named James W. Parker, Nat and his men met their first resistance. It was from a group of militia commanded by Captain Alexander P. Peete and Captain James Bryant. After first forcing the whites to retreat, the poorly armed blacks were dispersed. During the night and throughout the next day, Nat was unable to regroup his men in sufficient numbers to engage the alarmed whites who were being reinforced by militia from neighboring communities, not to mention soldiers from Fort Monroe.[46] Indeed, the whole Eastern seaboard was galvanized into action by the news of the revolt. The people of Southampton were offered assistance from as far away as Philadelphia and New London, Connecticut.

In the end Nat despaired of continuing the fight with the few men he was able to keep together. He made an escape and hid in the woods near the Cabin Pond. For six weeks he eluded the posses that scoured the area and was discovered only accidentally by two slaves whose dog was attracted by the smell of meat from a cave where Nat was concealed. The two men probably reported that they had seen him. But for ten days longer—an incredibly long time considering the alarm that was raised—Nat managed to baffle his pursuers by hiding out on the large Salathul Francis plantation.[47] He dug a hole under a fallen tree and remained there until Sunday, October 30, when a white man, Benjamin Phipps, stumbled upon his hideout and apprehended him at gunpoint. On the following day he was taken into Jerusalem and was tried and convicted in the course of five days. During those days he made his full confession to Thomas R. Gray and on November 11, 1831, was hanged. Nat told the court just before he was sentenced that he had nothing more to say. After the confession he made no appeal for mercy and showed no sign of penitence. Gray reported that when he asked the prisoner if he did not now believe that he was mistaken, the reply was simply, "Was not Christ crucified?"

Thus ended the great Southampton insurrection. Fifty-three blacks were arrested and tried. Twenty-one were acquitted, twelve transported out of the state, and twenty hanged. It has been estimated that more than one hundred slaves were killed before the back of the movement was broken. But it is more than likely that at least half of those were summarily lynched during the first few days when whites marauded through the countryside looking for suspected insurgents.[48] Drewry's earlier account, following Gray's statistics, says that seventeen blacks were executed. He adds that the body of Nat Turner was delivered to doctors who skinned it and made grease of the flesh.[49] Worse things have been known to happen to black offenders.

The Southampton revolt caused a paroxysm of fear throughout the South. It also inspired slaves everywhere to a new restiveness about liberty. Nat Turner was not the only black preacher during this period who wanted to lead an uprising. Governor Floyd of Virginia wrote: "From all that has come to my knowledge during and since this affair—I am fully convinced that every black preacher in the whole country east of the Blue Ridge, was in the secret."[50] Turner had said that the Southampton revolt was local, but he did affirm that more than likely the revelations he had received had also come to others, prompting them to similar undertakings. As could be expected, the effect on the free exercise of black religion and church life in the South was immediate. Du Bois reports:

A wave of legislation passed over the South prohibiting the slaves from learning to read and write, forbidding Negroes to preach, and interfering with Negro religious meetings. Virginia declared, in 1831, that neither slaves nor free Negroes might preach, nor could they attend religious services at night without permission. In North Carolina slaves and free Negroes were forbidden to preach, exhort or teach "in any prayer meeting or other association for worship—slaves of different families are collected together on penalty of not more than thirty-nine lashes." Maryland and Georgia had similar laws. The Mississippi law of 1831 said, it is "unlawful for any slave, free Negro, or mulatto to preach the gospel" upon pain of receiving thirty-nine lashes upon the naked back of the presumptuous preacher. . . . In the District of Columbia the free Negroes began to leave white churches in 1831 and to assemble in their own.[51]

Thus, from David Walker to Nat Turner, black religion in the United States—strongly fortified by Old Testament and New Testament apocalyptic—provided blacks with spiritual resources with which to resist oppression, if with tragic unsuccess. The southern whites who observed the slave preachers at close range knew about the possible amalgam of African religion and radical Christianity. They sensed the ability of those men and women to inspire revolt and threw up the ramparts of repressive legislation and the lynch law against them.

To insist that these remarkable persons were merely misguided fanatics and that the vast majority of humble black folk neither approved nor participated in their conspiracies—preferring "pie in the sky"—is to fail to appreciate one of the most significant undercurrents in the complex stream of black church life. In the next chapter we shall see how this undercurrent of rebelliousness and outrage over slavery expressed itself in the great independence movement that gave birth to the black denominations. The black church in this country has never been as militant as it was in the days of Denmark Vesey and Nat Turner, but new occasions teach new duties. The prophetic zeal of Turner continually erupted in other forms from the ranks of black preachers and ignited various movements for freedom and self-determination that, in one way or another, have been related to the black church. The great Negro spiritual—

> O Freedom, O Freedom
> O Freedom, over me,
> And before I'll be a slave,
> I'll be buried in my grave,
> And go home to my Lord
> And be free. . . .

—reveals, more than the institution-maintenance functions of Methodist general conferences and Baptist annual conventions, what is really at the heart of black religion. Even when the church was quiescent, the seed of resistance to tyranny and oppression was being harbored in its bowels against the day when the cup of patience would run over.

To say with William S. Drewry that a man like Nat Turner was given to gloomy fanaticism and possessed with a "love of self-importance, encouraged by the efforts of Negro preachers, who were influenced by external affairs . . ." is grossly to miscalculate the impact of the gospel of liberation upon those who could understand the existence of a God of love only as One who demanded uncompromising justice.[52] To recoil in horror at the intention of men like Denmark Vesey and Nat Turner and to argue that for all their religiousness they were certainly not Christians—that the black church should never dignify such deranged enthusiasm—

is to bargain for cheap grace in order to cover up the sin of white America. As much as white Christians might wish that there were some other way out, there is no escape from what Reverend Francis J. Grimke, the distinguished black Presbyterian of Washington, D.C., said in a sermon delivered in 1902 on the resemblance and contrast between the Hebrew people and African Americans:

> God is not dead,—nor is he an indifferent onlooker at what is going on in this world. One day He will make restitution for blood; He will call the oppressors to account. Justice may sleep, but it never dies. The individual, race, or nation which does wrong, which sets at defiance God's great law, especially God's great law of love, of brotherhood, will be sure, sooner or later, to pay the penalty. We reap as we sow. With that measure we mete, it shall be measured to us again.[53]

## CHAPTER 5

# The Black Church Freedom Movement

*The Church having opened the way for the development of the black man, other means have followed, and still others will follow, until his opportunities are equal to that of any other race. . . . The African Church will then have accomplished its special work—not till then.*

Bishop J.W. Hood,
*One Hundred Years of the A.M.E. Church,* p. 48

From 1750 to 1861 there were more black and white Christians worshiping in the same congregations, proportionate to their numbers as baptized Christians, than there are today. This should not, however, be taken to imply that prior to the Civil War American churches were racially integrated. Blacks enjoyed no real freedom or equality of ecclesiastical status in either the North or the South. It never occurred to white Christians that the equality that was denied to their brothers and sisters in civil society should at least be made available to them within the church. As a matter of fact, the relationship pattern of whites and blacks in the household of God made it difficult for Americans to perceive that there was anything wrong with inequality in the household of Caesar.

In the South it seemed rather a matter of prudence on the part of the planters not to permit the slaves to come together for religious services unless some white persons were present. That, rather than any desire for racial integration, is the reason why most slaves and their masters sought the blessings of God under the same roof for more than a hundred fifty years before the Emancipation Proclamation.

There was interracial worship before the Civil War, but it was never intended to suggest equality. Even if a few pious slaveholders sincerely believed that they benefited from worshiping with blacks, and were willing to be reminded of their sins by black preachers, they were wise enough to appreciate the fact that their presence in the services had a restraining effect upon black religion. It was expedient that inflamed passions not be permitted to get out of hand and be exploited by some dubious character who might fancy himself a witch doctor, or by some itinerant Yankee preacher.

The possibility of slave uprisings was invariably associated with religion, despite the pains that had been taken to make the faith an instrument of compliance and control. Black Christians who were ardent in their devotions had to be watched carefully. Although church mission boards received word from the field that the new converts were zealous in their beliefs and generally of good behavior, one could not be sure just how deep their christianization process had been, or how long it would last, particularly in view of the injustices that were tolerated within the church itself. Slaveholders and overseers knew that rebellion inspired by religion was always a possibility.

## INDEPENDENT BLACK CONGREGATIONS

When a few independent black congregations began to appear in the South almost a hundred years before the Civil War, there was actually more rather than less control over the situation. Unlike the clandestine meetings in the woods and slave cabins from sundown to sunup, these were religious institutions much like those of the whites. They were, after all, public places in full view of the whites and often erected with their blessing and financial assistance. In the South they remained under white control. White preachers officiated at the services of the earliest black congregations, though some of them had had black preachers before the Revolutionary War.[1] When these preachers began to be called to totally or predominantly black congregations, the fear of conspiracy heightened and black ministers were harried and persecuted until it was unmistakably clear that they posed no threat to the community. They were warned that they had a sacred trust from the white community. If they wanted to enjoy the privilege of preaching and a relaxation of the prohibitions against worshiping alone, they had to maintain the same deportment and discipline that the master's own preacher would exercise over black congregants.

The black minister, however, was not naive. He was likely, in fact, to be the most intelligent person in the community. He knew that he was being watched by the whites, but also how to make the best use of the opportunity to teach what blacks needed to know about themselves and their situation.

Philip A. Bruce, somewhat later than the period we are discussing, made an interesting observation about black preachers and politics that deserves quoting at length:

The preachers of the negroes are their most active politicians, as a rule, but even when they are not they have much political influences, for they constitute, individually, the natural leaders of their race, being elevated to their clerical position not because they are men of greater holiness of life or eloquence of tongue than the rest of their fellows, but because they have more energy and decision of character. Each one brings these qualifications to bear on all occasions of public agitation from that conspicuous coigne of vantage, his pulpit, which thus becomes a rostrum, the religious doctrines enunciated from thence, taking the color of his political principles, just as, on the other hand, his political harangues have a religious echo. The two parts of minister and orator are played so skillfully at one and the same time that it is impossible to distinguish them; and the affairs of the Hereafter and a contemporary political canvass are mixed in inextricable confusion. His church is thus converted into a political organization that is consolidated by the religious fervour that pervades it, and propelled towards a single political end by a religious enthusiasm that expects to be rewarded spiritually for the performance of partisan duties. The preacher playing alternately upon both at once, excites an emotional responsiveness that is prepared to obey his slightest injunctions; and he does not hesitate to turn this exalted state of feeling to the most useful account.[2]

White commentators who write so glibly about the "otherworldliness" of the black church fail to understand what was really going on. The preacher was most relevant to this world when he was telling his congregation what to expect in the next one, precisely because he whetted appetites for what everyone knew whites were undeservedly enjoying in the here and now. His congregation had no difficulty understanding that he wanted them to have the best of this world too, for what else could he mean by always talking about a just God from whom everyone—including black folks—gets his or her due? White preachers never made as rich and elaborate a use of religion as their black brothers of the cloth.

The disestablishment of the churches in the several states soon after Independence removed them from the center of public life, even though they continued to exercise a certain amount of authority in manners and morals. But for the slaves and their descendants, a religion that could unveil the reality of another world beyond "this vale of tears" and at the same time interpret what God was doing to redress the wrongs against blacks was an absolute necessity for survival. It was never really disestablished in the black quarters. It was precisely the mystique and so-called otherworldliness of black religion that gave it license to speak authoritatively about daily life, about oppression and liberation. "Going to church" for blacks was never as much a matter of custom and convention as it was for whites. It was rather a necessity. The church was the one impregnable corner of the world where consolation, unity, and mutual assistance could be found and from which the master—at least in the North—could be effectively barred if the people were not of a mind to welcome him.

Andrew Bryan was one of the pioneer black preachers in Georgia. Born as a slave in 1737 at Goose Creek, South Carolina, he was baptized by another early black preacher, George Liele, who escaped to Jamaica with the British during the Revolution. Subsequently Liele was to organize in Kingston the first black Baptist congregation of the Caribbean. Bryan at first preached to both races in Savannah, but on January 20, 1788, he was ordained by a white Baptist minister and became the pastor of the first African Baptist church of the city.

As pastor of one of the first recognized black congregations in the South, Bryan's reputation among the slave population grew rapidly. Hundreds of slaves made their way to his church every Sunday despite the necessity of obtaining passes, evading the sometimes lawless patrols, and other difficulties.[3]

In the early days of his ministry, whites feared that Bryan was going to foment insurrection. In addition to the dispersals of peaceful assemblies and frequent whippings in public, many of his members were arrested and severely chastised by the authorities. Bryan himself and his brother Sampson, a deacon in the Savannah congregation, were flogged, imprisoned, and dispossessed of their meeting place. Later they were exonerated through the intervention of their master, Jonathan Bryan, who permitted the meetings to continue in a barn on his property.

To have suffered such indignities in the name of Jesus Christ, as was the case with both Andrew Bryan and George Liele, could only have increased the preachers' conviction that if whites so desperately tried to curb its proclamation, the gospel must have something very important to do with the freedom and well-being of blacks. Reverend Bryan survived his ordeal and became the most highly regarded and influential black man in Georgia. When he died in 1812 the white Baptist Association of Savannah memorialized his passing with a public statement of respect and commendation.[4]

Did Bryan and others win approbation by softening their attitude toward slavery? Liele, for example, would accept no slaves into his Kingston congregation who did not have the explicit approval of their masters. It is difficult to know the extent to which the preachers actually conformed to repeated warnings not to stir up discontent, and to what extent they pretended to go along with the system while subverting it.[5] Certainly they were more vulnerable than the white preachers who limited themselves to mild encouragement of an occasional manumission in areas where it was lawful.

Like Bryan, two black Methodist preachers of the period, Henry Evans and Black Harry, were under constant surveillance. Their meetings were infiltrated by spies and informers who frequently were promised their freedom for reporting seditious information. These preachers could do and say very little that would not speedily be brought back to the whites who were their mentors and benefactors. In the worst of circumstances they would be reported to the civil authorities, who were in a state of nervousness about meetings of blacks for any purpose. The fact that many preachers, despite their lack of formal training, were popular among the whites would seem to indicate that they, at least ostensibly, stayed within bounds and behaved themselves.

But these pioneers were not blind to the degradation of themselves and their people. They would never have been tolerated for long by the people if they had seemed to favor the masters over the demands of the gospel. When the lash was cutting the backs of men like Bryan and Evans, the thought was burned into their flesh with every blow that, for all their protestations, the slaveholding Christians knew that their days were numbered, because what they were doing was abhorrent to God. Shame and guilt made whites want to silence the black preacher even when the danger of insurrection was remote. They knew that the argument that God had ordained the enslavement of the African was a lie. And they knew too that whatever could be done by black preachers to hasten the demise of slavery—whether from the open pulpit or in secret—was a part of their commitment to the ministry. In the North, as soon as Richard Allen, Absalom Jones, and James Varick had established their independence from white church bodies, they began to give moral and material support to their brothers and sisters in the South who were less fortunate in winning independence for their congregations.

## BEGINNINGS OF THE BLACK FREEDOM MOVEMENT

The independent church movement among blacks, during and following the period of the Revolutionary War, must be regarded as the prime expression of resistance to slavery—in every sense, *the first black freedom movement*. It had the advantage of being carried on under the cloak of ecclesiastical affairs rather than as an affair of the state or the economy. The movement, therefore, could pass as representing the more or less legitimate desire of the slaves to have "a place of their own in which to worship God under their own vine and fig tree." But it was, in fact, a form of rebellion against the most accessible and vulnerable expression of white oppression and institutional racism in the nation: the American churches.

It is another of the bittersweet ironies of history that the good white Christians who deplored the agitation of the black churches had long since declared that the struggle of the colonies against the British crown was a holy war. And so it was. During the bicentennial celebration in 1976 there was much boasting in some quarters that the Revolutionary War was sometimes called "the Presbyterian Rebellion."

The fever of liberty was very much abroad in the land when black ministers began to lay claim to their own independent congregations. Under the general impulse for freedom from tyranny, Virginia repealed its discriminatory tax on free Negroes and mulattoes in 1769, declaring that it was "derogatory to the rights of freeborn subjects." The first draft of the Declaration of Independence contained a passage that laid the sin of African slavery, somewhat hypocritically, on the doorstep of the king of England. The Quakers had consistently opposed the slave trade and before the war was over they had organized the first Abolition Society in Philadelphia in 1775. The abolition of slavery came in Vermont in 1777. In 1778 Virginia prohibited the external slave trade. All in all, the end of the war saw restraints on emancipation generally lifted, and manumissions in the South as well as the North were relatively numerous. In 1784, as we have seen, the famous "Christmas Conference" of the Methodist Church, meeting in Baltimore, passed a resolution against slaveholding. Throughout the decade emancipatory legislation was enacted in the northern states.[6]

In this short-lived but expansive atmosphere, blacks took measure of the sincerity of the founding fathers by the only recourse available to them for gaining a modicum of liberty without getting themselves exterminated in the process—namely, by petitioning the white denominations for control of their churches. It was the beginning of the black revolution in American history—the first stirring of rebellion in an organized, mass-based movement, and on a national scale.

Furthermore, it began—perhaps unconsciously but no less effectively—in the most respected institution of the American society. Even so, it was not an easy task to accomplish. Few white churches and judicatories were actually eager to let them go, and even when separate congregations were permitted, white clergy presided over most of them. Black congregations remained under the eyes of the civil government and the discipline of church bodies. Before the African Methodist Episcopal and the African Methodist Episcopal Zion churches finally won their unconditional freedom from white Methodism, Richard Allen in Philadelphia, Morris Brown in Charleston, and James Varick and Christopher Rush in New York City had to fight almost every step of the way to be dismissed properly from the mother church and retain rights to their finances and properties.[7] The Baptists, with a much less centralized control over individual congregations, put fewer obstacles in the way of separating memberships, and several independent black congregations were formed in the South and the border states before the turn of the eighteenth century.[8]

Probably the first black congregation of which we have record today was organized in 1758 on the plantation of William Byrd on the Bluestone River near what is now Mecklenburg, Virginia. It was constituted by followers of the separatist Baptist missionary Shubal Stearns, who was more responsible—directly and indirectly—than any other white preacher for bringing Christianity to the slaves of North Carolina, South Carolina, and Georgia. Under the leadership of David George and George Liele, a black church was founded on the plantation of George Galphin at Silver Bluff, South Carolina, between 1773 and 1775. The Black Baptist Church at Williamsburg and the Harrison Street church of Petersburg, Virginia, were both organized in 1776. In the North the Joy Street African Baptist Church of Boston dates from 1805 and blacks in Philadelphia separated from a conservative white Baptist congregation in 1809. In the same year, after conflict with reluctant white Baptists, Thomas Paul, who had been at Joy Street, organized the Abyssinian Baptist Church in New York City.[9]

### Richard Allen and the Free African Society

The earliest black Methodist church was the African Union Church incorporated in Wilmington, Delaware, in 1807—well before the first general conference of the African Methodist Episcopal Church and thus claiming the honor of being the first black denomination. It united with the First Colored Methodist Protestant Church in 1866 to form the African Union First Colored Methodist Protestant Church of America.[10] Once the dam had been opened by Richard Allen and Absalom Jones in 1787, the flood inundated the land. Blacks suddenly became aware of the fact that they no longer were obliged to suffer the indignity of segregation and the lack of opportunity for advancement in the white churches, even if there seemed to be no end to the denial of freedom and equality in secular society.

Philadelphia was a hotbed of ecclesiastical insurrection. Mother Bethel African Methodist Episcopal Church began as a protest against segregation in St. George's Methodist Episcopal Church in that city. Even though Allen at first agreed to keep the dissatisfied blacks in fellowship with the St. George congregation, he did so not because he was anxious to continue worshiping with whites, but because he believed in the evangelical theology and policy of Methodism. Inherently, he embraced a latitudinarian or low doctrine of the visible church. He believed that sanctification came to those who lived a pious life, rather than through adherence to rites and dogmas. In this he shared with the Wesleys, Asbury, and other Methodist fathers of the eighteenth century a bias for personal, noninstitutional religion. But Allen had something more. He had a desire for a church that would combine secular relevance with deep spirituality in a context of simplicity and spontaneity. He saw that the formal churchmanship that was gaining ground among whites of the northern cities, as the new middle class began to dominate churches such as St. George's, was not for poor blacks. Even though he finally adopted the discipline of white Methodism with few changes, he was interested in neither a legalistic nor a socially fashionable church.

Allen saw the creeds and ordinances of an ecclesiastical establishment as irrelevant to the spiritual, moral, and material needs of the community. His vision was of a well-ordered, but flexible, spirit-filled, community-oriented church that could move immediately into the arena of the movement for freedom and equality. His deep affection was for simple Methodism, like Blade Willgoose's class that met on Monday nights and was made up of poor, ignorant persons who needed help.[11]

The earliest development of black religious independence in Philadelphia was almost taken over by the Society of Friends, for at that time blacks had no better friends than the Quakers of Pennsylvania. But Allen was not inclined in that direction as the answer to the problem of a suitable church for blacks. He believed in the openness of Christian fellowship to anyone who would consent to the simple rules of a moral life, but he was not given to the quietness and individualism of the Society of Friends. More than anything else he wanted spirited preaching and singing, with congregational participation and the freedom of black worship evolving out of its African background. Throughout his life he was convinced that Methodism came closest to the form of worship desired by blacks, and it was obvious to him that he could not worship as he pleased at St. George's.

Therefore, when Allen saw "a large field open in seeking and instructing my African brethren," only a few of whom were attending public worship anywhere, he brought them together in prayer meetings in his own house.[12] When he and Absalom Jones were finally forced from St. George's as they knelt in prayer, they did not immediately establish a competing congregation, but what amounted to a Christian association—the Free African Society—including in it all sorts and conditions of persons regardless of their religious preferences. The society's preamble gives us some idea of the spirit and intention of the founders:

> Whereas Absalom Jones and Richard Allen, two men of the African race, who, for their religious life and conversation have obtained a good report among men, these persons, from a love to the people of their complexion who they beheld with sorrow, because of their irreligious and uncivilized state, often communed together upon this painful and important subject in order to form some kind of religious society, but there being too few to be found under the like concern, and those who were, differed in their religious sentiments; with those circumstances they labored for some time, till it was proposed, after a serious communication of sentiments, that a society should be formed, without regard to religious tenets, provided the persons lived an orderly and sober life, in order to support one another in sickness, and for the benefit of their widows and fatherless children.[13]

Although the Free African Society generally followed the pattern of the class meetings—the distinguishing characteristic of early Methodism—it had a broader and more secular purpose. The closing words of the preamble indicate the problems that were uppermost in the minds of Allen and Jones. One finds in this statement of purpose a certain ambivalence about religious and secular objectives in keeping with the best tradition of black religion in America. It was not the original purpose of the two men to organize blacks merely for community action and social welfare, as important as those concerns were to them. In his autobiography Allen writes plainly: "I established prayer meetings; I raised a society in 1786 of forty-two members. I saw the necessity of erecting a place of worship for the colored people."[14] In the face of resolute opposition from both blacks and whites, he never gave up the dream of a self-sustaining black congregation. But the nature of the Free African Society with its bilateral purpose indicates the direction of his thinking about the nature of black Christianity.

The suitability of the Free African Society pattern for meeting the multiple needs of the black community is amply demonstrated by the enthusiasm with which this form of organized activity spread from Philadelphia to other cities. Wherever such societies were founded, they began as tacit protests against white prejudice and neglect. It was usually their objective to provide not only for religious needs, but for social service, mutual aid, and solidarity among "people of African descent." They were typical immigrant organizations, such as have been established by every ethnic group coming to America—with one important difference. The Free African societies did not express the need for cultural unity and solidarity only, but the protest and resistance of a persecuted people. Richard Allen could see that black men and women were only slightly more free in the North than in the South, and he was persuaded that even in the City of Brotherly Love their churches would never be permitted to serve the social, political, and economic needs of blacks without a fight. Most of the members of the society in Philadelphia were as much, or even more, of the opinion that the group should move along secular lines. The others had no intention of being affiliated with the Methodists, whom they considered prejudiced, despite the fact that Allen devoutly wished for such affiliation.

The society was remarkably versatile in its style of life and work. Not only did it pass resolutions regulating the morals of its members—with particular attention to marriage and family life—but it also established a Committee of Monitors whose business it was to visit the membership regularly in order that they might "increase in grace and knowledge and every Christian virtue." The Philadelphia society became involved in abolitionist activity, and in 1790 another committee was organized to assist in an effort to take a census of the number of free blacks in Philadelphia. In that year it also decided to begin regular religious services. The direction in which it desired to move is indicated by this decision and the fact that the regular meeting room was considered no longer appropriate for this purpose. A special room was now assigned for worship at the Friends Free African School House, where the group met from 1788 to 1791.

Thus, in many respects the Free African Society, which represented the first bid for independence among blacks in the North, resembled an organized church without actually being one. Although Allen entertained hopes that a "preaching-house" would come out of it eventually, he never intended it to be a church as such, and yet he wanted it to serve the religious needs of those who joined. It was a fellowship of black citizens who craved independence and social progress without reference to the creeds and confessions used in most of the mainline white churches.

The interests of the Free African societies were both religious and secular, and never became exclusively one or the other. They created, therefore, the classic pattern for the black church in the United States—a pattern of religious commitment that has a double focus: free and autonomous worship in the African American tradition, and the solidarity and social welfare of the black community.

It was not until the Philadelphia group began to move in its religious life toward the style of Quaker devotion and churchmanship—under the friendly persuasion of well-meaning Quakers—rather than toward the spirit of primitive Methodism, that Allen raised objection and separated himself from it. Reconciliation took place by 1790 when the society finally decided to build a church. The result was St. Thomas' African Episcopal church, which was dedicated, with Jones as pastor, on July 17, 1794. Twelve days later, on July 29, Bishop Francis Asbury preached the dedicatory sermon at Mother Bethel where Allen and the group that followed him laid the foundation for African Methodism throughout the world.

In the public statement issued upon the establishment of the Bethel congregation, the founders said that they were aware that they had by their actions, "in some measure discriminated ourselves." But they regarded it also important to declare that they "had no other view therein but the glory of God and the peace of the Church, by removing what was in a measure treated and esteemed as a nuisance, on the one hand, and an insult on the other, endeavoring through grace to avoid the appearance of evil and to seek peace with all men, especially them that are of the household of faith."[15]

The spirit of African Methodism spread rapidly from its center in Philadelphia in a widening circle of rebelliousness. In 1787 the white members of the Log Meeting House, Lovely Lane, in Baltimore, refused to permit blacks to occupy the same pews with them or to participate in Holy Communion. The blacks withdrew and organized the Baltimore African church, which joined Allen's group in 1816. Reuben Cuff withdrew the black Methodists of Salem, New Jersey, in 1800. Forty-two members of the Asbury church of Wilmington, Delaware, under the leadership of Peter Spencer, organized the Union Church of Africans and considered joining the Allenites in 1813. Peter Spencer and William Anderson led the blacks out of the Methodist Church in Attleborough, Pennsylvania, between 1813 and 1816. Sixteen persons representing several different communities met at the Bethel church in Philadelphia in April 1816 and formed an Ecclesiastical Compact. The following resolution was adopted:

> That the people of Philadelphia, Baltimore, and all other places who should unite with them, shall become one body under the name and style of the African Methodist Episcopal Church.[16]

Several new groups had joined by 1818, including the Methodists in Charleston, South Carolina. In the conference that year, 6,748 persons were counted in the first detailed membership report. A strong organization, the first national institution organized and controlled by blacks in the United States, had evolved out of the spontaneous proliferation in several communities of the Free African Society concept. The new body was, of course, ecclesiastical and not primarily a self-help, benevolent society. But under the leadership of Richard Allen it never lost a basic concern for liberation and community welfare. As Richard R. Wright observed on the occasion of one hundred years of African Methodist history:

> The purpose in mind of the founding father of African Methodism . . . was, among other things, to exemplify in the black man the power of self-reliance, self-help by the exercise of free religious thought with executive efficiency. Hence, her spirit and practices have been, at all times and places, to encourage fraternal and economic organizations among the colored race; so that, upon any proper occasion, she throws open her churches and halls for funerals, anniversaries and conventions.[17]

### The AME and AME Zion Churches

Bishop Francis Asbury held an urgent meeting in 1796 with a small committee of black Methodists of New York City who were members of the predominantly white John Street church. The purpose was to discuss, at their initiative, the possibility of meeting separately in the interval between the regular preaching services of the whites.

The John Street congregation was experiencing a problem familiar to other white churches throughout the country. Blacks were joining in increasing numbers and creating a problem of seating—overflowing the sections reserved for them. Peter Williams, a former slave and a respected employee of the John Street church, had already entertained the idea of organizing an "African chapel" in order to minister more effectively to blacks.[18] The situation in New York was somewhat less hostile than in Philadelphia.

It may be safely assumed, however, that the matter of strained relations between the two groups went beyond the matter of deciding where black members could and should be seated on Sunday mornings. In his book *The Varick Family*, Wheeler makes the interesting comment that the white Methodists of John Street "did not persecute colored people, but simply denied them certain privileges."[19] In any event, steps were taken at the meeting with Asbury to form a new congregation.

A cabinetmaker's shop was secured for the first meeting place and the chapel was incorporated as the Zion Church over the signatures of Peter Williams and Francis Jacob on September 8, 1800. The first preachers to serve the chapel were Abraham Thompson, June Scott, and Thomas Miller.[20] When the Zionites, following the example of their brothers and sisters in South Philadelphia and Baltimore, decided to break completely with the white denomination, the New York Methodist Conference declined to ordain their preachers.

After two decades of exasperation over the obstructive tactics of splinter groups among their own number, and a schism led by a white minister, William L. Stillwell, into which they were drawn, the blacks made a crucial connectional decision. At a meeting on August 11, 1820, it was agreed to form the African Methodist Episcopal Church in America (later to become the African Methodist Episcopal Zion Church). On June 21, 1821, the original group, together with representatives from New Haven, Philadelphia, and Long Island, organized the new denomination.

They were, however, still plagued with difficulties. In September 1821 a special meeting was called to consider the problem of ordination in view of the obstacles presented by the white church. One group wanted to return penitently to the Methodist Church in return for securing ordination. Another favored receiving ordination from the Stillwellites, whose leader was a controversial white elder who attempted to lead the Zionites into his quarrel over the polity of the Methodist Episcopal Church. A third faction counseled the maintenance of elected elders until ordination could be obtained by some appropriate means. The problem was finally resolved in 1822 with "the imposition of hands" by three former elders of the mother church who had separated in the Stillwell schism—James Corvel, Silvester Hutchinson, and William L. Stillwell.[21] In the same year James Varick was elected the first superintendent (later bishop) and under his leadership the Zion Church grew and provided a strong counterpart movement, among black Methodists in the North, to the Allenites.[22]

Both the AME Church and the AME Zion Church were strongly opposed to slavery. The laws of both prohibited the retention of slaveholders in membership. We have already noted the complicity of the Allenites in the Charleston insurrection of 1822. One of the conspirators in that affair was Morris Brown, who, by being out of Charleston at the time, managed to conceal his involvement long enough to have escaped with his life. That might not have happened had not white friends warned him against remaining in the state and spirited him off aboard a ship leaving for Philadelphia. There he remained to become a shoemaker and later a bishop of the AME Church.[23] Bishop Payne makes it clear that AME members were well informed and supportive of the Vesey plot and that the church was feared by the slaveholders because of it.[24]

The Bethel church in Philadelphia and the parsonage of Bishop Allen were well known as stations of the Underground Railroad. Reverend Walter Proctor, one of the Allen's confidants, said that the "house of Bishop Allen was a refuge for the oppressed, and a house for the refugee from American oppression." This spirit of benevolence toward those who were still in chains infused the entire church. Denominational historians take it for granted that where the Allenites stood with respect to liberation is common knowledge among all blacks. As one of the elder statesmen of the denomination said at the General Convention in Cincinnati in 1856: "Every colored man is an abolitionist, and slaveholders know it."[25] Typical of the antislavery resolutions is the following adopted by the Western Conference of the AME Church, meeting in Pittsburgh on September 5, 1840:

We, the members of this Conference, are fully satisfied that the principles of the Gospel are arrayed against all sin, and that it is the duty of all Christians to use their influence and energies against all systems that rudely trample under foot the claims of justice and the sacred principles of revelation. And

Whereas, Slavery pollutes the character of the Church of God, and makes the Bible a sealed book to thousands of immortal beings, therefore,

Resolved, that we will aid by our prayers, those pious persons whom God has raised up to plead the cause of the dumb, until every fetter shall be broken, and all men enjoy the liberty which the Gospel proclaims.[26]

The General Conference of the AME church held in Cincinnati in 1856 is of particular interest because of the extended debate that took place over the question of revising the Discipline so that it would be unmistakably opposed to slaveholding. The original version read:

We will not receive any person into our society as a member who is a slaveholder. Any person now a member, having slaves, who shall refuse to emancipate them after due notice has been given by the preacher in charge, shall be expelled.

There were still a few black slaveholders in the South and the border states. Some had purchased slaves with the intention of setting them free immediately, but others expected the slaves to "work off" their purchase price before claiming full liberty. The report of the Committee on Slavery proposed to force immediate emancipation or expulsion from the church. It also offered for adoption the policy that no person who was a slaveholder be received into membership in the church under any condition. A minority of the committee objected that in some cases there were extenuating circumstances. They argued that in order not to penalize those church members or new converts who had bought slaves for the purpose of giving them freedom, due notice of expulsion should be given "by the preacher in charge," as already provided for in the Discipline. The minority warned that in establishing the denomination in a new area it was impossible always to know immediately who were slaveholders and who were not until after they had joined the church. Furthermore, there should be a period of "mercy" for such persons, untutored as they might be in the duties of Christians, that they might learn of God's will, repent, and emancipate slaves they may have acquired for whatever reason.

The matter was sharply debated. The whole issue of the church's position regarding black liberation was reopened for the first time since the Discipline had been adopted. Although there was unanimous agreement that the denomination should be against slavery and most of the conference assumed that the *de jure* position of the old Discipline had been maintained, there were others who questioned what had happened in the church over the years. There was wide disagreement over whether the church had actually cleared itself of slaveholders, whether those remaining should be summarily expelled no matter what their motives were, and whether or not the church's missionary activity and expansion into the slave states would be made even more difficult than it already was if a hard line was taken on this question. Just prior to the calling for the question, Reverend A. R. Greene made an eloquent address to the now almost disorderly audience, and said:

If the preachers having charge of churches in slaveholding states will not execute the laws, the fault is theirs, and not that of the Church. Where is the conscience of the preacher, with this rule in his hand, that does not exclude a slaveholder? To charge the Church with the sin of slavery under such circumstances is to charge God with the sin of Adam, who did previously transgress in the very face of the law which forbade him to eat the forbidden fruit. The Church is free from this accursed sin—standing forth as a beacon light, and as glorious as the unclouded sun![27]

The minority report, calling for the enforcement of the original position against slaveholding as it already stood in the Discipline, was adopted by a vote of forty to twelve. Thus, in the 1850s followers of Richard Allen encountered some of the same dilemmas the white Methodists had wrestled with in 1844, despite the fact that the question was presented in Cincinnati more as one of strategy than of principle.

The AME Zion Church from its founding was involved in the struggle against slavery. Its congregations along the Mason-Dixon line were known as stations of the Underground Railroad. Catherine Harris, Thomas James, Frederick Douglass, Harriet Tubman, Jermain Louguen, and Sojourner Truth were all associated with Zionite activity against slavery.[28] Catherine Harris of Jamestown, New York, was a member of the Zion congregation whose parsonage is today on the site of the house she used after 1831 as a sanctuary for fugitives. During the 1850s she had seventeen slaves in her house at one time, caring for their needs until they could be sent on to safety. The most famous story about her and the people of the Zion Church of Jamestown has to do with the concealment of a fugitive slave in a coffinlike box in which he was taken by wagon to Dunkirk and ferried across Lake Erie to Canada.[29]

The distinguished Syracuse minister Jermain Louguen was himself an escaped slave. He became a bishop of the Zion Church in 1864 after many years of abolition work in the North. It was the opinion of the late David H. Bradley, the denominational historian, that Louguen's enthusiasm for his work as an abolitionist lecturer so overshadowed his church affiliation that he should be remembered more for fighting slavery than for his administrative work as a bishop. Much the same could be said about many other black ministers of the period.

Thomas James, the AME Zion pastor at New Bedford, Massachusetts, when Fred Douglass arrived there, was born a slave in 1804 and escaped as a young boy. While working as a school teacher and preacher in Rochester, New York, in 1831, he was given some antislavery literature to read. It so impressed him that he launched out on a career that made him outstanding in western New York. It was after James had been transferred to New Bedford from a parish in Long Island that he met Douglass and had some influence on the latter's decision to engage in full-time antislavery work. In his autobiography he tells us that as a minister of the Zion branch of black Methodism he naturally took an active part in the freedom struggle.[30]

An incident illustrating the character of the man and the involvement of his church in antislavery agitation happened on a return journey he made to New Bedford from a visit to New York City. In the Jim Crow coach of the train he met a slave girl from Richmond traveling with her master and his family to New Bedford for a vacation. James invited the girl to visit the Zion congregation during her stay. But when he and a friend called upon her later to inquire why she had not attended services, her owner, Henry Ludlam, met them at the door and informed them that: "Lucy is my slave, and slaves don't receive calls." James applied in Boston for a writ of habeas corpus and took possession of the girl. It so happened that her master warned her that she was in danger with the minister and his friend, and that she should display a handkerchief as a signal for him to come and rescue her. James writes:

> We took the girl to a chamber on the upper floor of the residence of the Rev. Joel Knight, and that evening we prepared to lie down before the door. Lucy displayed the handkerchief as she had promised, and when we questioned her about it, answered, "Master told me to do it; he is coming to take me home." At this we quietly called together twenty men from the colored district of the place, and they took seats in the church close at hand, ready for any emergency. At one o'clock in the morning Ludlam appeared on the scene, with the backing of a dozen men, carrying a ladder, to effect the rescue. The sheriff hailed them but they gave no answer, whereat our party of colored men sallied forth, and the rescuers fled in all directions. The entire town was now agog over the affair.

The girl was finally escorted by the intervention of the local police to Boston, where she appeared in court, petitioned to be released, and received her freedom the next day. Another attempt by her owner to "rescue" her was foiled. The girl later married in the North, had children, and continued to live unmolested until her death.[31]

Reverend James was subsequently assigned to the AME Zion Church of Boston and in 1856 returned to the congregation in Rochester where he had first joined the denomination in 1823 as a runaway slave. In a testimonial preserved by Bishop Hood, Douglass speaks of Zionite ministers he respected and admired. It deserves quoting here not only to illustrate the quality of the Zionite preachers, but also to demonstrate the extent to which Douglass's commitment to the cause of black freedom was rooted and grounded in his earliest encounter with them and the church. The great black abolitionist writes:

> My connection with the African Methodist Episcopal Zion Church began in 1838. This was soon after my escape from slavery and my arrival in New Bedford. Before leaving Maryland I was a member of the Methodist Church in Dallas Street, Baltimore, and should have joined a branch of that Church in New Bedford, Mass., had I not discovered the spirit of prejudice and the unholy connection of that Church with slavery. Hence I joined a little branch of Zion, of which Rev. William Serrington was the minister. I found him a man of deep piety, and of high intelligence. His character attracted me,

and I received from him much excellent advice and brotherly sympathy. When he was removed to another station Bishop Rush sent us a very different man, in the person of Rev. Peter Ross, a man of high character, but of very little education. After him came Rev. Thomas James. I was deeply interested not only in these ministers, but also in Revs. Jehiel Beman, Dempsey Kennedy, John P. Thompson, and Levan Smith, all of whom visited and preached in the little school house on Second Street, New Bedford, while I resided there. My acquaintance with Bishop Rush was also formed while I was in New Bedford.

It is impossible for me to tell how far my connection with these devoted men influenced my career. As early as 1839 I obtained a license from the Quarterly Conference as a local preacher, and often occupied the pulpit by request of the preacher in charge. No doubt that the exercise of my gifts in this vocation, and my association with the excellent men to whom I have referred, helped to prepare me for the wider sphere of usefulness which I have since occupied. It was from this Zion church that I went forth to the work of delivering my brethren from bondage, and this new vocation, which separated me from New Bedford and finally so enlarged my views of duty, separated me also from the calling of a local preacher. My connection with the little church continued long after I was in the antislavery field. I look back to the days I spent in little Zion, New Bedford, in several capacities of sexton, steward, class leader, clerk and local preacher, as among the happiest days of my life.[32]

### The Presbyterians and Episcopalians

A few black congregations were established among the Presbyterians and Episcopalians after 1800. But the tenor of the preaching and the formality of the services of those denominations were not amenable to most blacks. Moreover, the white presbyters and Episcopal bishops exercised paternalistic inhibition over their black congregants. The Presbyterians had shown an early interest in the religious instruction of blacks, but "could never quite bring themselves to the place where they would recognize the ability of the Negro to be a responsible agent for his own salvation."[33] A succession of general assemblies, up to the division of the denomination in 1861, passed several eloquent resolutions that were generally supportive of the antislavery position, but the church refused to withhold fellowships from slaveholders and became embroiled in interminable debates over whether or not slavery was an affair of the state, and therefore outside the competence of the church. The first black Presbyterian church was formed with twenty-two members in 1807 as the First African Church of Philadelphia. Its pastor was an ex-slave named John Gloucester who had worked as a missionary under a white Presbyterian minister in Tennessee.[34]

The attitude of the Episcopalians may be deduced from the fact that, unlike the Presbyterians, they were not divided between North and South during the Civil War.[35] Although the Anglicans were the first to evangelize the African slaves, the Protestant Episcopal Church, which succeeded it in the independent nation, catered to its southern constituency in the interest of preserving the unity of the denomination. It confined itself, therefore, to urging slaveholders to see that their slaves received religious instruction.

The first black Episcopal church in the United States developed from the group that separated from the Methodists with Richard Allen and Absalom Jones. It was organized as the St. Thomas Church of Philadelphia and was received into the Episcopal Church on October 12, 1794. Jones was ordained its first deacon in 1795.[36]

Despite differences in the way they developed over the years, it is clear that the same independent spirit that impelled the Baptists and Methodists to separate from the whites led to the organization of black Presbyterian and Episcopal congregations.[37] In both instances it was a case of not being wanted in the white churches and needing a separate congregation in order to exercise the rights and privileges of membership.

The first decade of the nineteenth century saw a veritable hurricane of restlessness and rebellion blow through the black communities of the North. New churches were formed, divided, and subdivided as blacks sought to advance under their own leadership and control their own affairs. The decorous Episcopal and Presbyterian churches were no less affected by this restlessness. The blacks who were drawn to them, however, were fewer in number and more inclined to the quiet worship service and intellectual sermonizing than those who were attracted to the Methodist and Baptist churches. But denominational preferences aside, all were weary of being seated by tightlipped white ushers in the "African Corner," "Nigger Pews," in seats marked "B.M." (Black Members), or in the increasingly crowded galleries called "Nigger Heavens" by the most uncouth of the white members.[38]

The black Presbyterians, Congregationalists, and Episcopalians did not, however, go as far as the Methodists and Baptists in breaking fellowship with their white brothers and sisters. In the first place, being fewer in number, they did not precipitate the crisis over seating experienced during the large in-gathering of free persons and slaves into the Methodist and Baptist churches. Secondly, there were stronger class affinities and a greater similarity of complexion with the whites among those who were attracted to the other three denominations. Thirdly, the emphasis on an educated ministry in those denominations kept the number of black preachers small. Almost without exception they were able men who were not only capable of pastoring whites, but secure in their ability to hold their own with white clergy in the judicatories in which they participated and, to some extent, to reform the church from within. But they were eminently unsuccessful in developing truly integrated congregations in those denominations.[39]

The Presbyterians and Episcopalians administered their "Negro" or "colored work" separately from the rest of the mission program. The southern Methodists had a somewhat similar attitude toward the ministry to blacks, but in 1870 the church released about forty thousand to become the third largest black Methodist body in the United States—the Colored Methodist Episcopal Church (now called the Christian Methodist Episcopal Church).

The Presbyterians and Episcopalians attempted to hold on to their black constituencies without granting them relief from the discriminatory practices of the church. Even though black Presbyterian and Episcopal congregations were finally admitted to the white judicatories and were organic parts of the denominations, they met together in their respective black conferences and caucuses almost continuously from their inception.

It is fair to say, however, that minimal integration made these churches less independent and less aggressively black-oriented than the African Methodists and the Baptists. Most of their pastors depended to some extent upon the white denomination for their salaries, which were always below standard. Such discriminatory arrangements rarely fostered self-determination and divergence from the norms and desires of the parent institution. The real independence movement among black churches—which adopted the name "African" to signify its pride of ancestral heritage and solidarity—grew out of the mass appeal that the Baptists and Methodists had in both the free and the slave communities. These churches made the first radical thrust for self-determination, and their ministers and lay leaders set the tone for the earliest agitation of northern blacks against slavery and African colonization.

We must note, however, that not all the leadership of what we are calling the black church freedom movement came out of the two Methodist connections and the independent black Baptist bodies. The influence of Presbyterian preachers, and to a lesser extent those of the Congregational and Episcopal churches, began to be felt early in the nineteenth century. After the death of Allen, the Methodists began to lose control of the national black convention movement and some of the new reform groups in the cities. Moreover, the pressures of ecclesiastical affairs in the burgeoning new denominations distracted many of their ministers from a fuller involvement in secular affairs. From the 1830s black ministers in the predominantly white denominations began to play an important role in reform work and antislavery agitation.

*Development of the Convention Movement*

The practice of blacks holding state and national conventions to coordinate their opposition to slavery, to the forced colonization of free Negroes in Africa, and to various social ills began about 1830. Howard H. Bell, commenting on the basic factors in the development of the convention movement, writes:

> Insisting upon separate organizations so that they might worship as they chose without submitting to the humiliating practice of segregation within white churches, Negro leaders gradually built their new Zion during the early years of the 19th century. By 1830 there were many a Negro pastor, and layman as well, who was grounded in the principles of self-expression, and who could give a good account of himself in debate. These men were ready and willing to grapple with the problems of the antebellum era.[40]

In a sense, the convention movement was the secular adjunct of the black church. It became ideologically autonomous in the 1830s, but its contribution to the growing radicalization of abolitionism in the 1840s and 1850s cannot be separated from the influence of black religion. It was the spirit of uplift and self-reliance cultivated in the independent churches that originally infused the convention movement and, for a brief interim when a white agenda donimated it, served to secularize and institutionalize the black religious impulse. What the convention movement indicated was that the spirit of the religiously inspired insurrections, of Walker's *Appeal,* and of Allen's withdrawal from the Methodist Episcopal Church, was dislodged from domination by ministers and taken over by intelligent and capable lay persons who were both within and outside of the churches. The black clergy in the predominantly white churches found its true métier in that company.

The black clergy used the convention movement as their sounding board. They sent delegates from their congregations, provided meeting space, and, at least in the beginning, played the commanding role in all of its deliberations. The Allenites of Philadelphia and the Zionites of New York competed with one another in calling the first National Negro Convention. Bishop Allen, a shrewd organizer and a man who understood how to use power, won out and the convention met on September 15, 1830, at Mother Bethel. The national conventions then continued to meet annually until 1835. There was an interruption of seven years, until 1843, when the meetings were resumed in Buffalo, New York. Reverend Samuel E. Cornish, a New York Presbyterian, editor with John Russwurm of *Freedom's Journal,* and later editor of the *Colored American,* was an active participant in the movement, as was another Presbyterian preacher, J.W.C. Pennington of Brooklyn.

Some of the New York clergy wanted to prevent the convention movement from being subsumed by a group of laymen who were strongly influenced by the irrepressible white abolitionist William Lloyd Garrison.[41] The laymen included, among others, William Whipper, James Forten, Robert Purvis, and William Watkins—most of them Philadelphians. They were all highly competent leaders of the black community and represented the first reaction to the domination of autocratic black preachers. But their movement was not an unmixed blessing for the rapid development of a mass-based black institution that could continue to receive the spiritual nourishment of militant black religion, as opposed to the theoretical humanitarianism of middle-class white Christianity. The northern backgrounds and wealth of men like Whipper and Forten put them in a class more congenial to the moralism and reformist posture of white abolitionism. By 1835 they had taken over the Philadelphia wing of the convention movement and organized the American Moral Reform Society.[42]

Cornish strenuously opposed this accommodation to moderation and in reply to the society's effort to substitute the term "oppressed Americans" for "colored people," he wrote in the *Colored American*: "Oppressed Americans! *who are they?* Nonsense brethren!! You are COLORED AMERICANS. The Indians are RED AMERICANS, and the white people are WHITE AMERICANS and *you are as good as they, and they are no better than you.*"[43]

Although Cornish became more moderate as the years passed, a brilliant group of preachers (all of whom were members of predominantly white denominations)—Pennington, Wright, Ray, Alexander Crummell, Amos G. Beman, William C. Munroe, and Henry Highland Garnet—kept the convention movement ideologically black, oriented toward political action, and essentially radical in its perspective on the issue of slavery. If the mass black churches were too engaged in making blacks Christians and organizing denominations to insist upon a highly trained clergy, the predominantly white churches were too half-hearted about slavery and too prejudiced to utilize the talents and energies of these extraordinary black preachers. Consequently, these men found themselves more or less free to move into the arena of social action (although the Episcopalians had a problem with this for some time) where their influence was out of proportion to the size of the constituencies they represented.[44]

When the National Negro Convention resumed its meetings in Buffalo in 1843, it was well attended by members who wanted to move against the conservative stance of those who still hoped that their white allies would bring about the death of slavery by their own initiative and means. Accordingly, the meeting was convened by radical upstate New Yorkers rather than by the moderately nonviolent New York City contingent, which was a part of the abolitionist group led by the merchant philanthropist Lewis Tappan.[45] Theodore Wright and Charles B. Ray, Tappanites from New York City, were not as conservative in their views as the Philadelphia group, which decided to boycott the meeting. But neither were they as ready to take drastic action that would have annoyed their white friends as were the convention president, Samuel H. Davis, and the fiery pastor of a Presbyterian church in Troy, New York, Henry Highland Garnet.

Garnet attempted to lead the convention to a new aggressive position against slaveholders. His celebrated "Address to the Slaves of the United States," presented for adoption in Buffalo, is one of the boldest invitations to insurrection in the name of religion in the history of American slavery. He challenged the slaves to plead their own cause with their masters, to appeal to their enlightened self-interest and sense of basic justice, as one last effort to avoid catastrophe:

> Tell them in language which they cannot misunderstand of the exceeding sinfulness of slavery and of a future judgment, and of the righteous retributions of an indignant God. Inform them that all you desire is FREEDOM, and that nothing else will suffice. Do this, and forever after cease to toil for the heartless tyrants, who give you no other reward but stripes and abuse. If they then commence work of death, they, and not you, will be responsible for the consequences. You had far better all die—*die immediately*, than live slaves, and entail your wretchedness upon your posterity. If you would be free in this generation, here is your only hope. However much you and all of us may desire it, there is not much hope of redemption without the shedding of blood. If you must bleed, let it all come at once—rather *die freemen than live to be the slaves*. It is impossible, like the children of Israel, to make a grand exodus from the land of bondage. The Pharaohs are on both sides of the blood-red waters.[46]

Garnet recalled the example of black heroes who chose violence as a last resort rather than submit any longer to slavery—Vesey, Toussaint, Nat Turner, Joseph Cinque, and Madison Washington. He called them what so many others had been afraid to call them—"Noble men!" whose memories would be cherished by future generations of freedom fighters. And at the end, in a powerful peroration that left his hearers with no doubt about his intentions, he called upon the slaves to follow their example:

> Let your motto be resistance! *resistance!* RESISTANCE! No oppressed people have ever secured their liberty without resistance. What kind of resistance you had better make you must decide by the circumstances that surround you, and according to

the suggestion of expediency. Brethren, adieu! Trust in the living God. Labor for the peace of the human race, and remember that you are FOUR MILLIONS![47]

Reverend Amos Beman of New Haven later recalled that Garnet's speech shook "stern men . . . as the wild storm sways the oaks of the forest," and that "every eye" was "suffused with tears."[48] But the motion to adopt and distribute it in the South as an antislavery pamphlet failed by the narrow margin of one vote. The young Fred Douglass and the Garrisonian, Charles L. Redmond of Massachusetts, prevailed upon the convention to try "the moral means a little longer." A second vote was attempted by Garnet and his friends several days later, but by that time more of his upstate colleagues had suffered attacks of faintheartedness, and the Douglass majority was even larger.

Many black clergymen, however, reversed themselves on the issue of nonviolence after this and came to support Garnet. Six years after the convention he published the address himself, together with a good companion piece—David Walker's *Appeal*. Five hundred copies were circulated.[49]

### Black Churches and the Antebellum Freedom Movement

Born in protest, tested in adversity, led by eloquent and courageous preachers, the black church was the cutting edge of the freedom movement during most of the nineteenth century. It presented itself as a living witness against the ambivalence and conservatism of most white Christians up to the Civil War. Notwithstanding Douglass's refusal to believe that there was any place in the purposes of a just God for a racial church, the independent black churches had their own peculiar vocation. Their preachers were more concerned about the religious and social needs of their people and the challenge of developing important national institutions than they were about what some integrationists called the disgrace of building "exclusive or isolated organizations."[50]

It is true that the majority of black preachers were not Nat Turners and were more imitative of the moralizing and peacemaking of the white clergy than was necessary under the circumstances. Most of them were, of course, in the South and were marked men. They had little to do with the movement out of the white churches and the antislavery activity we have been reviewing. Even Richard Allen and other northern church leaders were not radicals in the Turner or Garnet sense of the word. Yet it is important to remember that, although they were usually irenic toward whites and did not use the rhetoric of black separatism, they were, nevertheless, unquestionably "race men." The equanimity of their spirits and the graciousness of their language should not mislead us to assume that they were "gentlemen of the cloth" in the grand

English manner, incapable of the acrimonious debate and passionate dissent of revolutionaries.

It is true that Allen himself and others in the circle of northerners did not believe that all whites were their enemies, nor did they champion insurrection as a matter of policy. But they hated slavery as much as, if not more than, they loved the church.[51] The subject of continuous anxiety among them was how to organize and make use of the embarrassingly small resources of their parishes to do what had to be done for the sake of freedom and self-respect. Although a twentieth-century judgment may question how radical they were, their churches were regarded by black and white alike as uncompromising on the immediate and total abolition of slavery—and that was radical indeed for the nineteenth century. In this regard Benjamin Quarles writes:

> The Negro church had no such squeamishness about bearing witness against slavery [as compared to the white churches]. The Negro church had its weaknesses—its services tended to be emotional with an abundance of "rousements," and many of its preachers given to substituting sound for sense. . . . But from the viewpoint of social reform, the distinguishing mark of the Negro church was its independence from the white control. Its money came from Negroes. Hence it could speak out on such an issue as slavery without fear of losing members or offending someone in the South.[52]

If not frequently enough in conventions and conferences, which were as rife with church politics and career-climbing as any white judicatory, certainly back home in their own communities individual pastors and lay persons were at the forefront of black abolitionism. The slaveholding class had no illusions about the opposition of the black church to everything it stood for and regarded the aggressiveness of black religion, particularly in the North and West, as one of the most dangerous threats to the system of slavery.

The distinguished African Methodist historian, Charles Wesley, reminds us that the name of the first and perhaps greatest of the antebellum church leaders—Richard Allen—lost some of its luster outside AME circles as the pressure for racial integration increased among blacks in the twentieth century.[53] The hope of many for a nonsegregated Christian church in the United States—an ideal to which laymen such as Frederick Douglass and William C. Nell were unreservedly committed—tended to cast a shadow of doubt over the wisdom of Allen's "separatism" as seen from the perspective of those mainly urban, middle-class blacks who felt that there was no longer any need for all-black congregations and denominations. Today, in the post-King era, after brave expectations have fallen upon the harsh realities of an inveterate racism, the pride and power of black institutions are being reasserted. Inasmuch as the church is one of the keys to black cultural revitalization, perhaps Allen's work can now be viewed in a somewhat more positive light.

Allen certainly never conceived of what he was doing as "reverse racism" or "Black Power chauvinism." He upheld the unity of the Body of Christ as the divine pattern for the oneness of the human family and never lost his esteem for the great white humanitarians who promoted that oneness and inveighed against slavery. Nor did he lack genuine appreciation for Methodism as the tradition most suited to the religious predilections of African Americans. But he was not given to evading practical necessities in the interest of abstract principles. Always willing to stand alone, he faced in his time, even more critically than many persons today, what some blacks now concede: the need for black institutions to be free of white control, no matter how benevolent that control might be and how uncertain it is that black control will be any less oppressive of some laity, particularly women.

Allen believed that the black community had to be organized to deal responsibly with its own problems as long as prejudice and the lack of compassion refused to erase the color line. He also believed that an independent church, which made every aspect of life its arena of witness, was the most widely accepted and the most effective instrument with which to pursue the twin goals of holiness and civil freedom. In the closing years of the twentieth century he should doubtless be reappraised for the pioneering and prophetic role he played in church history in the United States and his relevance to the antebellum church freedom movement. Those who are inclined to regard the church and its past leaders as historical oddities offering little inspiration for the present generation need to catch the spirit of this man as it was expressed in the obituary notice of his death on March 26, 1831:

> When the humble African was even dragged from the altar of God by the inhuman whites who disgrace the land, rendered sacred by the glowing recollections which arise at the mention of the name William Penn, Richard Allen stepped forth as their defender and protector, built, at his own expense and upon his own ground, the first African Church in America. He it was that through persecution, through malice and through envy, walked like the Savior upon the troubled waters, in favor of African Religious Independence.[54]

This was the work that began it all and made possible the later emergence of secular agencies of protest and reform such as the national and state conventions of black citizens. Without Allen and the pioneers who came out of the white churches in order to claim their humanity and create more effective instruments for confronting their many ills, even those who chose to remain outside the church, or chose as a matter of strategy to stay in the white denominations—the Garnets, the Bemans, and the Crummells—would probably not have found an audience for their antislavery radicalism. The foundation for black power and self-determination was laid down in the independent churches. It remains now for us to trace the further development of the motif of independence and solidarity through the outreach of the churches to the Caribbean and Africa, and the final transformation of these themes— freedom, self-reliance, and solidarity—into the quasi-religious black nationalism of the twentieth century.

## CHAPTER 6

# Black Religion and Black Nationalism

*If it be here shown beyond reasonable doubt . . . that the ancient Egyptians, Ethiopians and Libyans . . . were the ancestors of the present race of Ham, then the Negro of the 19th century may point to them with pride; and with all who would find in him a return to racial celebrity, when in the light of a Christian civilization, Ethiopia shall stretch out her hands unto God.*

Rev. Rufus L. Perry,
ex-slave Baptist pastor of Brooklyn, N.Y.,

Almost from the beginning of slavery in the New World, a process of repatriation and colonization back to Africa made it possible for a few slaves, who by one means or another had secured their freedom, to return to their homeland from South America and the Caribbean, and later from the English colonies in North America. The reverse movement facilitated the development of an early relationship between blacks in the New World and those who remained in Africa. During the Revolutionary War thousands of slaves who escaped to the British forces, or who had been liberated by loyalists, made their way to Canada and Nova Scotia, to the West Indies, or to the coastal areas of the South American mainland. Some of them later recrossed the Atlantic to take up their lives again in West Africa.[1]

John Kizzel, an escaped slave from South Carolina who became a minister and built a church in Sierra Leone, sailed from Nova Scotia at the end of the Revolutionary War with a group of American slaves and developed a prosperous settlement in the British colony. In 1818 Kizzel met Samuel J. Mills and Ebenezer Burgess, agents of the American Colonization Society (ACS). He conducted them to Sherbro Island, where it was decided to erect the first Sierra Leonean settlement of the society.[2]

The relationship between African-Americans and Africa was, of course, first established by the African slave trade itself. New England rum manufactured from the sugar and molasses of the West Indian plantations was exchanged for slaves in the markets of West Africa. The captives were shipped across the Atlantic and sold for the sugar cane and molasses they were enslaved to produce, beginning the whole process over again. By the end of the eighteenth and the beginning of the nineteenth century, this triangular commercial relationship was providing a network of contact and communication between Africa and the Americas that laid the foundation for the spiritual and intellectual exchange that was to follow under the sponsorship of black Christians on both sides of the Atlantic—the vision of African-African American solidarity projected by men such as Garvey and Du Bois.

One of the first persons to take advantage of the connection was Paul Cuffee, a New Bedford shipowner. Cuffee was a member of a small group of blacks in Massachusetts who made contact with the Free African Society of Philadelphia and founded the first African Baptist and Methodist churches in Massachusetts and Rhode Island. Inspired by African Methodism and his own talent for commercial ventures, Cuffee undertook a mission to Africa. It was his intention to colonize West Africa with American blacks who could not only carry out an evangelistic project among their non-Christian relatives, but would also lay the foundation of commerce between Africa and America that would compete with and finally bring an end to the slave trade.[3] In 1815, at his own expense, he took nine families and thirty-eight other persons to Sierra Leone to begin the realization of his dream of bringing Christian civilization and businesses owned and operated by blacks to the motherland.[4] Influences flowing from men such as Captain Cuffee, from the missionary aspirations of the new black churches in the United States and the West Indies, from political developments and anti-slavery agitation on both sides of the Atlantic, circulated back and forth and generated quite early a spirit of incipient black consciousness and anti-colonialism more than a hundred years before what came to be known as the Pan-African movement against colonialism.

Black religion and the newly independent churches played an important role in these developments. The emergence of black nationalism in America and Africa cannot be understood apart from the zeal of believers to christianize the land of their ancestors and to open up an administrative and communications network between churches for the promotion of Christian missions in both Africa and the Caribbean.[5]

From the early effort of former slaves to establish a Christian settlement and mission in the British colony of Sierra Leone, churchmen from the United States and West Africa turned their eyes to Africa as an object of evangelization. They intended to win Africa not only for Africans, but for Christ, by mass emigrations from the West and by forging bonds of friendship and collaboration between Africans and African Americans. This dream, as we shall see, was never shared by the majority of American blacks—especially those in the free states of the North who were rapidly becoming acculturated to the values and loyalties of white America—but it continued to plague the consciousness of the descendants of the slaves well into the twentieth century and is inseparable from the rise of black nationalism in the United States, the islands of the Caribbean, and on the continent of Africa itself.

## THE AMERICAN COLONIZATION SOCIETY

Whatever the motives of the ACS and other white-controlled colonization schemes, it must be conceded that these early efforts of whites, many of them sincerely motivated by Christian missionary zeal, opened up for blacks the whole issue of emigration. It helped to forge a connecting link between emigration, Christianity, and black nationalism. The Reverend Samuel Hopkins, a former slaveowner of Newport, Rhode Island, first conceived of the idea of black emigration to Africa in 1759. Feeling that some "remuneration was due Africa" for the plunder of its people, Hopkins devised a plan to educate some free blacks and send them back to bring the blessings of Christian religion and civilization to their unfortunate brothers and sisters.[6] The ACS grew out of this plan and was to play a central role in the founding of Liberia in 1822. The ACS was always controversial among both whites and blacks in the United States, but it cannot be doubted that the society gave impetus and continuity to the idea that black Americans had a contribution to make to the awakening of Africa, and that Africa and not North America was the natural homeland of black people.

To be sure, the motives of the southern supporters of the idea of colonization were suspect from the beginning. The presence of free blacks in the United States presented both southern slaveholders and northern politicians with an irritating and anomalous situation. Theoretically the natural increase of free blacks threatened white hegemony in the North and slavocracy in the South. In the North the specter of black franchise and competition for industrial jobs was combined with racial prejudice. In the South whites feared black inundation and a consequent rebellion of slaves. The very existence of a community of free blacks, such as in Charleston, Richmond, and New Orleans, reminded those who were still in bondage that slavery was not a natural and necessary condition of all blacks, and "uppity," querulous free blacks represented a potential seedbed of conspiracy and insurrection. The problem of what to do with the blacks was, therefore, conveniently if fraudulently solved by the idea of African or West Indian colonization in either Africa or the West Indies. Both those whites who favored slavery and those who were genuinely opposed to it found common cause in the proposal to remove this source of embarrassment and danger and salve their consciences about Africa at the same time.

In the very year that the AME Church was founded in Philadelphia, a group of white citizens representing several states and including some of the most distinguished men in America gathered in Washington to organize the ACS. In an atmosphere charged with both guilt feelings and noble aspirations the colonizationists plotted what many of them had come to believe was the ultimate solution to the American race problem. But through either stupidity or self-delusion, the manner in which the argument was framed aroused more fear and resentment among northern blacks than the support that might otherwise have been forthcoming from them. Leon F. Litwack writes concerning the crisis that was precipitated:

> One month after the organization of the Colonization Society, approximately three thousand Negroes crowded into Philadelphia's Bethel Church to give their reply: the colonization scheme violated professed American principles, it sought to stigmatize the free Negro population, and it countenanced the perpetuation of human bondage and encouraged it by seeking to remove the free blacks. Under these circumstances, it deserved to be repudiated by all Negroes, who should, instead, reaffirm their determination never to part voluntarily from their enslaved brethren.[7]

It should be understood that Richard Allen and the African Methodists who followed him were not so enamored of their situation in the North that they were unwilling to entertain any thoughts of renouncing American citizenship. The convention of 1830, which was dominated by Allen and other black churchmen, strongly recommended emigration to Upper Canada. Many who were opposed to the ACS, such as James Forten, the wealthy sailmaker and abolitionist of Philadelphia, were concerned about the future of Africa. They were privately of the opinion that the day would come when blacks would have to separate themselves from their oppressors and return to their native land.[8]

It was the arrogance of the whites, their miscalculation of the self-esteem of free blacks and their feeling of solidarity with the slaves, rather than aversion to the idea of emigration that made black leaders repudiate the ACS. It was the talk of "Negro inferiority" and "degradation," the obvious attempt by the colonizationists to dodge the question of the immorality of slavery, and the overenthusiastic participation of the slaveholders themselves in what purported to be a benevolent scheme, that turned the free communities in the North against the colonization proposal. They were well aware of the illogic of whites wanting to do "a great good" for a people they despised while continuing to hold their relatives and friends in chains. They shared their suspicions with their abolitionist friends, such as William Lloyd Garrison, and finally disabused them of the idea that such a scheme could ever be made compatible with antislavery.

The expulsory laws of Ohio in 1829 and the desirability of securing a place for fugitives outside the United States infused the first National Negro Convention with emigrationist sentiment. The convention rejected the ACS because its leaders suspected the real motives of the colonizationists, but the notion that it would be good to consider emigrating to some part of the world that was free from the curse of slavery was upheld. What those who attended the meeting at Mother Bethel church resented was the coercive, high-handed methods of the whites—who once again wanted to speak and act for blacks. Although they recognized the need of many to be relocated "in a land where the laws and prejudices of society will have no effect in retarding their advancement to the summit of civil and religious improvement," they refused to be settled "in any place which is not the object of our choice." In general, they also objected to emigrating to Liberia or Haiti, "believing them only calculated to distract and divide the whole colored family."[9]

After the white abolitionists of the North were convinced that black leaders were staunchly opposed to the Colonization Society, they abandoned it. Some of them, misunderstanding the real point at issue, then began to escalate their own campaign against African emigration, ridiculing blacks who favored it in succeeding years. In such a way well-meaning white friends exercised, in a backhanded manner, considerable influence over blacks who thoughtfully considered selective emigration but did not wish to appear to be betraying white friends and the grand cause of abolishing slavery in the United States.

However, there was ambivalence about the subject throughout the nineteenth century. If northern blacks had not been so convinced that the abolitionists could deliver what they promised without acrimony, and if they had not been so squeamish about offending Garrison and other friends, it is possible that some modified form of emigrationism may have caught on in the North as it did in many parts of the South. Black church leaders could never quite divorce their desire to carry the gospel to their brothers and sisters in the West Indies and Africa from a candid recognition of the intolerable condition of black life in America and the chance that there might be a better life abroad. Despite their public opposition to the idea of running away from the challenges at home, the missionary implications of the offers held out by the ACS and other state and local colonization groups continued to intrigue many.

Transatlantic travel was expensive and difficult to arrange. No less so was the founding of a settlement and church once the emigrants arrived at their destination. The newly independent churches, which had become the focal point of cultural activity and community organization, had little means with which to plant Christian colonies in Africa or anywhere else. It is not surprising, therefore, that the Allenites, for all their criticism of the colonization movement, could still justify utilizing it as an instrument for helping to relocate those who wanted to cut the umbilical cord and answer the Macedonian call from Africa.

With the obvious success of the English repatriation program for liberated and fugitive slaves and freed West Indian blacks—which eventuated in the establishment of Sierra Leone as a British crown colony in 1808—and with rising missionary fever in the ACS as more churches and prominent clergymen took an active role, the twin interests of missions and colonization oscillated back and forth in the minds of many church leaders. It was not easy to decide what was best. Although the majority continued to be skeptical about colonization, there was enough interest in what may be called "missionary emigrationism" to keep the colonization societies alive and kicking into the twentieth century.

Four years after the AME Church was founded, one of its ablest ministers, Daniel Coker of Baltimore, sailed for Africa with the help of the ACS as the first black Methodist foreign missionary.[10] Although he was not officially commissioned by the AME Church, he nevertheless "carried the unanimous consent and good will of his brethren."[11] Coker's destination was the island of Sherbro, a part of Sierra Leone where the Colonization Society planned to develop the first American settlement.

Coker accompanied the first group of slaves to be sent by the society. In the company was a group of free blacks who, like Coker himself, had hopes of finding greater freedom and opportunity in Africa than in the beleaguered free communities of the United States. Before the ship landed at Campelar, the brilliant and controversial minister had organized a church among the eighty-nine colonists aboard and was conducting worship services in accordance with the Discipline of the AME Church. Like the self-styled missionary John Kizzel who preceded him with another party of ex-slaves, Daniel Coker saw colonization not only as a bid for independence and opportunity for America's oppressed blacks, but as a part of God's plan to bring the Christian faith to the land of his ancestors through the ministry of a black church.

Mills and Burgess, emissaries of the ACS, had been helped by John Kizzel to locate a site for the settlement in 1817. Two years later they accompanied Coker and the little group of pioneers back to the area. The choice of location proved to be an unfortunate one because of the frequent inundation of the low-lying terrain. An epidemic broke out in the group, nearly wiping it out and taking the lives of the two white agents. Coker suddenly found himself heir to the responsibilities of the two officers of the ACS and decided to lead the survivors back to mainland Sierra Leone, where he later settled and built a church in Freetown. The resolute spirit and commitment of this man who almost became the first bishop of the AME Church may be gleaned from a remarkable letter he sent back to the Colonization Society:

We have met trials; we are but a handful; our provisions are running low; we are in a strange heathen land; we have not heard from America, and know not whether provisions or people will be sent out; yet, thank the Lord, my confidence is strong in the veracity of his promises. Tell my brethren to come; fear not; this land is good; it only wants men to possess it.[12]

The attitude of the first African Americans to colonize Africa was unquestionably one of condescension and paternalism. The Africans were regarded as a degraded race in need of nothing so much as the salvation and superior virtues others could bring. As unpalatable as such arrogance would be today, this was the missionary spirit of the time; black and white churchmen shared it alike. Daniel Coker and others believed it was nothing less than God's grace that had brought the black American church into an independent status and one of its great purposes was to return Africa's sons and daughters to their true homeland, in order to save the souls of millions who languished in darkness. As presumptuous as such an attitude was, it was nonetheless motivated by a sincere dedication to service, a wide compassion for the plight of Africa, and a willingness to take up the vocation of suffering for its redemption.

In a letter from Campelar to a friend in Baltimore, Coker eloquently expresses his deep tenderness and humanity toward his African brothers and sisters, and the hope he shared with other Christians for the day when "Ethiopia would soon stretch forth her hands unto God" and become one of the great nations of the world:

The millions in this land, are the thousands in America, and the thousands unborn are deeply interested in it. Oh! my dears, what darkness has covered the minds of this people. None but those who come and see, can judge. You would be astonished to see me travelling in the wilderness, guided by a little foot path, until, coming suddenly upon a little town of huts in the thickets; and there, to behold hundreds of men, women and children, naked, sitting on the ground or on mats, living on the natural productions of the earth, and as ignorant of God as the brutes that perish. You would see them coming round me, shaking hands, (but very different from our way of shaking hands) and gazing on me, and spreading a mat, and offering me of such food as they live upon. In a word, they are friendly and kind. Such is their conduct, that any one who loves souls would weep over them, and be willing to suffer and die with them. I can say, that my soul cleaves to Africa. . . . I expect to give my life to bleeding, groaning, dark, benighted Africa. I expect to pass through much, if I should live. I should rejoice to see you in this land; it is a good land; it is a rich land, and I do believe it will be a great nation, and a powerful and worthy nation; but those who break the way will suffer much.[13]

Another early black missionary effort in Africa was the work done by Reverend Lott Carey (1780–1828), a slave preacher from Richmond, Virginia, who took the second shipload of colonists from the United States to Liberia in 1821. Carey founded churches that were supported by the Baptists of Richmond. In 1815 he had organized the original African Missionary Society of Richmond and raised seven hundred dollars for its work. Six years later he sailed for Liberia, arriving before the agent of the ACS. His gifts were soon recognized by all, and he was appointed vice-governor. He later served as governor during the absence of Governor Jehudi Ashmun from the colony. The Baptists of Richmond, with whom he kept in close contact, were stirred by the prospect of missionary emigrationism in Africa, despite Carey's open criticism of the ACS. Carey became the symbol of African American involvement on the continent and of the independence and self-reliance of black missionary endeavor.

Like Samuel Hopkins, the Quaker pacifist Benjamin Lundy, who influenced the young William Lloyd Garrison to join the abolition movement in 1828, had an early interest in missionary emigrationism. It was Lundy who encouraged Bishop Allen to establish a branch of African Methodism in Haiti, where Lundy had already started a colony of free blacks from the United States.[14] In 1824 Haiti became the first official mission field of the AME Church. At the invitation of President Jean Boyer, two thousand emigrants settled in the new black republic. Many of them were members of Allen's own Bethel church in Philadelphia. With the assistance of Reverend Scipio Beans of the Baltimore conference, they built St. Peter's church at Port-au-Prince and selected Richard Robinson as their first pastor.[15]

By 1830 the black Methodists had mission congregations at Port-au-Prince, Samana, and Santo Domingo. Here again we have some indication of the foreign mission interest of the independent churches and the convergence of the spirit of missions with that of emigrationism in the nineteenth century. The spread of African Methodism in several parts of the Caribbean, and the consequences of that development for intensifying fraternal relations between the West Indies and the United States, is a matter requiring careful study. But there can be little doubt that African Methodism and the outreach of black Baptist churches and missionary societies in North America contributed to pride and self-determination throughout the area.

In British possessions, such as Barbados and Jamaica, where the former Georgia slave Reverend George Liele founded the first Baptist church in Kingston in 1782, black congregations helped to create a climate for rebellion in the early nineteenth century by developing new forms of leadership based upon church government among the slaves. The leaders of the insurrections in Demerara in 1823 and Jamaica in 1831 were strongly supported by church members. In all likelihood, blacks were emboldened by reports of AME involvement in the Denmark Vesey revolt of 1822. The Akan slave, Kwame, who led the revolt in Demerara, was first deacon of Bethel chapel in the town, and many of the participants in the 1823 uprising were members of that chapel. The revolt in Jamaica was known as the "Baptist War." The reference is to the native Baptists who evolved from the Liele congregations. Monica Schuler writes, "it is clear that in both Demerara and Jamaica, the slaves had detached the London Missionary Society and Baptist church organizations from missionary control, and used them as organizations of social protest."[16]

The news of slave revolts and the part played by Baptist and Methodist church members in instigating them encouraged blacks on the mainland and in the West Indies to shake off their chains and support one another. Christian missions and emigrationism thus worked hand in hand to foment unrest and a desire for independence throughout the Caribbean as well as the southern region of the United States.

The planting of congregations from the United States was widespread. Before the end of the nineteenth century, AME missions had been established in Haiti, Cuba, Jamaica, Antigua, the Virgin Islands, Tobago, Barbados, and Trinidad. There were also mission points in the Bahamas and Bermuda. From about 1850, missionaries from the African Methodists labored at Paramaribo, Dutch Guiana, and at Georgetown, British Guiana.[17] When Marcus Garvey traveled throughout the Caribbean and Central America preaching the gospel of black nationalism and the "Back to Africa" movement, he found some of his most sympathetic audiences among black Baptists and African Methodists whose families had emigrated from North America in the previous century, or whose congregations were influenced by those denominations and had taken pains to cultivate pride in their African heritage and a spirit of self-reliance.

The early missionary movement of the black denominations to Africa and the Caribbean should not be regarded as an expression of what we today call black nationalism. Even efforts linked with emigration and promoted by the ACS were not primarily political in nature, or related to a self-conscious rejection of American values and civilization. It is true, of course, that some of the first black preachers who took the gospel to foreign parts and encouraged others to follow had visions of a better life than blacks found anywhere in the United States. Yet their primary concern was not to found a black nation free of slavery, poverty, and racism, but the inauguration of a great evangelistic mission to heathens who happened to be black and among whom the proud African Methodist and Baptist traditions could take root and flourish.

After the Civil War, Edward W. Blyden, a Presbyterian, Henry M. Turner of the AME Church, Theodore Holly, an Episcopal bishop, and Lucius H. Holsey, a bishop of the Colored Methodist Episcopal Church, became powerful advocates of black separatism. They attempted, without notable success, to propagate a kind of religious black nationalism in the Caribbean and Africa. Their efforts bore fruit in the first third of the twentieth century, but whatever success they enjoyed cannot be attributed to the support they received from either their respective denominations or from the public at large.

The fact is that neither colonization nor foreign missions were effectively developed or promoted by the African American churches. To have instituted a strong and well-financed missionary program in Africa would have required considerably more resources than these struggling churches had available after taking care of urgent needs at home. The white colonizationists, having committed a strategic error in their approach to emigration, were never in a position financially, or in terms of influence, to generate much enthusiasm for Liberian emigration among the churches. Nor were they able to demonstrate the kind of effective nation-building in Africa that might have encouraged greater response from the denominations. The fiasco of naivete, broken promises, and stranded emigrants destroyed any real possibility for a mammoth encampment of black America at the doorstep of the colonization societies.[18]

The white churches, for their part, had the money and should have had the vision to undergird the development and expansion of black missionary activity overseas as one way of making a rather safe contribution to black freedom and independence. But it rarely occurred to white American Christians that what they hoped to do for Africa could have been done to better purpose for both Africans and African Americans by the black churches of the United States and the Caribbean. Torn with theological and sectional strife during most of the nineteenth century and having segregated their black constituencies or dismissed them to black denominations, the white churches studiously avoided giving anything more than paternalistic charity at the local parish level to black Christians. For the most part, they ignored what the black denominations were trying to do in both the United States and the overseas mission field.

The tragedy of black American missionary outreach in the Caribbean and Africa during the nineteenth century was its neglect by the churches themselves. The predominantly white denominations were relatively affluent and, in a spirit of ecumenism and fraternal cooperation, could have helped, but they looked the other way with their noses in the air. Although the black denominations wanted to maintain a healthy missionary enterprise outside the country, their aspirations far exceeded their ability to do so. It was not altogether because of a disaffection vis-à-vis missionary emigrationism among the free blacks of the North. By the time of the Civil War almost every leader of consequence favored or was at least open to the idea of colonization in Africa or the Caribbean, and Christian missions were thought to be the noblest and the best method for African colonization.[19] It was rather that there was never sufficient money and personnel to demonstrate that missionary emigrationism was realistic for the churches and that it could succeed without an enormously increased investment of time, energy, and money.

The work initiated by Daniel Coker, Lott Carey, and others could not be adequately supported with missionaries and settlers from the United States, or given sufficient funds to develop its full potential without greater help from the white churches than they were prepared to give. The demands upon the nickel and dime collections in the churches of the blacks were overwhelming. Normal requirements for building national denominations and strengthening home missions to care for the steadily mounting tide moving northward and into the southern cities drained off both personnel and funds. As a result the work so auspiciously begun in West Africa went begging most of the century.

At the New York annual conference of the AME Church in 1853, Bishop Willis Nazrey, a great promoter of African missions, proudly reminded his brethren that their church had as much responsibility in Africa and the West Indies "as any other Christian Church upon the face of the globe." However, it took the practical-minded Bishop Daniel Alexander Payne to bring the African Methodists back to reality by citing the formidable problems of establishing missions in foreign lands and caring for them without money. The recognition of black responsibility, he said, was no guarantee of the ability to perform it. Such was the sad acknowledgment of the impossibility of carrying on an elaborate program of foreign missions at a time when even wealthy white denominations were having problems with such work.[20]

The fact that most black ministers and their denominations did little to foster the emigration fervor prior to Emancipation does not mean, however, that religion played no significant role in the rise of black nationalism and Pan-Africanism. Quite the opposite is true. A black theology of missionary emigrationism and racial destiny evolved from the aggressive thrust of black folk religion toward liberation from slavery and an African homeland. This inchoate, unofficial theology gradually took the initiative from the churches and laid the groundwork for Garvey, Padmore, and others of the twentieth century who were less dependent upon the institutional church. This way of thinking about God and black destiny was by no means unrelated to the vision of young Hezekiah Grice, the man who started Allen thinking about colonization. It was also expressed by Willis Nazrey, and other churchmen who were basically orthodox in their understanding of the faith, but possessed great racial pride and black consciousness.

## MARTIN R. DELANY

The most intellectual expression of this rudimentary black theology of the antebellum period came from someone who was not a clergyman, but a prominent physician and journalist, Martin R. Delany. Delany represented a small group of nonclerics who were products of the church, but less conservative than either their pastors or the black integrationist laity who catered to Garrison. Although Delany said that he "had rather be a Heathen *freeman,* than a Christian *slave,*" he was nevertheless an African Methodist and a lay theologian of rare insight and ability.

Martin R. Delany was born in 1812, the son of free blacks, in Charleston, West Virginia. His parents fled from persecution and settled in Chambersburg, Pennsylvania, where he was educated until moving to Pittsburgh in 1831. There Delany began the study of medicine and commenced publication of *The Mystery*—later converted into a journal of the African Methodists.[21] From 1847 to 1849 he worked with Frederick Douglass in publishing the *North Star* in Rochester and in 1849 entered Harvard Medical School. Although he opposed the Colonization Society, Delany became a proponent of black emigration and was active in the Negro Convention movement, where he had close association with the prominent churchmen of the day. His outstanding contribution to black nationalism was a book published in 1852, *The Condition, Elevation, Emigration, and Destiny of the Colored People of the United States, Politically Considered.* It was sharply attacked by the white abolitionists for its advocacy of colonization. When Delany took measure of the fact that he was losing the support of those who were working for abolition, he ordered sales stopped. This did not, however, keep him from being a theoretician of black nationalism and emigrationism until his death in 1885.[22]

Notwithstanding his nationalistic leanings and belief that white Protestants were the cruelest oppressors of the blacks, Delany was an ardent supporter of the missionary outreach of Christianity. He believed that Protestant missions were the most important gift of Europe and America to Africa, and that they would eventually bring a "purer and higher civilization" to that continent. But he also believed that missionaries should be "homogeneous in all the natural characteristics, claims, sentiments, and sympathies—the descendants of Africa."[23] That is to say, he favored sending black missionaries to Africa. His problem with religion in the black community was that the churches, too imitative of the pietism of Protestant evangelicalism, were giving blacks the impression that they were in miserable conditions because of their immorality, and that what was necessary for salvation was "being good" like the "best" white people.

This exaggerated moralism and emulation of whites was never, in fact, central to black folk religion, although it could certainly be found in the mainline black churches. Delany, for all his erudition and sophistication, was closer to the realism and wisdom of folk religion than to the churches. It was sheer nonsense to him, and bad religion, to believe that God would prosper whites, but placed blacks in the condition in which they found themselves "for not half the wickedness as that of the whites."

Delany reasoned that the right use of religion required an understanding of its function and limitations as ordained by God himself. He thereby extrapolated a theological principle from folk religion that was not unknown to the American pragmatist and agnostic Benjamin Franklin—"God helps those who help themselves." Unlettered black Christians have always believed that those words were found in the Bible and were the essence of the Christian religion. They have agreed essentially with Delany that it is foolish to try to gain equality and the power to elevate a people by praying for it. The universe is governed by spiritual, moral, and physical laws, each restricted to effectiveness within its own sphere of operation. Hence, said Delany, a spiritual blessing is to be prayed for, a moral good sought by exercising one's sense of justice, and a physical end requires the use of might and muscle.[24]

Delany recognized the crucial significance of the church in lifting and ennobling the masses. But he faulted the church for teaching an excessive otherworldliness that expected spiritual means to equip the folk to compete with whites in the moral and physical areas of life. God, said Delany, did not provide mystical solutions for the hard problems of power and self-realization, nor did he expect blacks to accept white definitions of reality when those definitions presumed white jurisdiction over black progress. Thus, more than any other person of his period, he anticipated and developed one of the major emphases of black theology:

> We are no longer slaves, believing any interpretation that our oppressors may give the word of God, for the purpose of deluding us to the more easy subjugation; but freemen, comprising some of the first minds of intelligence and rudimental qualifications, in the country. What then is the remedy, for our degradation and oppression? This appears now to be the only remaining question—the means of successful elevation in this our native land? This depends entirely upon the application of the means of Elevation.[25]

The "means of Elevation" had to be in strict conformity with the laws governing politics and economics. Delany's rationalistic analysis of the situation led him to the conclusion that self-effort, plus what he called "attainments," and finally emigration, were the only means sufficient for equality and social progress.

Delany helped to clarify the cultural vocation of the black church during the 1850s—particularly its responsibility with respect to the continent of Africa. He was a member of the famous African Civilization Society, a group of very able men founded in 1858 with the explicit purpose of bringing about "the civilization and christianization of Africa and of the descendants of African ancestors in any portion of the earth, wherever dispersed." In 1861 he was influential in reformulating the purpose of the society to include the encouragement of selective emigration of persons "practically qualified and suited to promote the development of Christianity, morality, education, mechanical arts, agriculture, commerce and general improvement."[26]

Delany considered several possibilities for mass emigration from the United States. At first he favored colonization in Central America or East Africa. But later, after leading an exploration of the Niger Valley in 1859, he settled upon selective emigration to West Africa. Henceforth, his life and labors were devoted chiefly to that objective.

Throughout his career he retained an explicit theology of racial redemption, which he shared with such distinguished divines as Bishop James T. Holly and Alexander Crummell. It was essentially an understanding of God as liberator—a God who was calling oppressed blacks out of the land of their captivity to a place that he had appointed for them and their posterity forever. This was a salient contribution of an elite group of churchmen to the formulation of a theological perspective that explicated the subtle and clandestine meaning of much of the preaching and many of the spirituals of the folk religious tradition. It never became the official, recognized theology of any major black denomination, but had its systematizers and propagators in both black and white denominations. It was a theology of racial destiny achieved by struggle against the powers of evil—powers once represented by the mysterious forces of nature and spiritual beings that African religious specialists and early plantation preachers sought to control or manipulate. Those powers were now understood to represent and be operative in social and political events, but no less violent and intractable.

The focus of this perspective was the biblical revelation of the justice of God who "put down the mighty from their seats and exalted them of low degree" (Luke 1:52), who gathered the scattered children of Israel under Nehemiah and helped them to build the wall of Jerusalem—"because the people had a mind to work" (Neh. 4:6). Martin R. Delany believed in such a God. His conviction that God had decreed greatness for blacks and that they could claim a glorious future only by their own power is sung with lyrical passion in his writings:

> The time has now fully arrived, when the colored race is called upon by all the ties of common humanity, and all the claims of consummate justice, to go forward and take their position, and do battle in the struggle now being made for the redemption of the world. Our

cause is a just one; the greatest at present that elicits the attention of the world. For if there is a remedy; that remedy is now at hand. God himself as assuredly as he rules the destinies of nations, and entereth measures into the "hearts of men," has presented these measures to us. Our race is to be redeemed; it is a great and glorious work, and we are the instrumentalities by which it is to be done. But we must go from among our oppressors; it can never be done by staying among them. God has, as certain as he has ever designed any thing, has designed this great portion of the New World, for us, the colored races; and as certain as we stubborn our hearts and stiffen our necks against it, his protecting arm and fostering care will be withdrawn from us.[27]

By the time of the publication of his *Official Report of the Niger Valley Exploring Party* in 1861, Delany had shifted his sights from Nicaragua and New Grenada as possible sites for a colony to West Africa. In Lagos, Nigeria, he found a black Christian community that strengthened his belief in the divine election of African Americans for a special work in Africa, for which an enlightened and inspired church would be the vanguard. As he wrote as early as 1852:

"Princess shall come out of Egypt; Ethiopia shall soon stretch out her hands unto God." With the fullest reliance upon this blessed promise, I humbly go forward in—I may repeat—the grandest prospect for the regeneration of a people that ever was presented in the history of the world. The disease has long since been known; we have found and shall apply the remedy. I am indebted to Rev. H. H. Garnet, an eminent Black clergyman and scholar, for the construction, that "soon," in the Scriptural passage quoted, "has reference to the period ensuing *from the time of beginning*." With faith in the promise, and hope from this version, surely there is nothing to doubt or fear.[28]

The outbreak of the Civil War prevented the execution of Delany's grandiose plan for emigration and the redemption of Africa. During the war his energies were concentrated on the recruitment of black soldiers for the Union. He was commissioned a major in the medical corps and postponed his dream of emigration until the war could be won against slavery. After discharge he worked for the Freemen's Bureau during the Reconstruction period. Although the war revived his hopes that justice could be secured in the United States, those hopes were once again dissolved in the acid realities of the post-Reconstruction era, the Compromise of 1877, and the Supreme Court's repeal of the Civil Rights Act of 1875 only two years before he died.

## ALEXANDER CRUMMELL

Another great champion of missionary emigration and theologian of black liberation was Alexander Crummell, an Episcopal clergyman whose life also spanned the Civil War period. Crummell was born in New York in 1819, and one of the friends of his boyhood was the New York abolitionist Presbyterian, Henry Highland Garnet. After being refused matriculation at General Theological Seminary, the leading seminary of the Episcopal Church, Crummell studied privately in Boston for the priesthood and in 1844 was ordained in Philadelphia.

Throughout his life he was a brilliant spokesman of black pride and solidarity. In his early years he was one of the best-known supporters among black intellectuals of colonization and nationalism. He went to Liberia in 1853 as a missionary under the encouragement of supporters of the ACS even though, like Delany and others, he had been highly critical of its operations.

In preparation for his work in Africa, Crummell went to England and received a degree from Queen's College, Cambridge. It was at Cambridge that he matured as a scholar and developed a viewpoint on racial advancement that adumbrated the Du Bois theory of the "Talented Tenth." Crummell advanced the idea that black intellectuals had a special responsibility and leadership role in church and community. As the first president of the American Negro Academy, which he helped to organize shortly before his death in 1898, he helped to blaze the path for scholarship and the study of black life and culture, which many talented persons who gathered around Howard University in Washington, D.C., were to follow.

After spending twenty years in missionary and educational work in Liberia and Sierra Leone, Crummell returned to the United States in 1873, somewhat less visionary and optimistic about mass emigration. He became rector of the fashionable St. Luke's Episcopal Church in Washington and enjoyed in that setting a national pulpit for his controversial views regarding the advancement of blacks. Like Booker T. Washington, Crummell had little confidence in political agitation, although he consistently demanded civil rights for blacks. His major interest was in self-help, industrial education, and racial solidarity. He spoke out strongly for what he called "the Social Principle"—the natural law of association that "binds men in unity and brotherhood, in races and churches and nations"—without which, he believed, no nation or people could hope to achieve greatness.[29]

As a minister, Crummell's primary concern about Africa rested upon his conviction that the message of Jesus Christ had to be preached in all the world, as the Lord himself commanded. African colonization, however much he objected to the way some of its advocates promoted it, was for him one of the means by which "God's beneficent providence" chooses to work for the propagation of the gospel among all nations, and particularly among the heathen kinsfolk of American blacks. It was through the efforts of blacks to bring Christianity and civilization to Africa (and also to South America and the Caribbean) that they would be able to prove to the world that their "previous condition of servitude and the color of their skin" had no effect upon their capacity for progress and nobility of character. When blacks question the responsibility they bear for the destiny of Africa, they only reveal their lack of self-respect and pride. Liberia was the "land of their fathers," and the shame that many evidently felt because of their African origin, or that of their ancestors, was unworthy of intelligent people obliged to face the fact that America could never be their true home—that "*all* men hold some relation to the land of their fathers."

Alexander Crummell was one of the first black theologians to question the theology of totalistic agape, with its emphasis upon the unconditional love of the enemy, by speaking of self-love as a Christian principle that oppressed blacks must espouse if they are to cast off their chains and rise to equality with the white nations of the world. African Americans should not emigrate to Africa, said Crummell, merely for philanthropic reasons, but because of the natural desires and ambitions of people who have regard for themselves and the acquisition of power to accomplish something worthy of a great nation. Thus he wrote in 1860:

> I am referring to that sentiment of self-regard which prompts to noble exertions for support and superiority. I am aiming at that principle of SELF-LOVE which spurs men on to self-advantage and self-aggrandizement—a principle which, in its normal state and in its due degree, to use the words of Butler, "is as just and morally good as any affection whatever." In fine, I address myself to all that class of sentiments in the human heart which creates a thirst for wealth, position, honor and power.[30]

Such advice from a clergyman was a telling blow to the cloying pietism of the missionaries and subservient black preachers who taught people to humble themselves under the yoke of "Jesus, meek and mild" while whites claimed the glory and riches of this world that were created for all to enjoy. Christianity for Crummell was a religion for tough-minded, enterprising persons who developed their natural energies, skills, and "*worldly* talent" to serve their own needs first, precisely because only so could God, who had brought them out of bondage for that purpose, use them to serve the needs of others.

Thus, early in his career, Crummell developed ideas pointing toward the legitimate secularity of black faith and the institutionalization of the church as an agency in which secular and religious purposes coalesced.

The sacred and profane roles of the church were united in the promotion of economic and social progress through self-help and the execution of a civilizing and humanizing mission to the world. This was, in fact, a further extension of the concepts around which the first Free African societies, fraternal orders, and cultural organizations in black churches were founded, and a theme that runs through the quasi-religious black nationalism of the twentieth century.

Crummell's critique of the churches of his period had to do with their excessive moralism and refusal to take seriously the challenge of the mission to Africa. Throughout his life he had lingering doubts about the ability of African Americans to shake off the psychological encumbrances of the experience of slavery and rise to the stature of the manhood and womanhood that characterized the essential quality of true religiousness:

> But I say it deliberately, that the difficulties in the way of our brethren doing a goodly work for Africa, are more subjective than objective. One of *these hindrances is a want of missionary zeal.* This is a marked characteristic of *American* black Christians. I say *American,* for from all I hear, it does not characterize our West Indian brethren; and the infant church of Sierra Leone is already, in sixty years from its birth, a mother of missions. *This* is our radical defect. *Our* religion is not diffusive, but rather introversive. It does not flow out, but rather inward. As a people we like religion—we like religious services. Our people like to go to church, to prayer-meetings, to revivals. But we go to get enjoyment. We like to be made happy by sermons, singing, and pious talk. All this is indeed correct so far as it goes; but it is only *one* side of religion. It shows only that phase of piety which may be termed the "piety of self-satisfaction." But if we are true disciples, we should not only seek a comforting piety, but we should also exhibit an effective and expansive one. We should let our godliness exhale like the odor of flowers. We should live for the good of our kind, and strive for the salvation of the world.[31]

## EDWARD W. BLYDEN

A younger contemporary of Martin Delany and Alexander Crummell was the West Indian propagandist of emigrationism, Edward Wilmot Blyden. Blyden was born in St. Thomas in 1832 and came to New York in 1847. Like Crummell he was discriminated against by a white institution of higher education and the incident undoubtedly influenced his life as an ardent champion of black nationalism.

In 1850 he went to Liberia as a missionary. From 1881 to 1885 he was the president of Liberia College, where he distinguished himself as the leading Christian educator and scholar of West Africa. George Shepperson calls Blyden the "pioneer theorist of the African personality" and the outstanding example of the "three-way process" that bound together the intellectual contributions of militant black leaders of the United States, Africa, and the Caribbean in the evolving Pan-Africanism of the late nineteenth and early twentieth centuries.[32]

Blyden was widely traveled. He lectured to black and white audiences at some of the leading colleges and seminaries in the world. Between 1872 and 1888 he visited the United States eleven times, speaking in behalf of Africa and the solidarity of the black people, and maintaining contact with the leading intellectuals of his day. In the early years of this century he devoted himself to the study of the African past. With Carter G. Woodson and W.E.B. Du Bois, Blyden helped to create the black history movement in the United States.

Perhaps even more than Delany and Crummell, Blyden's writings represent a self-conscious and systematic development of the seminal theology that gave spiritual substance and inspiration to black nationalism and Pan-Africanism. He was convinced that Liberia was the place God had chosen for the stolen race of Africans in the Americas, and he spent many years trying to persuade the leaders of the church in the United States to sponsor Liberian emigration.

Like many others of the time, Blyden seems to have had no special problem with what today would be regarded as a misguided black American cultural and political imperialism in Africa. His understanding of the place of African Americans in the *Heilsgeschichte* of black faith justified such a position and made it the cornerstone of his theology. By means of their enforced sojourn with the Anglo-Saxon race in the New World, God had bequeathed to the blacks in North America and the Caribbean a cultural superiority over the native African, precisely for the purpose of lifting the veil of darkness from their less fortunate brothers and sisters and opening up the continent of Africa to modern civilization. At first Blyden believed that the native Africans were so tractable "that it would be a comparatively easy matter for civilized, Christianized Black men to secure all the land to Christian law, liberty and civilization." In this regard his early thinking was almost identical with that of Paul Cuffee and others who had assumed a providential relationship between Christian missions and the economic and political development of Africa by Afro-Americans.

Today organized Christianity is often criticized by black intellectuals because of its involvement with governmental and commercial interests in the oppression of Third World countries. It is no wonder that many find it difficult to understand the esteem in which radical protagonists of black nationalism such as Blyden, Delany, Crummell, Garnet, Walker, and other nineteenth-century intellectuals held the Christian religion. It is, however, necessary to observe that, for all its defects, Christianity provided what was the only familiar and coherent body of moral and ethical principles available to most of those leaders for organizing a distressed and undisciplined people. As practical men of affairs, they would not permit black chauvinism to prevent them from using the Christian faith as an instrument to serve their own purposes even as it had so well served the economic and political fortunes of the civilization of which they were the most recent and favored beneficiaries.

Blyden, much like Crummell, did not consider himself orthodox in the narrow sense of most American evangelicals. He felt a greater theological affinity to the nonconformist luminaries of New England Protestantism—the Channings, Parkers, and Emersons, all of whom, he believed, were more reliable as friends and allies than the camp-meeting evangelists and sanctimonious clerics of the mainline denominations.

In this the powerful bishops and the prominent though often poorly educated preachers of the established black churches did not follow Blyden and his theologically trained colleagues. Blyden, nevertheless, continued to respect the white missionaries and ministers who, despite the discrepancies of their form of Christianity—of which he studiously reminded them—were the means by which blacks were introduced to the gospel of the Kingdom. "The lessons they have taught us," he wrote in an encomium to American Protestantism, "for their uplifting effect upon thousands of the race, we have no doubt, contain the elements of imperishable truth, and make their appeal to some deep and inextinguishable consciousness of the soul."[33] It may be for this same reason that black religion in North America has remained essentially Christian and attracted, until well into the present century, the fidelity and respect of some of the most radical leaders of the race.

Blyden became one of the most distinguished Presbyterian ministers in the world, although he is still not well known among Presbyterian scholars. His lectures in some of the great churches and theological seminaries in this country have been forgotten, but in his own time they marked him as the outstanding theologian and theoretician of black advancement in the post-bellum period. His association with whites did not prevent him from being an unswerving proponent of "Africa for the Africans," a motto which he or Delany coined and which included African Americans as well as those born on the continent.

One must not be deceived by Blyden's expressed appreciation of the civilizing function of Christianity. He bitterly criticized the white-controlled missions in Africa, particularly because they refused to tolerate the practice of polygamy, and he encouraged the secession of African Christians from the mission churches in order to form their own native churches.[34] In Nigeria his effort to this end assisted in creating, together with Majola Agbebi, the Yoruba Baptist founder of the first independent church in West Africa, the United Native African Church.

Blyden's interest in the pioneering movement for promoting the study of black history grew out of his attempt to develop a biblical and theological interpretation of the origin and destiny of the race. It was this interpretation of the Christian faith that gave him a platform for his program of emigration to Africa. In a sermon entitled "The Call of Providence to the Descendants of Africa in America," he took his text from Deuteronomy 1:21:

> Behold, the Lord thy God hath set the land before thee: go up and possess it, as the Lord God of thy fathers hath said unto thee; fear not, neither be discouraged.

In typical fashion he proceeded in this sermon to develop what became the central motif of black religion in the latter half of the nineteenth century as black preachers sought to pierce the mystery of the enslavement and suffering of God's people at the hands of an unrighteous nation. What was the meaning of the forcible removal of the millions of Africans from their native land to these alien shores? How could a positive religious meaning for the present and future be extracted from the desperate situation they faced in America?

These were questions that haunted Blyden and others like him. One of the ways he tried to resolve them was by developing a doctrine of divine providence that could account for suffering as preparation for a great work. Accordingly, it must be that God speaks to us in two ways: by his word and by his providence. In the case of African Americans, he had spoken providentially in the following ways:

> First, by suffering them to be brought here and placed in circumstances where they could receive a training fitting them for the work of civilizing and evangelizing the land whence they were torn, and by preserving them under the severest trials and afflictions. Secondly, by allowing them, notwithstanding all the services they have rendered to this country, to be treated as strangers and aliens, so as to cause them to have anguish of spirit, as was the case with the Jews in Egypt, and to make them long for some refuge from their social and civil deprivations. Thirdly, by bearing a portion of them across the tempestuous seas back to Africa, by preserving them through the process of acclimation, and by establishing them in the land, despite the attempts of misguided men to drive them away. Fourthly, by keeping their fatherland in reserve for them in their absence.[35]

Behind this understanding of the operation of divine providence lay a distinctive interpretation of the origin of blacks in the history of peoples that Blyden made the basis for his attack upon the pretensions of white American theology. Many white Christians, fortified by the opinions of distinguished scholars and church leaders in the South, claimed that the black skin of the African was the dire consequence of the curse that Noah had invoked upon his youngest son, Ham, when he had the indiscretion to look upon the nakedness of his drunken father.

Actually the curse in Genesis 9 was upon Canaan, the son of Ham, who as a result of his father's sin was to become a "servant of servants" to his brothers—Cush, Mizraim, and Phut—and to his uncles, Shem and Japheth. Inasmuch as the curse was spoken to Ham and the Hebrew word *ham* meant "hot" and "black," and further, in view of the inclusion of the people of Ethiopia and Egypt among the descendants of Ham (Gen. 10:6–14), the accepted interpretation of the white scholars was that the blacks were of Hamitic origin and their skin color was divine punishment upon all the races descended from Ham.[36]

It was by this interpretation of the Genesis story of the origin of the world's peoples that black converts to Christianity first learned of the cause of their misery. Even though many preachers discounted such a convenient excuse for black enslavement, many others were too convinced of the absolute reliability of Scripture to dismiss it out of hand. Instead of flatly denying that the Bible was accurate about the Hamitic genealogy of the dark-skinned races, Blyden, Garnet, and others sought rather to reverse the significance of the passage by emphasizing the previous fulfillment of Noah's malediction and the fact that the regenerating and elevating power of the gospel superseded the judgment of the Old Testament. In other instances they emphasized the positive, even superlative, implications of the Hamitic genealogy.[37] This was all the more possible on the basis of a Hamitic hypothesis that recognized the Egyptians and Ethiopians as originally black peoples and their ancient civilizations as the achievements of a Hamitic race.

In accordance with this latter theory, Blyden wrote in 1862:

> The all-conquering descendants of Japheth have gone to every clime, and have planted themselves on almost every shore. By means fair and unfair, they have spread themselves. . . . The Messiah—God manifest in the flesh—was of the tribe of Judah. He was born and dwelt in the tents of Shem. The promise to Ethiopia, or Ham, is like that to Shem, of a spiritual kind. It refers not to physical strength, not to large and extensive domains, not to foreign conquests, not to wide-spread dominions, but to the possession of spiritual qualities, to the elevation of the soul heavenward, to spiritual inspirations and divine communications. "Ethiopia shall stretch forth her hands unto God." Blessed, glorious promise! Our trust is not to be in chariots or horses, not in our own skill or power, but our help is to be in the name of the Lord. And surely, in reviewing our history as a people, whether we consider our preservation in the lands of our exile, or the preservation of our fatherland from invasion, we are compelled

to exclaim: "Hitherto hath the Lord helped us!" Let us, then, fear not the influences of climate. Let us go forth [to Africa] stretching out our hand to God, and if it be as hot as Nebuchadnezzar's furnace, there will be one in the midst like unto the Son of God, counteracting its deleterious influences.[38]


## THE HAMITIC HYPOTHESIS

By searching the Scriptures and the works of historians of antiquity, black preachers and intellectuals at the turn of the century eloquently repudiated the argument that God had forsaken black peoples by permitting them to be enslaved in America. They believed that through the diaspora, Africa was destined to experience a revival of its ancient glories in the name of Jesus Christ. Martin Delany, for example, turned to the writings of the Greek historians, Herodotus and Diodorus Siculus, to prove that the world was indebted to Egypt and Ethiopia for the gifts of an enlightened and progressive civilization.[39]

There was no denying the fact that Egypt and Ethiopia were among the earliest and greatest of the ancient civilizations. In Genesis 10:6–20, Mizraim and Cush, the sons of Ham, were said to be the progenitors of the people of Egypt and Ethiopia respectively. By 1860, however, white scholars—particularly the group called the "American school of anthropology"—were loath to surrender ancient Egypt and Ethiopia to black peoples and began to undermine the implications of what seemed so obvious in the Bible and history about the origin of the Africans.[40] White biblical scholars and Egyptologists did not return to the original Hamitic hypothesis, but now insisted that the Hamites must have been a white race, and whatever can be found in African societies that is commendable must be traced to the invasion of the "white Hamites" who ascended the Nile valley from Europe and Asia Minor to begin the process of civilization in black Africa.

African American intellectuals and abolitionists persisted in the other point of view. "The ancient Egyptians," declared Frederick Douglass, "were not white people, but were undoubtedly, just about as dark in complexion as many in this country who are considered Negroes." In 1862 William Wells Brown, his fellow antislavery lecturer and friend, contended: "I claim that the Blacks are the legitimate descendants of the Egyptians." Other spokespersons pointed to the fact that the Egyptians called their country *Kemet*, "the black land," and that this did not refer to the color of the soil, but the color of the people. Similarly, they recalled Solomon's marriage to an Egyptian princess, immortalized in the Song of Solomon 1:5–6, and the clear meaning of Jeremiah 13:23: "Can the Ethiopian change his skin, or the leopard his spots?"[41]

Thus, black abolitionist preachers and the intellectuals of the postwar period, undaunted by the ethnology of Louis Agassiz of Harvard and the testimony of many books and pamphlets arguing for black inferiority, stubbornly relied upon what has been an ineradicable feature of black religion in America: an interpretation of Scripture rooted and grounded in the corporate experiences and perceptions of blacks. They identified themselves with the Canaanites, who built great cities across the Jordan and resisted the invading Israelites for centuries; with the Carthaginians, who produced Hamilcar and Hannibal and were related to the descendants of the Canaanites; with Nimrod, the great Cushite hunter and warrior whose might founded cities and conquered others from Babel to Nineveh; but most of all they identified themselves with Egypt and Ethiopia—the two great African monarchies that intrigued them the most and which they believed were the incubators of much of what is called Western culture and civilization.

The great prophecy of Psalm 68:31 became a forecast of the ultimate fulfillment of the people's spiritual yearning. It is impossible to say how many sermons were preached from this text during the nineteenth century, but we know that Richard Allen, Prince Hall, Lott Carey, Henry Highland Garnet, Alexander Crummell, Edward W. Blyden, James T. Holly, and Bishop Henry M. Turner were all eloquent expositors of Psalm 68:31. They made it the cornerstone of missionary emigrationism both in the United States and Africa.

In his own commentary on this crucial biblical text, Bishop Hood wrote in 1895:

> But the promise is that princes shall come out of Egypt, and that Ethiopia shall soon stretch forth her hands unto God. Whatever shall become of the two younger sons of Ham, this promise assures us that the two elder sons shall cast aside idolatry and return unto the Lord. That this prophecy is now in the course of fulfillment the Negro Church stands forth as unquestionable evidence. It is the streak of morning light which betokens the coming day. It is the morning star which precedes the rising sun. It is the harbinger of the rising glory of the sons of Ham. It is the first fruit of the countless millions of that race who shall be found in the army with banners in the millennial glory of the Christian Church.[42]

The black church in the United States, therefore, came to symbolize the ark of safety for the regenerate children of Ham—the "old ship of Zion," which would ride out the storms of oppression and deliver the sons and daughters of Africa to the Ararat of racial redemption. The mysterious purposes of God in making some of his children black and permitting them to be subjugated and persecuted by the white race was, after all, unfathomable. Some, like Bishop Hood, reasoned that it was because of the idolatry that had to be stamped out by the present generation under the feet of Christ. Others, like Delany and Blyden, wondered if God had not meant to toughen the black race for some great task in behalf of all humanity. Still others, like T. Thomas Fortune, the editor of the *New York Age*, held that the theory that God had brought blacks to America in order to evangelize Africa was "so much religious nonsense boiled down to a sycophantic platitude."

The problem of the divine intention continued to perplex black preachers for generations and has never been solved to the satisfaction of most Christians. In fact the problem was transcended by a metaphorical comparison of African Americans with the emancipated Hebrews, and identification with the critical importance of Africa in Judeo-Christian religious history. Many also believed that God had promised something better for those who trusted in him. The despoiled and despised peoples of Africa, who had been stolen from their homeland, had to be delivered from darkness by the light that shone in the face of Jesus Christ.

The seminal black theology that developed during the nineteenth century was neither superficial nor parochial. It taught that the descendants of the slaves were destined to be delivered not only from bondage to sin, but from injustice, prejudice, and oppression, and would be the means by which millions of their brothers and sisters who remained in Africa would someday be liberated from European colonialism.

The secular emigrationists who later articulated their aspirations in political rather than theological terminology should not be dissociated from this basically religious interpretation of the nature and destiny of the black race. They shared it even when, like Marcus Garvey, they were most critical of the failure of the church to give the leadership required to break away from obsequious adjustment to the American status quo. Emigrationism and the black nationalism that followed disillusionment over Reconstruction and appealed to landless farm laborers who poured into the cities after the First World War, was rooted in an ethos of blackness that, in large measure, had been created by the destiny motif in black religion. To some extent that motif was to be betrayed, but never totally expunged, by conservative forces within the church. It has been, nevertheless, nurtured by successive generations of black religionists and at the close of the twentieth century continues to be a deep undercurrent within the mainstream black churches.

## HENRY M. TURNER

Henry McNeal Turner, the vociferous and controversial bishop of the AME Church, was the most consistent advocate of this perspective in the closing years of the nineteenth century. More than any other single individual, Turner not only made a black theology of liberation the core of his preaching and writing, but also helped to implant the spirit of revolutionary religion in the independent churches of Africa that were taking up the struggle against colonialism and racism in the last quarter of the century. Turner was born free in South Carolina in 1834. For a time he worked on a cotton plantation as a laborer, then later as a porter in a law office where the young clerks, recognizing his intelligence, taught him how to read and write. In 1854 he was ordained by the Methodist Church and traveled all over the South. His life changed dramatically in 1858, when he happened upon an AME congregation in New Orleans and accepted an invitation to go to Baltimore for further training to become an African Methodist pastor.

During his stay in Baltimore before the Civil War, Turner became convinced that America would never do justice to black people and that emigration was the only solution to the race problem. In 1862 he heard an address by Alexander Crummell, and from that day the mission of the church in Africa and the repatriation of African Americans became the two great passions of his life.

His intense interest in emigration did not, however, preclude his enthusiastic involvement in the war—first as an advocate for the use of black troops, and later as a chaplain in the Union Army. After the war he went into Reconstruction politics as a Republican organizer in Georgia. He built a mass base for the party in Georgia and used it as a springboard for his ambitions within the AME Church, but not without difficulty. Like other black preachers of the postwar period, Turner astutely mixed religion and politics to the advantage of both himself and the community—a practice guaranteed to win as many enemies as friends.

By 1876 Turner had attained the powerful position of manager of the AME Book Concern, and his sermons and essays received national notoriety. He was, without question, the leading politician of the southern wing of the denomination and enjoyed an enormous following among the disillusioned and restless African Methodists of the South, many of whom were intrigued by the African emigration movement. With this support Turner was elected the twelfth bishop of his denomination in 1880 over the opposition of conservative northern churchmen who resented his brazenly unpatriotic attitude toward the United States and sharply disagreed with his emigrationism.[43]

Henry M. Turner was the first to raise seriously the issue of reparations for the years of black slavery and regarded it as necessary for financing the mass removal of blacks to Africa. In an article entitled "The Negro Has Not Sense Enough," which appeared during his editorship of the *Voice of Missions* in 1900, he wrote:

> We have worked, enriched the country and helped give it a standing among the powers of the earth, and when we are denied our civil and political rights, the fool Negro who has no more sense than

a jackass, yet he wants to be a leader, ridicules the idea of asking for a hundred million dollars to go home, for Africa is our home, and is the one place that offers us manhood and freedom, though we are the subjects of nations that have claimed a part of Africa by conquest. A hundred million of dollars can be obtained if we, as a race, would ask for it. The way we figure it out, this country owes us forty billions of dollars, and we are afraid to ask for a hundred million.[44]

Turner had little respect or affection for this country, although (or perhaps because) he had served as a token black in several positions for the government. "In this country," he wrote, "white represents God, and black the devil, but little thought is given to the Black man's future." He did not believe that every black person would or should emigrate to Africa. What he pleaded for was "a highway made across the Atlantic: upon which regular social and economic intercourse between Black America and Africa could be carried on and self-reliant, energetic Black people could be permanently settled if they chose to do so."[45]

It was his opinion that blacks needed a place where they could demonstrate their ability to build and govern a nation by themselves—a theater in which young black men and women could express the gifts of the manhood and womanhood denied to them in the land of their birth. As few as a half-million black Christians, he said, could build a new nation in Africa. But he was stringently demanding about the kind of persons who would be equal to the task. Only young men and women of courage, pride, ambition, and resourcefulness would be of any use to themselves or to Africa.[46]

Although he was a consummate politician, Turner was also a theologian. It was God, he said, who allowed the blacks to be transported to America, but for an inexorable purpose: to be equipped for a great missionary crusade in Africa. In this opinion he followed the view that had been popularized by Crummell and Blyden, and also by his colleague on the bench, AME Bishop R.H. Cain of South Carolina. But in the pages of the *Christian Recorder* and the *Voice of Missions*, powerful mouthpieces for the dissemination of his ideas throughout African Methodism, Turner made it clear that American whites had been disobedient to God's command by not receiving blacks as brothers and sisters, sharing with them the riches of the nation, and helping them to return to Africa with the education and resources necessary for their mission—the creation of a black nation free of imperialistic exploitation by the nations of Europe which were then dividing up the continent among themselves.

He expressed his most radical views in the *Voice of Missions* between 1893 and 1900 when mounting opposition from within the church removed him as its editor, and in an independent publication called, significantly enough, *The Voice of the People*, which he edited between 1901 and 1907.

Turner's theology culminated almost a hundred years of black theological reflection on the origin, destiny, and responsibility of blacks to demand their God-given rights in the United States and, at the same time, bring freedom and the Christian faith to Africa. By 1880 he believed that black religion was essentially a protest movement against the disobedient white church that had reduced African Americans to obsequious believers in their own spiritual inferiority and the right of whites to dictate the terms of religious faith.

When an "Observor" in a letter to the *Voice of Missions* offered the opinion that Turner was "becoming demented" because he taught that "God is a Negro," Turner replied:

We have as much right biblically and otherwise to believe that God is a Negro, as you buckra or white people have to believe that God is a fine looking, symmetrical and ornamented white man. For the bulk of you and all the fool Negroes of the country believe that God is white-skinned, blue-eyed, straight-haired, projecting nosed, compressed lipped and finely robed white gentleman, sitting upon a throne somewhere in the heavens. Every race of people since time began who have attempted to describe their God by words, or by paintings, or by carvings, or by any other form or figure, have conveyed the idea that the God who made them and shaped their destinies was symbolized in themselves, and why should not the Negro believe that he resembles God as much so as other people? . . . Yet we are no stickler as to God's color anyway, but if He has any we would prefer to believe that it is nearer symbolized in the blue sky above us and the blue water of the seas and oceans; but we certainly protest against God being white *at all*; abstract as this theme must forever remain while we are in the flesh. This is one of the reasons we favor African emigration, or Negro naturalization, wherever we can find a domain, for, as long as we remain among the whites the Negro will believe that the devil is black and that he (the Negro) favors the devil, and that God is white and that he (the Negro) bears no resemblance to Him, and the effect of such a sentiment is contemptuous and degrading, and one-half of the Negro race will be trying to get white and the other half will spend their days in trying to be white men's scullions in order to please the whites.[47]

Bishop Turner's first visit to Africa took place in 1891 under the authorization of the Council of Bishops. Accompanied by Reverend J. R. Geda, the bishop received an enthusiastic reception in Freetown, Sierra Leone. There he organized the first annual conference on the African continent, with a lay membership of four hundred and five tribesmen. Enraptured by this successful first encounter with the land and people who had been the object of his yearning for so many years, he went on triumphantly to

Liberia. There, following a brief visit with the leading officials in Monrovia, he sailed up the St. Paul River for Muhlenberg and convened the Liberian annual conference on November 23, 1891.[48] His letters back to the *Christian Recorder* were printed together as a pamphlet, and glowed with rapturous reports of the stability and prosperity of the places he visited, the accomplishments of the immigrants from America, and the myriad opportunities available to those who would follow them. "I get mad and sick," he wrote, "when I look at the possibilities God has placed within our reach, and to think that we are such block-heads we cannot see and use them."

With the economic and social problems Liberia was experiencing as the influence and funding of the ACS declined, and with adverse publicity being bandied about by his opponents, Turner's visit to Africa was a strategic contribution to the revival of missionary emigrationism within the AME Church. His exaggerated descriptions of what he found were calculated to make the most of a cause that had been rapidly losing its vitality.

Bishop Turner, even more determined to open up Africa and to cement ties between African Christians and the AME Church, returned to Africa in March 1898 on an episcopal visit that was to have far-reaching implications for relationships between Africans and African Americans and the development of nationalism through the independent church movement on the African continent. This time his travels took him to South Africa. Amid great celebration, he held conferences, organized churches, and ordained native ministers—charging them to dedicate their lives to a black church that stood for God, freedom, and independence from the control of whites.[49]

The stage for this development had been set prior to his arrival when a group of singers, brought to the United States from South Africa in 1893, included a Basuto girl, Charlotte Manye, whose uncle was Reverend Mangena M. Mokone, a Wesleyan Methodist who was disaffected with segregation in the Wesleyan mission and had withdrawn to form the Ethiopian Church in Pretoria. When the singers became stranded between engagements in the United States, Reverend Reverdy C. Ransom, an AME minister in Ohio who was to become a prominent bishop and theologian, arranged to have them go to Wilberforce University, where Ms. Manye graduated with honors before returning home. Through letters to her uncle in Pretoria, Charlotte Manye drew the attention of Mokone to the existence of a church "owned and operated" by black Americans—the AME Church. The South Africans requested further information, and after studying the Discipline, the hymnal, and other books concerning the church, decided to unite with the AMEs in the United States. Union was consummated by Turner at the Allen Temple church in Atlanta on June 19, 1896.

Reverend James M. Dwane, one of the Ethiopian Church's emissaries to the General Conference, was appointed general superintendent in

South Africa. Dwane later withdrew from the church over its failure to provide funds for a school and because of his dissatisfaction with the title of general superintendent. However, he never gave up his belief in the unity of the black church and became a powerful leader of the separatist movement throughout southern and eastern Africa—as well as in the Sudan, Egypt, and Ethiopia.[50]

The Ethiopian Church had been foreshadowed by the separatist Tembu National Church founded by Reverend Nehemiah Tile in 1884. Tile was accused by the white Wesleyans of "taking part in political matters and stirring up feelings of hostility against magistrates in Tembuland" (South Africa). The Ethiopians followed in this rebellious tradition and took their name from Psalm 68:31, which we have already noted as a favorite text among blacks on both sides of the Atlantic during the nineteenth century.

Originally Ethiopianism was a schismatic movement within the mission churches; it tried to bring black Christians together across tribal and national lines into one independent African church. From the beginning it had an implicit political appeal based upon a growing national consciousness among segregated and abused African churchmen—especially in the industrialized areas of southern Africa. Its antiwhite bias soon aroused the opposition of the colonial governments as well as the embarrassment of white missionaries who began losing hundreds of their converts to the new movement.

James M. Dwane, who by 1896 had successfully challenged Mokone's leadership to become, in effect, the bishop of the Ethiopians, told the African Methodists in Atlanta that "Africans would never allow the white man to ride roughshod over their country. Africans were rapidly imbibing civilized habits and would soon be able to run great civilized governments. Then they would say to the European nations, 'Hands off.' "[51]

Nothing could have pleased Bishop Turner more. He devoted his visit in 1898 and his subsequent contacts with Africa to the welding together of this potentially powerful native movement with his own nationalistic aspirations for the AME Church. The Ethiopians, for their part, made remarkable gains under the combined influence of Dwane and Turner. In 1896 the membership was reported to be 2,800. On June 17, 1898, Turner reported a membership of 10,800, and after he reached home word was received that it had grown by another 1,200. By then the church encompassed Cape Colony, the Orange Free State, and the Transvaal.

Although he had formidable opposition, Turner's efforts in behalf of Africa were generally supported by the AME Church in the 1890s. Already in 1892 the bishops of the church, responding to the growing feeling of kinship with Africans, had declared:

Africa is the largest and most important of the fields that lie before us. First, because of the number of persons involved in the work;

second, on account of the relationship that exists between our race and the inhabitants of the Dark Continent; third, because our church is better adapted to the redemption of Africa than any other organization among the darker races for the moral and religious training of the people. . . .

Thereupon followed nineteen specific items dealing with the mission to be undertaken by the AME Church. Item sixteen, for example, called for the formation of an organization that would bring unity among the blacks of North, Central, and South America and would promote their common moral and spiritual uplift. The statement continued:

And then pursuing our onward march for the Dark Continent, we will speak to more than 200 million of men and women, bone of our bone, and flesh of our flesh, and say to them, "Arise and shine, for the light of civilization is waiting for thee."[52]

The affiliation of the Ethiopian Church with the AME Church was the first significant achievement under this policy. The key role of Dwane was recognized by Turner, who created for him the office of vicar-bishop. Although the episcopacy supported this move, Dwane ran into difficulty with Bishop W. J. Gaines who raised objection to his holding such a title when he was introduced to the several annual conferences he attended in 1898. Dwane's disappointment over the objections raised about his appointment, and the failure of the denomination to send the $10,000 he believed had been promised for Queenstown College, provoked him to schism.

In 1899 he succeeded in leading about thirty Ethiopian ministers out of the AME Church and organized the Order of Ethiopia, which he then placed under the authority of the Queenstown Anglicans. Reverend Julius Gordon, rector of the local congregation, explained the doctrine of apostolic succession to Dwane and told him that the AME Church could not possibly pass on valid episcopal orders to anyone. Ironically, Dwane never became an Anglican bishop, and even his appointment as provincial was later withdrawn.

The emergence of revolutionary church movements in Africa as a result of the rebellious spirit inspired by black Christians from the United States went far beyond colonialist expectations. One group that appeared in Natal in the 1890s was the African Christian Union (ACU), which listed some of its officers as residing in America. In a 21-point manifesto the ACU announced that one of its intentions was "to solicit funds [from Europeans] to restore Africans [in America] to their father-land . . . and to pursue steadily and unswervingly the policy of AFRICA FOR THE AFRICANS, and look for and hasten by prayer and united effort, the forming of the AFRICAN CHRISTIAN NATION by God's power and in his own time and way."[53]

Shepperson and Price point out that similar developments were taking place in various black communities in the United States. For example, in Richmond, Virginia, in addition to the black Baptists, there were a "host of infinitely less orthodox sects, with their prophets and messiahs, which flourished in the atmosphere of open-air, river baptisms, with their associations of John and the Jordan."[54] In fact many members of the National Baptist Convention, which had been organized in 1895 as the largest black denomination in the world, were themselves very much at home in this chiliastic atmosphere.

Reverend Lewis G. Jordan and Reverend Charles S. Morris, among others, were ardent educators of young black preachers. The church schools of their denomination, in contrast to those of the white northern Baptists, "taught doctrines and inculcated attitudes which some call politely 'racial radicalism,' and others, more bluntly, 'sedition.' In this they anticipated the later trend of independent native schools in Africa."[55]

The influence of American blacks on nationalism among Africans at the turn of the century is best illustrated by the career of Reverend John Chilembwe of Nyasaland, who returned to Africa with Charles S. Morris after studying in the United States. Chilembwe led his people in the ill-fated Nyasaland Rebellion of 1915. He had come under the influence of a remarkable Australian missionary, Joseph Booth, who visited black Baptist churches in the United States for three months in 1895. During this time Booth evidently completed a book, *Africa for the Africans*, which was published in 1897 by the Morgan College Press of Baltimore. It was also during this period that Booth made contact with a pre-Garveyite group in Washington, D.C., and wrote to his daughter on April 9, 1897: "There are many signs that a great work will spring from this side of the ocean also. I am lecturing on 'Africa for the Africans.' "[56]

Young Chilembwe, whom Booth had met at Chiradzulu, British Central Africa, and had introduced to his ideas, accompanied him on this eventful visit to the United States. Both men readily perceived the similarities between the oppression blacks were suffering in South Africa and the situation in America. Moreover, they were well briefed by black preachers they met and talked with in both the North and the South. In Richmond Booth and Chilembwe were even attacked by a mob of young toughs for walking together in the streets and probably because they lived together for a time in the black section of the city.

Chilembwe later attended the Virginia College and Theological Seminary at Lynchburg. There he met many leading black Baptist ministers including Dr. Gregory W. Hayes and Dr. Lewis G. Jordan, secretary of the Foreign Mission Board of the National Baptist Convention, which financed his work in Nyasaland for fifteen years. Radical religious ideas were rampant at the school in those years, and Chilembwe transported them back to Africa where he subsequently founded an independent Baptist denomination. His church became increasingly hostile to the incursion of Europeans into the Nyasaland Protectorate. On Saturday evening, January 23, 1915, Chilembwe led a revolt in which three Europeans were killed and two wounded. The uprising was overwhelmed in ten days by white settlers. Chilembwe was killed as he tried to escape across the border into Portuguese territory.

## RESISTANCE TO WHITE RULE IN AFRICA

Religious resistance to white rule began to build up in South Africa, the Belgian Congo, Nyasaland, French Equatorial Africa, Kenya, and in West Africa in the 1880s. It continued with increasing strength through the first half of the twentieth century. The dramatic defeat of the Italians by the Abyssinians at Aduwa in 1896 greatly emboldened the Ethiopianists. The Italian invasion, discrimination in the mission churches, the pressure of the white settlers on tribal lands and traditional ways of life, and finally the influence of the churches of the United States—all these factors worked together to unleash a torrent of antiwhite sentiment and schismatic activity among African Christians.

In South Africa Ethiopian preachers were involved in the Zulu uprisings of 1906. In the Cameroons serious anti-European agitation was led by a rebellious Baptist preacher named Lotin Same. In the Congo, following the First World War, African separatists called for political emancipation and raised their prophets, Simon Kimbangu and Andre Matswa, to the level of black gods—or so it seemed at that time. In 1909 John Msikinya, a dismissed African Methodist preacher, visited the United States and returned to South Africa as bishop of the Church of God and the Saints of Christ, a black American denomination that exists today as an interesting synthesis of Judaic and Christian traditions. Msikinya died in 1918 and his second-in-command, Enoch Mgyima, split the church and organized a new sect called the Israelites, which rejected the New Testament altogether.

Mgyima's group saw themselves as followers of the Jewish patriarchs who, they believed, had been delivered by God from foreign oppressors. In May 1921 the government sent in police to destroy their sacred village, Bullhoek, near Queenstown in the Ciskei. A massacre occurred when the Israelites attacked with swords and spears. One hundred sixty-three members of the sect were killed and one hundred twenty-nine wounded. The incident was widely publicized and worldwide attention focused on racism in South Africa and the repressive policies of the Smuts government.[57]

In the Transkei another prophet, Wellington Butelezi, who said he came from America, organized a cargo cult. Butelezi told his followers that all Americans were blacks and that they would soon be coming to liberate their brother and sister Africans and put an end to the white man's rule. He promised that the Americans would arrive in airplanes and when they landed "the Europeans would be driven into the sea and the Bantu would not have to pay poll taxes anymore."[58]

In Kenya, between June 1921 and April 1922, Harry Thuku, leader of the Young Kikuyu Association, organized a protest against the reduction of native wages, rising taxation, and the seizure of ancestral lands by white settlers. Although Thuku was not an ordained minister, he had, nevertheless, strong religious motivations for making missionaries the target of his attack and gathering many lapsed Christians into his fold. His followers were reminded that:

> Our God brought the Children of Israel out of the house of bondage of King Pharaoh . . . and to Him let us pray again, for He is our God. And also let us have faith since in the eyes of God there is no distinction of white or Black. All are sons of Adam, and alike before Him, Jehovah our living God. . . . Thou Lord Jehovah, our God, it is Thou who hast set apart to be our Master and Guide Harry Thuku; may he be chief of us all.[59]

According to a study by Joseph S. Coleman, the hand of Blyden and other black American clergymen in Nigeria was reflected in the political disorder that broke out among the sectarian groups they had contacted after 1899. In the Delta region, for example, a movement began about 1914 led by a Nigerian who called himself the Second Elijah. It was essentially an ascetic Christian sect, but became openly anti-European when its leader was convicted of sedition.

Another movement that sought to combine Christianity with the traditional Yoruba religion was called Orunlaism. Its prophet, not unlike the leaders of African American sects and cults in the ghettos of the United States, exhorted his people:

> Scrap the imported religions. . . . [There can be no] political emancipation without spiritual emancipation. . . . Paint God as an African . . . the angels in Africans . . . the Devil, by all means, in any color than an African . . . and thou shalt be saved.[60]

The predominantly white churches of the United States and Europe—and particularly the Anglicans in South Africa—were not entirely without some salutary effect upon the growth of African political consciousness. Their influence was mainly through the schools, despite the fact that most of the mission schools were racist and paternalistic. But in South Africa the English missionaries were the first whites to fight against the enslavement of the aboriginal population. Under the pressure of white settlers and Afrikaaner domination, they gradually yielded to the application of the color bar in the churches as everywhere else. The practice of some of the Anglican clergy, however, made a contribution to African freedom and opposition to the prevailing discriminatory customs.

Both John Tengo Jabavu and Reverend Walter Rubusana, two out-standing black politicians in South Africa, were educated in mission schools and received guarded approbation if not a great deal of support from liberal churchmen. Rubusana was ordained by the London Missionary Society in 1884. He received a degree from a black college in the United States and went back to South Africa infected with nationalist sentiments for which the moderate Jabavu had little sympathy.

Thus, the *Zeitgeist* of sub-Sahara Africa at the turn of the century moved in a socio-religious climate favorable to revolutionary change. Such a climate must be attributed to a combination of many different factors, but among them must be included the teaching of Christianity by black and white missionaries, some of whom—such as the radical Joseph Booth and the American-based Watchtower Bible and Tract Society—introduced highly inflammatory elements into the African religious scene: ideas of political freedom and economic justice based on the implications for secular society of a radical evangelism and apocalypticism.[61]

As yet there has been little research on the effect of American missionary outreach on the development of nationalism and independence in Africa, but there is scattered evidence that the Americans were more sensitive to the injustices of the colonial regimes than were some Europeans. The American mission schools and churches were, of course, less directly related to colonial authorities with whom missionaries from Europe were involved by nationality ties. Moreover, in a few instances the American missions included highly competent black Americans who could identify with the plight of African Christians.

In 1909 ten American denominations and mission boards united in an attempt to get the United States government to use its diplomatic channels to support Reverend William M. Morrison, a white missionary, and Reverend William Henry Sheppard, a black missionary, in a libel trial brought against them by the Belgian *Compagnie du Kasai* in the Congo. Sheppard and Morrison, representatives of the Board of World Missions of the Presbyterian Church in the United States, had for several years given support to the cause of social justice in the Belgian colony. They had incurred the wrath of Leopold's administrators by protesting the brutalization of rubber workers in the Kasai region.[62] To these crusading missionaries must go much of the credit for the amelioration of conditions in the Kasai. Their trial and vindication were widely discussed at home and helped to make more Americans aware of the challenges of preaching the gospel in Africa. Sheppard was in great demand as a speaker in black churches all over the country, and many blacks first learned of Africa and its struggle from his lectures and sermons.

The major weight of African American contributions to the African independent church movement and the rise of black nationalism, of course, rests upon the black Baptist, Methodist, and Pentecostal churches in the United States. These churches, by their example as well as anything else they might have done, helped to introduce African Christians to the free spirit, prophetism, and millennialist passion for liberation in this world and the next, which were fundamental characteristics of black religion in the United States and the Caribbean.

Towering over all others was the figure of Bishop Henry M. Turner, who inspired Mokone and Dwane and implanted African Methodism—with its pride of origin and rich heritage from the days of Allen and Coker—among thousands of questing Africans from Monrovia to Cape Town. Turner was more political than either Crummell or Blyden and, with perhaps the exception of Marcus Garvey who was to come later, had a more profound and lasting influence on Africa than any other leader of the American churches.

In their authoritative work on John Chilembwe, Shepperson and Price appreciatively summarize the place of Turner and other African American ministers in the movement of radical religion in Africa:

Turner was a man full of the concept of the "manifest destiny" of coloured Americans to redeem their unhappy brethren in Africa. After the mid-1890s, American Negroes of like persuasion were to have a growing influence in South Africa and the regions to which it was allied. They added a new nuance to the concept of Ethiopianism, and for many whites in South and Central Africa their schools and colleges in the United States became nests of agitators, American or African Negro, who brought growing elements of political consciousness of a rebellious nature of the African separatist churches, from which, through the influence of the Negro minister, they spread out amongst the masses of the native people who only wanted inspiration and organization to raise them anew against their white masters.[63]

The nationalistic aspect of black religion in North America, Africa, and the Caribbean has been greatly neglected by scholars. E. U. Essien-Udom is one of the few who gave early recognition to the significance of the church in the development of black consciousness and the demand for racial justice.[64]

For many years the eminent sociologist E. Franklin Frazier commanded respect as the leading authority on black religion in the United States. Frazier had little appreciation of the contribution of the black church to what Delany and others of his time called "elevation." In recent years a few writers have begun to sense the deficiencies in his analysis, which preceded the height of church involvement in the struggle for human rights during the second half of the twentieth century. Horace Cayton, for example, attributes these deficiencies in his work to the fact that Frazier did not live through the civil rights period and had no opportunity to reassess his perspective on the basis of subsequent events:

Frazier did not live to witness the fervor of the continuing Negro rebellion and the position of leadership which the church and churchmen are taking in it. Perhaps, if he had, his final judgment on the importance and resilience of the Negro church might have been tempered.[65]

Essien-Udom, however, whose manuscript for *Black Nationalism* was completed before the civil rights movement reached its zenith in 1963–64, perceived the enmeshment of the church in the web of historical factors leading to the emergence of radical black nationalism in the United States.[66] He seems not to be aware, however, of its influence in Africa and the West Indies—the operation of the triangular connection upon the freedom movement in all three areas. St. Clair Drake and a few others have, intentionally and unintentionally, helped to fill that gap.

Essien-Udom asserts that the church gave the black person pride in success, grassroots participation in a national movement, independence from white control, and a physical center for social life in the black community. This is all well and good, but it does not go far enough in light of what we have discussed in this chapter. The black church, as the primary institutional expression of black religion, erected the politico-theological foundation for black nationalism and Pan-Africanism. Not only did it provide the organizational skills requisite for mass movements in the twentieth century, it provided also the spiritual inspiration and philosophical rationale—building blocks for the structure of African and African American solidarity as it developed from the early Du Bois to Malcolm X.

The thrust of missionary emigrationism, the search for roots in the pre-Mosaic history of Israel, the challenge to the ethical interpretation of love and redemptive suffering in white Christianity, the prefigurement of black liberation in the story of the Exodus, the willingness to speculate about the "color" of God and the meaning of a black Christ, and the development of Ethiopianism in Africa and in the Caribbean and North America—all of these developments and tendencies gave inspiration and ideological substance to the evolution of black consciousness and nationalism, a heightening sense of racial identity and messianism wherever blacks writhed under the heel of white oppression.

Before the end of the nineteenth century, what began as a theology was secularized as an ideology of political and cultural separatism that reached its most explicit articulation in resolutions of the Pan-African congresses and the philosophy of negritude. But well before that occurred, black ministers and lay persons had drawn cultural and political implications for colonization and self-determination—not from egalitarian ideologies of the Western democracies or from Marxism—but from the Bible and Christian theology as reinterpreted by men and women who believed that the gospel itself contains the most penetrating and provocative justification for racial solidarity and social change.

Read in the light of the policies for the world mission of the church, which most denominations have today, the books, sermons, and editorials on the need for solidarity with Africa sound curiously presumptuous and less than flattering of the ancient cultures and religions of that continent. We cannot, however, doubt the sincerity of those men and women, many of them exslaves with only a modicum of formal education, who tried to bring to the land of their ancestors whatever material assistance and enlightenment their poverty-striken congregations could afford at a time they themselves were struggling for survival. Whatever errors they committed in their estimate of the state of civilization in Africa, or the ability of a Christianity that had been corrupted for ages to correct African deficiencies, must be absolved by their intentions and the grace of the God they trusted to guide them.

We owe something inestimable to them for their teachings about what the church means in terms of self-respect, of meaningful participation in the affairs of the world, and as an institutional base for black enterprise and culture. It was their hope to share these gifts with all in obedience to the command to "go and make disciples of all nations . . . baptizing . . . and teaching," and especially with those to whom they were bound by a common ancestry and the experience of subjugation by the white people of Europe and North America. In so doing, they demonstrated the power of their conviction that God was using African American Christians of the United States in a special way to help fulfill the promised glory of the Ethiopian people, of whom they considered themselves a privileged remnant, singing their song in a strange land.

## CHAPTER 7

# The Deradicalization
# of the Black Church

*There are indications that a new church is arising among Negroes, a militant church, one that is concerning itself with the problems of the masses. . . . Yet it cannot be said that today even this church is an influential factor in the lives of the whole Negro working population. Extremely significant in Negro life, however, has been the inordinate rise of religious cults and sects.*

Ira De A. Reid, 1940

When Bishop Henry M. Turner died in 1915, there were no clergymen of his stature who could, by temperament or ideology, assume the leadership position he had occupied in a persistent but unsuccessful attempt to radicalize the black church. The possible exceptions among the Methodists might have been the Pan-Africanist bishop Alexander Walters of the AME Zion Church, and the young AME minister Reverdy C. Ransom of Boston and New York. Both were militants and had, by that time, attracted public attention, but neither was as tough-minded, unconciliatory, and pessimistic about the United States as Turner was at the height of his influence.

### DECLINE OF BISHOP TURNER'S INFLUENCE

Turner entered his seventieth year in 1904 somewhat less strident than he had been earlier, and four years later he was removed from the pivotal position of editor of the *Voice of Missions*. By 1910 he was still the acknowledged representative of a certain radical fringe among the unsophisticated masses of African Methodists, but his age and the weariness of the years had taken their toll. What was now called for was the reincarnation of his spirit in some younger member of the episcopacy if the

African American churches were to continue to shape the future by drawing upon the aggressive black consciousness and nationalism that characterized some of the leading spokesmen of the antebellum period. The talented Ransom became a bishop in 1924, but by that time other nonreligious factors had taken control.

Even though the first decade of the twentieth century saw a rising tide of opposition to the leadership of Booker T. Washington, those who had the courage to attack the great symbol of black accommodation from Tuskegee, with few exceptions, happened not to be clergymen. In fact, the thin line of anti-Bookerite churchmen were members of the new bourgeoisie of Atlanta, Washington, and Boston. They did not have the common touch that was indispensable for the kind of leadership Turner represented, and they regarded civil rights agitation more as a last resort for breaking into the American mainstream than as a means of precipitating a crisis that would confront the basic assumptions of the system and create a feeling of nationalism among the masses. The most promising successor to Turner was the brilliant Atlanta University professor W. E. B. Du Bois. Although he was a religious man in the broadest sense, he did not regard himself as a churchman and could command no popular following.[1]

Turner had never really taken up cudgels against Washington with the vehemence of Du Bois, the determination of two of the leading anti-Bookerite Baptist preachers—J. Milton Waldron and Sutton E. Griggs— or with the erudite radicalism of Reverdy Ransom, the unofficial chaplain of the Niagara Movement.[2] This is not to say that he approved of Washington's position of compromise with the white South. Turner's prestige among the burgeoning black church population of Georgia helped to create a climate unfavorable to Washington, which was turned to good account by Du Bois and others. Moreover, when a group of Boston radicals led by the irrepressible Monroe Trotter shouted down Washington at a meeting in 1903, Turner supported their protest, although he could not approve of the reasons behind their actions, which he judged to be basic optimism about the possibility of obtaining justice in the United States. As for the address, he wrote on that occasion:

> Washington's policy is not worth a cent. It accomplishes no racial good except as it helps a thousand students at Tuskegee. . . . [Although] we agree with our Boston friends in spitting on everything that would appear to underrate the value of the Negro in every particular, they are doing no more good than Washington. . . . Nothing less than a nation owned and controlled by the Negro will amount to a hill of beans.[3]

But Turner did not seek a position in the front line of the skirmishes with Booker T. Washington. When Frederick Douglass died early in

1895, Turner, if he had desired to do so, could have challenged Washington for national leadership. With his excellent connections among church people in the South and his willingness to say publicly what many undistinguished blacks felt privately, he might have toppled the pedestal of the Bookerite clan. But Turner was, after all, not a stranger to certain key aspects of Washington's thought: the emphasis on people raising themselves up by their own bootstraps, the concentration on agricultural and mechanical arts as the prerequisite to economic independence, and the rejection of Douglass's example that social intercourse with whites was the way to get ahead in the world. In these respects Turner and Washington understood one another well. And both were understood and appreciated by Marcus Mosiah Garvey—the true inheritor of Turner's mantle of black nationalist leadership, although the former lacked the dignity and prestige of the AME Church.

Booker T. Washington had little else in common with the bishop. Like Douglass, he was an implacable foe of emigrationism. He remained a loyal Republican. He was, first of all, a gentleman who impressed whites with his splendid manners and conciliatory demeanor, both of which he used artfully to manipulate them and enlist support for his favorite projects. Bishop Turner, on the other hand, never ceased mauling southern whites and the servile, fawning blacks whose criticism he labeled "the billingsgate of this young fungus class, and some of these old fossils." Although he began as a Republican he came to distrust them and was one of a growing number of leaders who turned to the Democrats with the election of Grover Cleveland. He had no confidence in America and thought it the highest folly to expect whites ever to give blacks their due. His experience in the aftermath of the Radical Reconstruction more than convinced him that whites were determined to reduce blacks to their former status and the only salvation was to return to Africa.

At the close of the century, when white hostility was greater than at any other period in American history, Turner's tower of strength was his willingness to take a public offensive. He refused to bow before the canons of respectability at a time when whites were all too willing to require blacks to grin and bear it while they turned the screws of oppression with the greatest dignity and pious pretense. Turner simply refused to play that game and struck out mercilessly against hypocrisy and deception. He was, as a matter of fact, not beyond violence and in a *Voice of Missions* editorial urged that "Negroes Get Guns" to defend themselves against the lynch mobs.[4]

Rather than counsel blacks to make themselves acceptable and work for eventual assimilation with whites, Turner confronted America with a demand for reparations. When it became obvious to him that the government would not finance black colonization in Africa, he turned to the community itself and involved himself in numerous ill-fated emigration schemes. He was so single-mindedly intent upon getting out of the United States that he had neither the time nor interest to mount a campaign against Booker T. Washington. Suffering a stroke at the turn of the century, he practically turned his back on the leadership struggle and devoted himself to emigration, even though he had to experience the embarrassment of having both Blyden and Crummell attack him publicly.[5]

Turner's influence was also diminished by his alleged connection with a New Orleans agent of the International Migration Society, Robert Charles, who avidly imbibed Turner's propaganda and harangued blacks in the South to arm themselves. When Charles was slain in the summer of 1900 by police, after killing six white men, authorities uncovered stacks of the *Voice of Missions.* The New Orleans *Times-Democrat* reported that "it was from these booklets that Charles originally derived his fiendish animosity against the white race in general."[6] Black leaders viewed the incident as just one more predictable by-product of Turner's excesses, and his authority in the denomination dwindled until his death in 1915.

But the Charles affair did not silence him. He shifted his editorship to *The Voice of the People* and promoted an emigration convention in Nashville in 1901. There he and William H. Heard, an AME pastor from Atlanta, organized the Colored National Emigration Association (CNEA), which for several years attempted to purchase a ship to take blacks to Liberia. After several disappointments and a storm of opposition from "responsible Negro leaders," Turner apparently abandoned the group and began publishing announcements of commercial fares to Africa. Unfortunately, he had been accused by Heard of misusing of the funds of the CNEA, which he served for a time as treasurer. By 1906 he had lost interest in the project altogether and became deeply involved in local politics.[7] But his interest in emigration did not disappear during this last period.

When Turner died, in his eighty-second year, he stood alone, as he always had, as the most original and independent black churchman of his time—a person who combined the acuity of a theologian with the passion of an indefatigable Pan-African activist. Although there were other radical churchmen in the Niagara Movement and later in the National Association for the Advancement of Colored People (NAACP)—such as Reverdy Ransom and Francis J. Grimke—none of them had the grassroots following or audacity of Turner. In commemoration of his life, W.E.B. Du Bois, whose spirit became more and more reminiscent of Turner's as the years sped by, wrote of him:

> The late Henry McNeal Turner who recently died at the ripe age of 82 was a man of tremendous force and indomitable courage. As army chaplain, pastor and bishop he was always a man of strength. He lacked, however, the education and the stern moral balance of

Bishop Payne. In a sense Turner was the last of his clan: mighty men, physically and mentally, men who started at the bottom and hammered their way to the top by sheer brute strength; they were the spiritual progeny of ancient African chieftains and they built the African Church in America.[8]

## DETERIORATION OF RACE RELATIONS

Turner's prophetic leadership was sorely missed during the turbulent years preceding and following the First World War. Brawley called those years just prior to the war "the Vale of Tears," but the period from 1918 to the Great Depression was no less trying for blacks and their churches, reeling under the impact of massive social and economic changes and increasing white hostility as black migrants made a torrential rush into the cities. The background of the crisis in race relations included unprecedented mob violence and acts of terrorism against black citizens between 1890 and 1914. Thirty-five hundred were known to be the victims of mobs between 1885 and 1915, with 235 lynchings in the year 1892 alone.[9]

In addition to intimidation and murder, the so-called redeemers of the South, relieved of the presence of federal troops in 1877 and encouraged by northern complacency, began to use chicanery and economic reprisals against defenseless black landowners and tenant farmers. The situation in the North was not much better. White industrial workers resented the rising demand of blacks for jobs and equal rights and violently resisted the threat that the black unemployed posed for the lily-white trade unions.

A formidable structure of Jim Crow laws grew up in the South after 1900 and erected new barriers of segregation and discrimination on trains, streetcars, steamboats, and in almost every other area of interracial contact. States and local communities passed legislation prohibiting the races from working together in the same room, using the same entrances, stairways, drinking fountains, and toilets. Blacks were excluded from public institutions such as theaters, auditoriums, parks, and residential neighborhoods. In Baltimore, Atlanta, and other cities all-white and all-black blocks were so designated. In 1909 Mobile passed a curfew law exclusively for black citizens that required them to be off the streets by ten o'clock at night. The journalist Ray Stannard Baker even found that Jim Crow Bibles were being used for black witnesses in the Atlanta courts.[10]

Blacks had enjoyed an abortive participation in politics in the South during Reconstruction. Many of their ministers held offices while pastoring, or had abandoned the pulpit altogether to take up politics. But with the defection of the northern Republicans in the election of

Rutherford Hayes in 1877, the complete disenfranchisement of blacks was rapidly consummated by southern legislatures. By the election of 1912 most states had purged their political systems of black voters and officeholders. Many activists—including Bishop Turner, Reverend T. McCants Steward of Brooklyn, and the radical New York journalist T. T. Fortune—became deeply disillusioned with the conservatism of the party of Lincoln.

In the realm of ideas the popular literature of the period reflected the philosophy of social Darwinism and the pseudo-scientific interpretations of race in Europe by Count de Gobineau and Houston Chamberlain. Theories of the innate inequality of the races, the superiority of Nordic blood in the Anglo-Saxon nations, and the dire necessity of maintaining its purity, were steadily gaining respectability. American racists seized upon these ideas to justify the determination of the South to wipe out the results of the Civil War and return blacks to subservience.

Charles Carroll's *The Negro a Beast* appeared in 1900. In quick succession other works provided the literary and intellectual basis for segregation: William P. Calhoun's *The Caucasian and the Negro* (1902), William B. Smith's *The Color Line* (1905), Robert Shufeldt's *The Negro: A Menace to American Civilization* (1907), and Madison Grant's *The Passing of the Great Race* (1916). White racists used these works and others to arouse public support for stemming the tide of immigration with the Quota Act of 1921 as well as keeping blacks in their places. The enormous popularity of this literature even reached the White House, where Warren G. Harding quoted Lothrop Stoddard's *The Rising Tide of Color Against White World Supremacy* in support of Booker T. Washington's doctrine of social separation. The novelist Thomas Dixon spewed out his antiblack invective in *The Leopard's Spots* in 1902 and *The Klansman* in 1905. Bishop Turner regretted only "that there will be a host of Negroes that will have to spend eternity in hell with Tom Dixon."[11]

The resistance of black leadership to the direction in which the nation was moving was consistent but moderate. Washington's gradualism, while opposed by a few who were not dependent upon his influence for personal advancement, was adopted by most black preachers not only because they lacked the courage to fight back, but because it was consonant with the ethics of the white Christianity by which they were increasingly influenced. The picture of the nonviolent, self-effacing, patiently-suffering white Jesus held up by the conservative evangelicals and revivalists at the turn of the century became for many black preachers the authoritative image of what it is like to be a Christian. That image provided irrefutable confirmation, supported by Scripture, of the wisdom and expediency of Washington's position.[12]

There were many blacks who were not entirely beguiled by this program of religious pacification. They retaliated against marauding whites who invaded their neighborhoods to enforce the codes of white supremacy. In 1917 serious riots broke out in Philadelphia and Chester, Pennsylvania, and in East St. Louis, Illinois, in which scores of blacks lost their lives. Black soldiers returning from France, where they had been decorated for their contribution to the war effort in 1919, refused to accept the injustices they thought they had fought to abolish for all peoples. Many of them were involved in over twenty race riots in the "Red Summer" of 1919. One of the causes of these riots, which found blacks responding with retaliatory violence, was the enormous influx into the cities and the resulting panic of lower-class whites who were terrified and embittered by the new competition for economic and political power.[13]

Although some found it necessary to abandon the pacifism and gradualism their preachers espoused and become more aggressive, most church members drew back from the hard line of Bishop Turner and Robert Charles. Instead they enlisted in church programs for community betterment, cultural enrichment, and only mild opposition to the most destructive aspects of white racism.

As a whole, black Christians eschewed the radical strategies of massive retaliation and confrontation. In commenting upon this characteristic of the black community generally, Nancy Weiss writes:

> The afflicted exercised unusual restraint and self-discipline, engaging in thoroughly polite, deferential opposition. In the second decade of this century, hardly more than a generation removed from the demise of Reconstruction, Negroes were in considerable part an ex-slave population. . . . It is a commonly accepted principle of social science that a submerged group must reach a certain plateau before it can even begin to rebel, and most Negroes of the Wilson era were still struggling toward that level.[14]

That something more than the economic condition of African Americans contributed to the passivity of the postwar years is suggested by the fact that the Niagara Movement, the NAACP, and the denominations exhibiting this "polite, deferential opposition" were not composed of the ragtag, down-and-out blacks who were so submerged economically that they could not mount a more forceful program to improve their situation. These organizations were certainly not to be compared with the mutilated rubber workers of the Belgian Congo who followed the prophet Simon Kimbangu, or the impoverished industrial laborers of South Africa who rallied around Ethiopianism. To the contrary, the leaders and many of the constituents of these primary representatives of organizational life in the black community were members of the new bourgeoisie, lower-class "strivers" who were rapidly gaining sufficient economic security to permit them to begin participation in social reform if an appropriate leader had been presented.

At the turn of the century an increasing number of blacks, particularly light-skinned mulattoes, were artisans and skilled laborers—mechanics, seamstresses, teamsters, barbers, expert domestics. Although they were discriminated against in countless ways, they were able to earn a living and raise families with some semblance of dignity. It was from this rising class, which had begun to move northward and westward after the Civil War and arrived in ever growing numbers in the twentieth century, that the churches, lodges, cultural associations, and the new civil rights organizations, received the bulk of their members.

There were, of course, millions of wretchedly poor blacks, particularly in those areas of the South that suffered most from the ravages of nature and the cyclical depression of the agricultural economy; they were to come to the urban ghettos later on, seeking a better way of life for themselves and their families. But many of them found that those who had preceded them occupied positions of prestige and power in the older institutions and looked down upon them with as much scorn as pity, quietly relegating them to a subordinate position.[15] School teachers, college educators, employees of the federal government, and most of the Northern-based bishops of the three major Methodist bodies were members of this relatively privileged class, which in some respects rivaled the white middle class in elegance and urbanity.

The church was closely related to the founding of the Niagara Movement, the National Urban League, and other organizations for community uplift. But the conclusion must be drawn that the fact that these groups were essentially moderate in their approach to social change had little to do with apathy and low morale. Nancy Weiss argues that the reason for the restraint in the way they dealt with the problems of blacks may be found in a symbiotic relationship to a church that exercised a morally elevating but politically conservative influence on the community organizations with which its members were associated. As Gary Marx has shown, the factors of social class and church membership overlap in their relationship to black militancy.[16] It is difficult to know which has priority, but from what is known about the white church's distrust of social radicalism, it should not surprise us that orthodox Christianity played some role in pacifying black Christians when their churches were trying to imitate the theology and lifestyle of the mainline white denominations.[17]

By the end of the First World War the independent black churches were becoming respectable institutions. Having rejected the nationalism of Turner, they moved more and more toward what was presented by the white churches as the model of authentic Christian faith and life. The dominant influence of clergy in the social betterment and civil rights groups helped to keep these organizations on an accommodationist trajectory.

The NAACP met in many churches immediately after the benediction was pronounced. It used to be a truism in many communities that "the black church is the NAACP on its knees." Few of its meetings opened and closed without prayer. Special deference was always given to the clergy present; it was not strange to hear a hymn or two, and without the volunteer services of church men and women few branches could operate. *Crisis,* the official organ of the NAACP, made church news a regular feature in each issue, and Du Bois, who was its first editor, in 1910, regarded the Council of Bishops of the AME Church as the most powerful and prestigious group of men in black America. He was, nevertheless, critical of the church for not fulfilling its special calling to edify and lead blacks. Thus he wrote in 1918:

> Everybody knows that the Negro church has a large number of disreputable scoundrels in its ministry. Against these venal, immoral men—the indirect heritage of the slave regime—the forces of honesty and uplift in the church are fighting and making gradual headway. But they have not won.[18]

The period of the "Great Migration," which includes the years following the war, had a decisive impact upon the churches. It brought them face to face with a larger number of newcomers than they had ever seen before, thereby straining both their capacity to assimilate the southern style of worship and the meager resources available for expanding their ministries. A propertyless, disoriented proletariat crowded into the northern cities. Many of them were young men and women who had experienced the harshness and degradation of racism in the South and had no great admiration for their oppressors, nor any desire to "be like white folks." That was more likely to be the attitude of the longtime residents of northern communities. These newcomers sought an independent existence, a better way of life. And not a few had already been intrigued with the possibility of emigrating either to Africa, or to some other place where they could spread their wings.

Between 1890 and 1910, the proportion of urban blacks in the United States rose from 20 to 27 percent. Between 1900 and 1910, increases in the black population were notable. Birmingham increased by 215 percent in that period, Atlanta by 45 percent, and New York by 51 percent. Philadelphia and Chicago reported gains of more than 30 percent. Even before the First World War migrants were pouring into other cities, North and South. The census of 1910 recorded over 90,000 each in New York City and Washington, D.C., and more than 80,000 each in New Orleans, Baltimore, and Philadelphia.[19] The city church was practically inundated by this deluge.[20]

The influx began in 1915 and continued in waves through the Second World War. In 1915 disastrous floods in Alabama and Mississippi upset the precarious economy of black farmers. Cotton suffered from the boll weevil. Northern factories advertised for black workers in the pages of the

*Chicago Defender* and dispatched agents to the South to recruit them with promises of unprecedented earnings. Estimates are that in the three years between 1915 and 1918, from 500,000 to 700,000 blacks migrated to the North, and another 360,000 entered the armed forces. It was undoubtedly the most dramatic population shift in American history.

Unlike the earlier "migration of the talented tenth," these wartime migrants were largely poor and uneducated, and had to be assisted in making a rapid adjustment to urban life. This first group of the period became the mass base of the northern churches. Some of their memberships came to be almost entirely composed of persons from one particular rural town or village. Preachers usually followed their flocks, and their members wrote home to entice relatives and neighbors to join them in the "promise land."

Baptist and Methodist congregations received the bulk of these newcomers, and they helped to swell the membership rolls and pay off the debts of the buildings that white congregations had vacated as the strangers flooded their neighborhoods. The black Presbyterian, Episcopal, Congregational, Disciples and Roman Catholic churches—to mention some of the major denominations in the North—were less besieged. Inasmuch as they were composed mainly of upwardly mobile middle-class families, uncomfortable with their rough-hewn brothers and sisters from the South, they became even less inviting and more selective than they had been.[21] However, a second group, a small minority mainly of lighter color, was joining the black congregations of the white denominations, and those churches also grew unprecedentedly after the war.

A third group flowed into the marginal Holiness and Pentecostal churches and the various cults that were spawned during the war years and continued to multiply through the Depression of the 1930s.

Still a fourth group remained outside the churches altogether. They formed the beginning of an expanding segment of the black urban population that was almost totally uninterested in church affiliation.

Migrants, many of them enterprising and resourceful young persons, who entered the major denominations, ascended rapidly toward middle-class status—particularly those in the Methodist Episcopal churches whose ministers tended to be slightly better educated and more acculturated than the Baptist clergy. The leadership of many of these black congregations was frequently the product of Negro colleges that the denominations had developed in the South and were strongholds of the Booker T. Washington doctrine of hard work, frugality, good manners, and in all things moderation. Despite the spirited preaching and emotionalism that such churches increasingly discouraged, the prevailing norms were those of the white Methodists and Baptists of the North: conservative, revivalistic Protestantism.

Joseph R. Washington, Jr., has examined the folk religion of the southern migrants and how it was repressed and transformed by the black churches in the North after the First World War.[22] His central thesis, modified somewhat in later writings, is that the folk religion of the Negro, suffused with a yearning for social justice and bearing the burden of protest and relief, was betrayed by moralistic and dictatorial preachers who had little appreciation for the authentic theology of historic Protestantism. One cannot help but detect the silent ghost of Frazier in this analysis.

According to Washington, the black preacher was isolated from the mainstream of American religious institutions and, ignorant of the authentic heritage of the Reformation, permitted the black church to become little more than a social club involved in meaningless activities and ecclesiastical politics. The irrelevance of the black church, he argued, is due to the curbing of the natural militancy of the folk tradition by the institutional church in the face of the resumption of rigid segregation in the South and increased discrimination in the North following Reconstruction. He writes:

> In that era of decline in the quest for freedom, the Negro minister remained the spokesman for the people with this difference— faced by unsurmountable obstacles, he succumbed to the cajolery and bribery of the white power structure and became its foil. Instead of freedom he preached moralities and emphasized rewards in the life beyond. . . . From this point on, the black contribution lay dormant while the white contribution was active and dominating.[23]

Despite the many difficulties that students of the African American church find in Washington's controversial views on black religion and theology, it cannot be doubted that what he has to say about black folk religion merits careful consideration. Particularly helpful is his analysis of its basic characteristics and what happened when it merged with the accommodating religiosity of black preachers who were poorly educated and convinced that they had to curry favor with whites if blacks were ever to be permitted entrance into the mainstream of American life.

The blame cannot, however, be placed entirely upon the clergy. The push and pull of secularized white urban society permeated the ghetto and drew the best prepared and most enterprising of the migrants irresistibly toward the norms and lifestyles that Frazier described in *Black Bourgeoisie*. The black ministers who may have been deeply troubled about the direction of Bookerism, and who were faced with the necessity of orienting their congregations to the requirements of city life, could not successfully hold back a deradicalization process without breaking with orthodox Christianity, as they understood and believed it. Moreover, the powerful white influence within the early NAACP and other groups with which the churches were allied also drew the community into a comfortable accommodation with the white middle class and mainline Protestantism. The ministers had little choice but to go along with their people if they were to remain within the orbit of acceptable social policy and political behavior. The church was no longer a primarily lower-class institution arbitrating the terms of black existence. It was becoming thoroughly middle-class and marginated.[24]

## MARCUS GARVEY

There was a segment of the black community that did not feel itself under these restraints. It was ripe for the kind of leadership that could transmute the radical impulses of the folk religious tradition, with its attenuated African background, into a way of self-actualization that would bypass the value system of whites and erect an alternative style—a way of lessening the injustices and frustrations of second-class citizenship and poverty through black consciousness and nationalism. That leadership came, first of all, from Marcus Garvey.

Garvey was born August 17, 1887, in Jamaica. His mother and father were members of the Wesleyan Methodist Church, but Garvey was impressed with Roman Catholicism and never lost an early respect for both traditions. Later in life he insisted that his children be baptized in the high-church tradition. As a young man he was tutored by two clergymen, Reverend W. H. Sloely and Reverend P. A. Conahan.[25] He attended church services regularly in Kingston and learned elocution and platform decorum from the various preachers he heard there. At the age of eighteen he was employed as the manager of a printing company and trained young persons in public speaking in his spare time.

Feeling the pull of organizational work, Garvey gave up his job as a printer and after 1910 devoted himself full-time to politics and the publication of his own paper *The Watchman.* For a period he left Jamaica and worked at various positions in Costa Rica, Panama, and Ecuador where he observed the oppressive conditions of blacks and Indians. It was this experience that began to shape his views on economics and black self-development. From South America he traveled to London in 1912 and there became acquainted with many African sailors and students, the seedbed of black disaffection. He worked for a time with Duse Mohammed Ali on the *African Times and Orient Review.*[26]

During those years in London he was introduced to Pan-Africanism and learned of the atrocities and political tyranny in colonial Africa. His wide reading brought him eventually to Booker T. Washington's *Up From Slavery,* and he determined to visit the United States, where he hoped to meet the great founder of Tuskegee Institute and obtain some advice on developing a trade school for Jamaican young men who would subsequently go to Africa as "technical missionaries."

Garvey left England on July 15, 1914, and returned to Jamaica. There he organized the Universal Negro Improvement Association (UNIA) and African Communities League, "with the program of uniting all the Negro peoples of the world into one great body to establish a country and Government absolutely their own."[27] Despite opposition from those who feared what its success might mean for the white minority on the island, he was able to get the association established in Kingston "with the assistance of a Catholic Bishop, the Governor, Sir John Pringle, Reverend William Graham, a Scottish clergyman, and several other white friends."[28]

After corresponding with Washington, he received an invitation to lecture in the United States. By the time he arrived, March 23, 1916, Washington had died, but Garvey traveled throughout the nation lecturing and studying the condition of black Americans. In New York City he organized a division of the UNIA, again meeting opposition—this time from Harlem politicians who tried to take it over, and also from various factions of the West Indian community within and outside of the organization. Such encumbrances only served to increase his popularity. The UNIA grew spectacularly to more than two thousand members.

In August of 1918 Garvey began publication of the *Negro World*, and the incisiveness of his writings and speeches made an instantaneous impression upon the masses of blacks caught up in the poverty and despair of the ghetto. His statistics have been difficult to confirm, but by June 1919, he claimed that the UNIA had reached a membership of over two million. Such a figure may be close to the truth, for there is little doubt that he led the largest and most successful mass movement of blacks in the history of the United States.

The UNIA was an organization of many facets—political, religious, social, recreational, cultural, and economic—serving a wide range of the needs of those who were disappointed with traditional Christianity, bitter about ostracism from the rising black middle class, and looking for a new black savior who could give their lives meaning and direction. The Liberty Halls where Garveyites met for their services were the new churches of the ghetto. The program included Sunday morning worship, afternoon Sunday school, public meetings and forums, dances and concerts. Those in need came to the Liberty Hall to find a job or a rooming house. The unemployed were welcomed by Black Cross nurses who organized soup kitchens and provided temporary housing.[29] The UNIA was in the best tradition of the Free African Societies and the early black church at a time when many mainline black congregations were caught up in institution building for a new middle class.

Garvey fought off his enemies with the ferocity of a tiger. But he constantly pleaded his own innocence and good intentions. He was, he said, a friend of black and white. He meant America no harm. He eschewed communists and "radicals," although he recognized the true meaning of that word for blacks. He preferred to use the language of traditional morality and religion and devoted himself sacrificially to the uplift of his people. It was his claim that the work he was doing would liberate blacks by peacefully removing them from the United States, thus saving the country from miscegenation and a destructive race war. The UNIA was a multipurpose spiritual movement by which this great exodus, under the unchallenged leadership of Garvey, was to be performed. The preamble to its constitution read:

> The Universal Negro Improvement Association and African Communities League is a social, friendly, humanitarian, charitable, educational, institutional, constructive, and expansive society, and is founded by persons, desiring to the utmost to work for the general uplift of the Negro peoples of the world. And the members pledge themselves to do all in their power to conserve the rights of their noble race and to respect the rights of all mankind, believing always in the Brotherhood of Man and the Fatherhood of God. The motto of the organization is: One God! One Aim! One Destiny! Therefore, let justice be done to all mankind, realizing that if the strong oppress the weak confusion and discontent will ever mark the path of men, but with love, faith and charity toward all the reign of peace and plenty will be heralded into the world and the generation of men shall be called Blessed.[30]

Garvey's program combined a tough-minded and accusatory attack upon the enemies of the race with an ethically, constructive, quasi-religious summons to unity and humanitarian service. No leader before him had criticized America so incisively and demonstrated the hopelessness of blacks ever obtaining their rights, while at the same time claiming, "We are not preaching a propaganda of hate against anybody. We love the white man; we love all humanity, because we feel that we cannot live without the other."[31] He argued, therefore, from strength rather than from weakness:

> We ask for nothing more than the rights of 400,000,000 Negroes. We are not seeking, as I said before, to destroy or disrupt the society or the government of other races, but we are determined that 400,000,000 of us shall unite ourselves to free our motherland from the grasp of the invader.... We are determined to unite 400,000,000 Negroes for their own industrial, political, social and religious emancipation.[32]

And yet within the position of strength from which Garvey argued, there was an inherent weakness that he skillfully turned to his advantage. "The Negro," he said, "is dying out.... We are the most careless and indifferent people in the world. We are shiftless and irresponsible." On the one hand, he denounced the unmanliness and groveling of blacks under the heel of white oppressors; on the other, he amazed and angered many by seeking the support of the Ku Klux Klan for the UNIA's "Back to Africa" program. He excoriated blacks for being "Uncle Toms," and at the same time praised them for their loyalty and sacrificial service to the nations of the world that had so misunderstood and misused them.

It was this subtle ambiguity that was intrinsic to Garvey's message—his love-separatism, his paramilitary pacifism, his conservative radicalism—that succeeded in grasping the complexity of black psychology and the situation in the United States, the West Indies, and Africa. It made room for men and women of every level of perceptiveness, temperament, and political aspiration, and confounded his detractors among both the Marxist intellectuals of Harlem and the NAACP. Garvey castigated both of these groups and held them up to ridicule. He wove an intricate yet transparent relationship between civil rights and political responsibility without conceding his primary motive of disengaging blacks from all the nations into which they had been scattered, gathering them again for the reclamation of their homeland.

Despite his repudiation of black politics, "The Declaration of the Rights of the Negro Peoples of the World," adopted at a New York convention in 1920, contains an emphasis upon protesting segregation in places of public accommodation, discrimination in employment, education, "political privileges," and the administration of justice. The declaration demanded that wherever blacks form a community they should have the right "to elect their own representatives to represent them in legislatures, courts of law, or such institutions as may exercise control over that particular community." It declared that all persons should live at peace, but affirmed unequivocally the right of self-defense and recognized that war is inevitable and justified whenever races or nations provoke the ire of peoples by the continual infringement of their rights.

Black ministers were disturbed by Garvey's religion, and yet many thought that his position was basically sound and made sense for blacks. At the Fourth International Convention of Negroes, sponsored in 1924 by the UNIA, the religious question came to the fore:

> When this subject came up, and was thoroughly aired by both Clergy and Laity, the pious and the worldlian, it was decided that, as there are Moslems and other Non-Christians who are Garveyites, it was not wise to declare Christianity the state Religion of the Organization; but by establishing the Temple of God in each heart, and letting our every word and action be motivated from that Source, we could reach a state of inner Serenity so as to enable us to establish on earth the Fatherhood of God and the Brotherhood of Man—a belief which is the basis of recognized

religions. Christians who were not members of a Church, could join the African Orthodox Church; but all Church members should bear this in mind: that God is everywhere, not just in Churches on Sundays; that attendance at Church was for Christian fellowship, and rededication to righteous living.[33]

Many individual ministers—particularly those who were Baptists or leaders of the smaller sects—were Garveyites. Although Garvey was critical of preachers as "so-called leaders of the race" who persuaded their people to postpone the blessings of this life for a future paradise, he did not mount a direct assault upon religion, or upon the black religious establishment.[34] Indeed, he thought of himself as a deeply religious man. "I would rather stand alone," he wrote, "and be framed for the prison a thousand times than deny the [black] religion of my mother— mark you, not the [white] religion—the religion that taught me to be honest and fair to all my fellowmen."[35]

He preached that inasmuch as man was made in the image of God, black persons ought to visualize a black God.[36] His approach to Christianity was pragmatic. "No hungry man," he said, "can be a good Christian. No dirty, naked man can be a good Christian for he is bound to have had wicked thoughts, therefore, it should be the duty of religion to find physical as well as spiritual food for the body of man."[37] His theology centered on a belief that he found in the folk tradition: "God helps those who help themselves." The idea that God works generally through human agencies was clearly in step with the teachings of the nineteenth-century theologians of the mainline black denominations:

> In His directed, inspired prophecy He promised that Ethiopia's day would come, not by the world changing toward us, but by our stretching out our hands to Him. It doesn't mean the mere physical test, but the universal and independent effort to surround ourselves with the full glory of man.[38]

To institutionalize his most radical conception of black religion, Garvey tapped Reverend George Alexander McGuire, an Episcopal priest, to become the chaplain-general of the UNIA in 1920. McGuire was born on the island of Antigua in 1866. After training for the ministry in the Moravian Church he came to New York and thence to Philadelphia, to be tutored for Episcopal orders by Reverend Henry Phillips of the Church of the Crucifixion. After four years in Philadelphia he served a pastorate in Cincinnati, an administrative position in Arkansas, and returned to Philadelphia to study medicine at the Jefferson Medical College. He later returned to Antigua, where for six years he served as rector of the Church of St. Paul. But hearing of Garvey's work, he determined to join him in the United States.[39]

McGuire first gathered a group of dissident black Episcopalians around him and founded the Independent Episcopal Church, but was unable to receive authorization from either the Protestant Episcopal or the Roman Catholic churches. His work with Garvey led him to seek authority for bringing into existence a new denomination. After corresponding with the Most Reverend F. E. J. Lloyd, archbishop and primate of the American Catholic Church, he presided over the organizing convention of the African Orthodox Church, at the Church of the Good Shepherd in New York City, on September 2, 1921. He was consecrated bishop of the new denomination on September 28 by the exarch and metropolitan of the American Catholic Church, the Most Reverend Joseph Rene Vilatte, and enthroned in the cathedral chapel of the Good Shepherd Church.

It is interesting to observe that despite the strong emphasis of Garvey and McGuire on black religion and independency, the Anglo-Catholic orientation of both men required that the African Orthodox Church be authorized and have apostolic succession passed on to its first bishop by a white denomination. Garvey himself had excellent connections in the Roman Catholic Church and carried letters of introduction from the Jamaican church when he first came to New York.[40] The AOC was and continues to be strongly West Indian and high-church in its liturgy. It maintained fraternal relations with the Russian Orthodox Church, and when the General Synod of the Independent Episcopal Church met to become the AOC, an unsuccessful move was made to omit "African" from its name and substitute "Holy."[41] The AOC admitted persons of all races, but according to its constitution "particularly [sought] to reach out and enfold the millions of African descent in both hemispheres."

In 1942 the church reported 30,000 members in the United States and overseas, 239 priests, 5 bishops, the Endich Theological Seminary in New York City, and the George A. McGuire Seminary in Miami. It had weathered a storm of opposition from clergy who objected to McGuire's demand that blacks worship a black Christ by urging them to "erase the white gods from your hearts . . . we must go back to the native church, to our own true God."[42] When that cry went out from New York it may have been muffled in the United States, but was clearly heard from Nigeria to Addis Ababa in black Africa.

At the session of the fourth international convention McGuire advised the audience to name the day when all members of the race would tear down and burn all pictures of the white Madonna and Child, and replace them with a black Madonna and Child. Both Garvey and McGuire were attacked repeatedly by black leaders for these "heretical views," but A. Philip Randolph wryly suggested that the preachers opposed the AOC "out of fear of losing their flocks, since their congregations had been conditioned to white religion and the white Christian God."[43]

The influence of Garveyism among the separatist churches of the Caribbean and Africa deserves considerably more study than has been given to it. The Kitawala movement, for example, grew out of the teachings of the American-based Jehovah's Witnesses and spread throughout southern and central Africa, but it was infused with Garveyite evangelism. In South Africa, the Pan-African Congress and other political groups were in contact with American blacks and adopted aspects of Garveyism. Professor James Thaele, the Basuto president of the Western Cape branch of the African National Congress and a graduate of Lincoln University in Pennsylvania, was a strong advocate of Garveyism, although, unlike Garvey, he turned to communism in 1929.[44] An even more famous graduate of Lincoln, Kwame Nkrumah of Ghana, was to become Garvey's most vigorous supporter in West Africa.

The Rastafari movement in Jamaica recognized Garvey as one of its principal prophets and maintained close connections with the Harlem-based Garveyite Ethiopian World Federation. Rastamen regarded Emperor Haile Selassie of Ethiopia as God. Since the early 1930s they looked forward to a return to Africa, and their passion for emigration outlived both of their heroes—Haile Selassie and Marcus Garvey. In November 1930, when Haile Selassie—also known as Ras Tafari—was crowned emperor, some Jamaicans read the text of Revelation 5:2-5 as the fulfillment of a prophecy attributed to Garvey: "Look to Africa, when a black king shall be crowned, for the day of deliverance is near." It was also said that Garvey believed that his people would be redeemed and return to Africa in the 1960s.[45]

The Rastafari movement, like the former Nation of Islam in the United States, represents an interesting development of a relationship between unreconstructed Garveyism, black folk religion, and political radicalism. It has many ramifications and imitators in a wide range of groups that fall into any one or all three of those categories. A study in Jamaica by Smith, Augier, and Nettleford shows that, in addition to the Rastafarians' belief in Garvey's prophecy, they were also influenced by two early Jamaican preachers who were Ethiopianist Christians—Joseph N. Hibbert and H. Archibald Dunkley. Hibbert formed a body called the Ethiopian Coptic Faith. This group may have been more representative of South African Ethiopianism than of historical Coptic Christianity, although Hibbert instructed his followers from extracts of the *Ethiopic Bible of St. Sosimas.* The early Ras Tafari missions were related both to Hibbert, who preached from the Ethiopian canon, and to Dunkley, who taught his followers from the Authorized Version of the Bible.

Between 1935 and 1940 Leonard P. Howell, the most successful Jamaican preacher at that time, drew the movement toward the so-called Niyabingi Order of Ethiopia and the Congo. After the Italians invaded Ethiopia in 1935, stirring up a storm of anger and public protest in black communities around the world, the *Jamaica Times* reported that the order, over which Haile Selassie was supposed to rule, was dedicated to the overthrow of white domination by a racial war. "This violent note," writes Smith et al., "had already been struck by Howell, and Niyabingi was defined in Jamaica as 'death to black and white oppressors.' Some of those people who worshiped the Emperor and were locally known as 'Ras Tafaris' or 'Rastamen' came to describe themselves as 'Niyamen.' "[46]

## FERMENT IN BLACK RELIGION

The period between 1890 and the Second World War was one of luxuriant growth and proliferation of many forms of black religion in the United States and Africa that challenged the bourgeoisification of the mainline black denominations. Black Holiness and Pentecostalism, arising from southern folk religion pressure-cooked in the teeming ghettos of the North, mixed in fascinating combinations with some of the black consciousness and nationalistic tendencies noted above. Garveyism, as a religious movement, is one of the permutations of these converging and polarizing aspects of black religion and radicalism.[47] Knowledge of black Baptist and Methodist bodies and beliefs suffers from the scholarly neglect of black church history generally, but until recently even less was known about black Holiness and Pentecostal churches and their distinctive contributions to the development of black Christianity in America and overseas. A few studies have shown that these marginal groups grew rapidly from the end of Reconstruction through the Great Depression and made a lasting imprint upon the black lower class.[48] There is increasing evidence that the most direct influence of the black church upon white Christianity may well have come through the black Pentecostal churches that emerged during this period.[49]

### Black Pentecostalism

Black Pentecostalism originated in Los Angeles with W. J. Seymour, a former Baptist preacher who attended a Holiness Bible school run by whites in Houston in 1905 and was convinced that God was repeating the miraculous experiences of Pentecost for a worldwide revival of Christianity. In 1906 Seymour was invited by Reverend Neeley Terry, a black woman preacher of the Nazarenes in Los Angeles, to preach in her pulpit. He arrived in the city with two assistants, J. A. Warren and Lucy P. Farrow, the latter going on to Liberia as a missionary sometime later.

Seymour immediately began to preach from Acts 2:4 that the baptism of the Holy Spirit had to be confirmed by the gift of speaking in tongues.[50] Terry's congregation rejected this as heretical and Seymour was locked out of the church. He then began to meet in private homes, and on April 9, 1906, an unusual display of religious fervor broke out as a result of one of his prayer meetings on Bonnie Brae Street and continued for several days and nights. This was the beginning of an unprecedented development in the history of religion in the United States. Seymour rented an old Methodist church building on Azusa Street, now considered by many Pentecostal historians to be the cradle of Pentecostalism in the present dispensation. The Apostolic Faith movement, organized by William J. Seymour at the Azusa Street revival, began to sweep across the nation, moving from one black community to another. Many white people were drawn into the movement. Today Pentecostals number between twenty-five and thirty million adherents throughout the world.[51]

The British Anglican A. A. Boddy, for many years the leader of British Pentecostalism, writes of the far-flung influence of Seymour's Azusa Street revival:

> It was something very extraordinary, that white pastors from the South were eagerly prepared to go to Los Angeles to the Negroes, to have fellowship with them and to receive through their prayers and intercessions the blessings of the Spirit. And it was still more wonderful that these white pastors went back to the South and reported to the members of their congregations that they had been together with Negroes, that they had prayed in the Spirit and received the same blessings as they.[52]

At first Seymour's Pentecostalism could boast that "the color line was washed away in the blood" of Christ, but that lasted only about two years. Not all black Pentecostals denounced their racial identities as a result of the third blessing. The Church of the Living God (Christian Workers for Fellowship), founded by William Christian in Wrightsville, Arkansas, in 1889, claims 276 congregations and 72,000 members. It can be found in almost every black community of the United States. Its catechism contains the following questions and answers:

Was Jesus a member of the black race?
Yes. Matthew 1.

How do you know?
Because He was in the line of Abraham and David the king.

Is this assertion sufficient proof that Christ came of the black generation?
Yes.

Why?
Because David said he became like a bottle in the smoke. Ps.119:83.

What color was Job?
He was black. Job 30:30.

Who was Moses' wife?
An Ethiopian (or black) woman. Num. 12:1.

What color was Jeremiah?
He said he was black. Jer. 8:21.

Should we make a difference in people because they are black?
No. Jer. 13:23.

Why?
Because it is as natural to be black as the leopard to be spotted. Jer. 13:23.

Triumph the Church and Kingdom of God in Christ, founded by "Father" E. D. Smith in 1897, differentiated between the church militant of the whites and the "peace-loving" church of the blacks. Smith led the denomination until 1920 when he moved to Addis Ababa and never returned. It nevertheless continued to grow from two congregations and only thirty-six members in 1936 to 420 congregations and a membership of 45,000 in 1967.

Hollenweger calls these black Holiness and Pentecostal bodies "the step-children of church history." His study of thirty-one black Pentecostal churches (including ten for which he was unable to find membership statistics or date of origin) reveals that twenty-one churches have a combined membership of 4,411,000. Only five of them were organized prior to 1900; fifteen were organized between 1900 and 1936; one was founded in 1947. The four largest communions in this preliminary study are the House of Prayer for All People, with three million members; C. H. Mason's the Church of God in Christ, which had 30,263 members in 1926 and by 1983 reported more than three million; the Apostolic Overcoming Holy Church of God, with 75,000 members; and William Christian's Church of the Living God, with 72,000 members.

Even if some of these statistics require more documentation than it is usually possible to obtain, any observation of religion in the black community will make it obvious that this movement, begun by Seymour at the beginning of the twentieth century, continues to be one of the most powerful expressions of black faith in the world. It is outstripping the historic black denominations in both membership and influence. Many of these groups were splits from the mainline denominations and represent the judgment of black folk religion upon an established institution which, as Hollenweger remarks, "has too long taken sides with the mighty ones, too long . . . told Black history in white, too long . . . destroyed the spontaneity and musicality of the Black people."

Today in Africa there are more than five thousand separatist church bodies, many of them transplants of black American religious movements dating from the beginning of the present century. Almost all of these African churches began as protest groups within the white mission churches.[53] David Barrett's data suggest that between ten and twenty thousand distinct groupings of renewal or dissidence, successful or unsuccessful, arose within the African churches during the missionary era. This situation is remarkably similar to what has happened in the central cities of the United States and the urban areas of the West Indies during roughly the same period.

The major difference between the African and American phenomena in this regard is that the thousands of "gospel tabernacles," storefront churches, and house churches that appear and disappear unendingly in the heart of the inner city in the United States are more nearly homogeneous in their theologies, rituals, and organizational structures than those in Africa. They are mainly fundamentalist sects of evangelical Protestantism, but with the historic idiosyncracies of the African American folk tradition. In Africa the traditional religions, still very much alive, compete with Christianity for ascendancy and synthesize with it in many exotic variations. The distinctive identity and coherence of African traditional religion greatly exceeds that of black folk religion in the United States in the twentieth century, although both are under extreme external pressures and are constantly changing.

During the colonial period the unsettling heterodoxy of the African separatist churches posed a threat to the political status quo. Many of them, as we have seen, developed as antiwhite, revolutionary movements that yearned for the destruction of the old white-dominated world and the birth of a new world of black power. On the other hand, the storefront sects and cults of the United States have been largely apolitical, or at least politically quiescent, because despite their grievances, blacks are generally more assimilated to the culture and ethos of contemporary American life than were their more alienated brothers and sisters, for example, in South Africa under apartheid.

There have been, however, indications that a similar development of political withdrawal and conservatism has taken place among African independent churches outside of South Africa, particularly since black governments have been established and many dissident religious leaders have accommodated to them. Some black governments, however, have found nonconforming groups no less difficult to handle than the white governments found them to be during the struggle for independence—as demonstrated in recent years by the Jehovah's Witnesses in Zambia.

Similarities and differences between independent churches and sects in black America and those in sub-Sahara Africa have not yet been adequately investigated. There are no empirical studies to show whether or not, or the extent to which, independent religious movements on both sides of the Atlantic are carriers of behavioral tendencies or cognitive motifs fundamental to black religions as such. Joint theological studies interested in such matters were proposed in the 1970s between the All

African Conference of Churches and the National Committee of Black Churchmen in the United States, but organizational problems in both groups precluded implementation. But enough is already known about what Durkheim called "collective representations" and other patterns of belief and practice among impoverished and oppressed peoples to assume wide commonalities in various parts of the world. It remains to be determined whether specific patterns of faith and action have been shaped by the peculiar institutionalization of white racism in both the cultures of the New World and Africa.

The socialization studies of churches such as the Mt. Sinai Holy Church of America, Inc., of Bishop Ida Robinson, the United House of Prayer for All People, and Father Devine's Peace Mission show basic similarities with various prophetic movements in South and Central Africa as described by Sunkler, Oosthuizen, and others.[54] The classification system made by Raymond J. Jones in his studies of black American cults still has value in showing a similarity between them and separatist and independent churches in Africa. Jones's list includes faith healing cults, holiness cults, Islamic cults, Pentecostal cults, spiritualistic cults, and others.

Bishop Ida Robinson's Mt. Sinai Holy Church of America, Inc., was founded in Philadelphia in 1924. It typifies many churches of the ghetto that practice faith healing, foot washing, and extensive female participation.

A similar movement headed by a prophet rather than a prophetess is the United House of Prayer for All People, founded by Bishop Marcelino Manoel de Graca, better known as "Daddy Grace." Daddy Grace came out of the South to develop a sect that raised him to the status of deity for many of his believers—a phenomenon not uncommon among African groups.

Both Robinson's and Grace's sects appear to have grown out of Pentecostal revivalism during the "Great Migration." They are Christian in their theology and provided the migrants to the city with a shouting, dancing religion when many Baptist and Methodist congregations were moving away from the African-based spirituality of the slave church toward a more restrained emotionalism.

Prior to the rise of Black Islam, the best known black American group was Father Devine's Peace Mission. About 1932 a man named George Baker, who was said to have come from one of the sea islands off the South Carolina coast, where African survivals persisted into the present century, opened a mission in Harlem. He had preached for a brief period in Sayville, Long Island, where he operated a lodging house and employment agency.[55] Beginning his work as Major J. Devine, he attracted immediate attention among poor blacks by distributing alms and being regarded as one who had used mysterious powers to cause the death of a white judge who had prosecuted him for disturbing the peace. He became known as God to his followers, and sermons and addresses in his weekly newspaper, *The New Day*, reinforced that belief by reiterating the familiar tenet of American spiritualism—God is everywhere, in everything and everyone.

There was little that was otherworldly about Father Divine's ministry. His disciples were estimated from a few thousand to several million blacks and whites—many of whom he fed, clothed, and housed at minimal or no cost to themselves. The mission practiced a form of ascetic love-communism in which all things were held in common. An extremely rigid morality demanded cleanliness, abstinence from liquor and sex, no profanity, and good citizenship. The movement had more political significance than either Bishop Robinson's or Daddy Grace's churches. Father Divine's followers supported civil rights and social welfare. They were urged to help institute "a plan for a 'righteous government' in which there will be equality for all mankind, with the abolition of such evils as lynching and Jim Crow practices."[56]

### The Church of God

Two other movements of the pre-World War I period that continued to function through the Depression were the Church of God (or Black Jews, not to be confused with the Church of God of Elder Solomon Lightfoot Michaux) and the Moorish Science Temple of America. Both were black consciousness groups, similar in cultural and political orientation, and illustrate the way the liberation motif in black folk religion—when neglected in the historic denominations—surfaces in a quasi-secular guise in Islamic, Judaic, or traditional African religious movements in the United States.

Prophet F. S. Cherry, the leader of the Black Jews, came, like so many of these early leaders, from the South, which he often referred to (with what his followers considered divine license to use profanity) as "a hell of a place." Cherry regarded the white Jew as a "fraud and interloper," and taught his followers, reminiscent of some black preachers of the nineteenth century, that blacks were the true Jews of the Bible. Both the Christian Scriptures and the Talmud were required reading for the prophet's people.

Cherry taught that Jesus was black. During his services he would frequently shout out: "Jesus Christ was a black man and I'm offering fifteen hundred dollars cash to anyone who can produce an authentic likeness of Jesus Christ and show I'm wrong!" He would then wave a picture of the white Christ and ask, "Who the hell is this? Nobody knows! They say it's Jesus! That's a damned lie! Jesus was black!"[57]

The Church of God prohibited secular dancing and other sins of the flesh, but made discretionary concessions to the creeping secularization of the masses by tolerating mild profanity and looking in disfavor upon speaking in tongues. Cherry also encouraged moderate drinking. In his movement, as in other groups such as the Universal Temple of Tranquility of Sufi Abdul Hamid in New York City and the Moorish Science Temple in Chicago, we see the flowering of blackenization and alienation themes originally developed by Bishop Turner and the radicals of the late nineteenth and early twentieth centuries.

These themes were taken up in another, more sophisticated context by the West Indian lawyer H. Sylvester-Williams of Trinidad. Sylvester-Williams convoked the first Pan-African Conference in London in 1900. Under his and Du Bois's auspices the congresses were political rather than religious in their purpose and style, but they were no less reflective of the mystique of blackness and the messianic destiny of black peoples.

The Pan-African Congresses that met under the leadership of such nationalists as Bishop Alexander Walters of the AME Zion Church, Blaise Diagne of Senegal, Sir Casely Hayford of the Gold Coast, and George Padmore of the West Indies, were the intellectual counterpart of the folk tradition's blunt indifference to white values and American cultural imperialism, and its clandestine interest in black pride and power. Although it is true that Pan-Africanism languished in a kind of British and American middle-class reformism until the Fifth Pan-African Congress in October 1945, it finally found the leadership to depart from moderate and ameliorative appeals for participation in the colonial regimes in a subordinate status. Instead, a revolutionary demand was made in Manchester for the outright, absolute independence of African peoples and an expression of Africa's solidarity with persons of color not only in the United States, but also in Vietnam, Indonesia, and India.[58]

The religious dimensions and significance of the struggle for black power and independence were marked by the presence of many black clergymen in Manchester. A petition of mutual support and "cooperation among the various African peoples and their descendants in America" was signed by D. W. Jemison, president of the National Baptist Convention, Inc., W. H. Jernagin, president of the National Sunday School Congress, and Bishop W. J. Walls, of the Second Episcopal District of the AME Zion Church. For a moment the mainstream of black Christianity in the United States was diverted into radical currents by the critical implications of the Second World War and the rising tide of movements for self-determination in both Africa and North America.

While the Black Jews and various sects and cults in the Caribbean continued this emphasis on solidarity with other black peoples, keeping it alive among alienated lower-class persons in the United States and the West Indies, the historic black denominations did not follow Du Bois and Padmore very far along the slippery path of radical black consciousness and Pan-Africanism. The promotion of African independence and the rejection of Anglo-American capitalism and racism were, of course, primarily middle-class and secular. They were fostered not so much by the African American churches as by the intellectuals who supported the *Messenger* in Harlem and the Black Peoples Alliance in the United Kingdom. Since the Second World War these and related causes have been oriented more to the lower classes by various abortive attempts to develop a strong mass movement—the Organization of Afro-American Unity of Malcolm X, the more recent Republic of New Africa, the Black Political Assembly, the African Liberation Support Committee, the Revolutionary Action Movement, and other groups of Marxist activists among black trade unionists.

### The Moorish Science Temples

The nearest religious approach to black consciousness to be expressed consistently in an organized form during the period between the wars was that of the various Moorish American or Islamic groups that grew up around the concept that salvation for blacks lay in the rediscovery of their origin outside America and white Christianity. These groups repudiated the name "Negro," "colored people," and even "black people." They referred to themselves simply as Asiatics, or Moors, and introduced into the traditional stream of black Christian theology an entirely new, non-Western perspective that was to become a tenacious element in the further development of black religion in the United States, offering a powerful attraction to many black youth.

The most significant of these groups was the Moorish Science Temple of America, formed about 1913 by Timothy Drew, a North Carolinian who was born in 1886. Drew came to be known as Noble Drew Ali, the Prophet, and established his first temple in Newark, New Jersey. The movement spread to Detroit, New York City, Philadelphia, Chicago, and numerous southern cities. In many places it existed in a symbiotic relationship with Garveyism. At the height of its popularity the membership may have risen to as many as twenty or thirty thousand persons.[59]

Drew's private study of oriental religions and philosophy gave him a key for dealing with the plight of African Americans. C. Eric Lincoln observes that Drew believed:

> If Negroes could somehow establish an identity with the Oriental peoples, whose religious philosophies either knew nothing of the "curse of Canaan" or found it irrelevant, they might become less susceptible to the everyday hazards of being "everyday-Negroes" in America.[60]

Accordingly, members of the Moorish Science Temples would frequently accost whites on the streets of Newark or Detroit with repressed hostility, show them their "Nationality and Identification Card," on which was imprinted the star and crescent, clasped hands, and the mystical number 7, and demand to be recognized with respect and immunity from the humiliations suffered by mere "Negroes." They were to be regarded as Muslims, "under the Divine Laws of the Holy Koran of Mecca, Love, Truth, Peace, Freedom and Justice," and followers not only of Mohammed, but also of Confucius, Buddha, and Jesus of Nazareth.

The new religion drew adherents from the poor and uneducated who found themselves cast adrift in an unfamiliar urban environment. It drew also from the growing number of restless, inquiring young men and women who were searching for an alternative belief system, greater knowledge and understanding of the world in which they lived, and a more satisfactory way of dealing with the tragic realities of color prejudice in a supposedly free and democratic society. For many of them traditional Christianity was wearing thin with repetitive sermons on loving the neighbor and irrelevant moralisms honored more in the breach than in the observance by those who professed them. The new faith, with its lapel buttons, red fezzes, and identification cards, opened up a whole unexplored and fascinating perspective on "the black race in Babylon" for black youth, new books to read, a new "scientific view" to conjure with, and a new lifestyle in the drab existence of the great industrial centers of the nation.

The Moorish Science Temples fell upon evil days when Noble Drew Ali permitted some of the parasitic denizens of the ghetto to invade the movement and make money from selling herbs, magical charms, and other paraphernalia of the occult that many blacks associated with religious devotion. His mysterious death was attributed to an unsuccessful attempt to purge the temples of racketeers.

The cult split into many smaller groups that scattered to the four winds the fecund seeds of disaffection with the Christian church. Many of these groups continued the practice of changing the names of believers, or attaching "el" or "bey" to their given names as a sign of Asiatic nationality. Other practices, such as dietary observances, abstention from cosmetics and conventional attire, worship on days other than Sunday, asceticism, and the study of esoteric literature, began to take root in the sensational religious life of the black community.

The economic and psychological pressures of the Depression and the brutality of racism drove blacks deeper into themselves for a spiritual reserve with which to survive. Movements such as Father Divine's Peace Mission, Garvey's UNIA, the Ethiopian World Federation, the Black Jews, and various spin-offs of Noble Drew Ali's Moorish Americans began to challenge the mainstream churches, winning more and more members from them as the American situation worsened. By so doing they forced the churches into even greater defensiveness.

## RETREAT OF THE MAINSTREAM CHURCHES

The social gospel movement had invaded a sector of the white church between the wars and found favor among certain educated black clergymen who believed that the first responsibility of the church was to provide a ministry of social service for the needy. A few large urban congregations, such as R. C. Ransom's Institutional AME Church in Chicago, H. H. Proctor's First Congregational Church in Atlanta, and the Abyssinian Baptist Church of Adam Clayton Powell, Sr., in New York, became, in effect, social welfare agencies serving a broad spectrum of the needs of the burgeoning urban populations. By 1919 the Olivet Baptist Church in Chicago, under Dr. L. K. Williams, had a membership of 8,743, forty-two departments and auxiliaries with 512 officers, and employed twenty-four staff persons.[61] The 14,000-member Abyssinian Baptist Church in Harlem, the largest black congregation in the world in its heyday, became internationally famous for its influence in labor relations, politics, housing, child care, and recreation.

These so-called "institutional churches" effectively adapted to the pulse of the cities as blacks arrived from the rural communities of the South and the urbanization and secularization processes accelerated. But other forces were at work that further offset the ability of the older black churches to maintain their hegemony as the ideological leaders and pacemakers of the masses.

In the first place, the number of congregations that had an adequately trained ministry and financial resources necessary for becoming effective community institutions was relatively small. The institutional churches that Woodson describes with such obvious satisfaction were very much in the minority. Several studies written since his book on the history of the black church have shown that, although there were a few large, community-conscious congregations in almost every city where blacks were concentrated, most churches were small, inefficient, and plagued with an inferiority complex in a losing battle to compete with the sects and cults. The problem of paying the minister's salary, meeting regular denominational claims and assessments, and making mortgage payments on old buildings at greatly inflated rates kept these churches in a continuous struggle for mere survival.[62]

The myth that all black preachers drove Cadillacs during the Depression and all black churches had plenty of money belongs to black folklore. The church was characteristically impoverished, paid its clergy less than any professional in the community, and was all but overwhelmed by the anomie and antisocial lifestyles that accompanied the rapid secularization of black life in the metropolis. The situation of the church has not greatly changed since that period.

During the 1920s and 1930s most black churches retained a basically rural orientation and retreated into enclaves of moralistic, revivalistic Christianity by which they tried to fend off the encroaching gloom and pathology of the ghetto. As far as challenging white society, or seeking to mobilize the community against poverty and oppression, most churches were too otherworldly, apathetic, or caught up in institutional maintenance to deal with such issues, even in the good years following the Second World War. The large, social action-oriented, institutional church was always the exception rather than the rule, although it must be acknowledged that it sometimes set the pace for entire neighborhoods or sections of a city.

Another factor contributing to the overall dysfunctionality of the mainline church between the wars is closely related to what has just been said. The extreme proliferation of churches weakened the total impact of black religion in the urban community by reducing the economic and political viability of individual congregations and shattering the institutional solidity of the historic denominations. Rivalry between denominations and congregations, and among elite ministers vying for the most desirable pulpits and preferments—such as powerful national offices and bishoprics—diverted energies and money from self-help and community welfare concerns to ecclesiastical gamesmanship and institutional housekeeping.

By the end of the 1930s, the black community was glutted with churches of every variety and description. In Cincinnati, where blacks comprised 10.6 percent of the total population, their churches accounted for 32 percent of the total. In Detroit and Philadelphia, where the population proportion was 7.7 and 11.3 percent, respectively, black churches comprised 24 percent of the total.[63] The increase in the number of Holiness and Pentecostal denominations and independent congregations of a quasi-Baptist variety swelled the number of worshiping units, scattering the tabernacles and storefront churches alongside the older edifices purchased from fleeing white congregations.

St. Clair Drake and Horace R. Cayton describe the situation in Chicago:

If you wander about a bit of Black Metropolis you will notice that one of the most striking features of the area is the prevalence of churches, numbering some 500. . . . On many of the business streets in the more run-down areas there are scores of "storefront" churches. To the uninitiated, this plethora of churches is no less baffling than the bewildering variety and the colorful extravagance of the names. Nowhere else in Midwest Metropolis could one find, within a stone's throw of one another, a Hebrew Baptist Church, a Baptized Believers' Holiness Church, a Universal Union Independent, a Church of Love and Faith, Spiritual, a Holy Mt. Zion Methodist Episcopal Independent, and a United Pentecostal

Holiness Church. Or a cluster such as St. John's Christian Spiritual, Park Mission African Methodist Episcopal, Philadelphia Baptist, Little Rock Baptist, and the Aryan Full Gospel Mission, Spiritualist.[64]

This scene could be duplicated in New York City, Washington, Birmingham, Miami, Detroit, Los Angeles, and a score of other cities. To a somewhat lesser degree, but with equal diversity, it also obtained in the urban areas of Africa, the Caribbean, and South America. The fact is that religion flourished in black communities everywhere during much of the twenieth century, and blacks, as a rule, clustered in small congregations in response to highly stylized, charismatic religious leadership. They searched for the associative and expressive opportunities denied to them by the segregated institutions of the dominant society.

In the United States the deterioration of the quality of religious life, the stratification of church publics, and the growing irrelevance of Christianity to the real problems of life were inevitable. The Cayton-Warner study during the Depression confirms the assumption that the masses were becoming increasingly disillusioned with the church even though millions participated in it. The popular criticisms among urban blacks were recorded:

(1) Church is a "racket," (2) Too many churches, (3) Churches are too emotional, (4) There's no real religion among the members, (5) Churches are a waste of time and money, (6) Ministers don't practice what they preach, (7) Ministers don't preach against "sin," (8) Church places too much emphasis upon money, (9) Negroes are too religious.[65]

A third factor related to the displacement of the mainstream churches from the center of radical critique and reformation was the rising competition they experienced from secular organizations for the socializing, ideologizing, and political action functions they used to perform for the community. The growth of the number and influence of "social clubs"— small, private groups offering escape from the loneliness and anonymity of city life and a substitute for public recreational activities from which blacks were barred—undermined the church as a melting pot and induction center for entry into the urban milieu. During the 1920s fraternal orders such as the Masons, Elks, and Odd Fellows, with their hyperactive women's auxiliaries, as well as the Greek-letter fraternities and sororities of the new college-educated class, undertook certain functions that had once been the almost exclusive domain of the church. These groups supplied mutual aid in times of crisis—such as unemployment or death—education and cultural development, economic education, orientation to city politics, and an outlet for emotional energy in wearing colorful uniforms, parading on holidays to the accompaniment of bugle and drum corps, and finding personal gratification in many forms of organized social activity.

Lodges and social clubs were frequently related to churches in unofficial ways and transmitted basic religious values to their members who could, thereby, justify their participation in such groups when they might have been at a church meeting. But they were also largely free from the control of the old line preachers and conscious of a responsibility to fill the gap in services caused by the incompetence and moralism of the churches. This was even more true for the NAACP, the National Urban League, and the black trade unions, which carried on the tradition of agitation that was more and more demanded by the upwardly mobile working class.

Scheiner has indicated that one competitor of the church that enjoyed wide appeal was public recreation:

> For the lower classes, who did not participate in organized social activity to the extent of other classes, public amusements were of particular value. A major portion of the recreational and cultural life that centered for many years around the church shifted to the public arena. As the urban black community spread over a wider area and included more people, it offered a market for theaters, cabarets, sports events, and other forms of public amusements.[66]

Thus the church, which throughout most of the nineteenth century had been able to integrate much of the activity of the masses around the core of its own ideology of racial uplift and moral development, now found itself relegated to the periphery of the closed circle that was the segregated black community. From that eccentric and unfamiliar position the church began to offer personal security for older adults—mostly female—of the lower middle class. Its preaching and teaching began to reflect this new status while the center was surrendered to the street people, the cabaret crowd, and the lower class—many of whom were new "strivers," becoming more politically conservative in order to comply with and enjoy the emoluments of white society. At the same time, the intelligentsia, whom Robert A. Bone has called "the second generation of educated Negroes . . . the wayward sons of the rising middle class," identified psychologically with the masses and rebelled openly against the authority and leadership of the church. Langston Hughes, Claude McKay, and Countee Cullen were three eloquent representatives of this class—the "New Negroes" of the Harlem Renaissance—who participated in this revolt. They announced in the incandescent pages of the *Messenger:*

> I am an Iconoclast
> I break the limbs of idols
> And smash the traditions of men.[67]

This was strange, new talk for the black church, and the clergy never quite found a way to respond to it. Although the literati of the renaissance, which included more communities than Harlem, recognized the historic importance of the church and even honored what they considered the primitive religious instinct of blacks reflected in the African-style ritual behavior and jazzy revival meetings, they initiated a thrust into an arena in which the ordinary black church rarely ventured: the arena of white literary society, of interracial social and cultural contacts.

Notwithstanding the "New Negroes'" interest in black roots and the culture of the folk, their association with white socialites and Marxist intellectuals pushed them toward a form of social criticism that was not only foreign to the black church's perspective, but tended to further its isolation within the cocoon of pietism and the "old-time" religion.[68] For the intellectuals, the NAACP activists, and the underclass hipsters of 125th Street in Harlem or South Park in Chicago, the church was simply out of style. Its perception of urban reality was naive and maudlin. Its program for racial progress was fettered by gradualism, middle-class morality, and the requirement that one had to "accept Jesus" by rejecting a world that stubbornly refused to be ignored. Its preachers were regarded, often unfairly, as racketeers and con men who could shout on Sunday morning about being saved and play around with the sisters during the week when the brothers were catching hell on the white man's job for scarcely enough money to pay the rent.

Attacked by both the "nigger on the block," who had abandoned the too exclusive, too unjust God of white Christianity, and by the educated elite of "New Negroes"—who imagined themselves superior to preachers and too sophisticated for religion—many black preachers retreated to what they knew best: preaching hell fire and damnation and raising money. With a few outstanding exceptions, their churches turned inward to satisfy the spiritual hunger of those dispossessed and exploited people who found emotional release from victimization in the ritualism and organizational effervescence of black church life. As one former member commented about this situation to his interviewer:

> I used to be active in the church; I thought we could work out our salvation that way. But I found out better. These Negro preachers are not bothered about the Race—about all they think of is themselves.[69]

The judgment is too harsh and does not take account of the many faithful men and women who tried to make the church face up to the challenges of the times. But the forces unleashed by the Great Migration, the Depression, and two world wars, were more than most of them and their congregations could sustain. They quietly adjusted themselves to what appeared to be an inevitable border guard responsibility. The deradicalization of the black church, like a similar development in the white community, was almost complete by the middle of this century. Although many perceptive observers recognized the unique role it continued to play and its freedom from some of the worst sins of the white church, it could nevertheless be said—with a note of disillusion and nostalgia—that "in relations with the white community [the black church] has been for the most part a defensive and accommodating institution."[70]

In her sympathetic study of black religion in the mid-1950s, Ruby F. Johnston found that traditional religion had significantly declined among blacks in favor of a faith characterized by empirical concerns with practical life. But her analysis concludes with the judgment that the movement of the black church toward the middle-class norms and values of the dominant society alienated it from the blacks with whom it began. She writes:

> In the empirical type of church . . . affinity is seen in the formation of associations of persons of education and money. Internal divisions in the structure of the church promote relegation of traditional Christians or economically insecure groups to an obscure position. Thus men seek new religions.[71]

In the next chapter we turn to one "new religion" of the black community that emerged sometime between the late 1950s and the mid-1960s. It was partly a response of the people to the brokenness and insipidity of the church and nearly transformed it. It may be that this new religion of black power was nothing more than a revival of old themes in the tradition of the folk—particularly the theme of black liberation. Indeed, it was the old-time/new-time religion of Dr. Martin Luther King, Jr., that troubled the surface toleration of life in the ghetto and released those deep-lying spiritual powers from the masses, exemplified in Malcolm X, James Forman, and the radical black churchmen who sought to bring about a renewal of the institutional church as an instrument of black liberation during the 1960s. The dry bones were to be knit together once again by the old grievances against racism, and blacks were to "hear the word of the Lord" from a young seminary-educated warrior, who could hobnob with the great without losing the ability to call forth the soul of the black folk.

## CHAPTER 8

# The Dechristianization
# of Black Radicalism

*Go to church on Sunday,*
*Sleep and nod,*
*Trying to duck the wrath of God,*
*Preachers filling us with pride*
*Telling us what he thinks is right.*
*He must be some kind of stupid nut,*
*Trying to make it real,*
*But compared to what?*

Gene McDaniels

To begin this discussion it is necessary to differentiate between radicalism as it developed in the black community in America after the first organized resistance to slavery, and radicalism as it developed in Europe after the publication of the *Communist Manifesto* in 1848 and the subsequent rise of the Soviet Union and national communist parties. It is also useful to note that a peculiarly American form of radicalism was mobilized in the movement of Populism, which arose among lower-class whites in the United States following Reconstruction and continued to find expression in American socialism and the early trade union movement. Radicalism in the two latter senses was motivated by an intense class consciousness and hatred for bourgeois societies. It projected bold and utopian schemes for the transformation of established political and economic institutions. In communism and syndicalism, radicals attempted to force a transfer of power by means of the violent overthrow of the existing authority of states.

## BLACK RADICALISM

Black radicalism, in contrast to the more classic model usually implied by the term, has been less political, less obsessed with ideology on the grand scale, and somewhat less committed to violence as a revolutionary strategy. From time to time it has flirted with socialist ideas but without submitting to doctrinaire Marxism. At times it has been violent, but without the misanthropic and genocidal tendencies that frequently accompany radical political movements in the West. Black radicalism has certainly fomented revolution, but usually without the anarchistic nihilism and terrorism that have characterized the most extreme forms of fascism and communism, or even some of the strategies of the New Left of the post-civil rights period.

Black radicalism, from the black abolitionists to the Student Non-Violent Coordinating Committee and, with some qualifications, the Black Panther Party, has been different. Basically it has been a home-grown, race-conscious, unsystematic attack on the roots of black misery in American life—racism. In its most extravagant, separatist form—as with Turner and Garvey—it despaired of any possibility of freedom in the United States and called for a return to the African homeland. In its more moderate, integrationist form—as with Douglass, James Weldon Johnson, and Walter White—it was an attack on institutional racism without calling into question the more or less permanent, underlying structures of American society.

Both forms of black radicalism have been penetrated, at one time or another, by Marxism as communists and socialists sought to make black industrial workers the mass base of a revolutionary proletariat after the Fourth World Congress of the Communist International in 1922. But for many reasons that we shall not go into here, communism has not been able to cohere with the indigenous radicalism of black Americans. Among preachers, intellectuals, trade unionists, and social activists generally, the doctrine of dialectical materialism was either rejected or obliged to serve the special interests of the black community at the risk of an embarrassing revisionism that orthodox revolutionaries could not abide.[1]

Although Marcus Garvey sometimes used the term to discredit his opponents, he once defined radicalism as "a label that is always applied to people who are endeavoring to get freedom."[2] For the most part, black Americans have been content to accept that definition, with the understanding that their radicalism has always been justified in Garvey's special sense. They have never permitted themselves to be more than temporarily distracted from the main objective of black freedom. Their experience with the radicalism of the Populists at the turn of the century convinced many leaders that in the final analysis political equality had little to do with shared power in the minds of the white working class—

and less to do with social equality. Just as blacks were used as a buffer zone between contending whites for purposes related to realignments of power—which nonetheless continued to remain in white hands—they would also be used to bring whites together again for the preservation of that power.

Black radicalism, therefore, has been and continues to be a form of protest specific to the black community in its struggle for freedom and a more humane existence. Accordingly, it has been consistent, in terms of objective and style, with the intrinsic meaning of the entire history and culture of the African American community. It has been an adjunct to black Christianity because it was precisely through biblical stories, the Negro spirituals, and the event of the worship of God in their own idiom, that blacks knew the experience of being bound together in the family of a loving Creator and Redeemer who destined them to break the bonds of oppression, to open the doors of the prison, and let the prisoners go free.

That this essentially religious response to reality has mainly been Christian is an accident of history—looked at in one way. It might well have been Judaic or Islamic. It happened that the nations of the Christian West were the ones to enslave Africans on a large scale and separate them from their ancient religions. Indeed, the Christian faith was used by whites as an instrument of control, and its pronouncements about the "brotherhood of man and the fatherhood of God" were perverted to justify the paternalistic domination of all people of color as the "Manifest Destiny" of the superior white race. As Richard Wright wrote in his introduction to *Black Metropolis*: "The apex of white racial ideology was reached when it was assumed that white domination was a God-given right."

Notwithstanding this perversion, the "invisible institution" of black religion and the independent black church discovered something at the core of faith that had been obscured by white Christians: a bias for justice and the liberation of the poor that stood in stark contrast to the benign conservatism of the white church and its sanctification of Euro-American hegemony over the darker races. It was this discovery, aided by conspiratorial white Christians such as Lovejoy and John Brown in this country, and Booth in Africa, that opened up the possibility of an African American radicalism that broke out first in independent churches and religious movements, and gradually worked its way into the most permeable institutions of the black secular community.

Bishop Henry M. Turner was the principal exponent of that genre of radicalism closest to a Christian view of the meaning and destiny of blackness. In a way, he was a voice crying in the wilderness of Negro servility and resignation to the hypocrisy of white Christians. Although rebuffed by the middle-class leadership of his own denomination and unable to persuade the majority of blacks to follow him, he nevertheless represented the heritage of resistance that began with the preacher-led revolts and was reinvigorated during the period of Henry Highland Garnet and the black abolitionists. He preserved in the hearts and minds of the folk an important relationship between black Christianity and a fundamental incompatibility with the prevailing values of a racist society. Turner pointed the way to a unique, blackenized form of the Christian faith that went far beyond anything that had developed out of the African American church thus far—a reinterpreted belief system that was essentially radical in both its analysis of the black condition and its programmatic solution to racism and oppression.

After Turner the mainstream of black radicalism in America split in three directions. The self-consciously Christian stream, which he represented, continued as a marginal excrescence of the church and as a quasi-religious black nationalism in Garveyism and the religio-political sects of the ghetto.

A second stream threw off religious influences altogether and continued as a belligerent and thoroughly secularized black racism, empty of any self-conscious ideological or redemptive significance. It was characterized by cynicism about and hatred of whites and could be found among the sporting and criminal elements of Harlem and other black communities. Many young men and women from this second stream found their way into nationalist groups and into the Islamic sects and cults that nourished their personal resentment and nonconformity.

A third stream arose in support of Du Bois and the Niagara Movement—later in support of the NAACP. Christians were, of course, members of this stream, but it was more ideologically mixed than the first stream. It included not only unchurched members of the black middle class who wanted only to remove the barriers to full participation in society, but also the social radicals and Marxist intellectuals who rallied around A. Philip Randolph's *Messenger* and the National Negro Congress of the late thirties. A part of this third stream overlapped or merged with the second and first groups, but they were the exponents of the avant garde esthetic of the Harlem Renaissance more than political adventurers—an essentially middle-class movement whose identification with the masses was primarily artistic and rhetorical.

This third development, although not entirely dissociated from the churches, moved in a secular direction and found its inspiration not in the apocalyptic vision of a black Christian civilization restoring the ancient glories of Africa, but in the vision of a democratic socialist society, unabashedly interracial, moving toward the realization of the American dream of equality for all. Its primary institutional manifestation was the NAACP—an organization in which the race consciousness of Du Bois was continually modified in favor of the egalitarianism of a few wealthy white integrationists, and finally proscribed altogether. On one flank it fought off black and white Marxists who at first tried to destroy it and then to make it the captive of their program to overthrow the American government. On the other flank, this bourgeois Negro integrationism battled against what it considered the unrealistic pan-Negroism of the ghetto nationalist movements and Garveyism—the main undercurrent of the first stream of black radicalism.

The NAACP's integration and revisionist policy became the dominant social outlook of the black middle class. But of far greater significance for the future were the other two streams of radicalism that have, through the years, maintained a closer relationship with the people. They continued into the late twentieth century as quasi-religious ideologies of cultural nationalism and separatism, repudiating both pro-Marxist and anti-Marxist integrationism, as well as the Christianity of the mainstream churches.

The dechristianization of the first two streams of radicalism began with the frustration and disillusionment of the masses whose hopes were shattered by the crassness and hypocrisy of existence in the great white world of the northern cities. Their alienation is described by the poets and writers—Langston Hughes, Claude McKay, Richard Wright—who, although they belonged to a relatively privileged class of blacks after they became successful, understood what was happening to the masses under the impact of urbanization and the grinding poverty of the great industrial areas. James Baldwin describes the metamorphosis of the migrants in his powerful novel *Go Tell It on the Mountain*, when he makes Elizabeth, in her reverie, reflect upon her lover Richard and his Harlem friends:

> Not one of them ever went to Church—one might scarcely have imagined that they knew that churches existed—they all hourly, daily, in their speech, in their lives, and in their hearts, cursed God. They all seemed to be saying, as Richard, when she once timidly mentioned the love of Jesus, said: "You can tell that puking bastard to kiss my big black ass."[3]

Instead of recoiling in horror at such irreverence, the bottom layer of blacks abandoned in the ghettos would have laughed—bitterly. The old-fashioned pietism was dissolving in the acids of their brutal life in the streets and many, like Richard, were prepared to curse God and die. They were becoming, in the years following the First World War, the most secularized population in America. Bereft of the moral cement and social pressures of the southern rural ethos, deeply disaffected by the unending betrayal of whites, and embittered by the antagonism of the Negro middle class, many newcomers to the city turned their backs on the Christian church. They found psychological security in the close-knit camaraderie of the corner beer gardens where black music wailed and the good times rolled, and one could become wise to the lore of the big city from cut-buddies and boon-coons. No group of immigrants to the American metropolis was more systematically exploited. And no group fought more desperately, and yet more joyfully, to survive.

The "deferred dream" of freedom and equality, and the difficulty of life in the teeming slums of the North, released the lever by which millions of Negroes were coupled to the norms and values of evangelical Protestantism. When they discovered not only that the dream was a nightmare, but that the church—with a few notable exceptions—was generally indifferent to their plight, it was as if a great earthquake had opened up a spiritual crevasse in their lives. Shock waves of disenchantment and unbelief swept the moorings of faith into the abyss. Thus, in her poem "The Sundays of Satin-Legs Smith," the poet Gwendolyn Brooks could write:

> The past of his ancestors lean against
> Him. Crowd him. Fog out his identity.
> Hundreds of hungers mingle with his own,
> Hundreds of voices advise so dexterously
> He quite considers his reactions his,
> Judges he walks most powerfully alone,
> That everything is—simply what it is.[4]

There is probably no place in the world where the Christian church was under a more sustained and demoralizing attack from those who were once on the inside than in the black communities of the United States between the wars. The attack was intensified after 1918. It was led in the 1920s and 1930s by the intelligentsia who identified religion with ignorance and superstition and looked upon preachers as the "lickspittle of their white masters."[5]

Although Garvey avoided a direct confrontation with the church, black nationalist leaders who regard Garveyism as the wellspring of their radicalism have not been sparing in their open criticism of the clergy and their flocks. In Harlem during the mid-1960s a street gang calling itself the "Five Percenters" demanded a minimum of 5 percent of the monthly salaries of ministers in their neighborhoods because "bloodsucking preachers and their churches" were believed to be draining off the wealth of the community and to be making no meaningful contribution to the struggle.[6] In other cities churches that had been unresponsive to community needs were defaced and vandalized. It is likely that more churches would have been destroyed during the ghetto rebellions from 1964 to 1968 had it not been for the new image of the ministry that was projected by clergymen such as Martin Luther King, Jr., Albert Cleage, Tom Skinner, and the active leadership given by some of the younger clergy in the northern cities' liberation movements.

The direct attack on the churches provoked by the Black Manifesto, released in Detroit in April 1969, was, in a sense, the culmination of a growing hostility to religious institutions among young revolutionaries. The fact that the Manifesto addressed itself primarily to "the white churches and synagogues of America" resulted from a last-minute tactical decision to avoid a divisive struggle with preachers and to enlist a certain faction among them to support the Black Economic Development Conference.[7] But there should be no doubt that the Negro church was a secondary target of the attack and was being called upon, like the predominantly white denominations, to make redress for its defection from the cause of liberation and black power.

During the 1960s the Nation of Islam was the most consistent critic of the Negro church. Although millions of blacks continued to attend church, many were secret admirers of Elijah Muhammad's denunciation of the sins of Christianity and, in public meetings with Muslims, were not opposed to giving a sober "Amen" to a biting attack on "chicken-eating nigger preachers." Muslims picketed churches and passed out literature to their members. C. Eric Lincoln reported that such action was not uncommon in many cities and that churches were known to seek police protection against Muslim interlopers. Paraphrasing the Muslim attitude toward Christian ministers, he writes:

> The black Christian preacher is the white man's most effective tool for keeping the so-called Negroes pacified and controlled, for he tells convincing lies against nature as well as against God. . . . The black preacher has taught his people to stand still and turn the other cheek. He urges them to fight on foreign battlefields to save the white man from his enemies; but once home again, they patiently present themselves to be murdered by those they have saved. . . . Thus, in an unholy and unnatural way, the "Negro clergy class is the white man's right hand over the so-called Negroes," and the Black preacher is the greatest hindrance to their progress and equality.[8]

This was not an isolated phenomenon among Muslims in the 1960s and early 1970s. For many years an offensive strategy against black preachers and their churches had been one of the characteristics of various black urban sects and cults. As the largest and most powerful institution in the community, the church presented a formidable obstacle to the takeover and radicalization of the community. And it enjoyed certain emoluments from the white power structure for doing so. Mass leaders, from Marcus Garvey to Huey P. Newton, recognized that the sacrosanct position of the Christian church in American society and the affiliation of blacks with Christianity made it difficult to get them to accept another form of religious belief, even after becoming thoroughly secularized and alienated from the organized churches. It is, however, possible to undermine the authority of the church by discrediting its leadership and proving that its teaching is nothing more than the echo of the white slavemaster who used black preachers to carry out his robbery and exploitation.

The central message of the cults and sects that emerged out of the charisma of Noble Drew Ali and Wallace D. Fard in the 1930s was that Christianity was the white man's religion and that no black can be a Christian without betraying the cause of black dignity and self-determination. The Bible was "a poisoned book" of a "slave religion." Its basic purpose was to teach blacks that a white man named Jesus was God, and that they are supposed to love their oppressors and "turn the other cheek" to brutality so they can go into heaven after a life of hell on earth.

In the pages of the Muslim tabloid *Mr. Muhammad Speaks*, the honored leader of the Nation of Islam reached thousands with a scornful critique of the false teachings of the Christian religion:

> You fear and love [white Christians] though you are even disgraced, beaten and killed by them, from your ministers of their slavery religion . . . down to the lowly ignorant man in the mud. You have made yourselves the most foolish people on earth by loving and following after the ways of the Slavemasters, whom Allah has revealed to me to be none other than real devils, and that their so-called Christianity is not His religion of Jesus or any other prophet of Allah.[9]

Islam, the religion of "peace, justice and equality," was commended to blacks as the faith by which the race could achieve fellowship—for all black persons are Muslims, whether they know it or not, and only their true religion could give them the knowledge and power to stand up to whites. The Muslims invited black Christians to attend their meetings, and so powerful was their threat to the churches of Harlem in 1963 that Reverend Adam Clayton Powell, Jr., pastor of the Abyssinian Baptist Church, began to link his own ministry with them.[10]

There is no evidence that there was widespread defection from the churches into the Nation of Islam, as the Muslims predicted, but since the rise of Islam in the black community churchgoers have often measured what their preachers say about the black condition by what they recognize as the painful truth from the late Malcolm X, Louis Farrakhan, and other Muslim ministers who continue to be heard on some local radio and TV stations. Many blacks who once followed Dr. Martin Luther King, Jr., as at least nominal Christians, joined the Nation of Islam, or changed to Arabic or African names—considering themselves Muslims without formally uniting with a mosque. Only the split between Malcolm X and the Honorable Elijah Muhammad in 1964 and the assassination of Malcolm on February 21, 1965, prevented the movement from making serious inroads into the ranks of organized Christianity.

## DR. MARTIN LUTHER KING, JR.

If the period from the end of the First World War to the middle of the century saw growing disillusionment with the church because of a reactionary traditionalism, it must be said that it was the young Baptist minister Martin Luther King, Jr., who reversed that trend and gave new vitality and relevance to black Christianity in the United States. Black radicalism in the late 1960s found its most conspicuous expression in the highly secularized Black Panther Party which was justifiably suspicious of the churches and their leaders. But King's contribution to the civil rights movement gave the lie to the allegation that black preachers were nothing but Uncle Toms and that Christianity was hopelessly out of tune with the times. Despite the fact that he was never able to muster the full power of the churches behind the movement and received only token support from many of the most prestigious ministers, King nevertheless projected a new image of the church upon the nation and a new awareness of the possibilities inherent in black religion. "The peculiar genius of Martin Luther King," writes Lerone Bennett, "is that he was able to translate religious fervor into social action, thereby creating political leadership under the rubric of his religious ministry . . . under . . . conditions of extreme danger and liability."[11]

Martin Luther King, Jr., came from a long line of Georgia Baptist preachers and was one with them in every respect except education.[12] When he arrived at the Dexter Avenue Baptist Church of Montgomery, Alabama, in 1954, he had earned degrees from Morehouse College in Atlanta and Crozer Theological Seminary—a predominantly white seminary then located in Chester, Pennsylvania—where he graduated at the head of his class in 1951. After Crozer he moved to Boston University where he received the Doctor of Philosophy degree in 1955.

As the son of one of Atlanta's leading ministers, a member of one of the most prominent families in the South, a graduate of a distinguished black college with advanced degrees in systematic theology from white graduate schools in the North, King had everything he would need for a successful if prosaic career as a privileged, pampered minister of a fashionable, middle-class congregation in a capital of the black South. It would have been reasonable to predict that he would remain in Montgomery for a few years, move up to a leading congregation in Birmingham or Atlanta, and after a few years of revival preaching for clergy friends and building up a reputation in the Baptist national conventions, would finally settle down in one of the great pulpits of New York, Los Angeles, or Chicago, with ten-thousand-dollar anniversary gifts, winter vacations in Nassau, and summer travel in Greece, Turkey, and the Holy Land.

As Joseph R. Washington remarked, King had "that Baptist hum which makes what is said only as important as how it is said."[13] He could moan and hoop in the finest black Baptist style and "get down" with the lowliest folk on Sundays, or he could soar to the heights of erudition with complex ideas, an impressive vocabulary, and cultured tones that would please the most highly educated in the congregation. He knew the right persons in black society. He married the right woman— Coretta Scott of Marion, Alabama, a graduate of Antioch College and a voice student at the New England Conservatory of Music. And he had the right credentials, in terms of background and breeding, to have gone as far in black society, which has always included the upper-class clergy and their wives, as he may have desired. All that would have been required was that he avoided getting into trouble with women, the Internal Revenue Service, and southern red-necks.

However, when Mrs. Rosa Parks refused to give up her seat on a city bus on December 1, 1955, and the blacks of Montgomery rose up with a weary acceptance of the inevitable, King knew he could not avoid that ultimate peril of black leadership: trouble with white folks. James Baldwin, who understood this situation well because of his own religious background, writes:

> Until Montgomery, the Negro church, which has always been the place where protest and condemnation could be most vividly artic- ulated, also operated as a kind of sanctuary. The minister who spoke could not hope to effect any objective change in the lives of his hearers, and the people did not expect him to. All they came to find, and all that he could give them, was the sustenance for another day's journey. Now, King could certainly give his congrega- tion that, but he could also give them something more than that, and he had. . . . Once he had accepted the place they had prepared for him, their struggle became absolutely indistinguishable from his own, and took over and controlled his life.[14]

The bus boycott began by agreement among a handful of the city's middle-class blacks and their preachers. The first meeting, which took place in King's church, was opened with devotions by Reverend H. H. Hubbard, president of the Baptist Ministerial Alliance, and was domi- nated, from that point on, by the clergy.[15] But it was the ordinary people of Montgomery—the laborers and domestic workers, "many of them well past middle age, trudging patiently to their jobs and home again, sometimes as much as twelve miles"—who gave it success.[16] It was the people, first in Montgomery and then in more than sixty communities across the South, who rose up together in an almost compulsive response to the call of their preachers—as if following the script of an old, half-remembered scenario that had been played long before, but had fallen into disuse since Emancipation. They defied the laws and tra- ditions of the South to demand the redress of their ancient grievances.

From the winter of 1955 to the winter of the following year, despite insults, physical assault, bombings, and shootings, they walked for freedom. And as they walked millions of their brothers and sisters took new courage and began what was certainly the most remarkable mass movement of nonviolence since the protests led by Gandhi in India during the 1930s.

King had been influenced by the great Indian barrister's concept of *satyagraha,* or truth-force, during his period at Crozer Seminary, after hearing an address by Dr. Mordecai W. Johnson, the president of Howard University, at Fellowship House in Philadelphia.[17] The bedrock of King's philosophy of non-violent resistance was, however, the Sermon on the Mount. He came to believe that Christian love, which did not return evil for evil but would turn the other cheek to the oppressor, was not only valid for individual relationships, but could be "a potent instrument for social and collective transformation." His study of Reinhold Niebuhr, the American neo-orthodox theologian, taught him that there was a radical evil in human societies, and in his doctoral studies in Boston he examined Hegel's analysis of dialectical process and the possibility of growth and reconciliation through struggle and conflict.

These stimulating ideas, honed and polished by Bayard Rustin, an extremely skilled staffer of the Fellowship of Reconciliation who joined King during the early days of Montgomery Improvement Association, provided the scaffolding for the strategy and tactics of his nonviolent direct action as a weapon for racial justice. The substructure was the Christian doctrine of agape—a love that relentlessly pursues its object through suffering and death, ultimately triumphing over enmity by its transcendent and redemptive power. These were the resources of mind and spirit that King appropriated. During his student days he had reserved them against the moment of truth that was to break like a summer storm over Montgomery. In *Stride Toward Freedom,* he recalls:

> When I went to Montgomery as a pastor, I had not the slightest idea that I would later become involved in a crisis in which nonviolent resistance would be applicable. I neither started the protest nor suggested it. I simply responded to the call of the people for a spokesman. When the protest began, my mind, consciously or unconsciously, was driven back to the Sermon on the Mount, with its sublime teachings on love, and to the Gandhian method of nonviolent resistance.[18]

King's effectiveness in those early days of the civil rights movement cannot be attributed solely to the cogency of his ideas about nonviolence as a mode of practical action. The real power of his southern campaign lay in his ability to combine dexterously a simple but profound philosophy with the folk religion and revival techniques of the black Baptist preacher. He was able to elicit from the thousands who flocked to hear him throughout the South the old-fashioned religiosity of the folk, converted into a passion for justice. But the passion for justice was already there. Suppressed by years of subjugation and domesticated by the prudence of a mute and cautious church, it was nevertheless deeply embedded in the religion of the masses. King made the familiar religious language and old biblical images burst into new life.

Lerone Bennett caught the spirit of what happened when King brought from his creative mind gifts new and old for the black peasantry of the South:

> The opening to Gandhi was facilitated by two factors: King's propensity—largely because of his philosophical training and his original choice of himself as a symbolic being—for large ideas and concepts; and the further fact that the movement was already based on the solid rock of the Negro religious tradition. What King did now—and it was a high achievement—was to turn the Negro's rooted faith in the church to social and political account by melding the image of Gandhi and the image of the Negro preacher and by overlaying all with Negro songs and symbols that bypassed cerebral centers and exploded in the well of the Negro psyche.[19]

The people instinctively understood what he was saying. They recognized in his sonorous words and symbolic actions something akin to what they had always believed, or wanted to believe, about Christianity. It was something they had heard their preacher saying—somewhat vaguely—every Sunday, but they had, at some point, ceased to believe that he took it seriously himself.

Between 1955 and 1960 the South experienced a revival of black religion—a revival that did not break out with sawdust trails and mourners' benches, but with picket lines, boycotts, and marches through the downtown sections of scores of southern towns and cities. King, Ralph Abernathy, Fred Shuttleworth, C. K. Steele, Matthew McCollum, J. Metz Rollins, and a hundred other black preachers, most of them still unknown and unsung, were there only as the instruments—sometimes the reluctant instruments—from which the theme of freedom rose like a great crescendo from the depths of the people.

The Southern Christian Leadership Conference (SCLC), which King helped to organize and served as president of in 1957, was dominated by Baptist preachers—aided by a second echelon of middle-class professionals from race relations and social welfare organizations, and a few ministers from other denominations—but its program rested upon the courage, discipline, and determination of the poor blacks of Albany, Danville, Tallahassee, Birmingham, Selma, and many other cities. Some of them were good church people, some were neither good nor church people. They were the marchers who forced the movement into the streets and made their preachers walk at the head of the line singing "We Shall Overcome."

The Montgomery bus boycott resulted in a Supreme Court decision against segregation in public transportation. It stirred up a whirlwind of protest activity in communities throughout the South, and in many other parts of the nation. Ministers, theology students, seminary dropouts, and lay leaders of the churches figured prominently in much of what took place as SCLC affiliates were organized in town after town. Black college students, many of them led by seminarians or preseminarians—John Lewis, Prathia Hall, Charles Sherrod—or sons and daughters of ministers—Leontine Kelly, Maulana Karenga, and Joseph C. Jones, Jr.—pressed the clergy and the adult generation to assume a more militant posture.[20] Student sit-ins broke out in Greensboro, Durham, and Winston-Salem, North Carolina, in 1960, and also in South Carolina, Georgia, Florida, Tennessee, and Texas. By the end of the year, public accommodation facilities had been desegregated by sit-ins in 126 cities. By January 1962 the number of cities had risen to 200.[21]

Out of this student movement, which received its initial inspiration from King, came the Student Non-Violent Coordinating Committee (SNCC). Formed in 1960, SNCC became—with SCLC and the older Congress of Racial Equality—the third national civil rights organization to emerge to the left of the traditional groups—the NAACP and the National Urban League.[22] SNCC soon represented a hard core of militant black and white students and former students who plunged into civil rights field work for subsistence—concentrating largely, after 1960, on voter registration projects in Mississippi and Georgia. Many of its early leaders were middle-class black students from northern as well as southern colleges, who quickly drew around them the poor, unemployed youth of the rural areas who drifted in and out of the program but gave it the flavor of a new populist movement, challenging the traditional leadership of the communities in which they worked.

In its pioneering days SNCC was closely aligned with King and fiercely loyal to him. He was their symbol of new black militancy that clashed with the authoritarian and overly cautious leadership they had known among other adults. But from the beginning there were young persons in the movement who mistrusted the orientation of the ministers. Fired with a social gospel of their own, but one practically devoid of theological content, these students had little confidence in what could be expected from the churches—many of which refused to grant them sanctuary or cooperate with their free-wheeling style of "living off the land" in communal groups and their program of agitation and confrontation. These young warriors sang and prayed when prudence dictated, but they relied much more on organizing and politicizing the masses, and upon a direct and frequently derisive confrontation with southern white power.

Many preachers in the South were impressed with their courage and vaguely identified them with King's church-centered SCLC, but the clergy were not prepared to follow or to regard as Christian any movement in which disrespect for local customs, profanity, and sexual laxity between black and white appeared to be so openly practiced. On their part, the SNCC field workers were increasingly aware that traditional Christian values did not have the same binding power in their movement as in the SCLC and its preacher-led affiliates. Hence, they became more and more hostile to the church and its leaders. One student, during the height of the 1960 protests, voiced what was undoubtedly the sentiment of other young leaders such as James Forman and Robert Moses: "We have been singing and praying for three hundred years. Now is the time we should do something for ourselves."[23]

Despite his close identification with the organized church, King himself became increasingly conscious of the fact that he could not depend upon the majority of ministers and their congregations. With the prominent exception of the National Baptist Convention, Inc., which simply refused to be identified with him, the national black denominations made polite gestures in his direction, but never mounted a strong program that would have thrown their full resources into the struggle. Individual congregations raised a great deal of money for SCLC, many ministers joined the marches, and others offered facilities for mass meetings, food and clothing collection points, "freedom schools" and other purposes. But it must be conceded that the black church in its national institutional form—almost as much as the white church—was more of a sympathetic spectator than a responsible participant in the events that marked the progress of the movement.

King was too loyal a churchman to voice a public complaint about the failure of the denominations to support him. But he did on occasion point out that "too many Negro churches . . . are so absorbed in a future good 'over yonder' that they condition their members to adjust to the present evils 'over here.' "[24]

His general criticism of the defection of organized religion from the cause of racial justice obviously included the black church.[25] The difficulty of getting massive and sustained support from the churches, both black and white, had somewhat to do with the clannishness of the clique of Baptists at the head of SCLC, the jealousies and rivalries of leadership, and the unstructured manner in which these groups worked, which made it awkward for bureaucratic organizations like the national denominations to effect a programmatic integration with them. But the fact remains that King was considered too radical by black as well as white clergymen, and many churches carried on business as usual, Sunday after Sunday, while SCLC and SNCC workers suffered for lack of bail money and program funds, and were harassed, beaten, and jailed throughout the South.

In 1963–64 the situation improved significantly when the National Council of Churches and several member denominations made an unprecedented effort to move to the center of the struggle. Some denominations began to shift to more militant tactics and now gave open support to the movement. The religious community as a whole played an important role in the "Mississippi Summer Program" for increasing voter registrations, the March on Washington, and the lobbying effort leading to the passage of the Civil Rights Act of 1964 and the Voting Rights Act of 1965.[26] But the stated clerk of the United Presbyterian Church and president of the National Council of Churches, Dr. Eugene Carson Blake, said at the Lincoln Memorial during the March on Washington, what everyone knew, "The churches come late. . . ." Perhaps it was too late.

During the early 1960s the teachings of the Black Muslims, the Revolutionary Action Movement (RAM), William Epton's Harlem Progressive Labor Movement, and various local united front groups began to infiltrate the civil rights movement. RAM was organized in the winter of 1963 by supporters of Robert F. Williams, the deposed NAACP leader of Monroe, North Carolina, who advocated organized violence. At the same time, the idea of an all-black political party once again surfaced among left-wing northerners such as William Worthy, a Detroit journalist, and Conrad Lynn, a civil rights attorney. The Freedom Now Party, as the new organization was called, brought together a mixed group of intellectuals, self-styled revolutionaries, black nationalists, Marxists, and civil rights integrationists, and centered mainly in New York and Detroit.[27] The philosophies that flowed out of this group of northern social radicals seeped into the SNCC leadership and gave further momentum to its gradual withdrawal from the ideological commitment of the King-Wilkins-Young coalition.

Finally, in 1963 the New York congressman and Harlem pastor, Adam Clayton Powell, Jr., began to attack the NAACP and, somewhat less vociferously, King himself, for what Powell considered their co-optation by the white liberal establishment. In May 1965 at a Chicago rally Powell spoke of black power as an indispensable ingredient of victory. On May 29, 1966, he declared in a baccalaureate address at Howard University:

> Human rights are God-given. Civil rights are manmade. . . . Our life must be purposed to implement human rights. . . . To demand these God-given rights is to seek black power—the power to build black institutions of splendid achievement.[28]

The Howard address set the radical circles of the North humming with excitement. When Stokely Carmichael of SNCC raised the cry of "black power!" on the James Meredith march between Memphis, Tennessee, and Jackson, Mississippi, in June 1966, the ground had already been prepared for an eruption of black nationalism within the freedom movement. It was nourished now by new revolutionary groups under grassroots leadership that had developed in the northern cities.

A series of devastating ghetto rebellions broke out across the country in the summer of 1964 and continued in succeeding summers through 1968. King and the ministerial leadership of his organization fought back, but without either great enthusiasm or effect. In *Where Do We Go From Here: Chaos or Community?*, King describes the debate he had with Stokely Carmichael, who replaced the former theological student John Lewis as national head of SNCC, and Floyd McKissick, who took over from former clergyman James Farmer as the national director of the Congress of Racial Equality (CORE). The center of gravity was shifting away from a religious orientation. The argument that took place on the march between Memphis and Jackson was symptomatic of the split opening up over the black power issue:

> Sensing this . . . I asked Stokely and Floyd to join me in a frank discussion of the problem. . . . For five long hours I pleaded with the group to abandon the Black Power slogan. . . . Stokely replied by saying that the question of violence versus nonviolence was irrelevant. The real question was the need for black people to consolidate their political and economic resources to achieve power. . . . Floyd insisted that the slogan itself was important. "How can you arouse people to unite around a program without a slogan as a rally cry? Didn't the labor movement have slogans? Haven't we had slogans all along in the freedom movement? What we need is a new slogan with "black" in it.[29]

The reaction within the middle-class, interracial coalition that controlled the civil rights movement was predictable. Dismay over the turn toward black nationalism spread a blanket of gloom over liberal whites in the National Council of Churches and the few denominations that had stepped up their involvement in the movement. Black church leaders such as Dr. Joseph H. Jackson, president of the five-million-member National Baptist Convention, Inc., deplored the trend just as he had deplored King's leadership prior to 1966.[30] Individual pastors who all along had stayed aloof from SCLC and SNCC, preferring the NAACP style of reformist activity through the courts, were more than ever convinced that there were radical, anti-Christian elements, with which the church was incompatible, working within the freedom movement.

By 1965 the northern city riots had unnerved the white denominations and the liberal Jewish community. During the winter of the next

year there were signs that a serious retrenchment in racial justice programs was developing in the white churches and synagogues and that
funds for civil rights groups were diminishing rapidly. King's smashing
attack in 1964 against U.S. military intervention in Vietnam had alienated some of his support. The violent resistance of whites in Cicero,
Illinois, during his ill-fated attempt to consolidate a beachhead in the
North by demonstrating against the housing discrimination in metropolitan Chicago, unmasked once and for all the naked reality of the
white power conspiracy of northern business interests, labor, and big
city machine politics.

The almost indifferent attitude of the urbanized masses of the northern ghettos to King's black Baptist brand of civil rights evangelism was
equally apparent. Thus, in 1967 he began to show signs of lessening his
earlier antagonism to black consciousness. That year he made prepara-
tions for the Poor People's Campaign with "Black Is Beautiful" and Che
Guevara posters plastered on the walls of the SCLC headquarters in
Washington and wondered if the black nationalist groups would join
him for a last-ditch assault on the Johnson administration.[31]

The first National Black Power Conference, which originated with
Powell in 1966, was held in riot-torn Newark, New Jersey, following the
rebellion in July 1967. It was conceived and directed by Chuck Stone,
Powell's legislative assistant, Dr. Nathan Wright, the Episcopal Church's
urban executive in Newark, Omar A. Ahmed and Isaiah Robinson of
New York, and Maulana Ron Karenga of Los Angeles—all of whom were
rising stars in the black power movement and outside of the SCLC orbit.
The conference was a notable success, but King was not present—nor
were Wilkins, Rustin, or Whitney Young.

It was becoming increasingly clear that the nonviolence-espousing
hegemony of the NAACP and religious groups over the black revolution
had fallen out of phase with a new development that was primarily
northern-based, cultural as well as political, self-righteously secular, and
alienated from traditional American values and the quest for black civil
rights. By late 1967 SNCC had completed an alliance with revolutionary
movements outside the United States and was deep into a relationship
with the independence movement in Puerto Rico and with Fidel Castro
in Cuba. Carmichael was the new prophet of a resurgent radicalism,
although he was soon upstaged by his SNCC associate H. Rap Brown,
who was even more committed to breaking out of the moralistic
restraints of the civil rights organizations and the churches.

The black Christian radicalism that the early SNCC had helped to
generate and had made Martin Luther King, Jr., the high priest of the
religion of civil rights was giving way to a somewhat less sanctified, less
clarified, and less American ideology of black power. Someone at a
meeting in Chicago asked Carmichael to move into the North and "help
us get rid of Martin Luther King":

Stokely broke into a smile. The mood of the meeting had shifted, and from that moment on there was no more criticism of Stokely. It became clear that the earlier criticism was something of a ritual. The full love which they all felt for him began to flow through the room, and you could feel it in the air. "We can't be everywhere at once," Stokely answered. "And we don't want to get into a fight with King. We have enough on our hands fighting the Man. Daley would like nothing better than for SNCC to get into a fight with King. That way he could get rid of us both. If you want to get rid of King—or anybody else—it's up to you to get together right here in Chicago. There are enough black people in Chicago to take over—if you get together and get rid of the Uncle Toms."[32]

His voluble detractors notwithstanding, Martin Luther King, Jr., ushered in the era of black power by making black Americans conscious of their ability to change America. He could not maintain dominance over the older Christian tradition, and before his assassination in Memphis on April 4, 1968, he was obliged to share the limelight with the aggressive secularity of Stokely Carmichael and H. Rap Brown. But even more significant than Carmichael or Brown for black power and the dechristianization of black radicalism that King unwittingly initiated was another son of a Baptist preacher. A man called Malcolm X.

## MALCOLM X

Malcolm Little—later to become Malcolm X—was born in Omaha, Nebraska, one of eleven children of a preacher who was an ardent disciple of Marcus Garvey.[33] Malcolm grew up in the ghetto of Lansing, Michigan, where his father met a violent death by whites as a result of his outspoken black consciousness. The family moved from Michigan to New York, where Malcolm learned to "become one of the most depraved parasitical hustlers among New York's eight million people—four million of whom work, and the other four million of whom live off them."[34]

After a brief career in various criminal pursuits, from con games and dope pushing to armed robbery, he was convicted of burglary in Boston and in February 1946, at the age of twenty-one, sentenced to ten years in the Massachusetts State Prison at Charlestown. It was in prison that Malcolm, through correspondence with his family, and later with Elijah Muhammad, learned of a religion that was to change the course of his life and exert a powerful influence on black America.

In his autobiography Malcolm recounts a remarkable ascent from the ignorance of a Harlem hoodlum to the knowledge of a self-made philosopher and prophet. He read everything he could get his hands on and, by the time he was released by the parole board in 1952, had educated himself beyond the limits of any degree he might have earned at the best New England colleges. Later he would tell an audience in London, England:

> . . . my alma mater was books, a good library. Every time I catch a plane, I have with me a book that I want to read—and that's a lot of books these days. If I weren't out here every day battling the white man, I could spend the rest of my life reading. . . . I don't think anybody ever got more out of going to prison than I did. In fact, prison enabled me to study far more intensively than I would have if my life had gone differently and I had attended some college.[35]

Malcolm's extraordinary gifts were quickly recognized by Elijah Muhammad. After a period of recruiting for the Muslims in the bars and poolrooms of Detroit—where he took up residence following release from prison—Malcolm was named assistant minister to Temple Number One of that city in the summer of 1953. His favorite topic for sermons was "Christianity and the horrors of slavery," and with his knowledge of the history of Western civilization, he was able to link slavery and the Christian church in a way that was to become the standard line of the Muslim polemic—an attack virtually irrefutable:

> My brothers and sisters, our white slavemaster's Christian religion has taught us black people here in the wilderness of North America that we will sprout wings when we die and fly up into the sky where God will have for us a special place called heaven. This is white man's Christian religion used to *brainwash* us black people! We have *accepted* it! We have *believed* it! We have *practiced* it! And while we were doing all of that, for himself, this blue-eyed devil has *twisted* his Christianity, to keep his *foot* on our backs . . . to keep our eyes fixed on the pie in the sky and heaven in the hereafter . . . while *he* enjoys *his* heaven right here . . . on *this earth* . . . in *this* life.[36]

Malcolm's most devastating indictment was his analysis of the religious hypocrisy of whites and the function of their religion in the enslavement and subordination of blacks. He never wearied of holding white Christianity up to the ignominy of its failure to make good its promises of peace, freedom, and brotherly love for the whole world. To him the abysmal failure of the church was self-evident. No intelligent man or woman could be persuaded that a faith that had tolerated the hatred and oppression of nonwhite peoples had anything of value to give the world. The spectacle, said Malcolm, of white deacons barring church doors to young civil rights workers who had come to pray for racial justice was more than enough proof that the white man's religion is blasphemously racist and "very close at hand is the *end* of Christianity."

What was the response of the church to this barrage of accusations from the son of a Baptist preacher? C. Eric Lincoln indicates that because of the freedom of the pulpit in most black churches and the openness of black theology to heterodoxy, Muslim ministers were, at first, welcomed and could speak frankly against Christianity in many churches across the nation.[37] More important than the traditional leniency of the black church, however, was the persuasiveness of the Muslim critique. When it was expeditiously modified to refer to *white* Christianity, it commanded the assent of many lower-class black Christians and threatened their ministers with an articulate competition for the loyalty of the people. It was obvious to many ghetto pastors that they would be at a greater disadvantage by refusing to allow Muslims to address their congregations than to admit them and cheerfully acknowledge the truth of what they were saying.

When the Muslims began receiving dramatic notices in the press and "fishing" increased the number of black Christians joining the sect in the 1960s, it became more difficult for Mr. Muhammad's clergy to gain access to black pulpits. In a genial, almost humorous vein, Malcolm stripped black churches of the last shred of dignity by pointing out, as Garvey had done before him, their responsibility for "the Negro's deplorable economic condition," and how preachers conspired with white power structures to keep the people impoverished. A reporter of the *Amsterdam News* heard him at a Los Angeles meeting:

> He said $90,000,000 is spent annually in Los Angeles in upkeeping Negro preachers and churches, while (only) $60,000,000 is spent for houses and furniture combined. . . . Malcolm X then pleaded with the Negro preachers to return to their churches and put their members' money to work "for the members" . . . building factories and supermarkets instead of (more) churches.[38]

The long-range goal of the Muslim movement was to entice persons away from the churches and bring the entire black population into the Nation of Islam. But a certain ambivalence in its operational strategy was forced on it by the massive reality of the organized church. For all its passivity in the face of the needs of the ghetto, the black church still occupied an almost impregnable position. There is evidence that Elijah Muhammad, cognizant of this fact, all but gave up the idea of a frontal assault upon the church and was satisfied, at least temporarily, to work with the churches in the name of racial unity. Appeals for cooperation across religious lines replaced the uncompromising hostility of the earliest years of the movement's development.

After his break with Muhammad in 1964, Malcolm founded the Muslim Mosque, Inc., and announced that it would welcome the participation of all blacks "despite their religious or non-religious beliefs." His association with several preachers—Detroit's Albert B. Cleage, New York's Adam C. Powell and Milton Galamison, Rochester's Franklin Florence—made him realize that there were Christian ministers whose commitment matched his own, and he could not afford to alienate them. It is significant that he organized a new religious movement—the Muslim Mosque, Inc.—before he founded the secular Organization of Afro-American Unity.[39]

Malcolm recognized the historic importance of religion in the lives of blacks and that, if his teaching turned many away from Christianity, they would require some spiritual foundation, a more profound anchorage for faith than was available from a purely secular movement for black solidarity. It is true that he once said "we [Muslims] don't mix our religion with our politics and our economics and our social and civil activities."[40] But that was an interim strategy—a calculated bid to remove the scandal of religious particularity from a group that he hoped would solidify the entire community—Christians, Muslims, and atheists—around the core idea of black liberation. He was too aware of the false dichotomy between the sacred and the profane, and the hypocrisy that dichotomy had produced in white religion. He knew the history of black peoples too well and had seen too much of the influence of religion as a motive force in the black community to discard it, either in his own personal life or as a means of inspiring the masses to adopt Islam as the true faith. Keeping Islam available as an alternative to Christianity provided him with one of his most potent ideological weapons for weaning persons away from the dominant Euro-American values and preparing them for solidarity with other nonwhite cultures around the world.

His assassination in 1965 brought to an end one of the great prophets of black liberation, a man whose influence extended far beyond the borders of the United States—to the Middle East, Africa, and Latin America. It is impossible to calculate the degree to which he would have redirected the course of history had he lived. The revolution he envisioned was primarily secular, but his incisive evaluation of the function of Christianity as an exploitive religion that went hand in hand with Western capitalism, and his understanding of the spiritual quality of an ultimate commitment—the power of the faith that had shaken the foundations of his own life and impelled him to spend himself in the struggle—give him unquestionable standing as a religious leader, if one appreciates the meaning of religion in the black experience.

No brainwashing appropriation of Marxist dogma or of some other purely materialistic philosophy of social change could have awakened the awe-inspiring sense of mission and prophetic gifts that were released in Malcolm X by his conversion to Islam. Even after his discovery of the apostasy of Elijah Muhammad, he cherished the experience of visiting Mecca and the confirmation of his faith that he received from the seers and scholars of his religion who welcomed him as a black brother. "The only true world solution today," he declared, "is governments guided by true religion—of the spirit. Here in race-torn America, I am convinced that the Islam religion is desperately needed, particularly by the American black man."[41]

The truth that he perceived was not only cognitive, but revelational in the deepest sense of that word. His study of Western civilization opened his eyes to the whole demonic structure that had been erected by the per-version of one of the world's great religions. By his own estimate of the depth of that perversion, he came to the conclusion that the distortions of Christian belief and the system of values extrapolated from it could never serve the purpose of restoring personhood and self-respect to blacks. But it was the compulsion of faith, not unrelated to the Bible itself, that caused him to prophesy what had been revealed to him as the judgment of a righteous God upon the unrepented sins of white Western societies:

> I believe that God is giving the world's so-called "Christian" white society its last opportunity to repent and atone for the crime of exploiting and enslaving the world's non-white peoples. It is exactly as when God gave Pharaoh a chance to repent. But Pharaoh persisted in his refusal to give justice to those whom he oppressed. And, we know, God finally destroyed Pharaoh.[42]

Since Malcolm's death, various movements inside and outside the black community have laid claim to his legacy.[43] But that legacy cannot be the exclusive possession of any one group. It belongs to all freedom-loving persons who continue to struggle against racism, neocolonialism, imperialism, and sexism. Malcolm X had a consummate respect for women despite the restrictions under which they lived in the Nation of Islam. His inheritance belongs to secularists and religionists alike, for during his brief lifetime he brought black religion and politics together for the edification and empowerment of the people.

Although he repudiated Christianity, his prophetic ministry con-tributed to the further development of the indigenous black religion that was never exclusively Christian anyway. And what he stood for as an exponent of that black faith—namely, faith in human justice and libera-tion for all—was the continuation of a great tradition of nativistic-messianic religions in the United States, Africa, and the Caribbean. Whatever else black Christianity may be, it is also a part of the tradition that Malcolm shared, and it is precisely for this reason that some black Christians were willing to say in those days, "The God who spoke by the prophets and in the fullness of time by his Son, now speaks to us through Brother Malcolm."[44]

No one outside the church spoke more clearly on the relationship of the faith of blacks to black awareness and empowerment than did Malcolm. His was a polemic directed against white Christianity, but its

real strength was not its negativity and sectarianism, but the demonstration it made of the difference religion could make in the life of a young
Harlem hipster who was bound for self-destruction until—as he wrote—
"every instinct of the ghetto jungle streets, every hustling fox and criminal wolf instinct in me . . . was struck dumb."[45] Its strength was in the
extraordinary insight it gave him into a truth about life that was validated in the experience of every black person, and the courage it gave
him to speak that unvarnished truth. The masses also heard him gladly,
and were purified and ennobled by his words.

## DECHRISTIANIZATION AND RECHRISTIANIZATION

The church, smug in its complacency and hiding behind the facade of
what Nathan Wright called "a honkyfied version of the faith," was forced
to acknowledge that its vision of an integrated, nonviolent America as
the *telos* of powerless love had alienated large numbers of blacks irre-
trievably. That acknowledgement was not to come, as is often the case
with prophets, until after Malcolm's death, and it must be admitted that
it has not yet come to the majority of black Christians in the United
States. But the religio-political legacy of Malcolm X awakened the spirit
of dissidence and rebellion in the black church, and Christianity will
never again find easy acceptance among black peoples without proving
itself worthy of their respect.

Despite the dechristianization process I have described, the separation of black radicalism from Christian roots was never completely
achieved during the 1960s. Even the Muslims were affected by patterns
of church life by former Christian ministers who crossed over into their
ranks with vestiges of their old faith still clinging to their preaching, and
particularly by the fact that these followers of Allah continued to make
an important place for Jesus. In a negative way their anti-Christian dia-
tribe backed them into a grudging esteem for authentic Christianity.[46]

In somewhat the same way, black nationalist groups took cognizance
of the civil rights movement and were affected by it even though they
renounced its goals. Rejecting the idea that blacks could "overcome" as
long as they desired to be integrated into a sick society, the nationalists
regarded every apparent victory within the system as mere tokenism that
simply blinded more persons to the real truth about their condition.
And the fact that the movement was led by a black preacher invited their
contempt. But again the popularity of Martin Luther King, Jr., and the
widespread response of the people to the day-to-day struggle to restrain
the lawlessness and violence of whites, made it impossible to mount a
frontal attack against King and maintain, at the same time, a good relationship with the thousands of average persons who respected him, even
after they lost faith in the efficacy of his strategy.

Moreover, the Muslims did not deny the need for justice and equality in American life. They differed with King and Wilkins over methods and goals. Elijah Muhammad said:

> We have not been opposed to the NAACP's cause for the National Association of the so-called Negroes. Only we feel that the NAACP should have at its head a Black Man, and not a white man . . . and should not at this late date seek integration of the Negroes and Whites. . . . Seeking love and equal recognition among this people is the most foolish and ignorant thing that a Negro leader could do in this late date and it would eventually prove the total destruction of us, as a people.[47]

Nor did the Muslims and other nationalists yield at the attempt of the white press to incite an internecine conflict in black leadership ranks. They were sometimes attacked publicly by black leaders, but more often they avoided public laundering of the movement's dirty linen and reserved their most vitriolic rhetoric for whites. Criticism of King, Wilkins, and Young continued in the relatively closed circle of the left-of-center movements and only occasionally seeped into the public arena. When it did, the exchange was usually sharp and brief.

The relationship between Muslim and Christian leaders, such as King and Abernathy, could be described, for the most part, as a restrained cordiality. Although King rejected what he called hate groups, he secretly admired the way the Muslims "took care of business."[48] On their part, both Malcolm and Muhammad welcomed dialogue with civil rights leaders, and occasionally Muhammad invited them to meet with him at his headquarters in Chicago. Wyatt T. Walker tells how once Malcolm and Martin happened to meet in an airport, and the Muslim leader told King that what he (Malcolm) was doing was actually helping the civil rights movement.[49] Muslim ministers still accept invitations to speak at church-sponsored forums, and although the areas of disagreement are recognized, there is, even more than formerly, fundamental concurrence on the desirability of black unity in the face of the white conspiracy to divide and conquer.

It is important to recognize that the relationship between the dechristianizing tendencies within the nationalist groups and the rechristianizing effect of King was one of both competition and interdependence. It is unlikely that one could have existed without the other. Although Malcolm was a converted Muslim three years before the Montgomery bus boycott, he did not reach the zenith of his ministry until the late 1950s, when the climate of resistance to institutionalized racism had been heated to the boiling point by King's direct action program. Northern blacks were elated over the successes in the South, but frustrated by the difficulty of transforming those victories into anything meaningful for the metropolitan areas of the North. Malcolm found a ready audience in this milieu because northerners were looking for a strategy of involvement more appropriate to their needs and experiences than the marches, rallies, and picketing that were desegregating lunch counters in five-and-dime stores.

Conversely, the international attention and the power of the middle-class coalition King was able to bring together by the time of the March on Washington received considerable impetus from blacks and whites outside the South who had been radicalized by the Muslims and other nationalist groups. King had, of course, already earned his reputation. But during the period 1963–64, resistance to his leadership was rising among those who were listening to Malcolm and beginning to push King toward a more radical posture—if he intended to keep younger blacks on his side. Their aggressive tactics and tougher ideological line also forced the federal government to take King's church-oriented movement more seriously as a desirable alternative to those who would not hesitate to use violence. Thus, pushed from behind by the radical sentiment building up outside SCLC, and pulled forward by his own diagnosis of fundamental issues, King took the offensive against the Vietnam War effort, and moved toward a more political stance in the sanitation worker's strike in Memphis and the Poor People's Campaign in Washington, D.C.

One cannot fully understand the black revolution of the 1960s and what has happened since then without grasping the complementary functions of independence and interdependence between Malcolm and King that bound them together in a dialectic of social action that was at once cultural and political, Christian and non-Christian, separatist and integrationist.[50] They learned from one another and received impelling power from one another. Little has been written about how they reacted to each other in private, or whether or not they were really aware of reciprocal roles in the drama being played out in the black community. But it does seem reasonable that their contributions cannot be evaluated separately with any accuracy.

These two young men, both of whom were struck down by assassins' bullets at the peak of their careers, approached the vocation of black liberation from two different politico-religious perspectives that had been growing silently, side by side, in the rich soil of the black folk tradition. But they shared the nourishment of that tradition together. They received enormous moral and spiritual power by calling forth from each other, perhaps quite unconsciously, the single, full-orbed interpretation of reality that caught hold of, and held in tension, the antinomies of the centuries-old yearning for black humanity and liberation.

The debate in some circles about whether there has ever been anything that could be called radical in the black religious tradition is misguided. What could have been a more radical understanding of America than Malcolm's call for blacks to give up the slave religion of Christianity and discover integrity and fellowship in the worship of Allah? Not only that, but to turn their backs, once and for all, literally and ideologically, on all that America offered or promised? And not only *that*, but joyfully to take up the gun, if it became necessary, to protect themselves and make their freedom secure? And what could have been more radical than King's belief that in twentieth-century America—after two world wars, a disastrous economic depression, and a series of ill-advised imperialistic adventures in Latin America and Southeast Asia—it was possible to make whites become Christian, to make love the operative agent of reconciliation between black and white, rich and poor, segregationist and integrationist? What could have been more radical than, after all the dismal trials and failures, to suppose that the church could become, once again, faithful to its Lord, transform itself into the church of the Sermon on the Mount and the Good Friday crucifixion?

It is no wonder that Harold Cruse could write that "the historically true, native American radicalism is black radicalism."[51] But what Cruse did not understand is that this unique black radicalism has religious roots that lie deep and unseverable in the soul of the black community. His otherwise perceptive analysis of the crisis of all thoughtful African Americans scarcely recognizes the existence of religion in the community. This stark and massive reality must not be overlooked in any examination of what occurred in the world of oppression and struggling people during the twentieth century. The radical faiths of Malcolm and King coalesce in the opaque depths of a black spirituality that is neither Protestant nor Catholic, Christian nor Islamic in its essence, but comprehends and transcends all these ways of believing and worshiping by experiencing God's real presence in the search for justice, by becoming one with God in suffering, struggle, and in the celebration of the liberation of the whole creation.

## CHAPTER 9

# Black Power, Black People, and Theological Renewal

*The message of liberation is the revelation of God as revealed in the incarnation of Jesus Christ. Freedom* IS *the gospel. Jesus is the* LIBERATOR!

National Committee of Black Churchmen, 1969

The civil rights movement began to show signs of serious disability when Martin Luther King, Jr., and the SCLC staff ran afoul of northern white power in the form of the Chicago Board of Realtors and the Daley machine during the long, hot summer of 1966. It managed to rally momentarily in 1967 when, with symptoms of desperation, it turned its attention to Washington, D.C., and the buildup for the Poor People's March. But finally, amid great consternation and confusion, it died with the tragic assassination of King on April 4, 1968. During those three fitful years—1966 through 1968—the African American community in the United States went through a hardening process from which it did not recover during the more placid 1970s, and, indeed, it has not yet quite recovered today.

When the shouts of anger, the sounds of violence, and the weeping died away, when the smoke cleared from the riot-torn streets of Washington and King was temporarily laid to rest on the campus of his beloved Morehouse College, a great and terrible silence settled down on black communities all across the nation. It was as if a dark shadow, as in an eclipse of the sun, was sweeping soundlessly and swiftly across the broad lap of the land—from the black upper-class neighborhoods of southwest Atlanta, across the tarpaper sharecropper shacks of the Mississippi delta, to the lonely, dilapidated rooming houses of the Albina area of Portland, Oregon. African Americans everywhere turned off their radios and television sets and settled back grimly to think in the gathering darkness. What was the meaning of the events just past? What could be made of the last ten or twelve years of the struggle that had claimed so much of the flower of black youth and now, in this swift and terrible way, had snatched away the most beautiful flower of them all—this brilliant, articulate young preacher who called himself a "drum major for justice"?

That rethinking of the black experience in America has not yet ended. It is a continuous process wherever racism persists. But it is now possible, at the end of the century, to assume that the great optimism of the period from the end of the Second World War to the shock wave that went out from Memphis, the city of King's assassination, in 1968, had been consigned that night of April 4 to the custody of an irreversible history, that a new tough-minded skepticism, racial self-interest, and a determination to survive, had slowly taken over black America.

At first there was burning anger, then frustration, and finally deep despair. But the long years of adamantine resistance and suffering had taught lessons that could not be easily forgotten. Those lessons— scarcely remembered during the almost lighthearted days of the Montgomery bus boycott—began to be dredged up from the depths of the collective unconscious of the masses, and the old feeling of having to close ranks, of insularity, and inner-directedness in the face of the overwhelming coercion and repression of the white community generated a new, almost brassy confidence and hope that rested on foundations deeper and firmer than anything white America had ever promised.

It would not again be possible to make African Americans forget who they were, whence they had come, and what were the requirements of true manhood and womanhood in the land soaked with the blood of their martyrs—a land whose majority had betrayed a sacred trust, perhaps for the last time. In community meetings, schools, and churches all over the nation, blacks were singing once again those magnificent words of James Weldon Johnson:

> Lest our feet stray from the places,
>     our God, where we met Thee,
> Lest our hearts, drunk with the wine
>     of the world, we forget Thee,
> Shadowed beneath Thy hand,
> May we forever stand,
> True to our God, true to our native land.

The year after King's death, NCBC held its third annual convocation in Oakland, California, with members of the Black Panther Party and other grassroots organizations, and while drawing from the wellsprings of King's deepest commitment, sounded a new, more radical note about the connection between black faith and black power. For all its now embarrassing insensitivity to the role of black women, a new theological and political challenge to the white church and community arose.

By the faith of our fathers, by the faith of Nat Turner and Denmark Vesey, of Allen and Varick, of Delany, of Garvey and Du Bois and Martin Luther King, Jr., and Malcolm X, and by the grace of God, the NCBC has undertaken, in cooperation with IFCO and BEDC, to call this nation, beginning with the white churches, which have a clear and acknowledged moral responsibility, to the conference table to negotiate in good faith the transfer of power to those segments of society which have been deprived of freedom, justice, and self-determination. It *can* be done. It can be done peacefully. *It must be done*, in any case, or peace, brotherhood, and reconciliation will remain empty, mocking words in an American wasteland of racial hatred and strife.[1]

## THE BLACK POWER MOVEMENT

The development generally described as the black power movement was consolidated and invigorated by the assassination of the one who had, in the hour of the movement's birth, opposed it with all his might. Black power was, in a way, the inevitable and historic response of the community to white perfidy—this time to a series of white backlashes beginning in 1964: the retreat of the federal government from the "War on Poverty" and enforcement of the Civil Rights Act of 1964 and the Voting Rights Act of 1965, the election of Richard M. Nixon in the fall of 1968, and his malicious decision to stamp out black radicalism, religious and secular. These developments were interpreted as clear indications that white America had taken all that it was willing to take of the drive for racial integration, and that it was time for blacks to get themselves together on some other basis than the good feeling of the King era.

Although the black power movement was born on Highway 51, between Memphis, Tennessee, and Jackson, Mississippi, its true home was in the great central cities of the nation's largest metropolitan areas, where there were in excess of twelve million African Americans in 1966, a population that increased by an average growth of over 316,000 through 1985.[2] This was unmistakably, as James Boggs called the American city, "the black man's land."

The most important contribution of the black power concept was the recognition of the crucial importance of the political and economic control of land, and that for those who lived on this increasingly blackenized terrain, which whites had declared, by a plebiscite of feet, unfit for white habitation—retreating to the suburbs—racial integration was an idle dream. Black power meant that only by solidifying their ranks through a new consciousness of history and culture, building political and economic clout and being willing to legitimize group self-interest, even defensive violence if necessary, could African Americans hope to survive the onslaught of repression in the wake of the collapse of white liberalism, and take control of their own future.

It was not that between 1966 and 1968 all African Americans became advocates of a sullen black nationalism. Never have all blacks been the advocates of anything, except the freedom to live and prosper like anyone else. But, in the mid-1960s, despite the white-controlled public polls which pretended to prove the contrary, blacks of all classes shared a general disenchantment with the professed goals of democracy. They took upon themselves a new sophistication about power—about what survival in the United States really required—and embraced a new pride in the strange and wonderful beauty of being black and "letting it all hang out," because the time for playing games with white folks, the time of humiliation and self-delusion, was over and gone forever.

Obedience to the old authoritarian leadership of the great national organizations, with their grand designs of making the nation live up to its ideals, was relegated to somewhere near the bottom of the black agenda. After King's death, highest priority was given to confronting white power in one's own private life and neighborhood or city. Ocean Hill-Brownsville, where a struggle for the control of Brooklyn's public schools took place, became a national symbol of localism and realism as citizens demanded control of all institutions claiming to serve them. New and younger leaders emerged from among the people themselves. They seemed to know, without having to be told, that they were accountable to the masses and could speak for them only when given permission.

From the first black power conference in 1967, meeting against the flickering backdrop of random fires during the closing days of the Newark rebellion, the white press and television news services were astonished at the decision to bar them from press conferences and to prohibit their receiving statements and personal interviews from the conference leaders. Ranks were closing around a new style of black activism. There was a feeling of obduracy and hipness in the air. African Americans had torn away the mask of white superiority and stared into the watery, lackluster eyes behind it to see fear, ignorance, and widespread white demoralization.

At a time when white morale was at its lowest ebb, with white youths running out of the control of their middle-class elders, with white communities reeling from daily exposés of drug abuse and sexual perversion, with a pervasive hopelessness over inflation and the Vietnam War gripping the nation, the black community was charged with a renascence of interest in black history and culture, a sense of pride and power, and a new feeling of identity with Africa and the Third World. It was a strange situation. White liberals bristled with indignation fed more by envy and a feeling of powerlessness than of rectitude. Conservatives made threatening statements about instituting detention laws and concentration camps. And the African American community, for the first time in years, ignored those reactions of the majority and went on getting itself together, planning ghetto economic development, community control, black studies, the rediscovery of black culture, and rapping about black power.

The final stage of the Meredith Mississippi Freedom March in June 1966 saw many black clergy from the North participating. They were, perhaps, less shaken than their brother and sister clergy from the South when the young SNCC workers defied King and invented the slogan of black power on the road between Memphis and Jackson. The northern city riots, which the people called rebellions, and the proliferation of ghetto community organizations in Chicago, Detroit, Philadelphia, New York, and a score of other cities had already heralded the shift toward a more hard-headed, race-conscious ideology.

Many of the ministers who worked within the bureaucracies of the predominantly white churches had been fighting a growing backlash in the Protestant establishment as the style of community organization, promoted by Saul Alinsky and the Industrial Areas Foundation, fell into disfavor and church funds began to be cut off.[3] Benjamin A. Payton, the executive director of the Commission on Religion and Race of the NCC, Edler G. Hawkins, pastor of St. Augustine Presbyterian Church in the Bronx and leader of the black Presbyterian caucus, and other northern Protestant ministers had already foreseen the breakup of the coalition of white middle-class liberals with black church leadership that had supported King and the SCLC since the March on Washington in 1963. The northern city rebellions had cooled down that relationship considerably.

Early in July 1966, Payton called a meeting at the Interchurch Center on the upper westside in Manhattan. It was attended by his associate, Anna Arnold Hedgeman, J. Oscar Lee, the NCC executive for racial and cultural affairs, H.R. Hughes, pastor of the Bethel AME Church in Harlem, and the author. The purpose was to discuss the hysterical reaction of some white clergy to black power, the way the slogan was being distorted by many whites and thoughtlessly bandied about by some blacks, and the obvious inability of SCLC to respond to the new situation. It was agreed that the time had come to mobilize the increasing numbers of radical black clergy in the North for more aggressive leadership in the next phase of the struggle. The group then decided to form an ad hoc group called the National Committee of Negro Churchmen (NCNC) and publish a carefully written statement on black power that would clear the air by clarifying the position of northern church leaders and point to some of the theological implications of the concept.

Within a few days a first draft was prepared by Payton. It was revised and adopted unanimously by a small group that met at the Bethel AME Church. The group pledged to raise $10,000 for a full-page advertisement in the *New York Times* and planned a second organizing meeting of the ad hoc committee at Mother Zion AMEZ Church. Those who formed the nucleus of the new organization, in addition to those who attended the first meeting in Payton's office, included Nathan Wright, an Episcopal urban specialist who later served as chairman of the first National Conference on Black Power, Methodist Bishop Charles F. Golden of Nashville, Reverend Horace Sharper of Newark, Reverend M. L. Wilson, whose Convent Avenue Baptist Church in Harlem became the first headquarters of the organization, and Reverend J. Metz Rollins, a Presbyterian race relations executive, soon to become the first executive director of the National Committee of Negro (later Black) Churchmen.

The black power statement was a signal success. It was published in the July 31, 1966, edition of the *New York Times* and simultaneously in the *Los Angeles Times*, and several other newspapers during the following weeks. It received widespread attention, particularly in black communities at home and abroad. It was the first carefully reasoned, analytical pronouncement on black power to get international publicity. That among its signatories were some of the best known and most powerful black ministers in the nation shocked and disquieted the white leadership of both the church and society. Although it was intended to be read by the masses, its real target was "the leaders of America"—the white ecclesiastical and secular establishments that molded public opinion regarding race relations and had reacted in horror to what it considered the dangerous trend toward lawlessness and "reverse racism" among African Americans. The July 1966 statement declared forthrightly:

> As black men [*sic*] who were long ago forced out of the white church to create and to wield "black power," we fail to understand the emotional quality of the outcry of some clergy against the use of the term today. It is not enough to answer that "integration" is the solution. For it is precisely the nature of the operation of power under some forms of integration which is being challenged. . . . Without . . . capacity to *participate with power*—i.e., to have some organized political and economic strength to really influence people with whom one interacts—integration is not meaningful. . . . We regard as sheer hypocrisy or as a blind and dangerous illusion the view that opposes love to power. Love should be a controlling element in power, but what love opposes is precisely the misuse and abuse of power, not power itself. So long as white churchmen continue to moralize and misinterpret Christian love, so long will justice continue to be subverted in this land.[4]

Despite its call for organizing the masses and the "rebuilding of our cities," the NCNC statement, by every measure, was a moderate document. Although by the standards of the time it read like a radical manifesto, Vincent Harding has correctly observed that it was far from any such thing:

Its definition of black goals was thoroughly American. The church-men repeatedly claimed that black people wanted power, "to par-ticipate more effectively at all levels of the life of the nation." At the same time they condemned programs of either "separation" or "domination," and made a point of referring to America as "our beloved country" and our "beloved homeland."[5]

But it is important to recognize that the theological and political defin-itions of the statement were considerably to the left of most black middle-class organizations and the mainstream black denominations. It placed the signatories in an unapologetic discontinuity with the civil rights move-ment and the interracial reconciliation theme of SCLC and the NAACP.

King had talked a great deal about Christian love, and many liberals rested easy in their compromises because they believed that it was still pos-sible to depend upon the love-of-the-enemy tradition among blacks not to embarrass white friends by putting them in an untenable position with their peers and superiors. The statement's critique of the agape ideal as the motivating force of the freedom movement cast a shadow of doubt across the minds of those who had been comfortable with the idea that the consciences of whites could be appealed to by the redemptive suffer-ing of blacks. The statement warned white America that power, not love, was the matter at issue. "Powerlessness," it declared, "breeds a race of beg-gars. We are faced now with a situation where conscienceless power meets powerless conscience, threatening the very foundations of our nation."

There is no evidence that King took more than a glancing notice of the black power statement or recognized in it a challenge to SCLC's domi-nation of the Christian forces for racial justice. It is significant, however, that some of his close associates in the North and members of SCLC's board of directors were among the signatories. The historic black Methodist denominations and the three major black Baptist conventions followed King in taking no official notice of NCNC. Indeed, one or two of the black denominations came close to repudiating black power.

The NCNC, however, went on to establish its headquarters at the Convent Avenue Baptist Church in Harlem and erected a permanent organizational structure at its first national convocation in Dallas, Texas, in November 1967. Although it was studiously ignored by the official hier-archy of the black churches, the black power pronouncement received enthusiastic support from nationalist groups. Stokely Carmichael quoted freely from it in several speeches around the country.

The National Black Power Conference in Newark, N.J., in 1967, fea-tured a workshop on religion that was well attended by nationalists and dominated by NCNC board members, together with disciples of Maulana Karenga's US—a Los Angeles–based group with a quasi-religious orienta-tion. Floyd McKissick, the national director of CORE, who himself had attempted to articulate a responsible interpretation of black power, entered into conversations with NCNC officials for the purpose of exploring possible areas of cooperation.

Finally, the National Council of Churches and a few white denominations, faced with the revolt of their own African American clergy and lay leadership, found it expedient to give at least tentative recognition to the legitimacy of the concept of black power and counsel white clergy to consider the need for power and self-determination in the African American community.[6] A few white pastors and lay church leaders were sympathetic. Occasionally NCNC spokespersons actually found more acceptance of black power in white than in some middle-class black congregations.

## A CRITICAL TURNING POINT: SEPTEMBER 1967

In September 1967 the NCC Division of Christian Life and Work sponsored a national conference on the urban crisis in America. It was held in Washington, D.C., and brought together black and white church activists and race relations executives from several denominations. The black delegates, many of them members of NCNC, which was still an ad hoc group representing both all-black and predominantly white denominations, insisted in the opening session that the conference be divided into two caucuses, one black and the other white. They further proposed that the caucuses meet separately for most of the three days and come together only for the final plenary session.

This was the first time such a format had been proposed in the history of the ecumenical movement in the United States. The white clergy made a weak remonstrance, but the blacks were firm and uncharacteristically aggressive for a meeting in which most of the whites present were known to be liberal allies. The motion to divide the conference was sustained and the two groups retired to separate rooms, with a strange feeling in the air that something of grave significance was about to happen—not unlike, perhaps, the action of Richard Allen and Absolom Jones in 1787 at St. George's Methodist Church in Philadelphia—and that this decision, in 1967, would be just as irreversible.

The discussions in the two meetings were essentially over the nature and feasibility of interracial alliances. After an agitated closing session the conference finally adjourned with the adoption of a statement prepared by each of the caucuses. The white group had divided in confusion over the issue of separate meetings after ejecting some of its most radical members. Later it was able to draft a statement for the final session. The statement of the black caucus supported black power, advocated the creation of African American caucuses in all predominantly white churches, and called for greater involvement of church bodies in the problems of the cities. The white caucus once again deplored the faithlessness of the white church, but in an unprecedented display of maturity affirmed the position of blacks unequivocally and called upon whites to stop trying to dominate liberal coalitions with African Americans and return to their own communities to deal with white racism.[7]

The Washington conference convened two months prior to the first convocation of the NCNC, which became the National Committee of Black Churchmen (NCBC) in Dallas later that year. There the group committed itself to a program that went beyond the usual pronouncement-making function of interchurch bodies. The rapid development of black consciousness in the churches and the desire of African Americans to organize pressure groups in almost every major denomination, including the Roman Catholic Church, is directly traceable to the Washington conference of the NCC in September 1967. Within a year black clergy caucuses had been established or revitalized (as in the case of the United Presbyterians and the United Church of Christ) in nine national churches, representing more than half of the organized white Protestants in the United States.[8] It was a dramatic demonstration of the influence of the black power movement within the precincts of the American religious establishment. The Washington conference inaugurated an era of confrontation and negotiation between blacks and whites unprecedented in twentieth-century American Christianity.

It should not be doubted that the dynamic for this turn of events in American Christianity came from the outside rather than inside the churches. It was the black folk of Watts, Newark, Detroit, Washington, D.C., and hundreds of other communities across the nation, and the young men and women of SNCC and northern-based nationalist groups, who convinced black ministers that the church was expendable if it proved unwilling to immerse itself in the vortex of the black power movement. It was not difficult to show that the movement was catching on everywhere or that its basic motif was pregnant with moral and religious meaning. African American believers could not evade its magnetic force once the people in the streets took the cause into their own hands.

Although King did not immediately participate in these developments, he gradually became aware of their significance for both the black revolution and the church. During the Poor People's campaign he strengthened his relationship with those black church officials at the Interchurch Center in New York who had led the action that took place at the Crisis in the Nation conference in Washington, D.C. The enormous work load of administering SCLC, organizing opposition to the war in Vietnam, and planning the second march on Washington, prevented King from joining the small group in the northeast that was plotting the course of dissident black Christians and making new contacts with secular black power leaders who were alienated from SCLC.

By late 1967 King was well on the way to a basic shift in his own theological and ideological posture and saw the merit of NCBC's attack on the entrenched power of the white denominations in the NCC. He called upon NCBC leadership for help in training cadres of black clergy in key cities, with a grant from the Ford Foundation, and sent SCLC staff members to NCBC meetings. Some of his closest lieutenants—Hosea Williams, T. Y. Rogers, Wyatt Tee Walker—became members of the New York–based organizations.

When the enemies of Adam Clayton Powell, Jr., succeeded in unseating him from his strategic position in the House of Representatives in January, 1967, the NCBC blasted the "arbitrary and cynical use of power" by the white member of Congress. It called for Powell's reinstatement and a uniform standard of ethics. The ministers argued for a code that would discipline every member of Congress, many of whom not only shared Powell's foibles, but exceeded him in manipulating the system for political favor and personal gain.

In the same year, NCBC announced plans for a National Renewal and Development Corporation to enable the African American community to establish an economic power base by controlling the selection of sites and personnel for urban renewal and community development, under Model Cities and other federal programs. Earlier Dr. Benjamin Payton, the first NCBC national coordinator, had conceived of a program for metropolitan development by government and private industry, calling for a minimum budget of $8.4 billion per year for a five-year period. Payton's plan pre-dated similar proposals by the National Urban League and the A. Philip Randolph Institute. It greatly influenced later NCBC efforts to mobilize a positive national response to radical black power proposals for urban economic redevelopment.

The collapse of Lyndon Johnson's Great Society program and the reluctance of NCC to support black power approaches to the urban crisis eventually forced NCBC to abandon the idea of a Renewal and Development Corporation and Economic Development Bank. The irony did not pass unnoticed in the board of directors that, its pretensions to black power notwithstanding, it had neither the expertise nor financial resources necessary to launch a national ghetto redevelopment scheme without massive private sector and governmental support. Neither would be forthcoming.

The logic of NCBC policies was inescapable although, as Harding's critique of its public statements argues, the group never proved that it was prepared to "find, educate, and mobilize [its] logical constituencies around the positions taken."[9] The day King was assassinated in Memphis, the NCBC board of directors was meeting in Chicago, where it declared support for the Poor People's March on Washington and released an important but much neglected statement to the white denominations. That statement, "Urban Mission in a Time of Crisis," raised serious questions about the mission of white denominations in black communities. It called upon white home missions agencies to surrender their hegemony over urban social welfare institutions and "come to the bargaining table" with African American churches for the transfer of power to those who were the legitimate religious leaders of the community.[10]

A continuing frustration for NCBC during the late 1960s was the problem of encouraging the creation of black caucuses within the predominantly white denominations while simultaneously welding them together under the banner of NCBC. For example, as the Unitarian, Methodist, and Lutheran caucuses received funds for program implementation they began to employ staffs and convene expensive national meetings that diverted much-needed resources that otherwise could have been used to strengthen NCBC. Money was desperately needed for developing a regional structure, but the issue of loyalty to the denomination or to NCBC presented a serious problem. The consequence was the inability of the new interdenominational organization to produce the infrastructure required by a national movement—regional offices, membership drives, fund raising, education and action programs, and the integration of African American lay persons, particularly women, into what continued to be a male clergy-dominated movement. Although several powerful bishops and pastors of key churches were NCBC members, the major African American denominations officially stood aloof and regarded it with suspicion.

In the first place, the NCBC was too closely identified with men and women who were pastors in the white denominations—especially the Methodists, Episcopalians, Presbyterians, and Unitarian-Universalists—whose congregations were largely the upper crust of the black middle class, and whose educational methods and styles of church work were influenced by white norms and standards. Second, the leaders of the black communions were no more willing to permit this new northern-based group of radical church leaders to encroach upon their power and prerogatives than they were prepared to be relegated to a subordinate status in their own communities by Dr. King's southern-based SCLC. Accordingly, many ministers assumed a "wait and see" attitude, keeping eyes and ears open for signals from their bishops and denominational officers.

American Christianity exists, like the society with which it is comfortably integrated, in two worlds—one white and the other black. Because the primary leadership and power of NCBC was in the white rather than the black world, the coolness of the black denominations might have been predicted. Some of that coolness, however, was dissipated by the historic relationship of most black churches to their immediate communities. Although black congregations of the white denominations were caught up in the program activities of their parent bodies, they could not escape responsibilities to their communities. This was recognized by both the official and grassroots black leadership as long as the pastors and congregations appeared to be fighting racism within their own denominational structures. During the 1950s and 1960s blacks in the white churches garnered a few committee memberships and chairs in important boards and agencies. In some churches blacks even acquired an impressive number of top-echelon staff positions. In such cases black power was not just an idle slogan.

Linkages between NCBC and these strategic outposts of power in the white religious establishment made it possible for the organization to continue if not thrive without the wholehearted support of the hierarchy of the black Baptists and African Methodists.[11] The caucuses of the white churches, while enlarging their own domains, were an important political factor in obtaining for NCBC and SCLC access to national and world decision-making bodies—such as the NCC Crisis in the Nation program and the Program to Combat Racism of the World Council of Churches—and in releasing white church funds for the administration of black organizations. For example, J. Metz Rollins of NCBC and Hosea Williams and Andrew Young of SCLC, were employed by funds their respective caucuses helped to get allocated from denominational sources.

Shortly after the creation of the Interreligious Foundation for Community Organization (IFCO) in 1966, a strong black caucus emerged in its interracial board of directors and took control of most of its deliberations.[12] The leaders of IFCO were active members of NCBC and the policies of the two organizations were usually in close agreement. When Lucius Walker, IFCO's director, introduced the idea of a National Black Economic Development Conference, to be convened in Detroit in April 1969, he was acting out of an ideological and institutional framework that had been in place for at least three years. Already in 1966, Benjamin Payton, Albert Cleage of the United Church of Christ, Bryant George of the United Presbyterians, and other clergy who were later instrumental in the formation of IFCO, had given priority to economic development as the next stage of the civil rights struggle. By 1968 NCBC had organized itself into five regional areas and was seeking funds for large-scale regional meetings to discuss the feasibility of church-sponsored economic development under the concept of a national economic development bank. The IFCO National Black Economic Development Conference (BEDC), which convened at Wayne State University in Detroit in April 1969, was a direct outgrowth of trends that had been in the making in black church circles and among mass-based community organizations for several years. But no one anticipated the radical upsurge of black power demands that would issue from this development.

## THE BLACK MANIFESTO

It was inevitable that African American clergy, particularly those from the predominantly white churches, would be deeply implicated in the most important action to come out of the Detroit conference—the

Black Manifesto. To understand why NCBC moved as it did to support the Manifesto, and the essential meaning of the crisis it precipitated, first it is necessary to understand the interlocking membership between the IFCO board and the mission agencies of the churches. Second, it is important to appreciate the central role that a few black clergy and laity played in NCBC, IFCO, and the NCC simultaneously during this period. Third, it needs to be understood that the Wayne State conference was deliberately planned to get maximum input from community organizations outside of, if not totally independent of, the churches.

For the most part, these leadership circles and the crisis of the Black Manifesto in which they were all involved, were outside the life and work of the historic black denominations. What occurred in Detroit, and later at the Riverside Church in New York City, was the culmination of many years of institutionalized racism in the structures of American Protestantism and the Roman Catholic Church. But it was also the curiously ironic consequence of an intricate pattern of good white intentions and bad white strategies, miscalculated power and incompetence, inaction and then overreaction on the part of the liberal establishment of the white churches. Black churches and black religion, as one genre of American religiosity, were drawn into the gravitational field of political and religious forces that were bound to come together for good or ill at some point during the late 1960s. That confluence occurred around the promulgation of a remarkable document called the Black Manifesto at IFCO's Black Economic Development Conference in Detroit on April 26, 1969.

The conference met on the campus of Wayne State from April 25 to 27. It was attended by more than 600 persons from all segments of the African American community, many coming as delegated representatives of ghetto community organizations and local churches. The purpose was to "help coordinate Black economic development and community organization effort, and to give members of the Black community a chance to develop an agenda for total community development."[13] The delegates heard James Boggs, the charismatic Detroit socialist theorist, Robert S. Brown, an economics professor from Fairleigh Dickinson University, Milton Henry, vice-president of the Republic of New Africa, Julian Bond, SNCC activist from Atlanta, Lucius Walker, the executive director of IFCO, and several leading exponents of black power.

In a series of resolutions BEDC rejected "black capitalism" and "minority entrepreneurship" as panaceas of the black condition in America and emphasized land ownership, cooperatives, and mass-based organizations for the political and economic control of urban areas where blacks predominated. It also voted for the continuation of the conference as a clearinghouse of national strategies for economic development. Thus BEDC began a separate existence alongside of NCBC and IFCO, the parent organization that called it into existence.

By far the most significant action to come out of the Detroit meeting happened on the night of April 26. James Forman, the international affairs director of SNCC and one of the architects of its famous Mississippi Project, in which the NCC had participated, presented a Black Manifesto, which he announced as the consensus of the conference.[14] Forman wrote the preamble and had discussed it with several persons, including some of the ministers present, before making it the substance of his address at the April 26 plenary session.

Because of rules of order there were some questions about the parliamentary correctness of the procedure by which the document reached the floor. But on the next day, the chairman, Lucius Walker, declared that the Manifesto had been approved by a vote of 187 to 63, with many abstaining.[15] In any case, Forman's dramatic presentation elicited the enthusiasm and expressed the feeling of most of the grassroots leadership attending the conference. Neither BEDC nor IFCO attempted to rescind or withdraw from the demands that Forman laid down, although some key members of both groups expressed reservations about the "highly inflammatory" nature of the preamble.

The preamble was a caustic indictment of black accommodation and white racism. It called for the identification of black America with Africa and the repudiation of capitalism and imperialism. "We are dedicated," said Forman, "to building a socialist society inside the United States . . . led by Black people . . . concerned about the total humanity of the world." He broadly hinted at the seizure of state power and guerrilla warfare and declared that the control of the conference was being justly seized by virtue of "revolutionary right."

At the same time Forman complimented IFCO, of which he was not a member, for "a magnificent job" and promised its leaders a place in the vanguard movement he envisioned. Lucius Walker, according to one observer, had studiously refrained from recommending a specific agenda for the conference in order that "it would be taken over" by creative grassroots leaders such as Forman who spoke for the people. "The hope was that something like a strategy of action and consensus would emerge from the delegates themselves."[16] Forman was a certified delegate and had a plan of action ready while others drifted in indecision.

Actually, it was the preamble, rather than the plan itself, that caused the greatest alarm and the strongest rebuttal from the white church. Rabbi Marc Tannenbaum, president of IFCO and national director of interreligious affairs for the American Jewish Committee, which subsequently withdrew from IFCO over the Manifesto, complained of its "Marxist-Leninist doctrine" and its acceptance of the "use of force."[17] Edwin H. Tuller, general secretary of the American Baptist Convention, could not agree with "the complete elimination of capitalism" and deplored "the military and guerilla stance taken by Mr. Forman."[18] Although it used the rhetoric of violence, the Manifesto somewhat qualified violence as a tactic by the denial "that [violence] is the road we want to take . . . but let us be very clear that we are not opposed [in principle] to force . . . and violence," and by the final paragraph, which declared, "Our demands are negotiable, but they cannot be minimized."

The main body of the Manifesto's text called for reparations to blacks in the modest sum of five hundred million dollars, to be paid through BEDC by white Protestant and Catholic churches and the Jewish synagogues of America. Repeating the theme that was dealt with more fully in the preamble, the document insisted that the white churches and synagogues are "part and parcel of the system of capitalism." "For the sake of the churches and synagogues," it continued, "we hope that they have the wisdom to understand that these demands are modest and reasonable."

Detailing the purposes for which sums from $10 to $200 million would be spent, the Manifesto listed the following:

— A southern land bank to secure land for black farmers;
— Black-controlled publishing and television facilities;
— Research and training centers for community organization needs and the development of various communication skills for young people;
— Funding of organizations that assist welfare recipients to secure their rights and influence the welfare system;
— Establishment of an International Black Appeal for financing cooperative businesses in the U.S. and Africa;
— Establishment of a National Black Labor Strike and Defense Fund for workers fighting racist employers;
— Establishment of a national black university.

These were to be the first installment on reparations due to African Americans by the United States and its racist religious institutions that participated in and reaped untold benefits from three centuries of uncompensated labor on the part of black men and women slaves. On June 8, in a discussion of these programmatic items, Forman said at St. George Episcopal Church in Manhattan:

Those are basically the uses we are talking about. . . . They are not a total solution [to the race problem in America], but they are a new departure. It's certainly a new departure to the Poverty Program whose funds are sapped up by the politicians making $25,000 to $30,000 a year. It's certainly a new departure to so-called Model Cities, and it is most definitely a new departure to whatever Nixon was going to propose about bringing business into the community, which is really a tax gain, you see, because he is going to give them the same kind of favored status that many other businesses have overseas.[19]

It is clear that the Black Manifesto went far beyond being merely a "new departure" from the Great Society program of the Johnson Administration and the proposals of Richard Nixon for "Black Capitalism." What the Manifesto contained, in fact, was the organizational and communications apparatus for institutionalizing black separatism and power in the United States. It was an almost comprehensive plan for the development of racial pride, solidarity, and self-determination as the first step toward systematic control of the black urban and rural communities—their land, institutions, and human resources.

It is not so much that the demands were new. Many of them had already been suggested by black church leaders. Some of the ideas, for example, the support of the National Welfare Rights Organization, the utilization of black-owned land in the southern states, and the development of research and training centers in community organization skills, had even been worked on by some of the white mission boards that were negotiating with black church strategists. The difference was that the Manifesto combined these programs in the context of black power and Third World revolutionary rhetoric and gave them a new urgency as totalistic approaches to liberation. Forman also backed up his demands with bold and coercive tactics that refused to permit the issues to be side-tracked by the usual bureaucratic procrastination and endless red tape of the religious establishment.

This was precisely the purpose of the confrontation on Sunday morning, May 4, 1969, a few days after the Detroit meeting, when Jim Forman walked down the aisle of Riverside Church in New York City and hurled a series of demands at its minister and congregation. During the ensuing months similar confrontations took place in various parts of the nation and overseas. African American expatriates in Europe took up the reparations issue with American churches in foreign cities and with the World Council of Churches at a crucial meeting in England.[20]

It was the dramatic appearance of Forman at Riverside Church, bearded and brandishing his staff like an Old Testament prophet, that galvanized the attention of the nation and brought a storm of outrage from white clergy and laity. The bold disruption of the Sunday morning worship at Riverside Church, one of the most prestigious congregations in the nation, alienated many liberal whites from the aggressive policies advocated by NCBC. Not a few black church leaders outside the organization also deplored Forman's action as "extreme and sacrilegious." The usually militant *New York Amsterdam News* of Harlem echoed the shocked reaction of the African American establishment with the observation that "busting up church services is not our idea of how to gain any demands, no matter how righteous they may be."

The fact remains, nevertheless, that the tactics used by Forman and BEDC in other cities achieved what years of gentle prodding by church executives and pulpiteers had not been able to achieve—a short circuit of the "business as usual" processes of the churches. The Manifesto sounded an unmistakable note of urgency and determination that sent officials scurrying into emergency meetings at the Interchurch Center at 475 Riverside Drive in New York and in many in other cities across the country.

It is of more than passing interest, in this regard, to note that when Charles Spivey, the ranking African American executive of the NCC after Payton's resignation, Leon Modeste, the executive of the Episcopal Church's Special Program to aid ghetto organizations, and J. Metz Rollins, NCBC's executive director, made an impassioned plea on the Crisis of the Nation Program to the May 1969 meeting of the General Board of the NCC, their addresses were received with polite but cool applause. But the docket was drastically amended in order for the Board to hear Forman repeat the Manifesto demands. Moreover, a committee was hastily formed to take the matter under advisement, and the General Board recorded "its deep appreciation to Mr. James Forman for his presentation of an explanation concerning the Black Manifesto." The Board then instructed its executive committee to bring "the most appropriate course of action that the Council should take on this important matter" to a special meeting on June 23. Hard-line and aggressive action, whatever might be said against it, obviously worked better than standard procedures.

Despite numerous expressions of penitence from denominational headquarters and the National Council of Churches, no major church body actually acknowledged the legitimacy of reparations, or publicly recognized BEDC as a negotiating agent for funding the specific demands made in various communications from Forman. The prophetic challenge thrown down—a modern-day reenactment of Amos before the temple at Bethel—only momentarily perturbed America's three great religious communions. Both black and white Amaziahs arose to defend the establishment. With profuse apologies and hard eyes, white church and synagogue leaders called upon mayors, police officials, private detectives, law firms, and ad hoc defense leagues to restrain this unruly black radical who talked about reparations to African Americans as if he really meant it. Church officials rapidly adjusted the delicate mechanism of their bureaucracies to absorb the impact and then went on with the usual business of being the church. One white commentator correctly observed:

> It was asking a great deal of churchmen and laity to rejoice in the opportunity for moral convolutions. God's choice of a black anti-church, a seemingly atheistic, revolutionary and socialistic mouthpiece, certainly did not make the task easier. Forman brought the judgment of Jeremiah down on the heads of Christians and Jews, who were supposed to respond by welcoming repentance and

embracing a radically new mission likely to turn America's churches upside down. To no one's surprise, the churches thanked God for the challenge and then went about business as usual. Institutional momentum may have been deflected briefly, but observers should not indulge any fantasies about the short or long-term impact of the Black Manifesto.[21]

The roles of IFCO, BEDC, and NCBC in this ecclesiastical brouhaha are matters of some dispute. IFCO and NCBC immediately supported the Manifesto. IFCO, of course, did so at great risk to its preferential position as the inconspicuous channel through which the white churches, against the wishes of some of their constituencies, were funding minority grass-roots community organizations. It paid for its indiscretion with what some hoped would be its life, but IFCO has nine lives and still exists today. NCBC would handle the matter with more aplomb. Its board of directors issued a statement in Atlanta on May 7 that had the intention of putting the organization on record in support of the Manifesto without giving it unqualified endorsement. The issue was whether or not Forman had selected the most strategic programs for meeting the needs of poor people, the specific processes by which his proposals could be implemented, and the viability of BEDC as the agency for negotiating with the complex bureaucracies of the churches. Nevertheless, NCBC clearly affirmed Forman as "a modern-day prophet" and called upon foundations, corporations, and other private sector institutions to join the national denominations in providing "millions of dollars for economic and social development in the Black community."

As the days passed it became increasingly evident that the major problem for the National Committee of Black Churchmen would be with the denominational caucuses. To a greater or lesser degree, all the caucuses supported the Manifesto, but the question was whether they could maintain credibility with their constituencies back home and the officialdom of their respective denominations if they did not force BEDC, Forman's conduit, to filter the demands of the Manifesto through NCBC's machinery rather than through Forman's.

For its part, NCBC—now in a tenuous relationship with the powerful Methodist, Episcopal, and Unitarian black caucuses—urged all caucuses to "unify their efforts of advocacy and implementation of the Manifesto—through coordination provided by the NCBC." It instructed J. Metz Rollins, its executive director, to "immediately begin this coordinating activity."[22]

By the end of May, Forman was closely coordinating his activity with Rollins and NCBC. The Black Economic Development Conference had now become independent of its parent, IFCO, and elected a member of NCBC's board of directors, Calvin Marshall of the AME Zion Church, as its new chairman. When it became apparent to everyone that by this action the line of separation between BEDC and NCBC had practically dissolved, the white churches began to yield to the demands of their caucuses, which had previously been held at bay and given only token recognition. This strategy served to draw the caucuses—fighting for their own lives—away from Forman. It made it possible for the churches to make smaller, indirect grants to BEDC *through* the caucuses without appearing to be caving in to Forman, thereby incurring the wrath of the white laity.

Throughout this period, Forman, completely overwhelmed by the bewildering convolutions of church politics, vacillated between a grudging endorsement of the idea of channeling funds through the caucuses and bitter denunciation of such a plan. In a report to BEDC on June 5, 1969, he related how he had accepted the advice of a group of black Methodists that their caucus would be the best and only acceptable conduit for reparations from the United Methodist Church. But, said Forman, something went wrong:

> Lo and behold, the next meeting when we came to the meeting where we were supposed to present our demands and argue them, we found out that a few well-chosen house niggers inside the Methodist Church who are on the paid staff of the masters inside that shop had agreed to accept a lousy $300,000 with a promise of a million more if the money was given to the Black task force.[23]

The accusation was not entirely correct or fair, but in any case, five days later he issued a memorandum to the steering committee and field staff of BEDC, urging:

> We must work with the staff and laymen of the denominations. We should touch bases with as many of them as possible. They are willing, for the most part, to help, and they can neutralize some of the flak from the local Toms. In addition, they know the church structure and can save us time in research and intelligence.[24]

This last point was the nub of the matter. Ironically, one of the main reasons why Jim Forman was rarely able to negotiate directly with the denominations and had so little success when he did, was his lack of knowledge and experience in dealing with white church structures. Although he was carefully briefed, caucus leaders became convinced that his reckless tactics had failed and that, left to his own devices, he would make it impossible for either BEDC or the caucuses to achieve a victory. They may have erred in this assumption and Schuchter's judgment that the Episcopal caucus and NCBC "prostituted themselves by taking money [which should have gone to BEDC] from the various Protestant denominations and the National Council of Churches" may be accurate. But the situation was more complicated than Schuchter suspected. Forman and Marshall concurred with this procedure as a last resort, and their concurrence made it possible for at least some funds to reach BEDC's coffers.[25]

The caucuses knew the labyrinthine channels of denominational funding better than Forman. They also understood the necessity of meeting some of the needs of their ghetto churches who were the original objects of their mission funding. To have totally evaded that responsibility would have robbed them of credibility with their own local people whom they needed in order to press the more national demands of the Manifesto on white Christians. The weakness in the caucuses' position was not in their playing the role of conduits for reparations while siphoning off some monies to repair their own crumbling defenses, but in their unwillingness or inability to allow themselves to be coordinated by NCBC in order to combine their aggregate strength in a single process of negotiation with funding sources.

Unreconstructed conservatism and a dismal failure of creative imagination are to be blamed for the depressing performance of the denominations in the Manifesto crisis. But most patently revealed are the naivete and vulnerability of black clergy when they are in competition for scarce resources—the lingering, divisive effects of welfare mentality and denominationalism within NCBC. The caucuses helped to bring NCBC into existence in 1967, and they were the advance guard from which a successful attack on racism in the churches had to begin. And yet the controversy taken up by NCBC with the white churches convincingly demonstrates that unless black caucuses are prepared to surrender their autonomy, black ecumenism cannot present a united front for social and political action on a national scale. The dynamic and integrity of the African American religious tradition cannot be sustained without the struggle for justice and liberation through some kind of interdenominational collective like NCBC.

Although black congregations of white denominations do not represent the mainstream of the justice and liberation tradition, they are only slightly marginal to it and have made their own contributions to the struggle over the years. Under the umbrella of a movement like NCBC the black clergy and laity of the predominantly white communions could have become an enormously important factor in the breakthrough of African American religious influence in the United States and the Third World after King's death. Their experience and power position within the executive offices of American Protestantism and, to a lesser degree in Roman Catholicism, gave them a peculiar aptitude for maneuvering within those structures and in national and international ecumenical bodies. They owe no apology for either their existence or political behavior as caucuses, for they and their ancestors have given much to those denominations of which they are a part, and what belongs to those denominations belongs also to them. But whether the black caucuses will ever be able to gain a more influential posture within American Christianity depends in large measure upon their rapprochement with the historic black churches, which in the 1990s showed no inclination to invite them to join the Congress of National Black Churches (CNBC). The future of the caucuses depends also upon their ability to come together in a new theological praxis that involves other ethnic caucuses and the grassroots of their respective denominations.

The Black Manifesto controversy illuminated, even more than the civil rights movement, the contours of America's civil religion. If it did nothing else, it spurred the formation of an ecumenical response on the part of African Americans to the religion of the rich and powerful. Thereby it accelerated the development of a black theology in NCBC and the caucuses of the predominantly white churches.

Even before 1966 a few clergy on the fringes of SCLC and CORE had begun to explore prospects for the revitalization of the black church and the restoration of its emphasis on the coherence of redemption and liberation in the African American religious tradition. The publication of Joseph R. Washington's *Black Religion* in 1964, by way of a generally negative rather than positive response, sparked this development. But the groundswell of political activism, ideological reflection, and cultural education among the masses in the ghettos was what finally produced the black power movement and provided the basis for a genuine theological renewal within the interlocking circles of African American church leadership.


## BLACK THEOLOGY

The Manifesto of 1969 served as the final booster stage for the theological renewal which had already been signaled by the 1966 statement of NCNC on black power. When that organization held its first annual convocation in Dallas in the fall of 1967 there was unanimous agreement that serious theological work needed to be done if the movement was to be solidly grounded in Scripture and the black religious experience. A theological commission was created in Dallas and instructed to bring back an outline of a new theological position to be presented at the St. Louis convocation in November of 1968.

The discussion in Dallas generated excitement about a theological position that would build upon the work of militant black preachers and scholars of the past, but break new ground for a dialogue between the religious and non-religious radicals in the black power movement. Most of the northern-based clergy who attended the organizing convocation believed that dialogue between NCBC and black power activists could not be carried forward unless the churches had something more to offer than the nonviolent, redemptive suffering position of Martin Luther King, Jr. Moreover, the charge by Joseph R. Washington, Jr., that the African American church had no authentic theology was regarded by many as an unjustified concession to the sociological reductionism of E. Franklin Frazier's analysis of the black church, an analysis that had already been rendered questionable by events since Frazier's death in 1962.[26]

The work group on theology rejected the positions of both King and Washington as the places to begin a theological renaissance in the African American churches. It recommended that its new commission conduct a survey among African American seminary professors and "scholarly pastors" to determine what might be the ingredients of a basic theological position that would clarify the growing interest in black power and determine its compatibility with the essence of the faith professed by most black Christians. The Dallas convocation called for a new dialogue with conservative, "whitenized" Negro Christians, liberal but frightened and paralyzed white Christians, and the black power movement.

NCBC leadership was convinced that these parties had to be brought together around a new sense of the relevance of the gospel for radical social change, a challenge to the religious and secular status quo that had robbed it of its vitality and credibility.[27] No one was prepared to argue that King had not already pointed the way to collaboration and operational unity among "the poor, the black, and the young." But the call for a new black theology meant that there was the feeling that something was needed that went beyond the universalism of the love ethic. What was sought for now was an interpretation of historic African American faith grounded in the experience of suffering and struggle, but also in a realistic appraisal of the depth of white racism and the possibility of black consciousness opening the door to countervailing economic and political power.

The publication of Washington's *The Politics of God* in 1967 clarified his revision of certain previous assumptions. Despite its integrationist flavor, it offered a new context for reflection on a theological basis for involvement with the poor in community organization and political action. But Washington's theology was a defensive polemic against the ghettoization of African Americans, and the reconstruction of his folk religion thesis moved toward a conception of the black person as the "suffering servant" who accepted the unenviable vocation to release white Christians from their ethnocentric bondage.[28] Washington did, however, indicate the possibilities of a radical theology that would incorporate the experience and passion of the masses for a new expression of the kingdom of God within the structures and institutions of white-dominated society.

In order to meet the needs of the Negro, which are the demands of the Kingdom of God, Negro ministers, laymen and denominational institutions required a conscious rejection of white theological and ecclesiastical doubletalk and a conscious acceptance of their black promise. . . . The inclusion of the Negro in the society is the demand of the Kingdom for the health of whites and blacks, but is dependent for extensity upon black cohesion in the present for the fullness of black dispersion throughout the society with equality in the future and as a whole.[29]

Between 1966 and 1976 articles and news items in the national religious press heralded the beginning of an unprecedented era of black theological reflection and sounded the themes that were to be further refined by a few scholars in both black and predominantly white seminaries. The interdenominational journal *Christian Century* published theologically astute articles by C. Eric Lincoln and Vincent Harding on black power. Harding's "Black Power and the American Christ" came to the defense of Carmichael and Floyd McKissick of CORE, declaring that for black Christians "Christ is the Lord of this [black power movement] too."[30] A Mennonite layman who chaired the department of history at Spelman College in Atlanta, Harding brought an impressionistic but keenly insightful view of what Nathan Wright, the black Episcopal theologian, called "the dehonkification of black Christianity."

Another of Harding's essays, "The Religion of Black Power," appeared in 1968 and caused a flurry of excitement. It brought to the fore the mixture of old and new black folk traditions in the religious ferment swirling around the black power movement. Harding's penchant had been to raise questions rather than propound answers, but he boldly affirmed that "Allah and other gods of Africa enter into competition with Yahweh, Jesus, and Buddha" in the theological winds that were rising in the black community. "It is," he wrote, "joyously difficult, but part of the affirmation of Black Power is, 'We are a spiritual people.' "[31]

His equation of black religion with the eclectic spirituality of black power was the contribution of an academician whose major interests were outside the sphere of organized religion. As such, it lacked the practical realism and authority of working clergy who could view the function of theology from within the institutional church and would be obliged to test its validity in the sanctuary as well as the streets.

Such a man was Albert B. Cleage, Jr., later to be known as Jaramogi Abebe Agyeman. In the 1960s Cleage was a minister of the United Church of Christ and pastor of the Shrine of the Black Madonna in Detroit—a nationalist congregation that experienced a new birth during the rise of black power. His first book, *The Black Messiah,* is a collection of sermons he preached during the tumultuous years of black uprisings in Detroit, where one of the most devastating riots of the period occurred in the summer of 1967. No black theologian was more controversial than Cleage. His thesis, drawn from some black preachers of the nineteenth century and the cults of the urban ghetto, was that Jesus is the Black Messiah—a descendant of the nation of Israel that became a nation of blacks during its sojourn in Egypt and Babylon. Cleage argued that Jesus was a member of a small underground movement, a Zealot, whose revolutionary message of racial separatism and liberation from Roman imperialism was corrupted by the Apostle Paul and the theologians of the white churches of the West. He told his Detroit congregation, which included many movement people:

> So then, I would say to you, you are Christian, and the things you believe are the teachings of a Black Messiah named Jesus, and the things you do are the will of a black God called Jehovah; and almost everything you have heard about Christianity is essentially a lie.[32]

Like other radical theologians, Cleage attacked the traditional Christian concept of selfless love and redemptive suffering. He declared that only the Old Testament was canonical for the black nation. He pressed the idea of African Americans as God's chosen people, called to purify the religion of Israel that the white man had despoiled, and to undertake revolutionary action "to build one Black community, one Black Nation, all stemming from the hub which is the Shrine of the Black Madonna."[33]

Intimately involved in the black power movement and much sought after as a spokesman and organizer, Cleage worked to assimilate the radical, anticlerical elements of the movement into a reconstructed black church that had been divested of the theology of white Christianity. A recurring proposition in his work is the brotherhood of blacks who prefer one another to the white enemy and who can rebuild the ghetto through self-help and mutual aid—a familiar theme in the history of the African American community.

"Jesus was black," Cleage wrote, "and he did *not* preach universal love. . . . God is working with us every day, helping us to find a way to freedom. Jesus tried to teach the Nation Israel how to come together as black people, to be brothers with one another and to stand against their white oppressors."[34]

Vincent Harding had also been emphatic about the pastoral care of blacks for each other and reiterated the theme of Cleage's polemic in a discussion of the alienation of young African Americans from the church.

> The issue of religion is constantly before many of the young persons who are drawn back into the ghettos by the urgent logic of Black Power. As they return—from college or from prison—to struggle against what can be reasonably described as "principalities and powers" which seem anonymously but fiercely to control the life of their people, they find themselves often insufficient as autonomous

sources of inner strength. . . . A few black Christian churches have responded fully to the call of Black Power. In Detroit, the pastor of one such congregation, the Reverend Albert B. Cleage, Jr., of the Central United Church of Christ, preaches of a black revolutionary Jesus who came to set the nonwhite peoples free. A Black Madonna is the focal point of worship, and the church has probably attracted more persons committed to Black Power than any single institution still connected to the Christian churches.[35]

It is a matter of speculation whether James Forman, who spent considerable time in Detroit, was influenced by Cleage before he penned the Black Manifesto in that city in April 1969. But it is unquestionably true that he and other young blacks who were drawn into the orbit of IFCO and BEDC were among those who returned to the North with humanitarian motives and tried to pursue, in the loneliness and anguish of their struggle, a mission to poor people and a more spiritual centeredness for involvement than the crass secularism that the white left provided.

The Manifesto controversy and Forman's cooperation with black church leaders, his willingness to see his ideas translated into theological terms, underscored the alienation of young black men and women from the kind of Marxism that dismissed religion as fantasy. It also indicated the alienation of African American religious thought from white liberal theology and the fundamentalism of much of the black church.

In the midst of the crisis a little-known scholar, James H. Cone from Bearden, Arkansas, with a doctorate in systematic theology from Northwestern University, was invited to join the faculty of Union Theological Seminary in New York City. Cone was to make a singular contribution to these developments. His first book, *Black Theology and Black Power*, appeared during the height of the debate over the Manifesto. Before its publication date, advance notices in the public press made it something of a sensation among black religionists. In 1969 Cone was the youngest of the new theologians and the first to suggest the broad outlines of what NCBC's theological commission was looking for: a theology that took the African American experience seriously, including the search for black economic and political power, but, at the same time, based upon an essentially classical interpretation of the Christian faith.

Calling upon Protestant theologians—from Karl Barth to Jürgen Moltmann—Cone showed how a radical but historically sound exegesis of the biblical story leads to the conclusion that black power can be an expression of the gospel in a particular situation of oppression.

In addition to a careful reading of Scripture, he arrived at his position by a thorough reading of Tillich, Camus, and Fanon, finding in their writings correlative ideas for the assertion that it is possible that black power is nothing less than the affirmation of black being against the nonbeing of white racism. Not only, therefore, must black power be accepted as indispensable to the formulation and praxis of a black theology, it is also necessary for a Christian understanding of freedom and authentic humanity.

> It would seem that Black Power and Christianity have this in common: the liberation of man! If the work of Christ is that of liberating men from alien loyalties, and if racism is, as George Kelsey[36] says, an alien faith, then there must be some correlation between Black Power and Christianity. . . . Black Power is the power to say No; it is the power of Blacks to refuse to cooperate in their own dehumanization. If Blacks can trust the message of Christ, if they can take him at his word, this power to say No to white power and domination is derived from him.[37]

Cone attended the meeting of the NCBC theological commission at the Interdenominational Theological Center in Atlanta on June 13, 1969. What had been demanded at the Dallas meeting two years earlier came to fruition at ITC—a brief statement of the main tenets of a black theology of liberation. Cone played a key role in the discussion, and the first public statement on the meaning of black theology, which issued from that meeting, shows his strong influence. The opening paragraph reflects one of the principal emphases of his work:

> Black people affirm their being. This affirmation is made in the whole experience of being black in the hostile American society. Black theology is not a gift of the Christian gospel dispensed to slaves, rather it is an *appropriation* which black slaves made of the gospel given by their white oppressors. Black theology has been nurtured, sustained, and passed on in the black churches in their various ways of expression. Black theology has dealt with all the ultimate and violent issues of life and death for a people despised and degraded.[38]

It was the contribution of Cone, augmented by substantive abstracts from Preston N. Williams, Henry Mitchell, and J. Deotis Roberts—all seasoned seminary professors—that came through in the statement and became generally endorsed as the basic theological position of NCBC. Their concept of black theology, formulated in Atlanta in 1969, was the baseline from which African American clergy defined their stance in the many debates with white clergy and seminary professors during the Manifesto crisis.

> Black Theology is a theology of black liberation. It seeks to plumb the black condition in the light of God's revelation in Jesus Christ, so that the black community can see that the gospel is commensurate with

the achievement of black humanity. . . . The message of liberation is the revelation of God as revealed in the incarnation of Jesus Christ. Freedom IS the gospel. Jesus is the LIBERATOR![39]

The NCBC interpretation of black theology arose from the existential situation that the organization faced in its attempt to make the white church acknowledge what African Americans believed to be God's judgment upon the American church and society as stated in the Black Manifesto. "Black theology," declared the theological commission, "must confront the issues which are a part of the reality of Black oppression." That reality was the refusal of white Americans, after years of tokenism in private sector and governmental programs, to make massive funding available for social and economic reconstruction in a black community that had been systematically underdeveloped for two centuries. The black theology statement, therefore, eschewed the abstractions of the debate among disengaged white theologians about the possibility of a race-conscious *black* theology that could, at the same time, be considered a *Christian* theology.

The issue at Atlanta was not whether a black theology could be authenticated by white churches as having universal applicability for all peoples and in every situation, but whether or not it could serve the needs of African Americans who were caught up in the oppressive and dehumanizing structures of the United States at the end of the 1960s. Because of the complicity of the American religious establishment in those structures, at the heart of the theological statement of NCBC was the issue Forman raised, as Bishop Henry M. Turner had raised before him— justifiable reparations for the years of chattel slavery. A new breed of African American theologians tried to elucidate the theological meaning of the Black Manifesto:

Reparation is a part of the gospel message. Zaccheus knew well the necessity for repayment as an essential ingredient in repentance. "If I have taken anything from any man by false accusation, I restore him fourfold" (Luke 19:8). The church which calls itself the servant church must, like its Lord, be willing to strip itself of possessions in order to build and restore that which has been destroyed by the compromising bureaucrats and conscienceless rich. While reparation cannot remove the guilt created by the despicable deed of slavery, it is, nonetheless, a positive response to the need for power in the black community. . . . As black theologians address themselves to the issues of the black revolution, it is incumbent upon them to say that the black community will not be turned from its course. . . . This is the message of black theology. In the words of Eldridge Cleaver: "We shall have our manhood. We shall have it or the earth will be leveled by our efforts to gain it."[40]

Afterward, an unpublicized and quiet controversy raged in academic circles about the justification of a black theology. The Atlanta theologians argued that its warrant was black oppression and that was sufficient justification for black people. The religion of Israel, moreover, depended primarily upon Israel's need for deliverance from Egyptian bondage. Thus, Yahweh was not the object of philosophical speculation, but the subject of a subjugated people. God refused to give Moses any epistemological arguments in answer to the question, "What shall I say to the people when they ask me, 'Who is this God who has sent you to summon us?' " God's response—"I am who I am. I AM has sent you"— abruptly terminated the discussion. Further inquiry on Moses' part would not only have been irrelevant but irreverent—even blasphemous. The God of the Hebrews delivers his people. The primal meaning of Jewish theophany and the warrant for both Judaism and black theology are the words of Exodus 3:16–17: "I have observed you and what has been done to you in Egypt; and I promise that I will bring you up and out of the affliction of Egypt, to the land of the Canaanites, the Hittites, the Amorites, the Perizzites, the Hivites, and the Jebusites, a land flowing with milk and honey."

James Cone, the leading exponent of black theology, took the brunt of the criticism that blackness, which most white theologians believed connoted nothing more than skin color, is an unacceptable basis for a Christian theology. His critics declared that they could find nothing unique in the historical experience of African Americans that could justify the particularity of the claim that the whole of biblical revelation points to the truth of what was being called black theology.[41]

In his first book Cone stated that "Black theology is Christian theology precisely *because* it has the black predicament as its point of departure."[42] White Christians must, therefore, "become black" in order to be Christians. But in an effort to prepare the groundwork for a systematic theology of the black experience that meets the requirement of universality, he added:

> Being black in America has very little to do with skin color. To be black means that your heart, your soul, your mind, and your body are where the dispossessed are. . . . Therefore, being reconciled to God does not mean that one's skin is physically black. It essentially depends on the color of your heart, soul, and mind.[43]

In *A Black Theology of Liberation*, Cone further developed this position by a reference to Paul Tillich's description of the symbolic nature of all theological discourse. Cone comments:

> The focus on blackness does not mean that *only* blacks suffer as victims in a racist society, but that blackness is an ontological symbol

and a visible reality which best describes what oppression means in America. . . . Blackness, then, stands for all victims of oppression who realize that their humanity is inseparable from man's liberation from whiteness.[44]

Cone's early struggle for academic legitimation of a black theology, as such, was commendable. He satisfied the norm of a certain emphasis on universality and avoided ideological presuppositions, a stance that he and his critics agreed was necessary for any systematic theology to be taken seriously. The question subsequently raised in this discussion, however, was whether the black religious experience requires such a validation by white systematic theology before it can be commended to African Americans who are being socialized away from their traditions, and whether the strain toward universality does not ipso facto rob black religion of the freedom to be one approach to God's revelation in Scripture. The white philosopher J. V. L. Casserley has a helpful comment to make in this respect:

> The advent of Christianity forced a new problem upon the attention of the ancient world—the problem of the singular. . . . There is a profound distinction between the term "particular" and the term "singular." The "particular" is the individual as seen by the man who is looking for the universal, and who will feel baffled intellectually until he finds it; the "singular," on the other hand, is the individual seen from the point of view of the man who is out to capture and enjoy the full flavor of its individuality.[45]

It is appropriate to ask whether black theology is simply the blackenization of the whole spectrum of traditional white theology, with particular emphasis on the liberation of the oppressed, or is it an independent formulation? In other words, does it find in the experience of the oppression of blacks by the Western world, *as blacks*, a singular religious meaning?

To say that being black in the United States has little to do with skin color is true (one has only to look at the color range of the African American population—from jet black to passing-white), but only half-true and capable of gross misunderstanding. It is possible to argue that in a world dominated by white power that is inextricable from white Christianity, being black, or "identifiably Negroid," is a unique experience. One that has, since the contact of African peoples with the Christian West, produced a unique religion—closely related to, but not exclusively bound by, the classic Christian tradition. That, in fact, is the reason for the emergence of a black theology. Simply being oppressed, or psychologically and politically in empathy with the poor and dispossessed, does not deliver one into the full experience of blackness any more than putting on a blindfold delivers one into the full experience of being blind.

This position does not intend to shut out white persons from the black religious experience or devalue the revelatory significance of the experience of other oppressed peoples. It is to affirm that black theology authenticates itself in the unique experience of being an African American in the particular circumstances of white, Euro-American civilization.

All oppression is an offense to the God who created all human beings, but there is a difference that makes a real *difference* between the way various groups of human beings experience oppression, vicariously and otherwise, and how they respond to it in religious and theological terms. Black theology is Christian theology, but it is a different way of responding to a singular, historical experience of poverty and oppression, and trying to reflect upon that experience theologically. That Cone himself also recognized this difference is clear.

> Black theology seeks to create a theological norm which is in harmony with the black condition and the biblical revelation. . . . Theology cannot be indifferent to the importance of blackness by making some kind of existential leap beyond blackness to an undefined universalism.[46]

Cone can even speak of "Jesus as the black Christ who provides the necessary soul for black liberation."[47] In so doing he opened up the possibility of a black theology of liberation that was neither Protestant nor Catholic, but the way black Christians think, feel, and act about their liberation with the intensity of an ultimate concern. Such a theology is rooted in the resistance to slavery and racism by the historic African American church, but it includes more than organized religion. It embraces also the attempt of black secular and non-Christian groups to express verbally and act out existentially the meaning and values of the black experience in the United States, Africa, South America, and the Caribbean.

In 1997 black theology continues to express both affirmation and negation. It affirms the real possibility of freedom and humanity for Africans and African Americans and negates every power that seeks to demean and rob them and other historically oppressed peoples of responsibility for their own futures. Black theology's contribution to the knowledge of God does not lie in being only the reverse side of traditional Christian theology—a white theology in black clothing. At the end of the twentieth century it continues to blaze its own trail.

In this regard, the veteran African American theologian, Leon E. Wright, was correct in his opinion that a judgment and protest against white Christianity is not enough. Rather, in its illumination of the religious significance of black liberation, black theology is obliged to break with the norms of white theology and unveil the most profound meaning of freedom for African Americans and, by extension, for all persons.[48]

The informal, unsystematic, and to a large degree, inarticulate theology of the masses still speaks to their urgent and distinctive needs and concerns. That "folk theology," confirmed and nourished not only in the African American church, but in many other institutions of the community, is still oriented toward an indestructible belief in freedom. The freedom toward which the experience of the people tends is rooted and grounded in the ancestral African environment. It is freedom as existential deliverance, as emancipation from every power or force that retrains the full, spontaneous release of the dynamism of body, mind, and spirit—freedom from every bondage that is not validated as contributing to the elevation of the whole person in the whole community. Here we are not referring simply to political and economic liberation, but to the freedom of the person as a child of God, the freedom to be herself and himself most fully, the freedom to realize the most creative potential of her or his psychosomatic nature and destiny in community with sisters and brothers.

I return to the more specific tasks of black theology in the next chapter, but—to summarize the foregoing discussion in one felicitous phrase—the freedom that black religion offers and celebrates, and black theology continues to explicate, is no less than the freedom to be a human being.

## CHAPTER 10

# Survival, Elevation, and Liberation in Black Religion

*This then is the Gift of the Black Folk to the new world. Thus in singular and fine sense the slave became master, the bond servant became free and the meek not only inherited the earth but made their heritage a thing of questing for eternal youth, of fruitful labor, of joy and music, of the free spirit and of the ministering hand, of wide and poignant sympathy with men in their struggle to live and love which is, after all, the end of striving.*

W. E. B. Du Bois, 1924

The three basic assertions of this book have been (1) that within American culture as a whole there was and continues to be an exceedingly complex and distinctive subculture that may be designated black or African American; (2) that despite sociological heterogeneity with respect to such secular factors as regional differences, education, gender, and socioeconomic background, religion has been and continues to be an essential thread interweaving the fabric of black culture; and (3) that religiousness, oscillating between conservatism and radicalism, has been and continues to be a persistent characteristic of black life not only in the United States but also in Africa, South America, and the Caribbean—or wherever the animating spirits of Africa have touched the quick of the human heart.

Religious institutions such as the church, therefore, are of the greatest importance in these societies. To them accrue the primary responsibility for the conservation, enhancement, and further development of that unique spiritual quality that has enabled African and black people of the diaspora to survive and flourish under some of the most unfavorable conditions of the modern world.

## THE AFRICAN AMERICAN EXPERIENCE

We have focused primarily upon the African American experience without excluding its original locus in Africa and its historic relationship to that continent. From the earliest years of their captivity, transplanted Africans, denied access to other forms of self-affirmation and collective power, have used religion and its various institutions as the principal expression of their peoplehood and their will both to exist and to improve their condition. Black religion, fluctuating between moods of protest and accommodation, and protesting in the context of accommodating strategies, has contributed considerably to the ability of African American people to survive the worst forms of oppression and dehumanization. Beyond mere survival, as leaders and followers became more sophisticated about how to make the most of their religion, it has helped them liberate themselves, first from chattel slavery, then from ignorance and degradation, and finally—though still imperfectly—from civil inequality and subordination, to go on to greater heights of personal and group achievement.

African American religion has not always and in all circumstances functioned in this way for the advancement of the masses. But it is difficult to understand how even the most skeptical observers of the black religious experience in America could deny that, on the whole, religion and its ancillary institutions have served the people positively. One can scarcely imagine how they would have fared without them.

In a sense not true of any other immigrant group in America, the irreducible problem of the Africans brought here was survival. For two hundred years slavery in Protestant North America, unlike human bondage in the Caribbean and Latin America, was practically devoid of mitigating influences from the side of either the church or state. Blacks, scattered in relatively small, isolated groups, were reduced to the level of beasts of burden. With but few exceptions they were treated with slightly more regard than animals who were fed, clothed, and sheltered to no greater degree than was necessary to protect the original investment made to procure them. Owners exploited such human property for the maximum amount of selfish personal gain their bodies would tolerate.

There is no way to palliate this inhumanity. Force and violence were required to establish and maintain the system. The argument that slavery in the South was mainly a paternalistic institution should not be permitted to disguise the fact that blacks reciprocated the blandishments of their supposedly conscience-stricken *paters* in the most effective ways they could devise. Eugene Genovese, a major proponent of the paternalism thesis, acknowledges that it should not be interpreted as evidence of how benevolent slavery was for most blacks, or how readily they acquiesced to it:

The slaves accepted the doctrine of reciprocity, but with a profound difference. To the idea of reciprocal duties they added their own doctrine of reciprocal rights. To the tendency to make them creatures of another's will they counterpoised a tendency to assert themselves as autonomous human beings. And they thereby contributed, as they had to, to the generation of conflict and great violence.[1]

The point needs to be made over and over. Paternalism, in fact, never really worked as it was supposed to. Slaveholders were obliged, sooner or later, to recognize that there was extreme insecurity in their situation. Only the most stupid among them could have mistaken the fact that they were not dealing with black "sons and daughters" who loved them as seignorial fathers and were willing to exchange that love for protection, but rather had on their hands sensible, thinking human beings who could never be trusted, precisely on that account, to respond in the same manner as children. Moreover, whatever feelings of warmth or tenderness may have been engendered in day-to-day relations, such feelings had to be subordinated to the hard, cold fact that the bottom line was the dollar. In the final analysis, the economic value was realistically calculated and made secure by the imposition of discipline and the monopoly of violent power that by law and otherwise remained in the hands of the masters. It is incredible that the slave did not know that the *noblesse oblige* of a fawning Christian master depended mainly on the slave's capability of producing wealth in the same sense that it was produced by the master's mule or cotton gin—a wealth to which the slave had no claim.

## THE SURVIVAL TRADITION

Against this reduction to the status of a thing, enforced by unpredictable cruelty and ruthlessness, the slave's obsession was to somehow "to make it"; to hold body and soul together for as long as possible; to engage in an unceasing interior struggle to preserve physical existence and psychological sanity—in short, to survive. Survival, therefore, became the regulative, moment-to-moment principle of the slave community, particularly among field hands. This single factor best explains the tenacity and functionality of black religion in the plantation South.

As a result of new research during the 1970s and 1980s we now have a better idea than previously of how this happened.[2] Drawn together in the quarters after sundown and on Sundays and holidays, the slaves pieced together the tattered remnants of their African past and new patterns of response to the American environment. They selectively chose for themselves attitudes of disbelief, codes of dissimulation and subterfuge, structures of meaning—in short, a view of reality and such coping skills that would make human survival possible under the conditions of their enslavement. Into this strategy of survival they invoked the protecting spirits of the gods of Africa, or in time, the new God of Christianity.

In the formation of a new common language, in the telling of animal tales and proverbs, in the leisure-time practice of remembered handicrafts, in the preparation of foods, homemade medicines, and magical potions and charms, in the standardization of rituals of birth, marriage, and death, in the singing, the use of instrumental music and the dance— by all of these and other means, the slaves wove for themselves the tapestry of a new African American culture. A culture of human survival in the face of legal oppression and forcible acculturation. A culture impregnated with spiritual and occult elements of African, European, and Native American origin, all integrated around a basically religious conception of human reality.

From the beginning, certain men and women who possessed power for both good and evil, skilled in sorcery and divination, exercised extraordinary influence over the slaves. In some slave narratives and reports of white missionaries, they occasionally appear as the first recognized leaders of the community, men and women respected and feared by both slaves and masters. Through these specialists in magic, conjuration, and the healing arts, what was left of the old African religions was transplanted and integrated into the new culture of enslavement.[3] To the misery and hopelessness of the slave quarters these specialists brought consolation and the possibility of transcending external circumstances to the extent that made physical and mental survival achievable. The invocation of mystical powers counteracted some of the magic of the whites and the wretchedness of daily existence. It gave a dimension of depth and ultimacy to the struggle for survival. At that deeper level the reinterpretation and synthesis of transplanted and newly acquired religious systems, mainly evangelical Protestantism, produced a distinctive African American religious consciousness.

Out of this mystical, survival-oriented consciousness, part African and part European, the shout songs and spirituals, expressing the loneliness and sorrow of a stolen people, emerged on the plantations. But with no less charismatic force the slaves' religion celebrated the sheer fact of survival despite constant brutalization in the fields and death and disease in the living quarters. The awakening of white evangelical Christianity during the second quarter of the eighteenth century made contact with this affirmative side of slave religion. Gradually a white-supervised black church evolved from the secret, shaman-led religious meetings in the cabins and brush arbors. But the white preachers and missionaries could never be sure what kind of religion their sermons and camp meetings were crafting.

The Christian faith did not sweep through the slave community with anything like the rate that some earlier scholars assumed.[4] The Society for the Propagation of the Gospel in Foreign Parts reported only 40 adult baptisms and 179 baptized children after some eight years of SPG labor among the relatively large slave population of New York City in the early 1700s. It is estimated that by 1750 there were only a thousand baptized slaves in Virginia—a mere 1 percent of the colony's black population.

Even those slaves who accepted white preaching and made a public profession of faith exasperated their mentors by the way they apparently drifted in and out of the state of grace, clinging to dreams, visions, belief in ghosts, good-luck charms, and the efficacy of the hoodoo man or root doctor. Some missionaries and travelers in the South simply branded black religion as childish superstition or insincerity, far distant from anything that they would call Christianity. They seem not to have been aware that the slaves were *surviving* rather than being swept away by the presumed cogency of Puritan theology.

If whites thought that they were dealing with children who could not discern the difference between white professions and white behavior they were sadly mistaken. As John Lovell, Jr., has observed, "The slave relied upon religion, not primarily because he felt himself 'converted' [to white Christianity], but because he recognized the power inherent in religious things."[5] That power had to do, first of all, with the necessity of survival— with the creation of an alternative reality system that could keep a person alive and possessed of some modicum of sanity. The protest and resistance elements we found in early forms of black folk religion in the Caribbean and the southeastern United States express the determination of the slaves to "make it" against all odds.

We should not be surprised to find, therefore, a dark and contrary side of black religion as it developed under the most trying circumstances. In Haiti it was the difference between the Arada and Petro rites of vodun that separated a religion of survival from one with more affirmative possibilities for inner peace, sociability, and edification. The same thing can be said about myalism and obeah, or about the religion of the black Methodists of Philadelphia and New York and that of the rebellious black Methodists of Charleston. This was during the first quarter of the nineteenth century, when the example of Haiti was most vivid in the minds of African Americans throughout the nation, but particularly in towns on the Atlantic coast.

The dark and contrary side of black religion must be understood as an alternative form of spirituality. It is a fundamental aspect of what we may call the survival tradition and was indelibly imprinted on a persistently heterodox form of Christianity that came down through the African American churches, sects, and cults into the twentieth century. Although it was often expressed as a curiously divergent version of Christianity, this African American spirituality should not be confused with the kind of white spirituality that was eventually translated into benevolent social reform. It often had, rather, a bitter unsentimentality about it. It was more often cynical, manipulative, and at the very least, ambivalent about spiritual things. Horace Clayton and St. Clair Drake found it in the Chicago black ghetto during the Depression years of the 1930s.[6] C. Eric Lincoln observed the same spirit, in contrast to orthodox Islam, in the bitterness and hatred of the early Black Muslim movement.[7]

This harsh realism and irony, that comes strangely mixed with religiosity, antedated the Great Migration. There were the "upstart crows" in the Southland. Churchgoers circulated songs and sayings that were irreverent of traditional religion:

> Our Father, who art in heaven
> White man owe me 'leven and pay me seven.
> Thy kingdom come, thy will be done,
> If I hadn't tuck that, I wouldn't got none.[8]

What Blassingame describes as making the best of a bad situation in the antebellum South is a good example of what we mean by the survival tradition in the literature.

> They simply had to make the best of the situation in which they found themselves. Henry Clay Bruce contended that there were many slaves "who though they knew they suffered a great wrong in their enslavement, gave their best services to their masters, realizing, philosophically, that the wisest course was to make the best of their unfortunate situation. . . ." Frederick Douglass spoke for many of them when he asserted, "A man's troubles are always half disposed of when he finds endurance his only remedy." William Grimes indicated the brutal realism and the will to survive of many slaves when he declared that slavery was a cruel institution, "but being placed in that situation, to repine was useless; we must submit to our fate, and bear up, as well as we can, under the cruel treatment of our despotic tyrants."[9]

There was a sense of the ironic and tragic in the slave secular songs and early blues. A sense that there is something out there that is in inexorable opposition to one's most ardent aspirations. But if we are not too "uppity, and remember that we are all, whether black or white, poor, ill-begotten creatures bound to die, it is possible 'to overcome someday.' " Other powers are always in the wings to help us survive.

W. E. B. Du Bois was probably the first to recognize this extraordinary duality in black folk religion. He speaks of "the peculiar ethical paradox" facing African American life at the turn of the nineteenth century that was transforming black Christianity. It was the paradox of the impotence, bitterness, and vindictiveness of migrants who still believed in God, but whose "religion, instead of worship, is a complaint and a curse, a wail rather than a hope, a sneer rather than a faith" as they faced the hopelessness and despair of the Northern ghetto.[10] The other side of the paradox was what he called the shrewd "Jesuitic casuistry" of the black farmhand who remained in the post-Reconstruction South, forced to take advantage of the inherent weakness of the white man by deception and hypocrisy, and willing, if necessary, to play the role of Uncle Tom—stooping in order to conquer.[11]

These two divergent tendencies in black ethics and religious life—the first tending toward a stubborn radicalism, the other toward a hypocritical compromise—represent two strands of the survival tradition. They belong to what Lawrence W. Levine differentiated from classical Christianity and called the slaves' "instruments of life, of sanity, of health, and of self-respect."[12]

Du Bois had an unfailing insight into this phenomenon. He recognized that what the white evangelical churches had passed on to African Americans had been thoroughly adulterated by the end of slavery and merged with a subterranean stream of African spirituality and the survival instincts of an impoverished and downtrodden people. In this condition, he wrote in his usual grandiloquent style, "broods silently the deep religious feeling of the real Negro heart, the stirring, unguided might of powerful human souls who have lost the guiding star of the past and seek in the great night, a new religious ideal."[13]

Perhaps it would be more accurate to speak of this form of African American religion as a tendency rather than an ideal toward which black believers strove. In any case, it was a persistent quality of the folk tradition that should disabuse us of the much too facile assumption that black religion was nothing more than an echo of nineteenth-century revivalism, a little louder, perhaps, and more given to raw emotionalism. Rather it had more to do with survival than with either elevation or liberation, although there is a complex relationship between the more aggressive form of survivalism and the left wing of the liberation tradition in the established black denominations. But the survival tradition was most characteristic of the "invisible institution," and gave the white missionaries much difficulty. By means of storefront religion and black Pentecostalism it laid the foundation for the paradoxical culture that Du Bois saw invading the Negro urban communities at the end of the nineteenth century.

He spoke of survival religion as the search for a "new religious ideal," breaking with the pietism and fundamentalism of the Southern Methodist and Baptist churches that tried to shape African American religiosity in its own image between the era of the plantation missions and the beginning of the Civil War. But whether powered by a "new ideal" or simply an instinctive recoil from white Christianity, the survival form was never completely domesticated by evangelicalism. It preserved an alternative tradition in the African American subculture that has served (to use Paul Lehmann's insightful phrase) "to make and keep life human."

Daniel Alexander Payne, the great patriarch of the AME Church, fought against lower-class, survival-oriented folk religion throughout his long ministry. The passion with which he attempted to drive it out of his denomination is proof of its tenacity even in that bastion of black Christian respectability. Bishop Payne was not mistaken in his assumption that what he was witnessing was not conversion to the religion of John Wesley, or fidelity to the discipline of Asbury and Allen, but something very different and possibly heretical. He encountered a mysterious form of virtue, in the sense of the Latin word *virtus*, or the term *mana*, as used by anthropologists—a power or force of causal efficacy and creative vitality. Something of which it is of the greatest advantage to possess. It was what West African priests would have recognized as both proceeding from and capable of influencing the gods and the ancestors. A power that could be used to ward off evil, to perform good, and to keep body and soul together against every destructive element of the universe—in other words, the sheer power *to be*, the power to survive.

Leonard E. Barrett writes that this kind of religion, to the consternation of British missionaries, asserted itself in the great Jamaican revival of 1860–61.[14] It also surfaced in several places in the United States in the early twentieth century: in the Azusa Street Revival of 1905, when Charles Fox Parham and his white followers split with William J. Seymour's black Pentecostals because of "heathen" manifestations; in the Universal Negro Improvement Association of Marcus Garvey, when West Indian survival religion sought synthesis with Anglo-Catholicism and Pan-Africanism in the African Orthodox Church; in the movement of the Cape Verdian prophet, Daddy Grace, who, from a small family congregation in New Bedford, Massachusetts, built one of the most powerful black religious organizations in the United States.

This survival motif is closely associated with authentic African American religion in its alternating phases of withdrawal from and aggressive opposition toward the white world. This is what the mysterious Detroit peddler W. D. Fard combined with a homegrown version of black orientalism to create the Nation of Islam. Elijah Muhammad's message attracted many alienated blacks because they recognized in it accents of a tradition they had known in the rural South where they and their ancestors had resisted the whitenization of the church. It is clear that Elijah Muhammad quoted as frequently from the Bible as from the Koran. His most gifted disciple, Malcolm X, whose father was a Garveyite Baptist preacher, received support from many black Christians who recognized those same accents when Malcolm drew upon a survival theme in folk religion to wean the masses away from evangelical Christianity.

The Harlem Renaissance poet Langston Hughes understood this survival tradition and used it as the basis of some of his most biting cultural criticism. He once wrote of those who were sustained by it:

But then there are low-down folks, the so-called common element, and they are the majority—may the Lord be praised! The people who have their nip of gin on Saturday nights and are not too important to themselves of the community, or too well fed, or too learned to watch the lazy world go round. They live on 7th Street in Washington, or State Street in Chicago and they do not particularly care whether they are like white folks or anybody else. Their joy runs, bang! into ecstasy. Their religion soars to a shout. Work maybe a little today, rest a little tomorrow. Play awhile. Sing awhile. O, let's dance! These common people are not afraid of spirituals, as for a long time their more intellectual brethren were, and jazz is their child. They furnish a wealth of colorful, distinctive material for any artist because they still hold to their own individuality in the face of American standardization.[15]

The connective links between black secular culture and black religion, which were forged by the survival tradition, are explored in much of the literature of black America and the West Indies. They can be found in the poetry of Claude McKay, Countee Cullen, Nikki Giovanni, and Sonia Sanchez; the novels of Richard Wright, James Baldwin, and Toni Morrison; and the essays of Alice Walker, Andrew Salkey, Derek Walcott, and the so-called "public intellectuals" of the late twentieth century. As ever, creative writers often see more clearly than theologians the dimension of depth in life and culture that yields more truth than philosophical speculation and exposes the raw, mysterious edges of existence in the language and symbols of the folk, mediated by artistic genius.

## THE ELEVATION TRADITION

What were the slaves trying to say when they mixed Old Testament allusions to Jacob's ladder and New Testament allusions to being "soldiers of the Cross," in the familiar words of one of the best-loved spirituals?

> We are climbing Jacob's ladder . . .
> Every round goes higher and higher . . .
> Soldiers of the Cross.

Most of us have assumed that the source of the inspiration for this song was the 28th chapter of Genesis where the patriarch Jacob names a lonely campsite in the desert, Bethel, because as he slept there he dreamed of angels ascending and descending a ladder stretched between heaven and earth. God stood at the top of that ladder and gave Jacob the solemn promise that the very land on which he lay would one day become his family's possession. That would seem clear enough to the slave poet, but John Lovell, in his monumental book on the spirituals perceives another, more profound meaning in the secret hearts and minds of the captive black men and women who first sang the lines of this spiritual. As humble as they were, they pictured themselves as climbing, one round at a time, out of their misery. They saw themselves, by the power of God and the dint of their own dogged determination, climbing out of downtroddenness, out of degradation, toward the God who called them to be soldiers of the Cross of Christ, working for a better world for themselves and their children. Lovell writes:

> The fact that there is a religious catchphrase in most songs (such as the name of the deity, or some other biblical character, or reference to a biblical event or to heaven) is not the significant thing at this point. The main thing is the pithy element of life suggested by the poetic grist of the title. For example, in "We Are Climbing Jacob's Ladder," the story of Jacob is just a point of departure. The really important expression the singer is pouring out is his determination to rise from his low estate and to progress up the material and spiritual ladder, "round by round." Jacob's experience has been chosen because it is the most available, the most dramatic, the most impressive and acceptable simile. And please note, his poetic point relates to his life on earth. In the mythical heaven, one is already as high as one can go.[16]

This spiritual, like many others Lovell analyzes, had a "morale-building function." Lovell compares it to other songs which suggest the slaves' determination to improve their earthly condition, to encourage individual and group initiative. He speaks of literally dozens of spirituals that focus on the perennial objective of both the slave and the free black— learning to read and write the English language. These spirituals include "My Lord's Writing All the Time," "My Mother Got a Letter," "O Lord, Write My Name," "Gwine to Write Massa Jesus," and "De Book of Revelation God to Us Revealed." "Jacob's Ladder" belongs to this genre of slave poetry. It expresses the longing and determination not to "go down," but rather to be "uplifted from slavery," by the power of God; to make a better life for one and one's children and grandchildren; to be "elevated" in body, mind, and spirit, above the vicissitudes and miseries of this life.[17]

The centrality of the idea of self-improvement, uplift, the "*advancement of colored people*," or elevation, is evident in much of the literature of the slave and the free African American in the nineteenth and early twentieth centuries. In many cases, it was closely connected with the comprehensive cultural vocation of the African American church. Elevation as a tradition is, of course, closely related to the tradition emphasizing liberation from slavery, for as AME Bishop Daniel A. Payne said he learned

from the abolitionist Lewis Tappan, "slavery and education were antagonistic and could not exist together . . . the one must crush out the
other."[18] But it is useful to differentiate between elevation and liberation
in order to make a closer examination of each. Elevation emerges as a
kind of second stage of self-development, for after the slave became conscious of the fact that despite the chains, he or she had a future, that
there was something beyond mere survival—something better in this
world as well as in the world to come—he or she began climbing the ladder of moral and material elevation. It was assumed that the church
would lead the way.

Throughout the slave narratives, testimonies, letters, essays, speeches,
sermons, and church resolutions, one finds the word elevation, or uplift,
used profusely—and, more frequently than not, in the context of religion.[19] Most black preachers were opposed to the moral anarchy
implied by slave carousing, indolence, feigned stupidity, or apathy,
which made slaves not only the victims of their oppressors but also of
their own ignorance and self-abnegation. The preachers, wanting desperately to read the Bible for themselves, tried to model the idea that
belief in Jesus Christ puts a person's life on a foundation of good morals,
manners, orderliness, and a growing ambition to learn and improve
one's station in life. Those who became Christians began their elevation
by learning how to read. The South Carolina slave James L. Bradley, who
entered Lane Seminary in 1834, explains how his conversion started him
on the Jacob's ladder of personal elevation:

> In the year 1828, I saw some Christians, who talked with me con-
> cerning my soul, and the sinfulness of my nature. They told me I
> must repent, and live to do good. This led me to the cross of
> Christ;—and then, oh, how I longed to be able to read the Bible! I
> made out to get an old spelling-book, which I carried in my hat for
> many months, until I could spell pretty well, and read easy words.
> When I got up in the night to work, I used to read a few minutes, if
> I could manage to get a light. . . . After I had learned to read a little,
> I wanted very much to learn to write; and I persuaded one of my
> young masters to teach me.[20]

C. H. Hall, a slave who was interviewed in Canada in 1863, intimates
the connection between conversion, elevation, and anti-slavery:

> It was a rule in that country [Maryland], that a slave must not be
> seen with a book of any kind; but old madam Bean, my mistress,
> belonged to the Baptist Church, and she said we might all learn to
> spell and read the Bible. The old man fought against it for some
> time, but found it prevailed nothing. . . . [I] got to know too much
> for the old boss himself, and he said it wouldn't do. He said I was

going just like my brother Bige, who had learned to read and was a preacher, and was raising the devil on the place. So after a little scorning, I stopped it, and gave up reading until I got to be 19 years old. But the more I read, the more I fought against slavery.[21]

Learning how to read and write did not, of course, work any magic for liberation, but it was the first rung of the ladder. The slave who could read soon discovered that there were other interesting things to read besides the Bible, such as Northern newspapers, pamphlets, and—if it was available—David Walker's insurrectionary "Appeal to the Coloured Citizens of the World." A whole new world was opened up and with it a new self-esteem, a new consciousness of identity and destiny.

In the North the independent black churches were freer to emphasize elevation and self-development. As a result they soon came together to uplift themselves by organizing burial clubs, lodges, churches, reading clubs, schools, and temperance and moral reform societies. The elevation motif stands out clearly in the statements of purpose and preambles of these fledgling organizations. They demonstrate how much freed men and women feared moral indifference and anarchy; how much they strove against ignorance, drunkenness, marital infidelity, and the neglect of widows and fatherless children. As we have seen, the Free African Societies or their counterparts in Boston, Newport, R.I., New York, and Philadelphia, became the scaffolding of the black churches, particularly that preeminent instrumentality of African American self-help and self-development, the AME Church. On the occasion of its 100th anniversary, Bishop Richard R. Wright explained its *raison d'être*:

> The purpose in mind of the founding fathers of African Methodism . . . was, among other things, to exemplify in the black man the power of self-reliance, self-help, by the exercise of free religious thought with executive efficiency.[22]

Some of the most ardent champions of the doctrine of racial elevation were black women. Concerned about the stability of the family, the education of children, and the cultivation of Christian morality, they organized female societies and auxiliaries alongside of the churches and other male-dominated institutions. The sermons and writings of Amanda Berry Smith, Maria Stewart, Frances Ellen Watkins Harper, Fannie Barrier Williams, Lucy Craft Laney, and Nannie H. Burroughs bear eloquent testimony to the special emphasis black women put upon uplifting black folk, making the church more responsible for "racial promotion," and training young women for parenting and leadership roles in church and community.

Delores Williams prefers to use the term "quality-of-life tradition" to describe essentially the same theme in African American religious history that we are calling "elevationism." Moreover, she links "quality-of-life" to survival as one of the primary contributions of biblically literate African American women to black culture and religion. Recent research in the writings of black women demonstrates that there is voluminous evidence to support her thesis. She writes:

> I concluded, then, that the female-centered tradition of African-American biblical appropriation could be named the *survival/quality-of-life tradition of African-American biblical appropriation.* This naming was consistent with the black American community's way of appropriating the Bible so that emphasis is put upon God's response to black people's situation rather than upon what would appear to be hopeless aspects of African-American people's existence in North America. In black consciousness, God's response of survival and quality of life to Hagar is God's response of survival and quality of life to African-American women and mothers of slave descent struggling to sustain their families with God's help.[23]

Before leaving the elevation, or "survival/quality-of-life tradition" we should note that women were the first to point out that the drive for self-improvement and uplift could be abused by selfish blacks who wanted only to distance themselves from those they considered beneath them. The very congregations that prided themselves on being models of respectability and uplift worthy of acceptance by whites were the ones that were cool to the bedraggled, poorly educated, and unsophisticated agricultural workers from the South who showed up at their doors on Sunday mornings. The elevation tradition was the lever by which some blacks lifted themselves up by their proverbial bootstraps and moved into the middle class, but when some of them shed the boots and donned the silk stockings and patent leather slippers, they regarded those not similarly blessed as unworthy of either their assistance or association. Maria Stewart, speaking in the African Masonic Hall of Boston in 1833, targeted the elevation-conscious black middle class:

> I am sensible that there are many highly intelligent gentlemen of color in these United States, in the force of whose arguments, doubtless, I should discover my inferiority; but if they are blest with wit and talent, friends and fortune, why have they not made themselves men of eminence, by striving to take all the reproach that is cast upon people of color, and in endeavoring to alleviate the woes of their brethren in bondage? Talk, without effort, is nothing ... this gross neglect on your part, causes my blood to boil within me.[24]

While Maria Stewart in the antebellum period criticized the affluent class of blacks in the North for refusing to share their upward-bound energies with their enslaved brethren, Fannie Barrier Williams in 1893 bemoaned the fact that by the end of the century the leadership of the mass black church, because of apathy or incompetence, seemed woefully unprepared to elevate the race:

> It is not difficult to specify wherein church interests have failed and wherein religion could have helped to improve these people. In the first place the churches have sent among us too many ministers who have had no sort of preparation and fitness for the work assigned to them. With due regard for the highly capable colored ministers of the country, I feel no hesitancy in saying that the advancement of our condition is more hindered by a large part of the ministry entrusted with leadership than by any other single cause.[25]

When it came to the elevation of the race no one was more critical of the defects of the black church than Booker T. Washington. By the time the great accommodationist of Tuskegee had reached the zenith of his power at the turn of the century, the ideals of moral elevation, self-help, and self-determination through industrial education had become the accepted antidote for the disappointment and despair that followed the rise of Jim Crow in every aspect of American life. Washington simply enunciated what almost all black religious leaders believed in both the South and the North: that rather than depend upon the political process to redress their grievances, blacks needed to get off their knees and elevate themselves morally, spiritually, and, especially, economically. Only then would God help them to help themselves and white America would relieve them of the onus of second-class citizenship.

## THE LIBERATION TRADITION

Many scholars have commented upon the complexity of the character of Booker T. Washington. Washington is difficult to categorize. Notwithstanding the self-development tone of his famous autobiography, *Up From Slavery*, published in 1901, the man was probably more of a survivalist than an elevationist. He came up the hard way and was shrewdly distrustful of progressive ideas that were more high-flying flights of the imagination than the result of a hard, calculating logic. Certainly he was no liberationist in the sense that Bishop Henry McNeal Turner, W. E. B. Du Bois, or Ida Wells Barnett were. All three of these and many other leaders of the black church, particularly the Baptist churches of the 1830s and 1840s in Virginia, Ohio, Illinois, and the border states, and the African Methodists of the North, particularly the Zionites of New York and Massachusetts, were solidly grounded in the liberation tradition.[26]

The liberation tradition stands out as the single most important and characteristic perspective of black faith from 1800 to the Civil Rights movement. It could not have been otherwise. From the landing of the first twenty Africans on the wharf at Jamestown, Virginia, in 1619, to the Emancipation Proclamation on New Year's Day, 1863, African American consciousness and culture were permeated with the idea of freedom. As tensions mounted toward the Civil War it was inevitable that the black quest for God and salvation would be greatly conditioned by an unquenchable desire to be rid of slavery. Even when individuals were manumitted, bought their own freedom, or escaped slavery and fled north, their consuming passion was to liberate the other members of their families who had been left behind. The main reason for the failure of the American Colonization Society was the refusal of free blacks, called to resistance by their churches, to leave the United States if that meant abandoning relatives and friends who were still in slavery.

Many of the spirituals speak about the yearning for liberation, and one of the most familiar expresses a willingness to die rather than submit to slavery:

> Oh, Freedom, Oh Freedom,
> Oh, Freedom over me,
> And before I'd be a slave,
> I'd be buried in my grave,
> And go home to my Lord
> And be free!

John Lovell, Jr., explodes with lyrical eloquence when he discusses this characteristic emphasis in so many of the slave songs and spirituals.

No more passionate songs have ever been written to proclaim the concept of freedom. Perhaps the American slave knew more about freedom than anyone who has ever lived. Whether or not this is true, his songs declare freedom as well as or better than it has ever been declared: "No more peck o'corn for me, No more, no more," "And why not every man?" "Tell ol' Pharaoh, let my people go!" "If I had my way . . . I'd tear this building down!" "Before I'd be a slave I'd be buried in my grave," "Done wid driber's dribin'," "No second class aboard dis train"—for the concept of freedom, where can you find their superiors! Who speaks today for freedom in such glowing terms? Who understands so well the soul of freedom? Who better ties together the dream and the reality![27]

Whether or not Lovell's assumption about the superiority of the spirituals as songs of freedom is correct is less important than the incontestable fact that the slaves thought a great deal about freedom and made it the keystone of their religion. Talitha Lewis, a slave in North Carolina, born in 1852 and interviewed when she was 86 years old, recalled:

> My master used to ask us children, "Do your folks pray at night?" We said, "No," 'cause our folks had told us what to say. But the Lord have mercy, there was plenty of that going on. They'd pray, "Lord, deliver us from under bondage."[28]

Black preachers in the North and their congregants—having somehow survived the ordeal of slavery and having concentrated their efforts on the educational, moral, and spiritual elevation of the race—began about 1800 to focus all their energies and resources on emancipation. These churches literally pushed and pulled their white friends and supporters toward the great war between the states. It is no accident that the first black Baptist churches on the frontier renamed their associations "Friends of Humanity" to indicate that abolitionism was their first order of business, or that Bishop William Paul Quinn of the AME Church, said that the first black Methodist denomination was "a veritable antislavery society."

This extraordinary emphasis upon the Christian religion as the foundation for a liberation movement and liberation itself as the primary message of the gospel is reflected in every African American institution of the nineteenth century. The Negro Convention Movement, which was an effective secular arm of the church from 1831 to the Civil War, brought together the leading men and women of the race in state and national conventions on political justice and economic issues. From its inception it was dominated by lay and clerical leaders of the churches. Nor did the black Methodists and Baptists have exclusive control of the Convention Movement. It was greatly influenced by clergymen like the three Presbyterians Samuel Cornish, Theodore Wright, and Henry Highland Garnet and the Congregationalists Charles B. Ray and J. W. C. Pennington. These ministers refused to spiritualize the concept of liberty as did so many white preachers and biblical exegetes of their day. They understood the freedom that Christ brought in very concrete terms. For them it was nothing less than freedom from chattel slavery. They ridiculed any attempt on the part of the white clergy of their denominations to use the Bible to spiritualize liberty, thereby making slavery a condition that referred primarily to being a slave of sin.

A white Methodist minister preaching to blacks in Charleston discovered later that he had completely misunderstood the meaning of the "Amens" they were giving him. A. M. Chreitzberg in his book on *Early Methodism in the Carolinas*, published in 1897, describes what happened.

> Though ignorant of it at the time, he remembers now the cause of the enthusiasm under his deliverances [about] the "law of liberty"

and "freedom from Egyptian bondage." What was figurative they interpreted literally. He thought of but one ending of the war; they quite another. He remembers the 68th Psalm as affording numerous texts for their declaration, e.g., "Let God arise, let his enemies be scattered;" His "march through the wilderness;" "the chariots of God are twenty-thousand." . . . It is mortifying now to think that his comprehension was not equal to the African intellect. All he thought about was relief from the servitude of sin, and freedom from the bondage of the devil. . . . But they interpreted it literally in the good time coming, which of course could not but make their ebony complexions attractive, very.[29]

The liberation tradition continued as a persistent emphasis through the years of the Civil War and into Reconstruction, when liberated black churchmen of the South became promoters of Radical Republicanism. Many pastors went into politics and enjoyed a brief if stormy tenure in state and national offices. Notwithstanding the bitter disillusionment over the withdrawal of federal troops from the South in 1877, the black churches continued to display the basic characteristics of the liberation movement—various forms of underground and open resistance to disfranchisement and racial segregation. While it is true, as we have already seen, that a wave of passivity and conservatism swept over African American churches in both the North and South between the First and Second World Wars, we are obliged to be cautious with that generalization when we examine more carefully the activity of what Carter G. Woodson called the "institutional churches" in many black communities.[30] These relatively large urban congregations across the country provided a social, economic, and political witness for liberation during the post-World War I period and into the Great Depression. They correctly understood that the vise of poverty and degradation in which the masses of their people were caught was the result of the deprivation of fundamental freedom and justice in the land of their birth. The liberation tradition slumbered in the black church from time to time, but it never slept.

## INTERRELATIONSHIPS BETWEEN THE THREE TRADITIONS

African Americans in the United States and the Caribbean are, for the most part, Christians. But they are Christian in a sense that is different from what the American public generally understands by the term. The nonsystematic, ambivalent Christianity of African Americans has been mistakenly identified by some scholars with occultism, otherworldliness, and primitive Protestant evangelicalism. Surely there is some of all three in black religion, but they have been transmuted by the experience of slavery and racism. That experience produced one of the most empirical, this-worldly, and culture-sophisticated religious traditions in the Western hemisphere. Moreover, the roots of this kind of religion are not in Rome, Geneva, or Canterbury, but in Calabar, West Kingston, Jamaica, and the plantation country of North America. It obscures the original, distinctive flair of this religion to equate it too easily with its subsequent institutionalization in the established black churches of the United States.

Many African Americans were converted to white Christianity, but many others were forced, by the sheer dint of an irrepressible humanity—and what Charles H. Long has called a "hardness of life"—to invent a religion of their own, a religion of survival.[31] As the Caribbean poet Walcott put the matter in an essay on black history, "What seemed to be surrender was redemption. What seemed the loss of tradition was its renewal. What seemed the death of faith was its rebirth."[32]

The liberation and elevation traditions began with the determination to survive, but they go beyond "make do" to "do more," and from "do more" to "freedom now" and "black power." All three strategies have to do with "making and keeping life human." They are basic to African American life and culture and intertwined in complex ways throughout the history of the diaspora. All three traditions are responses to hard reality in a dominating "white man's world." All three arise from the same religious sensibility that crystallized in African American Christian, Afro-Islamic, and Afro-Judaic sects and cults since the mid-eighteenth century.

Elevation and liberation arise after successful survival. The people could not concern themselves with either until they first learned how to stay alive. Of course, elevationism was grounded in the will to live, but it rose above the constraining and pessimistic attitudes of slavery and established itself on the higher ground of individual and group improvement, the search for moral rectitude, and disinterested benevolence. William Hamilton, addressing the New York African Society in 1809 from the relative safety of lower Manhattan, could declare:

> The gloomy hermit we pity and the snarling synic [*sic*] we despise, these are men who appear to be rubbed off the list of men, they appear to have lost the fine fiber of the mind, on which it depends for expansion and growth, they appear to be sunk into a state of insensibility of the extreme happiness growing out of social life.[33]

Although the situation of most free blacks like Hamilton was little better than slavery, the effort they made in Charleston, Boston, Philadelphia, and Baltimore with groups like the Free African Societies demonstrates that their immediate interest was not so much life and death as mutual encouragement along the path of "happiness growing out of social life." The historic decision of Richard Allen and Absolom Jones to transcend white denominationalism by organizing a nonsectarian society that could solidify the community for morality and mutual welfare led directly to the founding of the first black churches in the North. Allen and Jones were not, of course, so easily to divest themselves of denominationalism, but Allen at least was ultimately successful in wresting control from whites and establishing one of the first national organizations concerned about the elevation and liberation of all African Americans.

If the slave community of the South is where we find the most striking examples of survivalism and can trace it through the Christian churches of the nineteenth century to the heterodox sects and cults of the early twentieth, it is in the free communities of the North, in Charleston, Richmond, Atlanta, and New Orleans that we find incipient elevation and liberation traditions. They began, as we have seen, in the quasi-religious benevolent societies and independent Protestant congregations. They grew, side by side, in the Negro Convention Movement, the black press, black abolitionism, missionary emigrationism, the mission to the freedmen during Reconstruction, the Niagara Movement, the NAACP, National Urban League, and the Civil Rights Movement.

It would be too simplistic to suppose that the survival tradition was exclusively Southern, rural, and lower-class, while the other two were exclusively Northern, urban, and middle-class. Such regional and economic compartmentalization breaks down at several points. The connection between North and South, slave and free, field hand and house servant, rural peasantry and urban proletariat, is too complex for broad generalizations. And yet, with certain qualifications, it is instructive to observe that the survivalist strand, neglected and repressed in the South for more than two centuries, developed a stoical realism and inner strength consistent with its plantation environment. In the North, on the other hand, where the church soon found itself catering to a better-educated class, another set of religious norms and values developed. Radical-aggressive and conservative-avoidance patterns cannot be identified in the North any more than they can be shown among landless farm workers and share-croppers in the South, but the basic orientation of the elevation and liberation traditions was not so much to survive brutality as to liberate by uplifting and to uplift by liberating.

Nor can the latter two traditions be rigidly correlated with the division often made between black separatism and black assimilationism. In the controversy among the Baptists over the white American Baptist Publication Society and the development of independent black schools, many ministers in the South, although steeped in the survivalist tradition and the philosophy of Booker T. Washington, opted for cooperation with the Northern white church.[34] On the other hand, liberation-oriented black Presbyterians in the North demonstrated strong separatist tendencies by organizing a race-conscious ethnic caucus as early as 1894 and supporting the black power movement of the 1960s.

The connections are intricate. All we can say is that there are both separatists and integrationists, or conservatives and progressives in the broad spectrum of each tradition. Nevertheless, the general direction of survivalist strategies seems to incline toward an indifference about interracial cooperation while having a stronger interest in self-help. The general direction of elevationist and liberationist strategies seems to be toward interracial cooperation, but with a willingness to use coercive secular politics rather than church-sponsored charity to address the needs of the race. We may speak of the former tradition as conservative-separatist and the latter two as progressive-integrationist, but such labels must be employed cautiously and will not hold up in all historical contexts.

The elevationist and liberationist church leaders of the nineteenth century sought to free themselves from white control without necessarily rejecting the proffered friendship of whites. Second, they tried to promote the moral and cultural advancement of blacks *within* the American political and economic system. Third, it was their purpose not only to free brothers and sisters in the South by nonviolent means, but to champion the cause of oppressed peoples throughout the world. These characteristics were fairly continuous among clergy during the nineteenth century, for most of them wanted to build self-respecting black institutions and believed that it could not be done without cutting the umbilical cord with whites while continuing, in some respects, to emulate them. But after the death of Allen in 1831, and a secular challenge to the control that preachers exercised over organizations that grew up alongside of the churches, there was an increasing deference to white leadership. The close relationship between Northern church leaders and white allies who promised to secure their full civil rights continued to be problematic. Except for periodic disengagements, as when several leading black ministers broke with William Lloyd Garrison and the American Anti-Slavery Society in the 1840s and 1850s, this ambivalent, semi-dependent relationship continued up to the founding of the NAACP and the National Urban League.

It is important to note, with respect to the survivalist tradition, that the Southern wing of the churches was often closer to a conservative, apolitical form of Christianity than Northern clergy like Reverdy Ransom and S. L. Corrothers, both AME leaders, or Elias C. Morris, J. Milton Waldron, and Sutton E. Griggs, leaders of the National Baptists in the border states.

In any case, there is persuasive evidence that the role of the major African American denominations in activities that can be identified within the elevation and liberation streams contradict the allegation of E. Franklin Frazier that "the Negro church and Negro religion . . . have been responsible for the so-called backwardness of American Negroes."[35]

When we turn to the smaller denominations founded after the Civil War, most notably those that came out of the Holiness and Pentecostal movements, a somewhat different story emerges.[36] We know, for example, that most of their members were Southern in origin, less educated, and of a lower socioeconomic status. When they migrated to the North and West the basic survivalism of their religion went in one of two directions: either it persisted with a strong neo-African and rural flavor in an essentially urban milieu, or became secularized toward a new alignment of folk religiosity with a radically alienated race consciousness.

These smaller sects and denominations deserve much more study than they have received. They represent an important transformation of traditional black religion under modern urban conditions. Unlike many of the mainstream black churches, they had little interest in integration or emulating the standards of whites. They took new form and expression in the storefront churches that multiplied rapidly after the First World War. The challenges they threw up to the established churches in communalism, styles of dress and worship, prohibitions against the new fashions and immoralities of the city, etc., must be understood as a judgment upon what they regarded as dechristianizing influences in mainstream Christianity. They were to find, however, a more formidable obstacle to their own brand of religiosity in the dechristianizing misery and despair of the poor than in the creeping secularism of the black bourgeoisie.

It should come as no surprise that members of "Holy and Sanctified" churches and Pentecostalism turned up in the Garvey movement, the Moorish Science Temple of Noble Drew Ali, Father Divine's Peace Mission, and many of the nationalist and revitalization cults that were spawned in the ghetto. The dechristianization tendency in African American culture after the First World War was partly due to the demoralization of the masses by poverty and racism. If new sects and cults flourished it was because the survival mechanisms that their members found useful in the rural South went through a hardening process in the North that demystified black Christianity and produced a religiously motivated consciousness of color and racial destiny. The intellectuals and artists of the Harlem Renaissance perceived a rich, new culture developing out of this urbanization of survivalism. Their attempt to capture its aesthetic meaning and give it a voice helped create a new cultural nationalism.

Here we see the paradoxical interrelationship between the three traditions. What was happening in this development was their coming together in a new dialectic that was consonant with the demands of urban existence in a racist society. The black power movement, which emerged from secular activists in the North and a church-based Civil Rights Movement in the South, was the ideological consequence of this three-way convergence. Martin Luther King, Jr., personified the dialectical relationship of the three strands of black religion and culture that coalesced in the black power movement which he, paradoxically, rejected. In Dr. King's development as a national leader, nevertheless, we see the interweaving of a moral sternness fueled by the emotionalism of the mass-based black church of the South with the pragmatic, social action orientation of the North. The fact that the Dexter Avenue Baptist Church which he pastored was in Montgomery, Alabama, should not confuse the issue. It had an elevationist and liberationist "Northern exposure," and stands at one end of King's orientation, while at the other end stands the Mason Temple Church of God in Christ, where his involvement with a garbage workers' strike, made up largely of the members of that survivalist denomination, led to his death. That is why King is such a pivotal figure in African American religious history. At the beginning and the end, if not throughout his remarkable ministry, he wove together in his own charismatic personality, all three seminal traditions of black faith.

It was inevitable, therefore, that King would become a source of irritation to Joseph H. Jackson, the powerful leader of the National Baptist Convention, Inc., who was finally unseated from its presidency in 1982. Jackson represented the old-style, Bookerite leadership, essentially survivalist in character but certainly not opposed to racial advancement. This element of black Baptist leadership rather chose a nonconfrontational, conservative amelioration of the black condition. Such an orientation was bound to be threatened by a young Ph.D. from Atlanta who was educated at liberal Crozer Theological Seminary in Chester, Pennsylvania, and more liberal Boston University.

But it is also true, and points to the extraordinary character of King's leadership, that the more liberation-oriented clergy of the North—Adam Clayton Powell, Jr., of Harlem, Nathan Wright of the Episcopal Diocese of Newark, N.J., Bishop John D. Bright of the AME Church in Philadelphia, Bishop Herbert Bell Shaw of the AME Zion Church, and others—had their own questions about whether King's Southern Baptist piety was going to be tough and worldly enough to deal with the depths of white racism in the North. They supported his nonviolent strategy, but they still justified self-defense in a no-way-out confrontation with violent white power. In that regard these churchmen expressed, in a way that King made possible but never quite appreciated, the subtle interpenetration of the survival, elevation, and liberation perspectives among certain mainline clergy. These clergy opened the way to the convergence between the secular black power movement, the radical black studies movement, and black Christian theology.

Studies are still needed to show how black power and the mid-twentieth-century expression of black theology that was closely related to it illuminate the dialectical character of African American religion that was implied by King's leadership. He was never prepared to acknowledge those implications or admit that he had made a contribution to the radical rethinking of black Christianity. The new black theology, nonetheless, was grounded in the liberation tradition of one important segment of the mainstream church to which he belonged. It sought to learn from and assimilate the values of the black consciousness form of the survival tradition that King captured by his appeal to the urban masses.

The three traditions point to the diverse perspectives in the black theology movement. If that movement continues to hold together such divergent points of view as that of Jaramogi Abebe Agyeman, Cornel West, J. Deotis Roberts, and James H. Cone, it is partly because this way of doing theology in the post-Civil Rights African American community stands astride the shoulders of both Martin Luther King, Jr., the tender-hearted liberationist, and El-Hajj Malik El-Shabazz, the tough-minded survivalist.[37]

## WHAT OF THE FUTURE?

We have come full circle in what was intended to be a recapitulation and summary of the main themes and emphases of this book. We have seen that the development of black, womanist, and Afrocentric theologies is a culmination of more than two centuries of struggle and resignation, rejection and affirmation, action and reflection, on the part of men and women related to the subtle and often paradoxical connections between their peoplehood and the truth of biblical religion. It would be unwise to attempt here to predict what will happen to black religion in the twenty-first century, but as a contribution to the discussion about black theology over the past thirty years, I might venture now to indicate what I consider the starting point for fruitful and faithful reflection and praxis among the African American churches in the years ahead.

If we presuppose the central importance of Scripture and the witness of the early church (remembering our emphasis in Chapter 1, on the churches of ancient Egypt, Ethiopia, and Nubia), we can present the African American community itself as the first source of black theology. The generative traditions or motifs we have examined are still extant at the end of the twentieth century and are in the soil of the black community. They continue to resist total institutionalization, merging with the churches at times, but also maintaining a certain distance. They are still nurtured outside the churches by segments of the community that have never ceased resisting white oppression while the churches sometimes cringe behind walls of complacency and fear, or, in deference to an apolitical form of Christianity that belongs more to white evangelicalism than to black faith, retreat into silent neutrality.

Black faith as a folk religion is still available as a motivating force for revolutionary and nationalist movements. From the Ethiopian Manifesto of

Robert Young in the early nineteenth century to the pronouncements of Jaramogi Abebe Agyeman's Pan-African Orthodox Christian Church in the late twentieth century, a tenuous but persistent connection has been maintained to some of the most important elements of African and Afro-Caribbean culture. That connection, whether or not it was recognized by the masses, was particularly evident in nationalist struggles and movements between the 1960s and 1980s.[38] But it has also been reflected in more churchly developments such as the National Black Evangelical Association, the National Office of Black Catholics, the National Conference of Black Christians, Partners in Ecumenism, the Society for the Study of Black Religion, the Black Theology Project of Theology in the Americas, the Congress of Black Churches, and the Kelly Miller Smith Institute's national dialogue on "What Does It Mean to Be Black and Christian?"[39]

To the extent that these groups and those that will take their places continue to draw their main strength from the masses, they will foster the rationalization of certain elements of black religion toward freedom and social justice. Their ideological roots, however, must go down into the soil of the folk community, the life of the streets, if they are to maintain their credibility. That is why the poor people of the African American community who have been bypassed by advances made since the Civil Rights Movement must be considered the primary source for the further development of black Christian theology.

Black theologians must learn to appreciate and understand these roots before turning to white scholarship for the essential content of their reflection on the meaning of God, human existence, and freedom. Folk religion has been a constituent factor in every important crisis in the African American community. We ignore it only at the risk of being cut off from the real springs of corporate action. When the African American community is relatively integrated with white society, the folk religious elements recede from black institutions to form a hard core of inassimilable nationalism in the interstices of the community, biding its time. When the community is hard-pressed by poverty and oppression, when hopes are crushed under the heels of resurgent racism, then folk elements once again come to the surface and begin anew to infiltrate the power centers that ignored or neglected them. This is the significance of the development that Vincent Harding called "the religion of Black Power." It is what lies behind current efforts of groups like the National Congress of Black Churches and the Kelly Miller Smith Institute to create a new theology among the grassroots clergy and laity of the churches.

A second source of black theology should be found in the writings, sermons, and addresses of black preachers and public men and women of the past. Just as white theology has its Calvin, Luther, and Wesley, so black theology has its David Walker, Nathaniel Paul, Richard Allen, Sojourner Truth, and W. E. B. Du Bois. We have not made as much of the work of these heroes and heroines of our history as we should. We need to be reminded that not all African American thinkers for whom religion was a critical resource were members of the clergy or even active church members. But almost all were conditioned by sentiments that reflected the distinctive spirituality that is the essence of black religion and philosophy.[40] The interpretations of the African American experience by such powerful nonclerics as Martin R. Delany, Marcus Garvey, Maulana Karenga, and James Forman were influenced by great men and women of the past who laid a foundation for African American life and culture upon the bedrock of black faith.

Carleton Lee explored the religious roots of black secular protest by showing the significance of prophecy in the black community as spiritual vision, a way of "forth-telling" the transcendent meaning of history revealed to the inspired imagination.[41] To the extent that secular prophets draw upon the story of suffering and struggle to explain the meaning of the faith and hope of the people, they traffic with insights, motifs, and traditions of the African American religious consciousness. They interpret reality in ways that are either unabashedly religious or can be readily incorporated into a basically religious view.

As we have seen in earlier chapters, the writings of nineteenth-century African American philosophers and preachers about such topics as survival, self-help, elevation, chosenness, missionary emigrationism, unity, reparations for slavery, and political and economic liberation anticipate some of the foundational ideas of twentieth-century black theology. These are religiously charged themes with which Payne, Crummell, Henry M. Turner, and Garvey were concerned. The broad vistas of reality that these themes encompass need to be more carefully excavated for the richness of theological insight that they impart.

In 1970 James H. Cone made a beginning of this excavation by publishing a systematic theology based on the black experience. J. Deotis Roberts made a similar effort in 1974.[42] Since those years both scholars have produced further elaborations of their ideas without falling back on the insights of white theologians who have given little or no attention to the meaning of the African American religious experience. The use of white theological categories in black theology is certainly not prohibited, for there is no necessary incompatibility between African American Christianity and the tradition of the church of the first four centuries, particularly churches in Africa, which white scholarship is obliged to recognize, whether it wants to or not. At some point the work of African American theologians will be understood as illuminating the essentials of the Christian faith. While that work may have special relevance for black Christians in the United States, it will enrich and edify the Christian church everywhere in the world.[43]

In the meantime, what is needed to think theologically about the corpus of the black profession of faith in Jesus Christ—both written and oral—is a new consciousness of peoplehood, ethnicity, culture, and a new way of perceiving and ordering the data of the African American community. Our understanding of such data will be helped by using the categories of survival, elevation, and liberation. Of course, new sets of interpretive tools and paradigms will always be needed, and many of them should be sought in the religious history and experience of the African American people which have played such an exceptional, though neglected and depreciated role, in the shaping of American culture and religion. Even since the flowering of black theology in this century, white theologians have made almost no effort to use these data, which continues to make their work of less value to the African American churches. Henry H. Mitchell, as early as 1970, recognized the need for African American Christians to break with the interpretive conventions of history and theology written exclusively by white men and women.

> Just as the new hermeneutic of Ebling and others has sought to recapture the vital message of Luther and the Reformation Fathers for the benefit of their sons, so must the Black hermeneutic seek to look into the message of the Black past and see what the Black Fathers [and Mothers] could be saying to Black people today.[44]

Although Mitchell did not fully explain what such a hermeneutic might look like if we all learn how to communicate in the folk idiom of the uneducated black Baptist preacher and put the gospel on a "tell-it-like-it-is" basis, yet he helped create the interest in black biblical studies that culminated in the publication of articles by ten African American biblical scholars and the continuing work of the Society for the Study of Black Religion.[45] We are discovering that the problem of creating a black hermeneutic is infinitely more difficult than Mitchell's provocative comments suggested. It has to do with the intricate unpacking of the mythology, folklore, and ethics of the African American community as reflected in its oral and literary traditions. Something may have to be done for oppressed blacks in the United States like what Franz Fanon did for the people of Algeria and the French-speaking Caribbean in his *Black Skin, White Masks*.

A black hermeneutic would deal with the morphology of ebonics, the meaning of African American music, poetry, the novel, and the dance, and, as Mitchell recommended, not only with the content, but the accent and cadence of traditional black preaching. In other words, if God has identified with the struggle of black folks in special ways, then we need to know more about those ways, and more about the lifestyle and thought patterns of the community. We need to examine them through the eyes of formal and informal leaders and spokespersons of the past and present. Only so shall black scholars of religion unlock the secrets of the people's experience and develop a critical theology of humanization and liberation that will make contact with and be authenticated by that experience.

Du Bois reminded us that African Americans have been uniquely gifted as "a spiritual people." There is more disagreement with that bald statement today than when he wrote it. But our preeminent philosopher and interpreter of the black experience understood spirituality in a wider and deeper sense. For him it was more than a mood or disposition that belongs exclusively to organized religion.[46] Du Bois also understood theology in a broader, nontechnical sense than that term usually means today. In this nontechnical sense the theology of the African American community is properly developed not exclusively in theological seminaries, but in the streets, beauty parlors, barber shops, pool halls, and night clubs of the community, as well as in the churches.

What the brothers and sisters are saying around a late-hour bar in the community, or among thoughtful members of a harassed street gang, or when a group of hospital orderlies gather for lunch and talk about their patients, may more accurately reflect the operative, pragmatic spirituality and theology of the black community than the religious literature of its neighborhood Sunday Schools. By sensitivity to and knowledge of the variegated facets of African American culture—the thoughts, feelings, moods, and behavior of the people—a hermeneutic can be constructed that will help theologians formulate and read back to the community its own indigenous theology. Such a theology will both be recognizable by the people themselves and be the basis of their own self-criticism. This kind of reflective and self-correcting interpretation of black religion and culture will find that the most basic values of the folk are clustered around a core of beliefs that still includes the conviction that a righteous God ensures human justice in an inhuman and unjust world. Most African Americans still believe that this God of both wrath and mercy calls the poor and oppressed to a more abundant life in this world and in the world beyond.

A third source of black theology comprises the traditional religions of Africa—a knowledge of how they responded to and assimilated elements of Islam and Christianity—and the concepts by which African theologians, especially those in the independent churches, seek to make the Christian faith meaningful to Africa today. This is a source because African Americans are not only a spiritual people but also an African people. Despite the tragic and despotic conditions that prevail in so much of Africa today, conditions for which the former colonial powers must take a large share of responsibility, African Americans need to know what Africa has contributed to and continues to contribute to the knowledge of God and the liberation of the human race.

Of course, there will be differences of opinion about the relevance of Africa to African Americans today. The academic arguments about

African survivals will persist, and many ordinary African Americans will wonder about what contemporary Africa can possibly mean to them. But it should be clear by now that blacks in the United States did not originate *ex nihilo* on the auction blocks of Charleston and New Orleans. The common folk of both continents need to see that their experiences of capitalist exploitation and racism have been too similar to be purely accidental.

The question of an African religious connection—where it can be renewed and whether it can be justified—may be more difficult. But it is still possible and desirable to recover some of the great enduring values of the traditional religions of Africa for the revitalization and enhancement of religion in the United States. This is unlikely to happen, however, if African and African American scholars do not take the initiative to uncover the African religious inheritance for the benefit of the whole human family. The value of such collaboration, jointly sponsored perhaps by the All Africa Conference of Churches, the National Congress of Black Churches, and the Society for the Study of Black Religion, is incalculable. Charles H. Long, making a similar point, remarked:

> Our colleague Mircea Eliade said long ago that the West was in danger of provincialism through a lack of attention to the orientations and solutions of non-Western man. It would be difficult, if not impossible, to make the case for the non-Western identity of the black community in America, though several make this claim. The element of truth in this claim is that though we are Westerners, we are not Western in the same way as our compatriots, and thus we afford within America an entree to the *otherness* of America and the otherness of mankind.[47]

To what do we refer when we speak of the valuable contributions of African religions? Among other elements we should emphasize the following: a sense of the pervasive reality of the spirit world above, within, and beneath the artifactual world of every day; the blotting out of the line between the sacred and the secular; the practical use of religion in all of life; the surrender of excessive individualism for solidarity with the community and nature; the central importance of the family; reverence for the ancestors and recognition of their presence with the living to guide and inspire; the source of evil in the communal consequences of an act rather than in the act *per se;* the creative use of rhythmic movement of the body, singing, and dancing in the celebration of life and the worship of God.

All these elements and more of ATR were found in some form, however attenuated, in the slave community and were absorbed to some degree into black Christianity. Many of them are also found in Native American religions, and more effort should be made to recover values from that source. But it was mainly in the course of the development of the religion we have traced in the preceding chapters that a major effort was made by whites to nullify all African influences and substitute European. It will require another major effort to recover the beliefs and practices of our African American ancestors that defied total assimilation.

The emotionality, spontaneity, and freedom of black religion has much to do with its instinctive resistance to total whitenization, but that resistance is also related to intrinsic differences between African and European spirituality. Differences that have never been successfully reconciled by evangelization. African American scholars cannot continue to ignore these differences if they want to make a contribution to the black church and to American religion in general. More needs to be done in the future if we are to recover and enhance values, particularly those that reflect the affirmation of life, and the unity of all life in the unquenchable desire for survival, elevation, and the freedom to be *Muntu*, man and woman, in the most penetrating sense of that profound Bantu word.

The theological program of African scholars to Africanize Christianity has much to say to African American scholars who want to indigenize the Christian faith in the culture of the black America. In both instances, the purpose should not be a back door method of imposing a white Christianity in black vesture upon the unsuspecting masses in either Africa or in America. On the contrary, it should be a sincere effort to grasp a new revelation of old truths, to unveil the reality of Jesus Christ, the Liberator, in the life and destiny of a people who have suffered much, but who still have much to give to humankind. The future of Christianity in Africa probably belongs to the African Independent Churches. Only sympathetic, intensive, and critical dialogue between Africa, the Caribbean, and North America will be able to expose and explicate the harmonies and disharmonies in black religion on an intercontinental basis and forge theological and ideological linkages that can bind independent Africa and contemporary black America together for the enormous possibilities of the future.

We can only hope and pray that the black world, once it has gained its legitimate and long-denied power, will not repeat the errors of the white world. It is not altogether self-evident from current events that we will escape the mistakes our white brothers and sisters have made. But if Du Bois was right when he insisted that the gift of black folk "is a thing of questing for eternal youth, of fruitful labor, of joy and music," and perhaps other more indefinable qualities that he could not perceive, then the gift is worth preserving and making available to the whole world. If we are vindicated by these enduring characteristics of black faith, reconciliation between some of the world's oldest alienated and embittered peoples will be the eschatological event that all of us await with eager longing.

# Notes

## 1. African Beginnings

1. The Confession of Alexandria of the AACC can be found in Gerald H. Anderson and Thomas F. Stransky, C.S.P., eds., *Mission Trends*, No. 3 (New York: Paulist Press and Eerdmans, 1976), pp. 132–34.

2. The ignominy of the defeat at Adowa was never forgotten by the Italians. "Writing to a young man bound for 'the African war' in 1935, the veteran Gabriele d'Annunzio urged him to wipe out its memory, for he could still feel on his shoulder 'the scar, yes the shameful scar, of Adowa.' " Cited by A. H. M. Jones and Elizabeth Monroe, *A History of Abyssinia* (New York: Negro Universities Press, 1969), p. 145.

3. In 1985 a historic conference on the relationship of African American churches to the churches of Africa was held at Gammon Theological Seminary in Atlanta, under the leadership of Professor John W. Bown of the Gammon faculty. Significantly, the First Pan-African Christian Church Conference, bringing together African and African American Christian scholars and church leaders, was held at the Interdenominational Theological Center in Atlanta, which includes Gammon as one of its six constituent seminaries, from July 17–23, 1988. The theme of African and African American church solidarity was renewed at this important conference organized and chaired by Professor Ndugu Ofori-Atta of the ITC faculty. The papers and addresses of the 1988 conference are contained in a double issue of the *Journal of the Interdenominational Theological Center*, Vol. 16, Nos. 1 and 2, Fall 1988, Spring 1989.

4. See, Cheikh Anta Diop, *The Cultural Unity of Black Africa* (Chicago: Third World Press, 1978).

5. George W. Williams, *A History of The Negro Race in America, 1619–1880*, 2 vols. (New York: G. P. Putnam's Sons, 1883). This remarkable work by the first black graduate of Newton Theological Seminary, Newton Center, Massachusetts, is in nine parts and over a thousand pages. Williams began and concluded his history with Africa. At the end he shares his vision of its glory restored, after the ravages of slavery and paganism, by Christianity, education, and modern technology, contributed by the rest of the world, including African Americans.

6. William J. Walls, *The African Methodist Episcopal Zion Church: Reality of the Black Church* (Charlotte: A.M.E. Zion Publishing House, 1974), pp. 13–22.

7. Among works by Africans and African Americans, dating from the Second World War to the present, are Cheikh Anta Diop, *The African Origin of Civilization: Myth or Reality* (New York: Lawrence Hill, 1974); J. C. deGraft-Johnson, *African*

*Glory: The Story of Vanished Negro Civilizations* (Baltimore: Black Classic Press, 1986); Ivan van Sertima and Larry Williams, eds., *Great African Thinkers: Cheikh Anta Diop* (New Brunswick: Transaction Books, 1986); John G. Jackson, *Introduction to African Civilizations* (Secaucus, N.J.: Citadel Press, 1980); Willis N. Huggins and John G. Jackson, *An Introduction to African Civilization: With Main Currents in Ethiopian History* (New York: Negro Universities Press, 1969); Yosef ben Jochannan, *African Origins of the Major "Western Religions"* (New York: Alkebu-Lan Books, 1970); Molefi Kete Asante, Kemet, *Afrocentricity and Knowledge* (Trenton: Africa World Press, 1990); Maulana Karenga, *Selections from the Husia: Sacred Wisdom of Ancient Egypt* (Los Angeles: University of Sankore Press, 1984); and Chancellor Williams, *The Destruction of Black Civilization: Great Issues of Race from 4500 B.C. to 2000 A.D.* (Chicago: Third World Press, 1974).

8. Also of relevance to this area of study, which cannot be dealt with in this book, are recent works by African American biblical scholars—particularly scholars of the Hebrew Bible. See, for example, Alfred G. Dunston, Jr., *The Black Man in the Old Testament and Its World* (Philadelphia: Dorrance, 1974); Charles B. Copher, *Black Biblical Studies* (Chicago: Black Light Fellowship, 1993); Cain H. Felder, *Troubling Biblical Waters* (Maryknoll, N.Y.: Orbis, 1989); Cain H. Felder, ed., *Stony the Road We Trod: African American Biblical Interpretation* (Minneapolis: Fortress Press, 1991); and Walter A. McCray, *The Black Presence in the Bible* (Chicago: Black Light Fellowship, 1990).

9. John S. Mbiti, *African Religions & Philosophy* (New York: Praeger, 1969), p. 48.

10. Noel Q. King, *Christian and Muslim in Africa* (New York: Harper & Row, 1971), p. 3.

11. John G. Jackson, *Introduction to African Civilizations* (Secaucus, N.J.: Citadel Press, 1970) p. 134, citing E. A. Wallis Budge, *Osiris: The Egyptian Religion of the Resurrection*, 2 vols. (New Hyde Park, N.Y.: University Books, 1961), vol. 1, p. 174.

12. The Solomon-Sheba story is preserved in the treasured Ethiopian work, *Kebra-Nagast* ("Glory of Kings"), said to be a translation of a Coptic original found in Constantinople before A.D. 325. See Jean Doresse, *Ethiopia* (New York: Frederick Ungar, 1959), pp. 13–14.

13. The proximity to Palestine made it possible for a strong Jewish presence in both Egypt and Ethiopia during the centuries following the Exodus. Philo reports that the Jewish population of Egypt reached a million, with 200,000 dwelling in Alexandria alone. C. P. Groves, *The Planting of Christianity in Africa* (London: Lutterworth Press, 1948), vol. 1, p. 36.

14. We learn that the eunuch's name was Judich from the historian, Eusebius of Caesarea, *Ecclesiastical History*, II, 1, 13.

15. Bishop Athanasius of Beni-Suef and Bahnasa, *The Copts Through the Ages* (Arab Republic of Egypt Ministry of Information, n.d.), p. 5. One of the greatest public celebrations in modern Egypt was held in the new Cairo Cathedral on June 25, 1968, in recognition of the 1900th anniversary of the martyrdom of the founder of the Egyptian church.

16. For a brief but excellent treatment of the invention of monasticism in the Egyptian desert and the exploits of black Christians in the earliest days of the African church, see Martin de Porres Walsh, O.P., *The Ancient Black Christians* (San Francisco: Julian Richardson, 1969). Also, Cyprian Davis, *The History of Black Catholics in the United States* (New York: Crossroad, 1990), pp. 1–27.

17. Walsh, *Ancient Black Christians*, pp. 5–6. The story is also found in the Acta Sanctorum of the Roman Catholic Church.

18. *The Church of Ethiopia: A Panorama of History and Spiritual Life* (Addis Ababa: A publication of the Ethiopian Orthodox Church, 1970), pp. 3–6.

19. Doresse, *Ethiopia*, p. 64.

20. Groves, *Planting of Christianity in Africa*, p. 139.

21. Cited by Groves, ibid., pp. 141–42.

22. Giovanni Fantini, *Christianity in the Sudan* (Bologna: EMI, 1981), p. 25.

23. Ibid., p. 27.

24. Groves, *Planting of Christianity in Africa*, pp. 49–50.

25. Fantini, *Christianity in the Sudan*, pp. 199–202. Rumors persisted through the Middle Ages that small communities of Christians were scattered west and north of Dongola as far as Bornu and the Lake Chad area. Several hopeful missions were dispatched from Rome to contact them, but without success. Nevertheless, Nubian Christianity may have existed in an attenuated form as late as the eighteenth century. See William Y. Adams, *Nubia: Corridor to Africa* (Princeton: Princeton University Press, 1984), pp. 542–543.

26 Ibrahim Abu-Lughod, "Islam in Africa," in the *World Encyclopedia of Black Peoples*, vol. 1, Conspectus (St. Clair Shores, Mich.: Scholarly Press, 1975), p. 284.

27. The Oneness of God, prayer five times a day, the giving of alms to the poor, the annual pilgrimage to Mecca, and fasting from dawn to sunset during the sacred month of Ramadan. Some Muslims add the jihad, or holy war against the enemies of Allah.

28. King, *Christian and Muslim in Africa*, pp. 23–24.

29. Sir Harry H. Johnston, *The Colonization of Africa* (Cambridge: Cambridge University Press, 1930), p. 85.

30. Groves, *Planting of Christianity in Africa*, p. 129. For important detail on developments in the Western Sudan during the period of the great empires of Ghana, Mali, and Songhai to the nineteenth century, with suggestions for teaching this history to African Americans, see Willis N. Huggins and John G. Jackson, *An Introduction to African Civilizations* (New York: Negro Universities Press, 1969), pp. 122–39.

31. Elizabeth Isichei, *A History of Christianity in Africa: From Antiquity to the Present* (Grand Rapids: Eerdmans, 1995), p. 54.

32. Groves, *Planting of Christianity in Africa*, p. 131.

33. Lamin Sanneh, *West African Christianity: The Religious Impact* (Maryknoll, N.Y.: Orbis, 1983), p. 53.

34. Ellen Gibson Wilson, *The Loyal Blacks* (New York: G. P. Putnam's Sons, 1976), p. 151.

35. Ibid., p. 222.

36. For detailed discussions of the evangelization of West Africa by Africans and African Americans, see Sanneh, *West African Christianity*; David B. Barrett, *Schism and Renewal in Africa: An Analysis of Six Thousand Contemporary Religious Movements* (Nairobi: Oxford University Press, 1968); Sandy D. Martin, *Black Baptists and African Missions: The Origins of a Movement, 1880–1915* (Macon: Mercer University Press, 1989); Leroy Fitts, *Lott Carey: First Black Missionary to Africa* (Valley Forge: Judson Press, 1978); Walter L. Williams, *Black Americans and the Evangelization of Africa, 1877–1900* (Madison: University of Wisconsin Press, 1982); E. A. Ayandele,

*Holy Johnson, Pioneer of African Nationalism* (London: Frank Cass, 1970); and St. Clair Drake, *The Redemption of Africa and Black Religion* (Chicago: Third World Press, 1970).

37. A standard source of information about independency in Africa is David B. Barrett, *Schism and Renewal in Africa.* See also Nathaniel I. Ndiokwere, *Prophecy and Revelation: The Role of Prophets in the Independent African Churches and in Biblical Tradition* (London: SPCK, 1981), and Adrian Hastings, *African Christianity* (New York: Seabury Press, 1976).

38. Johnston, *Colonization of Africa,* pp. 48, 51.

39. Cited by Albert J. Raboteau, *Slave Religion: The "Invisible Institution" in the Antebellum South* (New York: Oxford University Press, 1978), p. 47.

40. Kofi Asare Opoku, "The West Through African Eyes," in the *International Journal of Africana Studies,* vol. 4, nos. 1 and 2, December 1996, p. 87.

41. King, *Christian and Muslim in Africa,* p. 113.

### 2. The Religion of the Slave

1. James Ramsey, *An Essay on the Treatment and Conversion of American Slaves* (London, 1784), p. 173.

2. See a seminal article in the early 1970s by Charles Long, "Perspectives for a Study of Afro-American Religion in the United States," *History of Religions,* vol. 11, no. 1, Aug. 1971. An important early book was that of Joseph R. Washington, Jr., *Black Religion: The Negro and Christianity in the United States* (Boston: Beacon, 1964). See also C. Eric Lincoln, ed., *The Black Experience in Religion* (Garden City, N.Y.: Anchor/Doubleday, 1974); Emmanuel L. McCall, ed., *Black Church Lifestyles* (Nashville: Broadman, 1986); Henry H. Mitchell, *Black Belief: Folk Beliefs of Blacks in America and West Africa* (New York: Harper & Row, 1975); George Eaton Simpson, *Black Religions in the New World* (Columbia University Press, 1978).

3. Newbell N. Puckett, *Folk Beliefs of the Southern Negro* (University of North Carolina Press, 1926), p. 545.

4. W. E. B. Du Bois, *The Negro Church* (Atlanta University Press, 1903), p. 5. A more recent study of obeah, different from but closely related to what was called "voodoo" in North America, is that of Tim McCartney, *Ten, Ten, The Bible, Ten: Obeah in the Bahamas* (Nassau: Timpaul Publ. Co., 1976).

5. See Benjamin Brawley, *A Social History of the American Negro* (New York: Macmillan, 1921), p. 7.

6. See ibid., pp. 4–5.

7. See Melville Herskovits, *The Myth of the Negro Past* (Boston: Beacon, 1958), p. 106.

8. Ibid. The Herskovits thesis has been widely debated in recent years. Most commentators see exaggerations in his theory of African survivals, but take a more positive view of his overall perspective. An excellent discussion is found in Norman E. Whitten, Jr., and John F. Szwed, eds., *Afro-American Anthropology: Contemporary Perspectives* (New York: Free Press, 1970), pp. 23–60.

9. See Carter G. Woodson, *The History of the Negro Church* (Washington: Associated Publishers, 1945), p. 7; Lorenzo J. Greene, *The Negro in Colonial New England* (Columbia University Press, 1942), p. 282.

10. Eugene D. Genovese, *Roll, Jordan, Roll: The World the Slaves Made* (New York: Pantheon, 1974), p. 211.

11. W. E. B. Du Bois, *The Souls of Black Folk* (Chicago: A.C. McClurg & Co., 1929), p. 141.

12. E. Franklin Frazier, *The Negro Church in America* (University of Liverpool Press, 1963), p. 11.

13. Clifton H. Johnson, *God Stuck Me Dead* (Philadephia: Pilgrim, 1969); Harold A. Carter, *The Prayer Tradition of Black People* (Valley Forge, Pa.: Judson, 1976); Benjamin E. Mays, *The Negro's God* (Boston: Chapman and Grimes, 1938); Miles M. Fisher, *Negro Slave Songs in the United States* (New York: Russell & Russell, 1968); John Lovell, Jr., *Black Song: The Forge and the Flame* (New York: Macmillan, 1972); LeRoi Jones, *Blues People* (New York: William Morrow, 1963).

14. Charles C. Jones, *The Religious Instruction of Negroes in the United States* (Savannah: T. Purse Co., 1842), pp. 125 ff.

15. Ibid.

16. See Henderson H. Donald, *The Negro Freedom* (New York: Schuman, 1952), pp. 110–111, quoting C. Stearns, *The Black Man of the South and the Rebels* (New York: American News Co., 1872).

17. See Donald, *Negro Freedom.* See also B. A. Botkin, ed., *Lay My Burden Down: A Folk History of Slavery* (University of Chicago Press, 1945), pp. 25–60.

18. Jones, *Religious Instruction*, p. 126.

19. This testimony is not uncommon in reports of slave religion; see, e.g., William Jay to Bishop Ives, Dec. 1846, in *Miscellaneous Writings on Slavery* (Boston: John P. Jewett & Co., 1853), p. 471.

20. Joseph B. Earnest, *The Religious Development of the Negro in Virginia* (Charlottesville: Mitchie, 1914), p. 134.

21. Puckett, *Folk Beliefs*, p. 526. For a more recent discussion of the relationship between slave religion and conjuration, see Albert J. Raboteau, *Slave Religion: The "Invisible Institution" in the Antebellum South* (New York: Oxford University Press, 1978), pp. 275–88.

22. See Botkin, *Lay My Burden Down*, p. 37.

23. See Leonard E. Barrett, *Soul-Force: African Heritage in Afro-American Religion* (Garden City, N.Y.: Anchor, 1974), pp. 63–69.

24. Quoted in Donald G. Matthews, *Slavery and Methodism* (Princeton University Press, 1965), p. 76.

25. Jones, *Religious Instruction*, p. 126.

26. Ibid., p. 127.

27. See George P. Rawick, *The American Slave: A Composite Autobiography* (Westport, Conn.: Greenwood, 1972) vols. 1, 6, 10, 18; Georgia Writers' Project, Works Project Administration, *Drums and Shadows* (University of Georgia Press, 1940); Simpson, *Black Religions;* Roger Bastide, *African Civilizations in the New World* (New York: Harper Torchbooks, 1971); Janheinz Jahn, *Muntu: An Outline of the New African Culture* (New York: Grove, 1961); LeRoi Jones, *Black Music* (New York: William Morrow, 1967); Ulysses D. Jenkins, *Ancient African Religion and the African-American Church* (Jacksonville, N.C.: Flame International, 1978). Although there have been numerous articles and unpublished monographs on the subject during the last decade, a definitive work on the African roots of black religion in North America still needs to be written.

28. The older works by Woodson, Du Bois, Cromwell, and Huggins are still important—e.g., Du Bois, *The World and Africa* (New York: International Publishers, enlarged ed., 1965), and Willis N. Huggins and John G. Jackson, *An*

*Introduction to African Civilizations* (New York: Negro Universities Press, reprint, 1969). See also Yosef ben-Jochannan, *African Origins of the Major "Western Religions"* (New York: Alkebu-lan Books, 1970), and Chancellor Williams, *The Destruction of Black Civilization* (Chicago: Third World Press, rev. ed., 1976). Works on African religion relevant to slave religion include: John S. Mbiti, *African Religions and Philosophy* (New York: Praeger, 1969); Geoffrey Parrinder, *West African Religion* (New York: Barnes & Noble, 1970); E. Bolaji Idowu, *African Traditional Religion* (Maryknoll, N.Y.: Orbis, 1973); Kofi Asare Opoku, *West African Traditional Religion* (Singapore: FEP International Private, Ltd., 1978); Kwesi A. Dickson and Paul Ellingworth, eds., *Biblical Revelation and African Beliefs* (London: Lutterworth, and Maryknoll, N.Y.: Orbis, 1969); J. V. Taylor, *The Primal Vision* (London: SCM Press, 1963).

29. See Mbiti, *African Religions*, pp. 15–16, 29–67.

30. Ibid., p. 52.

31. Ibid., p. 170. See also, Mechal Sobel, *Trablin' On: The Slave Journey to an Afro-Baptist Faith* (Westport, Conn.: Greenwood Press, 1979).

32. See George P. Rawick, *From Sundown to Sunup: The Making of the Black Community* (Westport, Conn.: Greenwood, 1972), pp. 37–38; Genovese, *Roll, Jordan, Roll*, pp. 216–18; and Sobel, *op. cit.*, pp. 33–34.

33. Herskovits, *Myth*, p. 107. See also William C. Suttles, Jr., "African Religious Survivals as Factors in American Slave Revolts," *Journal of Negro History*, vol. 56 (April 1971), pp. 99–104.

34. See Joseph J. Williams, *Voodoos and Obeahs* (New York: Dial, 1933); Jahn, *Muntu*, esp. chap. 2; Alfred Metraux, *Voodoo in Haiti* (New York: Oxford University Press, 1959); Bastide, *African Civilizations*, pp. 138–49; Maya Deren, *Divine Horsemen: Voodoo Gods of Haiti* (New York: Dell, 1970).

35. See the article in the *New Catholic Encyclopedia*, vol. 14, p. 752, and Metraux, *Voodoo*, pp. 30 ff.

36. See Parrinder, *West African Religion*, pp. 35 ff. However, Herskovits in his study *Trinidad Village* (New York, 1947) reports a native as saying that "all obia-men keep snakes," p. 225. J. J. Williams refers to an official document published in London in 1789 that says that obeah (witchcraft or sorcery) derives from the Egyptian *Ob* ("serpent"), which applies to "one particular sect, the remnant probably of a very celebrated religious order in remote ages" (Williams, *Destruction*, p. 109).

37. Metraux, *Voodoo*, p. 28.

38. See ibid., p. 34. Metraux follows the early descriptions of Moreau de Saint-Méry, but doubts the centrality of snake worship, which he says, in any case, died out in the nineteenth century.

39. See ibid., p. 364.

40. Mbiti, *African Religions*, pp. 209–10.

41. See Metraux, *Voodoo*, p. 48. Lerone Bennett says that Toussaint's nephew tells of the deposed general's renunciation of Christianity when he walked to the altar of a village church and hurled the crucifix to the floor with the words, "You! You are the God of the white man, not the God of the Negroes! You have betrayed men, and deserted me! You have no pity for my race!" (*Before the Mayflower* [Baltimore: Penguin, 1966], p. 108).

42. See Vittorio Lanternari, *The Religions of the Oppressed* (New York: Knopf, 1963), p. 140.

43. Bellgarde, *Histoire de peuple haïten*, cited in Metraux, *Voodoo*, p. 41.

44. Matthews, *Slavery*, p. 77.

45. Anson West, *A History of Methodism in Alabama* (Nashville: Publishing House, Methodist Episcopal Church, South, 1893).

46. Quoted by Du Bois, *The Negro Church*, p. 11.

47. Ibid.

48. For a discussion of the concept of freedom in primal religions, see Mircea Eliade, *Myths, Dreams and Mysteries* (New York: Harper & Row, 1967), pp. 103–6.

49. Joseph R. Washington, Jr., *Black Religion* (Boston: Beacon, 1964), p. 33. Although Washington raised a storm of protest and subsequently shifted his views on the inauthenticity of the theological credentials of the independent black churches, he was the first scholar during the civil rights period to examine the unique nature and function of black religion in the United States as differentiated from white Protestantism, Roman Catholicism, and Judaism. His work led to fruitful debates among black scholars and in the NCBC in 1966–67. He sought to correct some of his earlier negative appraisal in his second book, *The Politics of God* (Boston: Beacon, 1967).

### *3. Not Peace, but the Sword*

1. See Herbert Aptheker, *American Negro Slave Revolts* (New York: International Publishers, 1943), p. 162. Aptheker reports some 250 "revolts and conspiracies" during the history of American slavery. He does not include many that took place in the Caribbean and Central and South America. See W. E. B. Du Bois, *The World and Africa* (New York: International Publishers, 1965), pp. 60–62.

2. James Redpath, *The Roving Editor, or Talks with Slaves in the Southern States* (New York: A. B. Burdick, 1859), pp. vi–vii.

3. Several new studies, however, have appeared since the 1960s. See, e.g., William F. Cheek, *Black Resistance Before The Civil War* (Beverly Hills: Glencoe, 1970); Peter H. Wood, *Black Majority* (New York: Knopf, 1974), pp. 308–26; Vincent Harding, *There Is a River: The Black Struggle for Freedom in America* (New York: Harcourt Brace Jovanovich, 1981).

4. Quoted by Joe Grady Taylor, *Negro Slavery in Louisiana* (Baton Rouge: Burns and MacEachern, 1963), p. 222.

5. Aptheker, *American Negro*, p. 177.

6. Ibid., p. 190.

7. Quoted by James Hugo Johnston, "The Participation of White Men in Virginia Negro Insurrections," *Journal of Negro History*, vol. 16, 1931, p. 159.

8. Aptheker, *American Negro*, pp. 106–7; Vincent Harding, "Religion and Resistance Among Ante-Bellum Negroes, 1800–1860," in August Meier and Elliott Rudwick, eds., *The Making of Black America* (New York: Atheneum, 1969); Eugene D. Genovese, *Roll, Jordan, Roll: The World the Slaves Made* (New York: Pantheon, 1974), pp. 259–61.

9. Sterling Stuckey, in an article that throws new light on the protest role of the Negro spiritual and folk song, writes: "There seems to be small doubt that Christianity contributed in large measure to a spirit of patience which militated against open rebellion among the bondsmen. Yet to overemphasize this point leads one to obscure a no less important reality: Christianity, after being rein-

terpreted and recast by slave bards, also contributed to that spirit of endurance which powered generations of bondsmen, bringing them to that decisive moment when for the first time a real choice was available to scores of thousands of them" ("Through the Prism of Folklore," in *Black and White in American Culture*, Jules Chametzky and Sidney Kaplan, eds. [University of Massachusetts Press, 1969], p. 183).

10. See Carter G. Woodson, *The History of the Negro Church* (Washington: Associated Publishers, 1945), pp. 32–33.

11. Herbert Aptheker, *A Documentary History of the Negro People in the United States* (New York: Citadel, 1951), p. 9.

12. Ibid., p. 11.

13. For the attitude and activity of black church leaders, esp. those in New York, regarding slave revolts in contrast to the nonviolent philosophy of Garrison and the Quakers, see Carleton Mabee, *Black Freedom* (Toronto: Macmillan, 1970), pp. 51–56, 276 ff., and Benjamin Quarles, *Black Abolitionists* (New York: Oxford University Press, 1969), pp. 224–30.

14. Aptheker, *Documentary History*, pp. 91–92. See also Sterling Stuckey, *The Ideological Origins of Black Nationalism* (Boston: Beacon, 1972), pp. 7–8, 32–38.

15. Aptheker, *Documentary History*, p. 92.

16. It is not known whether or not Nat Turner, who certainly read widely, ever came into possession of the Ethiopian Manifesto. He did, however, have certain strange marks at birth that he and his parents took to be signs of a divine commission to do some great work for his people. The Bashilele people of the Congo, under anti-European prophetic movements dating back to 1904, looked for a black messiah to fight against the whites. Andre Matswa, the successor of Simon Kimbangu, was regarded as the messiah during his lifetime. After his death (1942) he was called Jesus Matswa—"the Black Christ" (Vittorio Lanternari, *The Religions of the Oppressed* [New York: Knopf, 1963], pp. 24–27).

17. See Aptheker, *"One Continual Cry," David Walker's Appeal* (New York: Humanities Press, 1965), pp. 45 ff.

18. See Henry Highland Garnet, *Walker's Appeal, With a Brief Sketch of His Life* (New York: J. H. Tobitt, 1848), p. v.

19. See Charles M. Wiltse, *David Walker's Appeal* (New York: Hill and Wang, 1965), p. viii.

20. See ibid.

21. Garnet, *Walker's Appeal*, p. vii.

22. Ibid. Wiltse says that Walker was found dead near the doorway of his shop, suggesting that death was sudden and without warning. There are grounds for suspicion that he met a violent end either in Boston or Richmond. Aptheker cites a letter that appeared in January 1831, over the signature of "A Colored Bostonian," which alleges that after painstaking investigation the writer learned that southern planters had spread the word in Boston that $3,000 would be given for the life of David Walker (*"One Continual Cry,"* p. 53).

23. Garnet, *Walker's Appeal*, p. viii.

24. Aptheker, *"One Continual Cry,"* p. 138.

25. Ibid., p. 80.

26. Ibid., p. 104.

27. Ibid., pp. 128–29.

28. Ibid., p. 89.

29. Ibid., p. 137.

30. Ibid., p. 133.

31. Ibid., p. 137.

32. Walker was able to get some copies into southern ports by slipping them into the pockets of black sailors who reclaimed their clothing at his shop on Brattle Street.

33. Wiltse, *David Walker's Appeal*, p. x.

34. See ibid. See also Samuel J. May, *Some Recollections of Our Antislavery Conflict* (Boston: Fields, Osgood & Co., 1869), pp. 133–34.

35. Quoted by Mabee, *Black Freedom*, p. 277.

36. See Quarles, *Black Abolitionists*, pp. 47–50, 53.

37. See Aptheker, *American Negro*, pp. 105–6. For an excellent discussion on the black preacher as revolutionary leader, see Genovese, *Roll, Jordan, Roll*, pp. 265 ff.

38. Aptheker, *American Negro*, p. 139.

39. See W. E. B. Du Bois, *The Souls of Black Folk* (New York: Avon, 1965), p. 146.

40. Ibid., pp. 147–48; italics added.

41. Joseph C. Carroll, *Slave Insurrections in the United States, 1800–1865* (Boston: Chapman & Grimes, 1938), p. 14; Aptheker, *American Negro*, p. 166. Slave revolts in the Americas, however, began as early as 1522 in Haiti; 1530 in Mexico; 1523, 1537, and 1548 in Santo Domingo; 1649 in the British West Indies. Roger Bastide writes: "Many of them, it is true, were spontaneous risings, a violent and passionate reaction to systematic torture or inhuman working schedules. Others, however, were most carefully organized and planned over a long period; and the leaders of such movements tended to be religious figures" (*African Civilizations in the New World* [New York: Harper Torchbooks, 1971], p. 47).

42. See Joseph B. Earnest, *The Religious Development of the Negro in Virginia* (Charlottesville: The Machine Co., 1914), p. 27.

43. See Joshua Coffin, *An Account of Some of the Principal Slave Insurrections* (Westport, Conn.: Negro Universities Press, 1970), p. 9.

44. Carroll, *Insurrections*, p. 18.

45. See ibid. See also Woodson, *The Education of the Negro Prior to 1861* (Washington, D.C., 1919), p. 27, and Benjamin Brawley, *A Social History of the American Negro* (New York: Macmillan, 1921), pp. 36–40.

46. Carroll, *Insurrections*, p. 14.

47. See Faith Vibert, "The Society for the Propagation of the Gospel," *Journal of Negro History*, vol. 18, p. 176.

48. In order to allay the fear that conversion would require manumission, the bishop of London laid down a fundamental principle in 1727 that was to become the basis of law in the British colonies: "The freedom which Christianity gives is a freedom from the bondage of sin and Satan and from the dominion of men's lusts and passions and inordinate desires; but as to their *outward* condition, whatever that was before, whether bond or free, their being baptized and becoming Christian, makes no matter of change in it" (quoted in Charles C. Jones, *The Religious Instruction of Negroes in the United States* [Savannah: T. Purse Co., 1842], p. 20).

49. See Aptheker, *American Negro*, p. 179.

50. See Gooch to the bishop of London, May 28, 1731, in the *Virginia Magazine of History and Biography*, vol. 32, pp. 322–23.

51. See Carroll, *Insurrections*, p. 22.

52. See C. L. R. James, *A History of Negro Revolt* (New York: Haskell House, 1969), p. 22. For much of the eighteenth century St. Augustine was a haven for escaped slaves and after the Revolutionary War served as a collection point for many black loyalists who followed the British to the Bahamas, Jamaica, and Nova Scotia.

53. See Aptheker, *American Negro*, pp. 188–89.

54. Ibid., p. 190.

55. Carroll, *Insurrections*, pp. 27–30. See also Brawley, *A Social History*, pp. 43–47. Aptheker cites a letter from a Massachusetts correspondent to one Cadwallader Colden in which the hysteria that seized the populace is compared to the Salem witchcraft panic. In this connection see also Charles A. Beard and Mary R. Beard, *The Rise of American Civilization—The Agricultural Era* (New York: Macmillan, 1927), p. 81.

56. Benjamin E. Mays, *The Negro's God* (Boston: Mt. Vernon Press, 1938), pp. 26 ff. See also James H. Cone, *The Spirituals and the Blues: An Interpretation* (New York: Seabury, 1972), pp. 38–39.

57. See R. A. and Alice Bauer, "Day to Day Resistance to Slavery," *Journal of Negro History*, vol. 26, pp. 388 ff.; Herbert Aptheker, "Slave Resistance in the United States," in *Key Issues in the Afro-American Experience*, Nathan I. Huggins, Martin Kilson, and Daniel M. Fox, eds. (New York: Harcourt Brace Jovanovich, 1971), vol. 1, pp. 164–65.

### *4. Three Generals in the Lord's Army*

1. See Joseph C. Carroll, *Slave Insurrections in the United States, 1800–1865* (Boston: Chapman & Grimes, 1938), p. 49.

2. Benjamin Brawley mentions that during this unusual storm the original force dwindled to three hundred men, and many of them were paralyzed by fear and superstition (*A Social History of the American Negro* [New York: Macmillan, 1921], p. 87).

3. See Carroll, *Insurrections*, p. 50; see also Aptheker, *American Negro Slave Revolts* (New York: International Publishers, 1943), p. 225. Gerald W. Mullin writes, "He [Gabriel] only talked of 10,000 men before gatherings of slaves of all kinds; in the privacy of Prosser's blacksmith shop, he carefully assessed his limited resources and planned accordingly. . . . A small guerrilla force of about two hundred men would enter Richmond at midnight, thoroughly terrorize the city by burning its warehouse district and (initially) killing indiscriminately, capturing stores of arms, and taking the governor as a hostage" (*Flight and Rebellion: Slave Resistance in Eighteenth-Century Virginia* [New York: Oxford University Press, 1972], p. 150).

4. See Aptheker, *American Negro*, p. 222.

5. Carroll, *Insurrections*, p. 56.

6. See Aptheker, *American Negro*, pp. 226–61.

7. Carroll, *Insurrections*, p. 63. The preceding year St. George Tucker wrote a letter to a member of the General Assembly of Virginia in which he said, "Fanaticism is spreading fast among the Negroes of this country, and may form in time the connecting link between the black religionists and the white. Do you not, already sir, discover something like a sympathy between them? It certainly

would not be a novelty, in the history of the world, if Religion were made to sanctify plots and conspiracies" (Mullin, *Flight*, p. 203).

8. See Carroll, *Insurrections*, p. 70.

9. See Aptheker, *American Negro*, p. 246.

10. Carroll, *Insurrections*, p. 74. Gabriel Prosser's brother Martin was a preacher and played an important role in the conspiracy. It was he who spoke of their cause as being "similar to [that of the] Israelites." In the light of the appeals made to religion by Gabriel, Martin, and Ben Woolfolk, the coordinator, it is difficult to understand Mullin's judgment that the rebellion lacked "a sacred dimension" (*Flight*, p. 160).

11. See John Loften, *Insurrection in South Carolina* (Yellow Springs, Ohio: Antioch Press, 1964); John O. Killens, ed., *The Trial Record of Denmark Vesey* (Boston: Beacon, 1970); Robert Starobin, "Denmark Vesey's Slave Conspiracy of 1822: A Study in Rebellion and Repression," in John Bracey et al., eds., *American Slavery: The Question of Resistance* (Belmont, Cal.: Wadsworth, 1970), pp. 142–57.

12. See Carroll, *Insurrections*, p. 85.

13. See J. Victor Orville, *The History of American Conspiracies* (New York: J. D. Torrey Co., 1863), p. 377. Sierra Leone blacks, both African and Creole, were sullen and rebellious several times during the century. A revolt among the Mende occurred in 1898 because of corporal punishment and the poll tax. The insurgents killed every missionary they could find and also certain Europeanized blacks. See C. L. R. James, *A History of Negro Revolt* (New York: Haskell House, 1969), p. 42.

14. See Victor, *The History*, p. 376; Carroll, *Insurrections*, p. 86.

15. Note the use of the number seven also in Vesey's battle plan. There were seven attack forces or groups prepared, with Vesey himself in command of the seventh, which was to march on the main guardhouse. A coincidence? See Loften, *Insurrection*, p. 141.

16. See Carroll, *Insurrections*, pp. 87–88.

17. Loften, *Insurrection*, p. 136.

18. See ibid., p. 91.

19. Ibid., p. 92; W. E. B. Du Bois, *The Negro Church* (Atlanta University Press, 1903), pp. 11–12.

20. See Carroll, *Insurrections*, p. 87; C. C. Jones, *The Religious Instruction of Negroes in the United States* (Savannah: T. Purse Co., 1842), p. 214.

21. See Charles H. Wesley, *Richard Allen: Apostle of Freedom* (Washington, D.C.: Associated Publishers, 1969, reprint), pp. 185–88; George Shepperson and Thomas Price, *The Independent African* (Edinburgh University Press, 1958), p. 107.

22. See Loften, *Insurrection*, p. 92.

23. See Carroll, *Insurrections*, p. 96.

24. See Victor, *The History*, p. 378.

25. Henry Bibb, *Slave Insurrection in 1831 in Southampton County, Virginia* (New York: Wesleyan Book Room, 1850), p. 3.

26. See Carroll, *Insurrections*, pp. 100–101.

27. Brawley, *A Social History*, p. 139. Peter Poyas deserves more attention than has been given him. He was a devout layman of the AME Church and had 600 names on his assault group's list, yet not one of them was arrested or betrayed his companions; see Victor, *The History*, p. 385.

28. Carroll finds no discontent among the slaves until 1826. Aptheker pre-

sents evidence that there were risings in Virginia, South Carolina, and North Carolina before that date (*American Negro,* pp. 276–77).

29. See Aptheker, *American Negro,* p. 275.

30. William Styron, *The Confessions of Nat Turner* (New York: Random House, 1966). A comprehensive documentary account of the event is that of Henry Irving Tragle, *The Southampton Slave Revolt of 1831: A Compilation of Source Material* (University of Massachusetts Press, 1971). See also, with a full text of "The Confessions," Herbert Aptheker, *Nat Turner's Slave Rebellion* (New York: Humanities Press, 1966); Stephen B. Oates, *The Fires of Jubilee: Nat Turner's Fierce Rebellion* (New York: Harper & Row, 1975).

31. John Henrik Clarke, ed., *William Styron's Nat Turner* (Boston: Beacon, 1968), pp. viii–ix.

32. Charles V. Hamilton, "Our Nat Turner and William Styron's Creation," in Clarke, *Styron's Nat Turner,* p. 74.

33. See F. Roy Johnson, *The Nat Turner Insurrection* (Murfreesboro, N.C.: Johnson Publ. Co., 1966), p. 16. Johnson, more than Aptheker and others, appreciates the African background of Turner's religion. He also recognizes the influence of West Indian spirituality in black religion and reports that voodoo was present in the area of Virginia where Turner preached. See also Oates, *The Fires,* p. 12.

34. William S. Drewry, *The Southampton Insurrection* (Washington, D.C.: The Neale Co., 1900), pp. 31–33.

35. Mike Thelwell, "Back With the Wind: Mr. Styron and the Reverend Turner," in Clarke, *Styron's Nat Turner,* p. 86.

36. This parable is also recorded in Matt. 24:45–51.

37. See Johnson, *Turner Insurrection,* p. 76; Oates, *The Fires,* pp. 36–39.

38. Drewry, *Southampton,* p. 114.

39. See ibid., p. 115.

40. Ibid., p. 33n. It is an interesting conjecture, which only Mr. Styron could validate or deny, whether upon finding the word "intercourse" in Drewry's account, Styron's imagination leaped to the idea of substituting Willis for Brantley in the baptism scene and linking Turner with homosexuality. See the novel, pp. 203–7 and 238–39.

41. See "The Confessions," in Tragle, *Slave Revolt,* pp. 361–62.

42. See Carroll, *Insurrections,* p. 133.

43. Nelson Williams was thought to be a sorcerer, like Gullah Jack, the companion of Denmark Vesey; see Oates, *The Fires,* p. 53.

44. George W. Williams, *A History of the Negro Race in America, 1619–1883* (New York: Putnam, 1883), vol. 1, pp. 88–90.

45. See Aptheker, *American Negro,* p. 298.

46. See ibid., p. 300.

47. See Carroll, *Insurrections,* p. 137.

48. See ibid., pp. 139–40.

49. See Drewry, *Southampton,* pp. 101–2.

50. Aptheker, *American Negro,* p. 305.

51. Du Bois, *The Negro Church,* pp. 25–26. On the reign of terror following the insurrection, see Tragle, *Slave Revolt,* pp. 374–76; on legislative activity, see Aptheker, *Nat Turner's Slave Rebellion,* pp. 74–83.

52. See Drewry, *Southampton,* p. 116.

53. Carter G. Woodson (ed.), *The Works of Francis J. Grimke* (Washington, D.C.: Associated Publishers, 1942), vol. 1, p. 354.

## 5. The Black Church Freedom Movement

1. Mechal Sobel, in her *Trabelin' On: The Slave Journey to an Afro-Baptist Faith* (Westport, Conn.: Greenwood, 1979), lists six churches that had black pastors before the end of the war (p. 250). Her research shows that the African Baptist or Bluestone church of Mecklenburg, Va., was the first to be organized, in 1758.

2. Philip A. Bruce, *The Plantation Negro as a Freeman* (New York: Putnam, 1889), pp. 73–74.

3. See Carter G. Woodson, *History of the Negro Church* (Washington, D.C.: Associated Publishers, 1972, 3rd ed.), p. 42.

4. See James M. Simms, *The First Colored Baptist Church in North America* (New York: Negro Universities Press, 1969, reprint), pp. 71–75.

5. For an interesting discussion of Christian ethics and slave rebellion, see Nathan I. Huggins, *Black Odyssey: The Afro-American Ordeal in Slavery* (New York: Pantheon, 1977), pp. 230–36.

6. See Benjamin Brawley, *Social History of the Negro in the United States* (New York: Macmillan, 1921), p. 51.

7. See Carol V. R. George, *Segregated Sabbaths: Richard Allen and the Emergence of Independent Black Churches, 1760–1840* (New York: Oxford University Press, 1973), pp. 61–62, 65–71; David H. Bradley, Sr., *A History of the A.M.E. Zion Church: Part I, 1796–1872* (Nashville: Parthenon, 1956), pp. 71–90.

8. See Sobel, *Trabelin' On*, pp. 182–217.

9. See Owen D. Pelt and Ralph Lee Smith, *The Story of the National Baptists* (New York: Vantage, 1960), pp. 49–52.

10. Valuable new research on the African Union Church of Wilmington has been done by Lewis Baldwin. Lewis V. Baldwin, *Invisible Strands in African Methodism* (Metuchen, NJ: Scarecrow Press, 1983) and *The Mark of A Man: Peter Spencer and the African Union Methodist Tradition* (Lanham, MD: University Press of America, 1987).

11. See Marcia M. Mathews, *Richard Allen* (Baltimore: Helicon, 1963), p. 47

12. See Richard Allen, *The Life Experiences and Gospel Labors* (Philadelphia: Ford and Ripley, 1880), p. 13; Milton C. Sernett, *Black Religion and American Evangelicalism* (Metuchen, N. J.: Scarecrow Press, 1975), p. 117. Sernett questions the accuracy of Allen's memory by the time he wrote his autobiography. He believes that the incident at St. George's church could not have occurred until after 1791, when the construction of the galleries was begun.

13. Mathews, *Richard Allen*, p. 55.

14. Allen, *Life Experiences*, pp. 14–21. See Charles H. Wesley, *Richard Allen, Apostle of Freedom* (Washington, D.C.: Associated Publishers, 1935), p. 81.

15. Quoted by Wesley, ibid.

16. Daniel A. Payne, *History of the African Methodist Episcopal Church* (Nashville: Book Concern of the A.M.E. Church, 1891), p. 14. On the beginning of African Methodism, see also Grant S. Shockley and Leonard L. Haynes, "The A.M.E. and the A.M.E. Zion Churches," in *The History of American Methodism*, E. S. Bucke, ed. (New York: Abingdon, 1964), vol. 2, pp. 527–63, and George A. Singleton, *The Romance of African Methodism* (New York: Exposition Press, 1952), pp. 19–24. An important new addition to the literature on the AME Church is Clarence E.

Walker, *A Rock in a Weary Land: The AME Church During the Civil War and Reconstruction* (Baton Rouge: Louisiana State University Press, 1982).

17. Richard R. Wright, Jr., *The Centennial Encyclopedia of the African Methodist Episcopal Church, 1816–1916* (Philadelphia: A.M.E. Church, 1916), p. 11.

18. See Bradley, *A History*, pp. 45–46. See also William J. Walls, *The African Methodist Episcopal Zion Church: Reality of the Black Church* (Charlotte: A.M.E. Zion Publ. House, 1974), pp. 45–48. The question of how long a group of blacks may actually have been meeting under Williams's auspices is a matter of debate. The controversy over which group of the various branches of black Methodism was the first to move toward the organization of a separate congregation is still unresolved. The Allenites of Philadelphia are generally considered to have been the first. It is nevertheless true that at least five denominations have claimed that honor. See J. W. Hood, *One Hundred Years of the African Methodist Episcopal Zion Church* (New York: A.M.E. Zion Book Concern, 1895), p. 6.

19. B. F. Wheeler, *The Varick Family* (published by Bishop W. J. Walls, 1966), pp. 6–7.

20. See Bradley, *A History*, p. 48.

21. See Shockley and Haynes, "The A.M.E.," p. 563.

22. Hood calls Varick "the first regularly elected bishop of the connection," but Bradley states that the Zionites did not change the name of superintendent to bishop until 1864 (Bradley, *A History*, p. 156).

23. See James A. Handy, *Scraps of A.M.E. History* (Philadelphia: A.M.E. Church, 1901), p. 78. See also D. A. Payne, "Morris Brown," in *Lives of Methodist Bishops*, Theodore L. Flood and John W. Hamilton, eds. (New York: Philips & Hart, 1882), pp. 669–74.

24. See Payne, *History*, pp. 45, 50, 84.

25. Ibid., p. 339. But the protracted debate at the Cincinnati meeting illustrates that the problem of slaveholding presented ethical ambiguities for black as well as white Christians.

26. Handy, *Scraps*, p. 141.

27. Payne, *History*, pp. 344–45.

28. See Bradley, *A History*, p. 108.

29. See the Jamestown, N.Y., *Sun*, Sept. 3, 1950.

30. See Thomas James, *Autobiography*, special edition of *Rochester History*, vol. 37, Oct. 1975, p. 7. Bradley writes: "The A.M.E. Zion Church not only was foremost in the carrying on of this struggle for freedom but appears to have been the leader along this line" (ibid., p. 107). This is interesting in view of the New York origin of the denomination as compared with the more conservative climate in Philadelphia where the AME Church originated. Carleton Mabee comments on the difference between the blacks of the two cities and the militancy of the New Yorkers in his *Black Freedom* (London, Ontario: Macmillan, 1970), p. 58. See also Leon F. Litwack, *North of Slavery* (University of Chicago Press, 1961), pp. 239–46, and Gerald Sorin, *The New York Abolitionists: A Case Study of Political Radicalism* (Westport, Conn.: Greenwood, 1971).

31. See James, *Autobiography*, p. 12.

32. Hood, *Hundred Years*, pp. 541–42.

33. W. D. Weatherford, *American Churches and the Negro* (Boston: Christopher Publ. House, 1957), p. 195.

34. See Andrew E. Murray, *Presbyterians and the Negro* (Philadelphia: Presbyterian Historical Society, 1966), pp. 32–33.

35. At least the southern wing, which met in Montgomery, Alabama, in 1861, was treated with the utmost deference by the northern bishops, and the designations of the southern dioceses remained on the convention rolls throughout the war (Weatherford, *American Churches*, pp. 43–44). See also Robert A. Bennett, "Black Episcopalians: A History from the Colonial Period to the Present," *The Historical Magazine of the Protestant Episcopal Church*, vol. 43, no. 3, pp. 238–39.

36. See George Bragg, *History of the Afro-American Group of the Episcopal Church* (Baltimore: Church Advocate Press, 1922), pp. 61–64.

37. See Murray, *Presbyterians*, pp. 29, 32, 239. See also, *All-Black Governing Bodies*. A report prepared by Darius L. Swann for the Presbyterian Church (U.S.A) Louisville, KY, 1996.

38. See Litwack, *North of Slavery*, p. 196.

39. It is difficult to understand how Frederick Douglass, who rejected the idea of a black church, could have persuaded himself—given what he saw of the Presbyterians and Episcopalians—that the white churches of the North were ready to accept blacks on a basis of equality. The situation that obtained in the Methodist Church when Allen and Jones withdrew continued to exist in many white churches into the twentieth century. Even after segregated seating was abolished in the North, blacks continued to be discriminated against in many subtle ways, such as being passed over for pastoral visitation and elective offices, and being excluded from the more fashionable and intimate functions of the society-conscious city congregations.

40. Howard H. Bell, "A Survey of the Negro Convention Movement," Ph.D. dissertation, Northwestern University, 1953, pp. 7–8. See also William H. Pease and Jane H. Pease, "The Negro Convention Movement," in *Key Issues in the Afro-American Experience*, Nathan I. Huggins, Martin Kilson, and Daniel M. Fox, eds. (New York: Harcourt Brace Jovanovich, 1971), vol. 1, pp. 191–205; George W. Williams, *History of the Negro Race in America* (New York: Putnam, 1883), vol. 2, pp. 61–63; John W. Cromwell, "The Early Negro Convention Movement," *Occasional Papers, No. 9*, The American Academy, 1904.

41. After Allen's death (1831), Cornish, Wright, and Charles B. Ray, a Methodist and later Congregational minister, sought to prevent the convention movement from falling under the control of more conservative laymen who were influenced by Garrison and other white friends (Mabee, *Black Freedom*, p. 58).

42. See Howard H. Bell, "The American Moral Reform Society, 1836–1841," *Journal of Negro Education*, vol. 27, Winter 1958, pp. 34–35.

43. *The Colored American*, March 15, 1838.

44. Seminary education and frustrations related to their relatively low status in the white denominations have continued to be factors in the militance of Presbyterian and Episcopal clergy in recent black church movements.

45. See Mabee, *Black Freedom*, p. 59.

46. Carter G. Woodson, ed., *Negro Orators and Their Orations* (Washington, D.C.: Associated Publishers, 1925), p. 155.

47. Ibid., p. 157.

48. Mabee, *Black Freedom*, p. 60.

49. See John H. Bracey, Jr., August Meier, and Elliott Rudwick, *Black Nationalism in America* (Indianapolis: Bobbs-Merrill, 1970), p. 67. Litwack claims that the pamphlets were published at the expense of John Brown (*North of Slavery*, p. 243). See also Arthur Zilversmit, "The Abolitionists," in James C. Curtis and Lewis L. Gould, *The Black Experience in America* (University of Texas Press, 1970), pp. 61–63. Zilversmit's comment on Garnet's effect upon black abolitionism strikes a note of sober warning for the church. He writes: "For other abolitionists the frustrations of their situation, the frustrations engendered by not having an audience that would respond to reasoned argument, led to the conclusion that a society so immoral, so impervious to reasoned argument, was not worth saving and had to be destroyed. They were led finally to a commitment to violence as a substitute for reason."

50. Douglass, in a speech in Rochester in 1848, had said, "I am aware of the anti-Christian prejudices which have excluded many colored persons from white churches, and the consequent necessity for erecting their own places of worship.... But such a necessity does not now exist to the extent of former years. There are societies where color is not regarded as a test of membership, and such places I deem more appropriate for colored persons than exclusive or isolated organizations" (quoted in Brawley, *Social History*, pp. 239–40). Douglass, however, found it impossible to dissociate himself from such organizations in the discharge of his duties as a professional abolitionist.

51. For a perceptive interpretation of Allen and others of the period, see Charles V. Hamilton, *The Black Preacher in America* (New York: William Morrow, 1972), pp. 47–50.

52. Benjamin Quarles, *Black Abolitionists* (New York: Oxford University Press, 1969), p. 82.

53. See Wesley, *Richard Allen*, p. 267.

54. *The Genius of Universal Emancipation*, March 1831, vol. 1, p. 185. See also Daniel M. Baxter, *Bishop Richard Allen and His Spirit* (Philadelphia: A.M.E. Church, 1923), passim.

### 6. Black Religion and Black Nationalism

1. See James W. St. G. Walker, *The Black Loyalists: The Search for a Promised Land in Nova Scotia and Sierra Leone, 1783–1870* (New York: Dalhousie University Press, 1976).

2. See Benjamin Brawley, *Social History of the American Negro* (New York: Macmillan, 1921), pp. 174–76.

3. See John H. Bracey, Jr., August Meier, and Elliott Rudwick, *Black Nationalism in America* (Indianapolis: Bobbs-Merrill, 1970), p. xxxi; Benjamin Brawley, *Negro Builders and Heroes* (University of North Carolina Press, 1937), pp. 35–39.

4. See Brawley, ibid.

5. Black churches in the West Indies played their own part in sending money and missionaries to Africa. The missionary societies in Jamaica, for example, trained men for work in Africa as early as the 1840s, and individual Jamaicans, such as Thomas Keith and James Keats, went to Africa on their own initiative to bring Christianity to Nigeria. Nettleford writes: "A Mr. Jameson, a missionary who worked at Goshen between 1836 and 1846, wrote in 1839 that 'the people's hearts are turning to Africa' and it was not surprising that as early as 1841 the Jamaica Presbytery decided to train 'black and coloured' Jamaicans for the

African missions" (Rex Nettleford and John Hearne, "The Africa Connection—the Significance for Jamaica," in *Our Heritage* [University of the West Indies, 1963], p. 44).

6. See Edwin S. Readkey, *Black Exodus* (Yale University Press, 1969), p. 17.

7. Leon F. Litwack, *North of Slavery* (University of Chicago Press, 1961), pp. 24–25.

8. See Forten's letter to Paul Cuffee in Bracey et al., *Nationalism*, p. 46.

9. George W. Williams, *History of the Negro Race in America* (New York: Putnam, 1883), vol. 2, pp. 69–70.

10. See Daniel A. Payne, *History of the African Methodist Episcopal Church* (New York: Arno Press and the New York Times, 1969, reprint), pp. 88–93; Artishia W. Jordan, *The A.M.E. Church in Africa* (New York: A.M.E. Press, 1960), p. 45.

11. James W. Rankin, "The Missionary Propaganda of the A.M.E. Church," *The A.M.E. Review,* Jan. 1916, p. 175.

12. Quoted by Payne, *History*, p. 91.

13. Daniel Coker to Jeremiah Watts, April 3, 1820, *Journal of Daniel Coker* (Baltimore: Press of Edward J. Coate, 1820), quoted in Bracey et al., *Nationalism*, p. 47.

14. See Booker T. Washington, "The Mission Work of the A.M.E. Church," *The A.M.E. Church Review,* Jan. 1916, p. 186.

15. See L. L. Berry, *A Century of Missions of the A.M.E. Church, 1840–1940* (New York: Missionary Dept. of the A.M.E. Church, 1942), p. 44.

16. Monica Schuler, "Akab Slave Rebellions in the British Caribbean," in *Savacou*, vol. 1, June 1970, p. 24, George Shepperson and Thomas Price write: "The slave disturbances of 1831 in Jamaica were spoken of as 'the Baptist war,' and after the abolition of slavery two years later, the Baptist name was linked to the whole train of troubles which resulted in the Jamaica Rebellion of 1865 under Governor Eyre" (*The Independent African* [University of Edinburgh Press, 1958], p. 423). See also Ernest A. Payne, *Freedom in Jamaica: Some Chapters in the Story of the Baptist Missionary Society* (London: Carey Press, 2nd ed., 1946).

17. See Grant S. Shockley and Leonard L. Haynes, "The A.M.E. and the A.M.E. Zion Churches," in *The History of American Methodism*, E. S. Bucke, ed. (New York: Abingdon, 1964), vol. 2, pp. 554–55.

18. See Redkey, *Exodus*, pp. 73–126.

19. See August Meier, *Negro Thought in America, 1880–1915* (University of Michigan Press, 1963), p. 63.

20. See Payne, *History*, pp. 293–94.

21. See ibid., p. 220.

22. See Martin R. Delany, *Official Report of the Niger Valley Exploring Party* (New York: Thomas Hamilton, 1861), pp. 50–51. Delany was also critical of white missionaries. He often accused them of destroying African culture—e.g., by changing the names of converts, which he believed led to a loss of identity. He vigorously upheld black identity, and either he or Edward W. Blyden was the first to use the slogan "Africa for the Africans." See Victor Ullman, *Martin R. Delany: The Beginnings of Black Nationalism* (Boston: Beacon, 1971), pp. 247–59.

23. Brawley, *Negro Builders*, p. 93.

24. See Martin R. Delany, *The Condition, Elevation, Emigration and Destiny of the Colored People of the United States, Politically Considered* (Philadelphia, 1852), p. 38.

25. Ibid., p. 40.

26. *Minutes of the African Civilization Society*, Nov. 7, 1861.

27. Delany, *The Condition*, p. 183.

28. Ibid., pp. 61–62.

29. See Meier, *Negro Thought*, p. 43.

30. Howard Brotz, ed., *Negro Social and Political Thought, 1850–1900, Representative Texts* (New York: Basic Books, 1966), pp. 174–75.

31. Ibid., p. 176.

32. George Shepperson, "Notes on Negro American Influences on the Emergence of African Nationalism," *Journal of African History*, vol. 1, no. 2, 1960, p. 299. See also Hollis R. Lynch, *Edward Wilmot Blyden: Pan-Negro Patriot, 1832–1912* (New York: Oxford University Press, 1967).

33. Edward W. Blyden, *Christianity, Islam and the Negro Race* (Edinburgh: Aldin Publ. Co., 1967), p. 45.

34. See Shepperson, "Notes," p. 310; James C. Coleman, *Nigeria—Background to Nationalism* (University of California Press, 1963), pp. 176 ff.

35. Edward W. Blyden, *Liberia's Offering* (New York: John A. Gray, 1862), pp. 71–72.

36. A thorough discussion of the Hamitic hypothesis and its use by American Christians is found in Thomas Virgil Peterson, *Ham and Japheth: The Mythic World of Whites in the Antebellum South* (Metuchen, N.J.: Scarecrow Press, 1978). One of the best analyses of this question is an unpublished paper by Edith R. Sanders, "The Rape of African History: The Hamitic Hypothesis."

37. See Blyden, *Offering*, p. 8; James W. C. Pennington, *A Text Book of the Origin and History of the Colored People* (Hartford: L. Skinner Co., 1841), pp. 9–13. An excellent example of this literary tradition continued by black church leaders into the twentieth century is in Bishop William J. Walls, *The African Methodist Episcopal Zion Church: Reality of the Black Church* (Charlotte: A.M.E. Zion Publ. House, 1974), pp. 15–22. See also F. S. Rhoades, *Black Characters and References of the Holy Bible* (New York: Vantage, 1980), pp. 12–19.

38. Brotz, *Thought*, pp. 121–22.

39. See James M. McPherson, "The Negro: Innately Inferior or Equal?," in Melvin Drimmer, ed., *Black History: A Reappraisal* (Garden City, N.Y.: Doubleday, 1969), p. 243. This theme continues in the more recent work of Cheikh Anta Diop, *The African Origin of Civilization: Myth or Reality* (New York: Lawrence Hill, 1974), pp. 1–9; Chancellor Williams, *The Destruction of Black Civilization* (Chicago: Third World Press, 1976), pp. 92–100; John G. Jackson, *Introduction to African Civilizations* (Secaucus, N.J.: Citadel, 1970), pp. 10–12, 63–70.

40. See John Henrik Clarke's Introduction in Jackson, *Introduction*, pp. 3–35.

41. Other key texts are Psalm 16:21–22; 105:23, 26–27.

42. James W. Hood, *One Hundred Years of the African Methodist Episcopal Zion Church* (New York: A.M.E. Zion Book Concern, 1895), p. 55.

43. See Redkey, *Exodus*, pp. 30 ff. See also Turner's response to the criticism of powerful church leaders such as Alexander Crummell, J. T. Jenifer, and Francis J. Grimke, in Edwin S. Redkey, ed., *Respect Black: The Writings and Speeches of Henry McNeal Turner* (New York: Arno Press and the New York Times, 1971), pp. 161–63.

44. Bracey et al., *Nationalism*, pp. 172–73. Turner's radicalism was without peer in the early twentieth century. He spoke of the United States as "this

bloody, lynching nation," and President Theodore Roosevelt, according to a letter written to the bishop by Booker T. Washington in 1906, once suggested to the latter that Turner might be tried for treason for referring to the American flag as a "bloody rag."

45. Henry M. Turner, "The Races Must Separate," in Willis B. Parks, ed., *The Possibilities of the Negro—In Symposium* (Atlanta: Franklin Co., 1904), pp. 91–92.

46. See *The Christian Recorder*, Feb. 22, 1883.

47. *The Voice of Missions*, Feb. 1, 1898. This position was roundly criticized by white theologians, but to compare a contemporary discussion of the Christian symbolism of color against which Turner inveighed, see Roger Bastide, "Color, Racism and Christianity," in John Hope Franklin, ed., *Color and Race* (Boston: Houghton Mifflin, 1968), pp. 34–49; also Gayraud S. Wilmore, "The Black Messiah: Revising the Color Symbolism of Western Christology," *The Journal of the Interdenominational Theological Center*, vol. 2, no. 1, Fall 1974, pp. 8–18.

48. See Berry, *Century*, pp. 72–73. Josephus R. Coan's unpublished doctoral dissertation "The Expansion of Missions of the A.M.E. Church in South Africa, 1896–1908" (Hartford Seminary, 1961) was the first authoritative work on Turner and his contribution to Ethiopianism in South Africa. See also J. M. Batten, "Henry M. Turner: Negro Bishop Extraordinary," *Church History*, Sept. 1938. More recent research on the bishop is in Edwin S. Redkey's *Black Exodus: Black Nationalist and Back to Africa Movements, 1890–1910* (Yale University Press, 1969).

49. Turner ordained 31 elders and 29 deacons—a total of 60 ministers during his 6-week whirlwind visit. This, naturally, became a matter of anxiety among the white missionaries. AME agents were designated by them as unwelcome and dangerous interlopers in South Africa. The government's Native Affairs Commission shared this view. See Coan, "Expansion," pp. 169–72, 174; see also Redkey, *Exodus*, pp. 248–49.

50. See Jordan, *A.M.E. Church*, pp. 59–60. For a discussion of Ethiopianism in this relationship, see Vittorio Lanternari, *The Religions of the Oppressed* (New York: Knopf, 1963), pp. 40–41; Bengt G. M. Sundkler, *Bantu Prophets in South Africa* (London: Oxford University Press, 1961), pp. 53–59; Thomas Hodgkin, *Nationalism in Colonial Africa* (London: Frederick Muller, 1960), pp. 99 ff.

51. Edward Roux, *Time Longer Than Rope: A History of the Black Man's Struggle for Freedom in South Africa* (University of Wisconsin Press, 1964), p. 81.

52. *General Conference Minutes for 1892*, p. 83. See Coan, "Expansion," p. 50.

53. Roux, *Time Longer*, p. 85.

54. Shepperson and Price, *Independent African*, p. 98.

55. Ibid.

56. Ibid., p. 91.

57. See Roux, *Time Longer*, pp. 135–39; Robert I. Rotberg and Ali A. Mazrui, eds., *Protest and Power in Black Africa* (New York: Oxford University Press, 1970), pp. 701–8.

58. Roux, *Time Longer*, p. 140.

59. Rotberg and Mazrui, eds., *Protest*, pp. 427–28.

60. Coleman, *Nigeria*, p. 177.

61. For an analysis of factors affecting African independence movements, see David B. Barrett, *Schism and Renewal in Africa* (Nairobi: Oxford University Press, 1968), pp. 142–50; G. C. Oosthuizen, *Post-Christianity in Africa* (Grand Rapids:

Eerdmans, 1968), pp. 30–61; for a more negative assessment, see Daniel Thwaite, *The Seething African Pot: A Study of Black Nationalism, 1882–1935* (Westport: Negro Universities Press, 1970, reprint).

62. See Stanley Shaloff, "Presbyterians and Belgian Congo Exploitation," *Journal of Presbyterian History,* June 1969, pp. 173–94.

63. Rotberg and Mazrui, eds., *Protest,* pp. 427–28.

64. See E. U. Essien-Udom, *Black Nationalism: A Search for Identity in America* (New York: Dell, 1962), pp. 30–75. Benjamin E. Mays should also be mentioned in this connection because of his work on the black church and his recognition that its emphasis on justice, though sometimes muted, was never totally absent: *The Negro's God* (Boston: Chapman & Grimes, 1938). For an excellent short study following the themes in Essien-Udom, see St. Clair Drake, *The Redemption of Africa and Black Religion* (Chicago: Third World Press, 1970).

65. Horace Cayton, "E. Franklin Frazier: A Tribute and a Review," *Review of Religious Research,* vol. 5, no. 3, 1964, p. 141. See E. Franklin Frazier, *The Negro Church in America* (New York: Schocken, 1963).

66. See Essien-Udom, *Black Nationalism,* pp. 37–38.

### 7. The Deradicalization of the Black Church

1. In support of Du Bois's liberal religious orientation, see his *Prayers for Dark People,* edited by Herbert Aptheker (University of Massachusetts Press, 1980). Du Bois also recognized and respected the strategic importance of the black church; see *The Souls of Black Folk* (Greenwich, Conn.: Fawcett, 1970, reprint), pp. 140–51; *The Gift of Black Folk* (New York, Washington Square Press: 1970), pp. 178–90; *The Philadelphia Negro* (University of Pennsylvania Press, 1899), pp. 201–7. His religion obtrudes through his secular writings under a nimbus of African spirituality and transcendental mystique. He was once Knight Commander of the Liberian Order of African Redemption, which had strong religious overtones. On his 25th birthday he vowed to become the Moses of black people and improvised a ritual of regeneration, using wine, candles, oil, and oranges. In the throes of the rite he prayed, sang, and made "a sacrifice to the *Zeitgeist* of Work, God and Mercy" (Lerone Bennett, Jr., *Pioneers in Protest* [Chicago: Johnson Publ. Co., 1968], pp. 241–42).

2. See August Meier, *Negro Thought in America, 1880–1915* (University of Michigan Press, 1963), pp. 218–19.

3. Edwin S. Redkey, *Black Exodus* (New York: Yale University Press, 1969), p. 277.

4. *Voice of Missions,* March-May, 1897.

5. See *Respect Black: The Writings and Speeches of Henry McNeal Turner,* Edwin S. Redkey, ed. (New York: Arno Press and the New York Times, 1971), pp. 161–63.

6. New Orleans *Times-Democrat,* July 29, 1900.

7. See Redkey, *Exodus,* pp. 258–76.

8. *Crisis,* July 1915.

9. See Benjamin Brawley, *Social History of the American Negro* (New York: Macmillan, 1921), p. 295; Ray Stannard Baker, "What Is a Lynching?," *The American Magazine,* Jan. and Feb. 1905, in Donald P. NeNevi and Doris A.

Holmes, eds., *Racism at the Turn of the Century, Documentary Perspectives, 1870–1910* (San Rafael, CA: Leswing Press, 1973), pp. 304–19.

10. See C. Vann Woodward, *Strange Career of Jim Crow*, 2nd rev. ed. (New York: Oxford University Press, 1966), pp. 97–102.

11. *Voice of the People*, March 1903. Racist literature of the post-World War I period is summarized in Thomas F. Gossett, *Race: The History of an Idea in America* (Dallas: Southern Methodist University Press, 1963), pp. 370–408.

12. The AME conference of 1912, however, after hearing Washington speak, approved a report from H. T. Kealing's committee calling upon blacks to resist manfully the mob violence to which they were being subjected (Meier, *Thought*, p. 220).

13. See August Meier and Elliott M. Rudwick, *From Plantation to Ghetto* (New York: Hill & Wang, 1966), p. 194.

14. Nancy J. Weiss, "The Negro and the New Freedom," in Allen Weinstein and Frank O. Gatell, eds., *The Segregation Era, 1863–1954* (New York: Oxford University Press, 1970), p. 194.

15. See De Berry's 1901 study of St. John's Church, Springfield, Mass., in Du Bois, *The Negro Church* (Atlanta University Press, 1903), pp. 149–51. Also report #37 on an Atlanta AME church: "As the church grew a cleft appeared between the richer and poorer members and the result was that some thirty or more members of the poor class withdrew" (ibid., p. 77). This was not untypical. An examination of Du Bois's and other studies will bear out the contention that social stratification within congregations and class churches was developing at the turn of the century and before. See also Gunnar Myrdal, *An American Dilemma* (New York: Harper, 1944), vol. 1, p. 196n., and E. Franklin Frazier, *Black Bourgeoisie* (New York: Collier, 1962), pp. 98–110, 173.

16. See Gary Marx, *Protest and Prejudice: A Study of Belief in the Black Community* (New York: Harper & Row, 1967).

17. A typical statement of the black middle-class position on the role of religion is Dean Kelly Miller's essay "Religion as a Solvent of the Race Problem," in Kelly Miller, *Radicals and Conservatives: And Other Essays on the Negro in America* (New York: Schocken, 1968, reprint), pp. 147–65.

18. *Crisis*, Jan. 1914.

19. See Meier and Rudwick, *Plantation*, p. 190.

20. The dramatic increase in the black church population of the North and West is illustrated by the fact that in twelve states of the South in 1890 there were 2,348,549 black church members and only 225,428 in the rest of the nation. By 1926 the black church population of the South had not quite doubled, with a total of 4,288,621, whereas the numbers in the North and West had more than quadrupled to 914,866 (from comparisons of the U.S. Eleventh Census report and statistics in *Negroes in the United States, 1920–1932* [Bureau of the Census, 1931], p. 536).

21. See Frazier, *Bourgeoisie*, p. 99; Vattel Elbert Daniel, "Ritual and Stratification in Chicago Negro Churches," in Hart M. Nelson, Raytha L. Yokley, and Anne K. Nelsen, eds., *The Black Church in America* (New York: Basic Books, 1971), pp. 123–28.

22. See Joseph R. Washington, Jr., *Black Religion* (Boston: Beacon, 1964), pp. 30–162.

23. Ibid., p. 35.

24. See James H. Cone, *Black Theology and Black Power* (New York: Seabury, 1969), pp. 103–15.

25. See Edmund D. Cronon, *Black Moses* (University of Wisconsin Press, 1962), p. 7. Cronon's reliable and well-known work on Garvey has been superseded by more recent research: see Tony Martin, *Race First: The Ideological and Organizational Struggles of Marcus Garvey and the Universal Negro Improvement Association* (Westport, Conn.: Greenwood, 1976); John Henrik Clarke, with Amy Jacques Garvey, *Marcus Garvey and the Vision of Africa* (New York: Random House, 1974); Elton C. Fax, *Garvey: The Story of a Pioneer Black Nationalist* (New York: Dodd, Mead, 1972); Shawna Maglangbayan, *Garvey, Lumumba, Malcolm* (Chicago: Third World Press, 1972).

26. For a penetrating study of Garvey's first visit to England and his relationship to Duse Mohammed Ali, see Robert A. Hill, "The First England Years and After, 1912–1916," in Clarke, *Garvey*, pp. 14–37.

27. Amy Jacques-Garvey, ed., *The Philosophy and Opinions of Marcus Garvey*, (New York: Arno Press and the New York Times, 1969), vol. 2, p. 126.

28. Ibid., p. 128.

29. See Amy Jacques-Garvey, *Garvey and Garveyism* (Kingston: United Printers, Ltd., 1963), p. 91; Martin, *Race First*, pp. 33–37.

30. Jacques-Garvey, *Philosophy*, vol. 2, pp. 37–38.

31. Ibid., p. 98. Garvey was, of course, not without guile, but for a discussion of the weaknesses of his strategy with groups such as the Ku Klux Klan, see Richard B. Moore, "The Critics and Opponents of Marcus Garvey," in Clarke, *Garvey*, pp. 210–35.

32. Jacques-Garvey, *Philosophy*, vol. 2, p. 95.

33. Jacques-Garvey, *Garvey and Garveyism*, pp. 133–34.

34. Garvey's frequent criticism of preachers was that they were tools of politicians and real estate interests. The latter talked them into putting the energies of "religious suckers" into buying new buildings that wasted money. For more on this particular problem among black city churches, see Woodson, *History of the Negro Church*, pp. 230 ff., and St. Clair Drake and Horace R. Cayton, *Black Metropolis* (New York: Harcourt, Brace, 1945), pp. 414–29. For black clergy in the movement, see Randall K. Burkett, *Black Redemption: Churchmen Speak for the Garvey Movement* (Philadelphia: Temple Univ. Press, 1978).

35. Martin, *Race First*, pp. 69–71.

36. See Jacques-Garvey, *Garvey and Garveyism*, p. 133. The most helpful work on Garveyism and its significance for black religion has been done by Randall K. Burkett, *Garveyism as a Religious Movement: The Institutionalization of a Black Civil Religion* (Metuchen, N.J.: Scarecrow Press, 1978), and *Black Redemption: Churchmen Speak for the Garvey Movement.*

37. Jacques-Garvey, *Garvey and Garveyism*, p. 61.

38. Jacques-Garvey, *Philosophy*, vol. 2, p. 16.

39. See A. C. Terry-Thompson, *The History of the African Orthodox Church* (New York: African Orthodox Church, 1956), pp. 49–50. Also, Gavin White, "Patriarch McGuire and the Episcopal Church," in Randall K. Burkett and Richard Newman, eds., *Black Apostles: Afro-American Clergy Confront the Twentieth Century* (Boston: G.I. Hall & Co., 1978), pp. 151–180.

40. See Cronon, *Black Moses*, p. 42. Jamaicans were not rigidly attached to

mainline denominations, and in the eclectic, revivalistic atmosphere of the island many Roman Catholics and Church of England communicants participated in other sects.

41. Terry-Thompson, *History*, p. 55.

42. Cronon, *Black Moses*, p. 178.

43. Ibid., p. 182.

44. See Edward Roux, *Time Longer Than Rope: A History of the Black Man's Struggle for Freedom in South Africa* (University of Wisconsin Press, 1964), p. 112n., 236; Vittorio Lanternari, *The Religions of the Oppressed* (New York: Knopf, 1963), p. 39; Sheridan W. Johns III, "Trade Union, Political Pressure Group, or Mass Movement? The Industrial and Commercial Workers' Union of Africa," in Robert I. Rotberg and Ali A. Mazrui, eds., *Protest and Power in Black Africa* (New York: Oxford University Press, 1970), pp. 714–16.

45. See M. G. Smith, Roy Augier, and Rex Nettleford, *The Rastafari Movement in Kingston, Jamaica* (Kingston: University College of the West Indies, 1960), p. 12. See also George E. Simpson, *Black Religions in the New World* (Columbia University Press, 1978), pp. 124–30.

46. Smith, Augier, and Nettleford, *Rastafari*, p. 7. See also Rex M. Nettleford, *Mirror, Mirror: Identity, Race and Protest in Jamaica* (Jamaica: William Collins and Sangster, 1972), pp. 41–111.

47. See Walter Rodney, *The Groundings With My Brothers* (London: Bogle-L'Ouverture Publ., 1969), pp. 60–67.

48. See Nils Bloch-Hoell, *The Pentecostal Movement: Its Origin, Development and Distinctive Character* (Oslo: Universitetsforlaget, 1964); *God's People: West Indian Pentecostal Sects in England* (London: Oxford University Press, 1965); Walter J. Hollenweger, *The Pentecostals: The Charismatic Movement in the Churches* (Minneapolis: Augsburg Publ. Co., 1972); *Pentecost Between Black and White: Five Studies on Pentecost and Politics* (Belfast: Christian Journals Limited, 1974); Leonard Lovett, "Perspective on the Black Origins of the Contemporary Pentecostal Movement," paper presented to the Society for the Study of Black Religion, Oct. 1972; James S. Tinney, "Black Origins of the Pentecostal Movement," *Christianity Today*, Oct. 8, 1971; "Competing Theories of Historical Origins for Black Pentecostalism," paper presented to the American Academy of Religion, Nov. 1979.

49. See Hollenweger, "Black Pentecostal Concept," in *Concept*, World Council of Churches Studies in Evangelism, June 1970, p. 11. See also Stanley H. Frodsham, *With Signs Following: The Story of the Pentecostal Revival in the Twentieth Century* (Springfield, Mo.: Gospel Publ. House, 1946), p. 31.

50. See Hollenweger, "Black Pentecostal," p. 9; James S. Tinney, "William J. Seymour: Father of Modern-Day Pentecostalism," *Journal of the Interdenominational Theological Center*, vol. 4, Fall 1976, p. 38.

51. See ibid., p. 34. Also, Iain MacRobert, *The Black Roots and White Racism of Early Pentecostalism in the USA* (London: Macmillan Press, 1988).

52. Hollenweger, "Black Pentecostal," p. 45.

53. See David Barrett, *Schism and Renewal in Africa* (Nairobi: Oxford University Press, 1968), p. 34.

54. See Raymond J. Jones, *A Comparative Study of Religious Cult Behavior Among Negroes with Special Reference to Emotional Group Conditioning Factors* (Washington, D.C.: Howard University Graduate School, 1939), pp. 7–34; Arthur E. Paris, *Black*

*Pentecostalism: Southern Religion in the Urban World* (University of Massachusetts Press, 1982); Melvin D. Williams, *Community in a Black Pentecostal Church* (University of Pittsburgh Press, 1974).

55. See Arthur H. Fauset, *Black Gods of the Metropolis* (University of Pennsylvania Press, 1944), p. 55; Joseph R. Washington, *Black Sects and Cults* (Garden City, N.Y.: Doubleday, 1972), pp. 121–27.

56. Fauset, *Black Gods*, p. 55; Washington, *Black Religion*, pp. 122–25.

57. Richard R. Mathison, *Faiths, Cults and Sects of America* (Indianapolis: Bobbs-Merrill, 1960), p. 246.

58. See George Padmore, *History of the Pan-African Congress* (London: Hammersmith Bookshop, 1947), pp. v, 13.

59. See C. Eric Lincoln, *The Black Muslims in America* (Boston: Beacon, 1961), p. 51.

60. See ibid.

61. See Woodson, *History*, p. 254. For an excellent biography of the pastor and the story of Olivet, see Lillian B. Horace, *"Crowned With Glory and Honor": The Life of Rev. Lacey Kirk Williams* (Hicksville, N.Y.: Exposition Press, 1978).

62. Mays and Nicholson estimated that the average black church membership was 586 in the year 1930. A 1930 investigation by the Greater New York Federation of Churches was probably closer to the real situation in that city: it found three out of four black churches with an average membership of 122. These smaller churches were largely supported by women, and their primary activities were Sunday worship, Sunday school, and choir. They had small effect upon the political and economic life of the community.

63. See Seth M. Scheiner, "The Negro Church and the Northern City, 1890–1930," in William G. Shade and Roy C. Herrenkohl, eds., *Seven on Black* (Philadelphia: Lippincott, 1969), p. 99.

64. Drake and Cayton, *Black Metropolis*, p. 381.

65. Ibid., p. 419.

66. Scheiner, "Negro Church," p. 105.

67. See Harold Cruse, *The Crisis of the Negro Intellectual* (New York: William Morrow, 1967), pp. 40–42; Nathan I. Huggins, *Harlem Renaissance* (New York: Oxford University Press, 1971).

68. See Archibald Robinson, *That Old Time Religion* (Boston: Houghton Mifflin, 1950), pp. 195 ff.

69. Drake and Cayton, *Black Metropolis*, p. 429.

70. Liston Pope, *The Kingdom Beyond Caste* (New York: Friendship Press, 1957), p. 115.

71. Ruby F. Johnston, *The Religion of Negro Protestants* (New York: Philosophical Library, 1956), p. 212.

### 8. The Dechristianization of Black Radicalism

1. See Wilson Record, *Race and Radicalism* (Ithaca: Cornell University Press, 1964), pp. 8–31; also Cornel West, *Prophesy Deliverance! An Afro-American Revolutionary Christianity* (Phila.: Westminster, 1982), pp. 138–47.

2. Amy Jacques-Garvey, ed., *The Philosophy and Opinions of Marcus Garvey* (New York: Arno Press and the *New York Times*, 1969), vol. 1, pp. 18–19.

3. James Baldwin, *Go Tell It on the Mountain* (New York: Dell, 1952), p. 163.

4. Herbert Hill, ed., *Soon One Morning: New Writing by American Negroes* (New York: Knopf, 1963), p. 560.

5. Record, *Race*, p. 60.

6. Reported to the National Committee of Negro Churchmen by New York pastors at a meeting in November 1966. Despite the close association of the Blackstone Rangers, a street gang, with the First Presbyterian Church of Chicago, some of the church's leaders believed that they were hostages to the Rangers' contempt for all churches, and if the building were closed to them they would "burn it down to the ground." Claims that the Young Lords, a Puerto Rican street gang, made upon a Methodist church in East Harlem, led to the seizure of the building.

7. Forman sought the advice of some clergy who had worked with him in the Conference of Federated Organizations (COFO) in Mississippi in 1964. He decided to seek the collaboration of the black clergy rather than risk alienation by an indiscriminate assault on them.

8. C. Eric Lincoln, *The Black Muslims in America* (Boston: Beacon, 1961), p. 79.

9. *Mr. Muhammad Speaks*, May 2, 1959.

10. See Gertrude Samuels, "Two Ways: Black Muslims and N.A.A.C.P.," in August Meier and Elliott Rudwick, eds., *Black Protest in the Sixties* (Chicago: Quadrangle Books, 1970), p. 40.

11. Lerone Bennett, *What Manner of Man: A Biography of Martin Luther King, Jr.* (Chicago: Johnson Publ. Co., 1964); see also August Meier and Elliott Rudwick, *From Plantation to Ghetto* (New York: Hill & Wang, 1966); August Meier, "The Conservative Militant," in C. Eric Lincoln, ed., *Martin Luther King, Jr., A Profile* (New York: Hill and Wang, 1970), p. 147; Kenneth L. Smith and Ira G. Zepp, Jr., *Search for the Beloved Community: The Thinking of Martin Luther King, Jr.* (Valley Forge, PA: Judson, 1974), pp. 126–27.

12. One of the best biographies of King is that of Stephen Oates, *Let The Trumpet Sound: The Life of Martin Luther King* (New York: Harper, 1982); see also David L. Lewis, *King: A Critical Biography* (Baltimore: Penguin, 1970).

13. Joseph R. Washington, Jr., *Black Religion* (Boston: Beacon, 1964), p. 3.

14. "The Highroad to Destiny," in Lincoln, *A Profile*, p. 96.

15. See Martin Luther King, Jr., *Stride Toward Freedom* (New York: Harper, 1958), p. 46.

16. Ibid., p. 54.

17. Ibid., p. 96.

18. Ibid., p. 101. See also King, *Strength To Love* (New York: Harper & Row, 1963), pp. 137–39.

19. Lerone Bennett, *What Manner*, p. 72.

20. See Claude Detton, "Sheriff Harasses Negroes at Voting Rally in Georgia," *New York Times*, July 27, 1962. King's influence on American theological seminaries has been great. During the 1970s and 1980s many theological students, both black and white, named him as the source of their aspiration to enter the ministry as a vocation.

21. See W. Haywood Burns, *The Voices of Negro Protest in America* (New York: Oxford University Press, 1963), p. 43.

22. See Howard Zinn, *SNCC: The New Abolitionists* (Boston: Beacon, 1964). The Congress of Racial Equality (CORE) came into existence during a sit-in protest in a downtown Chicago restaurant in 1942. Antedating both SNCC and SCLC, it

was interracial from the beginning with strong participation from white pacifists and members of A. J. Muste's Fellowship of Reconciliation. CORE was founded by James Farmer, a former black Methodist minister, who became its first national director. Farmer focused his activity in the North, but as early as 1947 CORE was sponsoring "freedom rides" through the South to test compliance with Interstate Commerce Commission regulations and Supreme Court rulings regarding segregated transport facilities.

23. Burns, *Voices*, p. 46.

24. Martin Luther King, Jr., *Where Do We Go From Here: Chaos or Community?* (New York: Harper & Row, 1967), p. 124.

25. Ibid., p. 96. See also *Stride Toward Freedom*, pp. 205–11, *Strength To Love*, p. 47, and his "Letter from the Birmingham Jail," April 16, 1963, in *The Christian Century*, vol. 80, no. 24, June 12, 1963, pp. 767–73.

26. See Robert W. Spike, *The Freedom Revolution and the Churches* (New York: Association Press, 1965).

27. Harold Cruse discusses the clash of the old communist left and the Socialist Workers Party in the leadership of the Freedom Now Party in *The Crisis of the Negro Intellectual* (New York: William Morrow, 1967), pp. 414–19. Despite the internal conflict that doomed the Freedom Now Party, it was probably from this source that the concept of black power first arose in the period 1963–64.

28. Chuck Stone, "The National Conference on Black Power," in Floyd B. Barbour, ed., *The Black Power Revolt* (Boston: Porter Sargent, 1968), p. 189.

29. King *Where Do We Go*, pp. 30–31.

30. Joseph H. Jackson, pastor of the Olivet Baptist Church in Chicago, led the convention from 1953. His position among rights-conscious black ministers was enigmatic. He was instrumental in the attempt of the National Baptist Convention, Inc., to develop farms on 100,000 acres in Liberia and in the purchase of 400 acres in Fayette County, Tennessee. He supported civil rights, but was also strongly anticommunist and critical of black militancy. His opposition to King centered on his belief in King's complicity in a revolt that led to the founding of the Progressive Baptist Convention. See Joseph H. Jackson, *A Story of Christian Activism: The History of the National Baptist Convention, U.S.A., Inc.* (Nashville: Townsend Press, 1980), pp. 422–32, 483–95, and Robert Miller, *Martin Luther King, Jr.* (New York: Weybright & Tally, 1968), p. 295.

31. See José Yglesias, "Dr. King's March on Washington," part 2, *New York Times Magazine*, March 31, 1967.

32. Eldridge Cleaver, *Post-Prison Writings and Speeches* (New York: Ramparts, 1969), p. 50.

33. See Malcolm X, *Autobiography*, with the assistance of Alex Haley (New York: Grove, 1964); George Breitman, ed., *Malcolm X Speaks* (New York: Grove, 1965), and *The Last Year of Malcolm X: The Evolution of a Revolutionary* (New York: Schocken, 1967); John Henrik Clarke, ed., *Malcolm X: The Man and His Times* (New York: Collier, 1969); for an analysis of his thought and a comparison of it with others, see Peter J. Paris, *Black Leaders in Conflict: Martin Luther King, Jr., Malcolm X, Joseph H. Jackson, Adam Clayton Powell, Jr.* (New York: Pilgrim, 1978).

34. *Autobiography*, p. 75.

35. Ibid., p. 180.

36. Ibid., p. 200; see also pp. 220, 241–42, 368 ff.

37. See Lincoln, *Black Muslims*, pp. 155–56.

38. New York *Amsterdam News*, April 26, 1958, quoted by Lincoln, *Black Muslims*, pp. 157–58.

39. See Breitman, *The Last Year*, p. 73.

40. Ibid., p. 74.

41. *Autobiography*, p. 369.

42. Ibid., p. 370.

43. The Muslim Mosque, Inc., the Organization of Afro-American Unity, the Black Economic Development Conference, the National Black Power Conference, the Republic of New Africa, the Black Panthers, certain factions of the Socialist Workers Party—and others.

44. Gayraud S. Wilmore, "The Black Church in Search of a New Theology," in Kendig B. Cully and F. Nile Harper, eds., *Will the Church Lose the City?* (New York: World, 1969), pp. 137–39.

45. *Autobiography*, p. 163. His experience of conversion is strikingly reminiscent of St. Paul's on the Damascus road. He speaks of the truth coming to him as "a blinding light" (p. 164).

46. See Breitman, *Malcolm X Speaks*, p. 24.

47. "Mr. Muhammad Speaks," Los Angeles *Herald-Dispatch*, Nov. 21, 1959.

48. King, *Where Do We Go*, p. 125.

49. See Breitman, *Malcolm X Speaks*, p. 125.

50. See James H. Cone, *Martin & Malcolm & America: A Dream or a Nightmare* (Maryknoll, N.Y.: Orbis Books, 1991).

51. Harold Cruse, *The Crisis of the Negro Intellectual* (New York: William Morrow, 1967), p. 328.

## 9. Black Power, Black People, and Theological Renewal

1. From "A Message to the Churches from Oakland, California," in Gayraud S. Wilmore and James H. Cone, *Black Theology: A Documentary History, 1966–1979* (Maryknoll, N.Y.: Orbis, 1979), p. 105.

2. See *Report of the National Advisory Commission on Civil Disorders* (New York: Bantam, 1969), p. 390.

3. Saul D. Alinsky, leader of the Industrial Areas Foundation, organized The Woodlawn Organization (TWO) in Chicago and other "mass-based" community organizations in the northern ghettos in the early 1960s. See his *Reveille for Radicals* (New York: Vintage, 1969), and *Rules for Radicals* (New York: Vintage, 1972). Alinsky's most successful efforts were in Chicago. On TWO and the West Side Organization (WSO) see, Arthur M. Brazier, *Black Self-Determination: The Story of the Woodlawn Organization* (Grand Rapids: Eerdmans, 1969) and William W. Ellis, *White Ethics and Black Power: The Emergence of the West Side Organization* (Chicago: Aldine Press, 1969).

4. *New York Times*, July 31, 1966; see also Wilmore and Cone, *Black Theology*, pp. 23–30.

5. Vincent Harding, "No Turning Back," in *Renewal*, Oct.–Nov. 1970, p. 8.

6. For example, the 179th General Assembly of the United Presbyterian Church (1967) encouraged Presbyterians "to view the phenomenon of Black power within the context of the White power we exercise, seeing in it both the legacy of frustrated aspirations and the promise of a newly assertive self-identity." The Assembly also commended the NCNC statement to the churches and rec-

ommended the study of its "action implementations" by predominantly white congregations.

7. See Wilmore and Cone, *Black Theology*, "The Church and the Urban Crisis, Statements from Black and White Caucuses . . . September 27–30, 1967," pp. 43–47.

8. The denominational black caucuses included the United Methodists, three Lutheran bodies, the United Church of Christ, the Episcopal Church, two Presbyterian churches, the American Baptist Convention, the Disciples of Christ, and the Unitarian-Universalists. Several of these caucuses were still meeting in the 1990s. Added to their number are at least two Roman Catholic caucuses and one among black evangelicals. During the 1960s the AME Zion Church had a group of radical younger churchmen called the Sons of Varick. Other African American churches did not have formally organized caucuses, but many NCBC members met informally within their respective denominations. See Leon W. Watts, "The National Committee of Black Churchmen," in *Christianity and Crisis*, Nov. 2 and 16, 1970, pp. 237–43.

9. Harding, "No Turning Back," p. 13.

10. The statement, drafted by John Hurst Adams, later to become presiding bishop of the AME Church, held it to be a "tragic mistake for well-meaning whites to attempt to bypass the black church in an effort to relate directly to the ghetto." It was adopted April 4, 1968, the very day King was assassinated, and mailed to more than 800 denominational executives, inviting them to negotiate with grassroots church and community leaders and "surrender power." Many of them replied that they resented the language of confrontation and polarization.

11. It is true, nevertheless, that the majority of the more than 1,000 NCBC members belonged to all-black denominations. They were generally younger seminary graduates who were disillusioned with the conservatism of the churches they pastored and their denominations.

12. IFCO was created by ten national white churches, under pressure from the caucuses, as a coalition for the development and funding of community organizing in African American and Hispanic American communities—usually along the lines of the Alinsky model. In 1969 its board of directors consisted of twenty-three black and Hispanic, and seventeen white representatives of national religious and social service agencies. The first IFCO executive staff persons—Lucius Walker, Jr., a Baptist minister, and Louis Gothard, a Unitarian layman—were among the founding members of NCBC.

13. IFCO News Release, May 5, 1969.

14. James Forman was born in Chicago in 1928. He was baptized and confirmed in the AME Church. After serving in the military for four years and earning a B.A. in political science and public administration at Roosevelt College, he did graduate work in government and African studies at Boston University. Between 1963 and 1965, Forman took over the SNCC program in Hattiesburg, Mississippi, from Bob Moses, and met with many black and white clergy who came from the North to participate in the project under the auspices of the NCC, and later, the Commission on Religion and Race of the United Presbyterian Church. See Michael Hamlin and the staff of the Black Star, Publishing Co., *The Political Thought of James Forman* (Detroit: Black Star, 1970), and James Forman, *The Making of a Black Revolutionary* (New York: Macmillan, 1971).

15. See Arnold Schuchter, *Reparations: The Black Manifesto and Its Challenge to*

*White America* (Philadelphia: Lippincott, 1970), p. 4. Also, Robert S. Lecky and H. Elliott Wright, eds., *The Black Manifesto* (New York: Sheed and Ward, 1969), pp. 66–67, 102–3. For the full text of the Manifesto, see Wilmore and Cone, *Black Theology*, pp. 80–99.

16. Stephen C. Rose, "Putting It to the Churches," in Lecky and Wright, *Black Manifesto*, p. 102.

17. *Tempo*, June 1, 1969, p. 7.

18. Ibid.

19. "Rationale for Restitution," a pamphlet published by St. George's Episcopal Church, Stuyvesant Square, New York City, n.d.

20. A "Declaration of Revolution" presented on May 23, 1969, to the WCC meeting at Notting Hill, England, demanded 500,000 pounds sterling to be used to set up a defense fund for political prisoners in South Africa and the "Panther 21" in the U.S., various sums for African liberation movements, developing an international publishing house, and the public disclosure of WCC assets and investments. A direct outgrowth of the Notting Hill action was the creation of the WCC Programme to Combat Racism, which has allocated over a million dollars to liberation movements and racial justice programs all over the world. See John Vincent, *The Race Race* (New York: Friendship Press, 1970), pp. 42–48.

21. Schuchter, *Reparations*, p. 62.

22. Minutes of the NCBC board of directors meeting, May 7, 1969.

23. *Action Training Clearing-House Notes*, Metropolitan-Urban Service Training Facility, June 1969, pp. 4–5.

24. Ibid., p. 53.

25. The major portion of BEDC's funding finally came through unrestricted grants to IFCO by the churches and through NCBC, which accepted Episcopal grants for this purpose by agreement with the Episcopal black caucus and BEDC.

26. E. Franklin Frazier, *The Negro Church in America* (New York: Schocken, 1962), pp. 44–46, and 85–86; see also Joseph R. Washington, Jr., *Black Religion: The Negro and Christianity in the United States* (Boston: Beacon Press, 1964), pp. 140–43. For a different view of the black church during the civil rights period, see C. Eric Lincoln, *The Black Church Since Frazier* (New York: Schocken, 1974), pp. 103–34; Hart M. Nelsen and Anne K. Nelsen, *Black Church in the Sixties* (Lexington: University Press of Kentucky, 1975); and for an overall analysis, Peter J. Paris, *The Social Teachings of the Black Churches* (Philadelphia: Fortress Press, 1985).

27. See NCNC, *Theological Commission Project: A Summary Report*, November 4, 1968, p. 4.

28. Joseph R. Washington, Jr., *The Politics of God* (Boston: Beacon Press, 1967), pp. 170–71.

29. Ibid., p. 185. For further development of Washington's thought, with the obvious influence of Fanon, see his *Black and White Power Subreption* (Boston: Beacon Press, 1969), pp. 124–27.

30. *The Christian Century*, Jan. 4, 1967, p. 10.

31. Vincent Harding, "The Religion of Black Power," in Donald R. Cutler, ed., *The Religious Situation: 1968* (Boston: Beacon Press, 1968), p. 31.

32. Albert B. Cleage, Jr., *The Black Messiah* (New York: Sheed and Ward, 1968), p. 37. See also his *Black Christian Nationalism: New Directions for the Black Church* (New York: William Morrow, 1972).

33. Cleage, *The Black Messiah*, p. 277.

34. Ibid., p. 111. On the concept of the Black Messiah, see James H. Cone, *A Black Theology of Liberation, Twentieth Anniversary Edition* (Maryknoll, N.Y.: Orbis, 1990), pp. 119–24; William L. Eichelberger, "Reflections on the Person and Personality of the Black Messiah," in *The Black Church*, vol. 2, no. 1, pp. 51–63; Gayraud S. Wilmore, "The Black Messiah: Revising the Color Symbolism of Western Christology," in the *Journal of the Interdenominational Theological Center*, vol. 2, no. 1, Fall 1974, pp. 8–18.

35. Harding, "Religion of Black Power," pp. 29–30.

36. George D. Kelsey was one of the first black ethicists to teach at a major white theological seminary. A professor at Drew Theological Seminary in Madison, New Jersey, his principal work, *Racism and the Christian Understanding of Man* (New York: Scribner's, 1965), antedates the modern black theology movement.

37. James H. Cone, *Black Theology and Black Power: Twentieth Anniversary Edition*, p. 39.

38. "Black Theology—A Statement of the National Committee of Black Churchmen," in James H. Cone and Gayraud S. Wilmore, *Black Theology: A Documentary History*, vol. 1, 1966–1979, 2d ed., rev. (Maryknoll, N.Y.: Orbis, 1993), p. 37. A bibliography of black theological writings between 1979 and 1993, compiled by Mark L. Chapman, is appended to volumes 1 and 2. See also an excellent bibliographical essay by J. Deotis Roberts, "Black Theological Ethics," in the *Journal of Religious Ethics*, vol. 3, Spring 1975, pp. 69–109; also Diana L. Hayes, *And Still We Rise: An Introduction to Black Liberation Theology* (New York: Paulist Press, 1996), pp. 198–214.

39. Ibid., Cone and Wilmore, *Black Theology* (1993), p. 38.

40. Ibid., p. 39.

41. Not all black theologians agreed with Cone. Leon E. Wright, former Howard University Divinity School professor, wrote: "It would be hazardous to insist . . . that one has made a case for a uniquely oriented world-view—'Black Theology'—whose posture consists essentially in judgment and protest of 'White Christianity' and/or 'racist' society. Though such judgment can be shown to be supremely righteous and just and the protest seem to stem from deep prophetic depths, there is involved in all this no distinctive alternative to the traditional approaches to 'God-talk' and man's self-understanding." *Journal of Religious Thought*, Summer 1969, p. 54.

42. Cone, *Black Theology and Black Power*, p. 118; italics added.

43. Ibid., p. 151.

44. Cone, *A Black Theology of Liberation*, p. 7.

45. J. V. Langmead Casserley, *The Christian in Philosophy* (New York: Scribner's Sons, 1951), p. 31. Perhaps more to the point is Franz Fanon's view: "The natives' challenge to the colonial world is not a rational confrontation of points of view. It is not a treatise on the universal, but the untidy affirmation of an original idea propounded as an absolute." (Franz Fanon, *The Wretched of the Earth* [New York: Grove Press, 1963], p. 41).

46. Cone, *A Black Theology of Liberation*, p. 36. For a more recent contrasting view by a black theologian at Vanderbilt Divinity School see Victor Anderson, *Beyond Ontological Blackness: An Essay on African American Religious and Cultural Criticism* (New York: Continuum, 1995).

47. Cone, *A Black Theology of Liberation*, p. 38.

48. For more recent developments in black theology, beyond the full corpus

of Cone's work, see the books and articles of black womanist theologians and ethicists. For example, Jacquelyn Grant, *White Woman's Christ, Black Woman's Jesus* (Atlanta: Scholars Press, 1989); Katie Cannon, *Black Womanist Ethics* (Atlanta: Scholars Press, 1988); Kelly Brown Douglas, *The Black Christ* (Maryknoll, N.Y.: Orbis, 1994); Diana L. Hayes, *And Still We Rise: An Introduction to Black Liberation Theology* (New York: Paulist Press, 1996); Marcia Riggs, *Awake, Arise, and Act: A Womanist Call for Black Liberation* (Cleveland: Pilgrim Press, 1995); Cheryl J. Sanders, ed., *Living the Intersection: Womanism and Afrocentrism in Theology* (Minneapolis: Fortress Press, 1994); Emilie Townes, *Womanist Justice, Womanist Hope* (Atlanta: Scholars Press, 1994); and Delores Williams, *Sisters in the Wilderness* (Maryknoll, N.Y.: Orbis, 1993). During the 1980s and 1990s a second generation of black male theologians has also been productive. See, for example, James H. Harris, *Pastoral Theology* (Minneapolis: Fortress Press, 1991); James Evans, *We Have Been Believers: An African American Systematic Theology* (Minneapolis: Fortress Press, 1993); Dwight Hopkins and George Cummings, eds., *Cut Loose Your Stammering Tongue: Black Theology and the Slave Narratives* (Maryknoll, N.Y.: Orbis, 1992); Dwight Hopkins, *Shoes That Fit Our Feet: Sources for a Constructive Black Theology* (Maryknoll, N.Y.: Orbis, 1993); Mark L. Chapman, *Christianity on Trial: African-American Religious Thought Before and After Black Power* (Maryknoll, N.Y.: Orbis, 1996); Peter J. Paris, *The Spirituality of African Peoples: The Search for a Common Moral Discourse* (Minneapolis: Augsburg-Fortress Press, 1995); and the two-volume work by James H. Cone and Gayraud S. Wilmore, eds., *Black Theology: A Documentary History*, Vol. 2, 1979–1992 (Maryknoll, N.Y.: Orbis 1993). A more recent work by the senior theological scholar J. Deotis Roberts is *The Prophethood of Black Believers: An African American Political Theology for Ministry* (Louisville; Westminster Press, 1995).

## *10. Survival, Elevation, and Liberation in Black Religion*

1. Eugene D. Genovese, *Roll, Jordan, Roll: The World the Slaves Made* (New York: Pantheon, 1974), p. 91.

2. In addition to Genovese's monumental work (note 1 above), for a broad selection of books related to the themes of this chapter see John W. Blassingame, *The Slave Community: Plantation Life in the Ante-Bellum South* (New York: Oxford University Press, 1972), and Blassingame, ed., *Slave Testimony: Two Centuries of Letters, Speeches, Interviews, and Autobiographies* (Baton Rouge: Louisiana State University, 1977); Henry H. Mitchell, *Black Belief: Folk Beliefs of Blacks in America and West Africa* (New York: Harper & Row, 1975); Lawrence W. Levine, *Black Culture and Black Consciousness: Afro-American Folk Thought from Slavery to Freedom* (New York: Oxford University Press, 1978); Albert J. Raboteau, *Slave Religion: The "Invisible Institution" in the Antebellum South* (New York: Oxford University Press, 1978); George E. Simpson, *Black Religion in the New World* (New York: Columbia University Press, 1978); Sterling Stuckey, *Slave Culture: Nationalist Theory and the Foundations of Black America* (New York: Oxford University Press, 1987); Margaret Washington Creel, *"A Peculiar People": Slave Religion and Community-Culture Among the Gullahs* (New York: New York University Press, 1988); Vincent Harding, *There Is a River: The Black Struggle for Freedom in America* (New York: Harcourt Brace Jovanovich, 1981); Dwight N. Hopkins and George Cummings, eds. *Cut Loose Your Stammering Tongue: Black Theology in the*

*Slave Narratives* (Maryknoll, N.Y.: Orbis, 1991); and C. Eric Lincoln and Lawrence H. Mamiya, *The Black Church in the African American Experience* (Durham: Duke University Press, 1990).

3. See Mechal Sobel, *Trabelin' On: The Slave Journey to an Afro-Baptist Faith* (Westport, Conn.: Greenwood Press, 1979), pp. 99–135.

4. See, e.g., Willis D. Weatherford, *American Churches and the Negro* (Boston: Christopher Publishing House, 1957), and Carter G. Woodson, *The History of the Negro Church* (Washington, D.C.: Associated Publishers, 1972).

5. John Lovell, Jr., *Black Song: The Forge and the Flame* (New York: Macmillan, 1972), p. 229.

6. St. Clair Drake and Horace R. Clayton, *Black Metropolis: A Study of Negro Life in a Northern City* (New York: Harcourt, Brace, 1945), pp. 650–57.

7. C. Eric Lincoln, *The Black Muslims in America* (Boston: Beacon Press, 1961), pp. 217–20.

8. Sterling Brown, Arthur P. Davis, and Ulysses Lee, *The Negro Caravan* (New York: Arno Press and the New York Times, 1941), p. 422.

9. Blassingame, *The Slave Community*, pp. 205–06.

10. W. E. B. Du Bois, *The Souls of Black Folk* (Greenwich, Conn.: Fawcett, 1961), p. 149.

11. Ibid.

12. Lawrence W. Levine, *Black Culture and Black Consciousness* (New York: Oxford University Press, 1977), p. 80.

13. Du Bois, *The Souls of Black Folk*, p. 151.

14. Leonard E. Barrett, *Soul-Force: African Heritage in Afro-American Religion* (Garden City, N.Y.: Doubleday, 1974), p. 115.

15. Langston Hughes, in Francis Broderick et al., *Black Protest Thought in the Twentieth Century* (New York: Bobbs-Merrill, 1970), p. 92.

16. Lovell, *Black Song: The Forge and the Flame* p. 119.

17. Ibid., p. 122.

18. Cited by AME historian Paul R. Griffin, *The Struggle for a Black Theology of Education: Pioneering Efforts of Post Civil War Clergy* (Atlanta: ITC Press, 1993), p. 17.

19. The word "elevation" and cognates expressing the idea of moral and material uplift are sprinkled liberally throughout the many sermons, addresses, resolutions, and other documents in Dorothy Porter, ed., *Early Negro Writing, 1760–1837* (Boston: Beacon Press, 1971). For example, in that collection, see the address of Prince Saunders before the Pennsylvania Augustine Society, pp. 90–92; an 1828 address by William Whipper, p. 117; 1832 address by an unnamed woman to the Female Literary Association of Philadelphia, p. 128; 1833 address by Maria Stewart, p. 134; address in 1834 by Joseph M. Corr of Bethel AME Church in Philadelphia, pp. 150 and 153; address to the Moral Reform Society of Philadelphia in 1836 by William Watkins, pp. 156, 161, and 165; address of Bishop Richard Allen to the 1830 Convention of People of Color, p. 179; the Minutes of the American Moral Reform Society, pp. 202, 205, 209, 226, 229, 238, and 242. For similar emphases on elevation, uplift, and "promotion" of the race in writings by black women, see Bert James Loewenberg and Ruth Bogin, eds., *Black Women in Nineteenth-Century American Life: Their Words, Their Thoughts, Their Feelings* (University Park: Pennsylvania State University Press, 1976), passim. See also frequent citations of "elevation" from the *Christian Recorder*, in Clarence E. Walker, *A Rock in a Weary Land: The*

*African Methodist Episcopal Church During the Civil War and Reconstruction* (Baton Rouge: Louisiana State University Press, 1982), pp. 16, 42, 44, 52, 90, and 93. As mentioned in Chapter 6 the concept of "elevation" is most fully developed by Martin R. Delany in *The Condition, Elevation, Emigration, and Destiny of the Colored People of the United States* (1852, Baltimore: Black Classic Press, 1993), pp. 36–48. In the revision of his 1982 doctoral dissertation Edward L. Wheeler used the term "uplift" in the same sense as Delany used "elevation," and examines its theological, sociological, political, and educational implications for the careers of black clergy after the Civil War; see Edward L. Wheeler, *Uplifting the Race: The Black Minister in the New South, 1865–1902* (Lanham, Md.: University Press of America, 1986).

20. Cited in Blassingame, *Slave Testimony*, p. 689.

21. Ibid., p. 417.

22. Richard R. Wright, Jr., *The Centennial Encyclopedia of the African Methodist Episcopal Church, 1816–1916* (Philadelphia: AME Church, 1916), p. 11.

23. Delores S. Williams, *Sisters in the Wilderness: The Challenge of Womanist God-Talk* (Maryknoll, N.Y.: Orbis, 1993), p. 6.

24. Maria Stewart, cited in Loewenberg and Bogin, *Black Women in Nineteenth-Century American Life*, p. 196.

25. Fannie Barrier Williams, cited in ibid., p. 269.

26. See James Melvin Washington, *Frustrated Fellowship: The Black Baptist Quest for Social Power* (Macon: Mercer University Press, 1986), pp. 28–45; Benjamin Quarles, *Black Abolitionists* (New York: Oxford University Press, 1969), pp. 68–89; James M. McPherson, *The Negro's Civil War: How American Negroes Felt and Acted During the War for the Union* (New York: Vintage Books, 1967), pp. 33–53; David E. Swift, *Black Prophets of Justice: Activist Clergy Before the Civil War* (Baton Rouge: Louisiana State University Press, 1989), pp. 1–18 and passim; and Randall K. Burkett and Richard Newman, eds., *Black Apostles: Afro-American Clergy Confront the Twentieth Century* (Boston: G. K. Hall, 1978).

27. Lovell, *Black Song: The Forge and the Flame*, p. 386.

28. Talitha Lewis, cited in B. A. Botkin, ed., *Lay My Burden Down: A Folk History of Slavery* (Chicago: University of Chicago Press, 1945), p. 27.

29. Cited in William B. McClain, *Black People in the Methodist Church* (Cambridge: Schenkman, 1984), p. 37.

30. Carter G. Woodson, *The History of the Negro Church*, 3d ed. (Washington, D.C.: Associated Publishers, 1921), p. 251.

31. Charles H. Long, "Freedom, Otherness and Religion: Theologies Opaque," in the *Chicago Theological Seminary Register*, vol. 63, no. 1, Winter 1983, p. 23. Long speaks of a form of consciousness as "lithic" (Hegel) . . . "that mode of consciousness that in confronting reality in this mode formed a will *in opposition*. . . . The hardness of life or of reality was the experience of the meaning of their own identity as opaque."

32. Derek Walcott, in Orde Coombs, ed., *Is Massa Day Dead? Black Moods in the Caribbean* (Garden City, N.Y.: Doubleday, 1974), p. 7.

33. William Hamilton, "An Address to the New York African Society for Mutual Relief," in Dorothy Porter, *Early Negro Writing*, p. 37.

34. Washington, *Frustrated Fellowship*, pp. 159–85.

35. E. Franklin Frazier, *The Negro Church in America* (New York: Schocken, 1964), p. 86.

36. The reference here is to the Colored Primitive Baptists (1865), the reunited African Union Methodists (1866), the Second Cumberland Presbyterian Church (1869), and the Colored Methodist Episcopal Church, about which considerably more has been written, founded in 1870. Among the Holiness and Pentecostal churches of the turn of the century were William Christian's Church of the Living God (1889), C. H. Mason's Church of God in Christ (1895), and William Crowdy's Church of God and Saints of Christ (1896).

37. For the best treatment of the significance of King's and Malcolm's lives and ministries for American religion and culture, see James H. Cone, *Martin & Malcolm & America: A Dream or a Nightmare* (Maryknoll, N.Y.: Orbis, 1991).

38. Some of the most publicized examples were movements led by Amiri Baraka, Maulana Karenga, Milton Henry and Brother Imari of the Republic of New Africa, Jaramogi Abebe Agyeman of the Shrine of the Black Madonna, and Louis Farrakhan of the Nation of Islam.

39. See representative statements from some of these groups in Gayraud S. Wilmore and James H. Cone, eds., *Black Theology: A Documentary History, 1966–1992*, vols. 1 and 2 (Maryknoll, N.Y.: Orbis, 1993); also articles in Larry G. Murphy, J. Gordon Melton, and Gary L. Ward, eds., *Encyclopedia of African-American Religions* (New York: Garland, 1993); and Jack Salzman, David Lionel Smith, and Cornel West, eds., *Encyclopedia of African American Culture and History*, vols. 1–5 (New York: Macmillan Library Reference USA and Simon & Schuster Macmillan, 1996).

40. For philosophy in the African American community and its relation to folk religious beliefs, see Denis Hickey, *Contemporary Black Philosophy* (Pasadena: Williams and Williams, 1971). A work linking Marxist philosophy and black theology is Cornel West, *Prophesy Deliverance! An Afro-American Revolutionary Christianity* (Philadelphia: Westminster Press, 1982), and *Prophetic Fragments* (Grand Rapids: William B. Eerdmans and Africa Third World Press, 1988). An important contribution to the dialogue between African American philosophers and theologians is Molefi Kete Asante, *Afrocentricity: The Theory of Social Change* (Buffalo: Amulefi, 1980) and *The Afrocentric Idea* (Philadelphia: Temple University Press, 1987). For trenchant critiques of black theology by African American philosophers and ethicists see Victor Anderson, *Beyond Ontological Blackness: An Essay on African American Religious and Cultural Criticism* (New York: Continuum, 1995), and Anthony B. Pinn, *Why, Lord? Suffering and Evil in Black Theology* (New York: Continuum, 1995).

41. Carleton L. Lee, "Religious Roots of the Negro Protest," in Arnold Rose, ed., *Assuring Freedom to the Free* (Detroit: Wayne State University Press, 1964).

42. See the 20th Anniversary Edition, with critical reflections by six scholars, of James H. Cone's *A Black Theology of Liberation* (Maryknoll, N.Y.: Orbis, 1990) and J. Deotis Roberts, *A Black Political Theology* (Philadelphia: Westminster Press, 1974).

43. For a thorough analysis of the wider influence of black American theology and the surprising development of its counterpart in Great Britain see Roswith I. H. Gerloff, *A Plea for British Black Theologies: The Black Church Movement in Britain in Its Transatlantic Cultural and Theological Interaction*, vols. 1 and 2 (Frankfurt am Main: Peter Lang, 1992).

44. Henry H. Mitchell, *Black Preaching* (Philadelphia: Lippincott, 1970), p. 27.

45. Ibid., pp. 29–31. The articles mentioned were published in Cain Hope

Felder, ed., *Stony the Road We Trod: African American Biblical Interpretation* (Minneapolis: Fortress Press, 1991).

46. See Herbert Aptheker, ed., *W. E. B. Du Bois—Prayers for Dark People* (Boston: University of Massachusetts Press, 1980).

47. Charles H. Long, "The Black Reality: Toward a Theology of Freedom," in *Criterion: Journal of the University of Chicago Divinity School,* September 1969.

# Index